CODIFICATION OF MARITIME LAW

MARITIME AND TRANSPORT LAW LIBRARY

Ship Building, Sale and Finance
Edited by Bariş Soyer and Andrew Tettenborn

The Modern Law of Marine Insurance
Volume 4
Edited by D. Rhidian Thomas

Air Cargo Insurance
Malcom A. Clarke and George Leloudas

Offshore Oil and Gas Installations Security
An International Perspective
Mikhail Kashubsky

International Trade and Carriage of Goods
Edited by Bariş Soyer and Andrew Tettenborn

Maritime Law and Practice in China
Liang Zhao and Lianjun Li

Maritime Law
Fourth Edition
Edited by Yvonne Baatz

Maritime Cross-Border Insolvency
Lia Athanassiou

The Law of Yachts and Yachting
Second Edition
Edited by Filippo Lorenzon and Richard Coles

Maritime Liabilities in a Global and Regional Context
Edited by Bariş Soyer and Andrew Tettenborn

New Technologies, Artificial Intelligence and Shipping Law in the 21st Century
Edited by Bariş Soyer and Andrew Tettenborn

The Law of Wreck
Nicholas Gaskell and Craig Forrest

Codification of Maritime Law
Challenges, Possibilities and Experience
Edited by Justyna Nawrot and Zuzanna Pepłowska-Dąbrowska

CODIFICATION OF MARITIME LAW

CHALLENGES, POSSIBILITIES AND EXPERIENCE

EDITED BY JUSTYNA NAWROT AND
ZUZANNA PEPŁOWSKA-DĄBROWSKA

informa law
from Routledge

First published 2020 by Informa Law from Routledge

2 Park Square, Milton Park, Abingdon, Oxon OX14 4RN

and by Informa Law from Routledge
605 Third Avenue, New York, NY 10017

Routledge is an imprint of the Taylor & Francis Group, an informa business

First issued in paperback 2021

All rights reserved. No part of this book may be reprinted or reproduced or utilised in any form or by any electronic, mechanical, or other means, now known or hereafter invented, including photocopying and recording, or in any information storage or retrieval system, without permission in writing from the publishers.

British Library Cataloguing-in-Publication Data
A catalogue record for this book is available from the British Library

Library of Congress Cataloging-in-Publication Data
Names: European Colloquium of Maritime Law Research (10th : 2018 : Toruń, Poland). | Nawrot, Justyna, editor. | Pepłowska-Dąbrowska, Zuzanna, editor.
Title: Codification of maritime law : challenges, possibilities and experience/edited by Justyna Nawrot, Zuzanna Pepłowska-Dąbrowska.
Description: Abingdon, Oxon ; New York, NY : Informa Law from Routledge, 2020. | Series: Maritime and transport law library | "This book is a collection of presentations from the European Colloquium of Maritime Law Research in Torun, Poland, September 20–21, 2018" — ECIP forword. | Includes bibliographical references and index.
Identifiers: LCCN 2019033491 (print) | LCCN 2019033492 (ebook) | ISBN 9780367343613 (cloth) | ISBN 9780429351792 (ebook)
Subjects: LCSH: Maritime law—Codifiation—Congresses.
Classification: LCC K1150.A6 .E87 2020 (print) | LCC K1150.A6 (ebook) | DDC 341.4/5—dc23
LC record available at https://lccn.loc.gov/2019033491
LC ebook record available at https://lccn.loc.gov/2019033492

ISBN: 978-0-367-34361-3 (hbk)
ISBN: 978-1-03-208196-0 (pbk)
ISBN: 978-0-429-35179-2 (ebk)

Typeset in Times
by Apex CoVantage, LLC

TABLE OF CONTENTS

FOREWORD

This book is a collection of presentations from the European Colloquium of Maritime Law Research in Torun, Poland, 20–21 September 2018. This seminar was the tenth of these biannual colloquia, and the hosts did a wonderful job of organizing the seminar practically and scientifically as well as taking extremely good care of us individually and collectively. They even had a good cultural program to entertain us and broaden our horizons beyond the law. This was certainly a colloquium to remember with great fondness.

I learned a lot at this colloquium by listening and by participating in discussions in the plenary and on the fringes. Some of the presentations were excellent. I cannot imagine anyone actively participating in the colloquium without profiting from it.

The theme in 2018 was Codification of Maritime Law (Challenges, Possibilities and Experience). This echoes the 2000 Oslo theme, Legislative Approaches in Maritime Law. Much has changed over this period. Nevertheless, it is still important that academics reflect on the methods and design of the systems of maritime law, looking beyond individual conflicts.

This was the goal of the seminars from the start in Oslo. The seminars soon became a joint project of the Scandinavian Institute of Maritime Law at the University of Oslo and the Institute of Maritime Law at the University of Southampton. In the early years, Professor Charles Debattista was the director in Southampton, and I was the director in Oslo. The seminar series was an immediate success, and it has never been difficult to find local organizers of the individual seminars. Indeed, a problem over the years has been that so many attend and present at the seminars that they can lose their character as real colloquia with ample time for discussion.

The local hosts over the years have been our sister institutes in Bologna, Nantes, Athens, Swansea, Messina/Palermo, Rotterdam, Bilbao and now Toruń. All have organized excellent seminars. The participants are very grateful, as are we.

The European colloquia are different from the many seminars for practitioners that academics and others organize in maritime law. There is room to discuss principles and tendencies and even academic questions. Discussions can be of a comparative nature, not bound to one legal system. We all love studying the law in action and the cooperation and dialogue with practitioners, and having a good grasp of practical issues is certainly necessary to being a good academic lawyer. However, sometimes it is fruitful to change one's perspective.

An academic perspective is important to lifting the discussion from black-letter law. These days, the pendulum has perhaps swung to the other extreme, so clarifying the law and organizing the case materials in black-letter style are not considered appropriate research for academic lawyers. Today, blue-sky visions and grand perspectives are in fashion. Personally, I believe that there should and must be room for both approaches, and that should certainly apply in the European colloquia as well.

Just as the European colloquia have helped shape an identity for maritime law researchers and academics as different from practitioners, they have also focused on the European legal culture. It is important to see what unites across language barriers and, for example, across common law and civil law.

A major influence in European law in this century has obviously been the European Union. However, it is fair to say that its influence on contract law in general and maritime law in particular has not been substantial. It is easier to form a political union than a unified system of law or even commercial law. Still, European maritime law academics are confronted with aspects of European Union law every day, particularly in relation to jurisdiction; enforcement and recognition of judgments; and consumers, including passengers. This is a new, common (play)ground for European maritime law academics.

However, Europe is a lot more than the European Union. We have tried to locate the European colloquia in the north and south of Europe as well as the east and west. This has made it possible for us to learn about the differences in legal and general cultures and for every participant to expand his or her network. To me, this has been a particularly fascinating aspect of the European colloquia. I think we know each other better today than we did when the colloquia started.

This book is a reflection of this long process. I believe it is well worth reading – as the culmination of this process and for a number of other reasons.

Oslo, 3 May 2019
PROFESSOR ERIK RØSÆG

PREFACE

As noted by Professor Erik Røsœg in the Foreword, this book is a collection of papers presented at the Xth European Colloquium on Maritime Law Research, organized by the Maritime Law Unit of the Nicolaus Copernicus University in Toruń, Poland, between 20 and 21 September 2018. The conference was held in cooperation with the Scandinavian Institute of Maritime Law at the University of Oslo and the University of Southampton's Institute of Maritime Law. The underlying theme of the conference was 'Codification of Maritime Law. Challenges, possibilities and experience'. Moreover, the book includes several papers which were not included in the conference proceedings, but complement the book, making it more comprehensive.

The issue of maritime law codification can be analyzed from many perspectives. Accordingly, the book is divided into four parts which represent different views on the main topic. The chapters in Part I are dedicated to the problems specific to different aspects and methods of unification of maritime law on a global scale, as well as several specific issues of maritime law from the regulatory point of view. Professor Francis Reynolds discusses difficulties in unification of maritime law deriving from considerable differences between the legal cultures of civil and common law countries. Professor Dr Eric Van Hooydonk provides a historical view on the unification process, raises the contemporary difficulties of maritime law unifications and considers methods of preserving uniformity. Professor Erik Røsæg submits critical analysis of the current state of commercial maritime law unification via international conventions. Professor Andrew Serdy evaluates the drafting technique adopted in respect of the Rotterdam Rules from the perspective of a public international law specialist. Professor Andrew Tettenborn provides pros and cons of different types of maritime law codifications: via national codes, international conventions, soft law and standard forms. Professor Juan Pablo Rodríguez Delgado refers to advantages and obstacles to the harmonization of maritime law by international conventions and comments upon the success of the 2001 Cape Town Convention on International Interests in Mobile Equipment, deliberating on whether that success may be replicated in the field of maritime law. Milagros Varela Choucíño discusses discrepancies between EEA and EU maritime transport law and challenges it creates, as well as suggesting some legislative simplification techniques. Dr Julia Constantino Chagas Lessa shares an analysis of the Maritime Labour Convention's characteristics, justifying its success as the codification of seafarers' minimum rights at an international level.

Part II of the book consists of those papers that centre on the issue of transport of goods. Professor Rhidian Thomas provides a critical review of the Rotterdam Rules, emphasizing their lack of the quality of commercialism. Dr Jingbo Zhang presents her thoughts in connection with the Uniform Customs and Practice for Documentary Credits and its shipping provisions, arguing that they are not entirely satisfactory. Dr Elena Orrù explores the issue of a suitable legal regime for electronic bills of lading. Dr Daniel Dąbrowski and Dr Konrad Garnowski provide a critical view on regulation of the multimodal carriage of goods under the Rotterdam Rules, pointing to deficiencies of adopted solutions. Patryk Ciok analyzes national solutions in respect of the multimodal carrier's liability regime.

Part III is dedicated to codifications of carriage of passengers, cruise law and leisure navigation. Professor Juan L. Pulido Begines discusses codification of sailing and leisure navigation, referring to Spanish and Italian legislation. Richard Coles analyzes the legal framework for the commercial yacht charter industry in the United Kingdom. Dr Olena Bokareva examines the international and regional codification of liability and compensation issues in relation to cruise passengers.

Finally, Part IV addresses national codifications of maritime law. Professor Souichirou Kozuka analyzes reform of Japanese maritime law. Professor José Manuel Martín Osante explores legislative techniques adopted in the Spanish Maritime Navigation Law in order to coordinate national maritime law with international conventions, as well as indicating its consequences. Dr Justyna Nawrot and Dr Zuzanna Pepłowska-Dąbrowska provide a comparative research into the reasons for adoption of new maritime law codes, as well as their scope and methods to provide uniformity on an international scale.

We should like to take this opportunity to thank all who contributed to the success of the conference: the speakers and chairs, as well its Partners: Kuyavian-Pomeranian Voivodeship, Polish Maritime Law Association and Polish Ship Managers' Association.[1] Moreover, we express our gratitude to the Scandinavian Institute of Maritime Law at the University of Oslo and the University of Southampton's Institute of Maritime Law for entrusting us with organization of the Xth European Colloquium on Maritime Law Research. Finally, we would like to acknowledge the work of our publisher, whose active role allowed the book to come to existence.

Gdańsk, 10 May 2019

DR JUSTYNA NAWROT, UNIVERSITY OF GDAŃSK, POLAND
DR ZUZANNA PEPŁOWSKA-DĄBROWSKA, NICOLAUS COPERNICUS UNIVERSITY IN TORUŃ, POLAND

1 The colloquium constituted a part of broader research on Problems of contemporary maritime codes, conducted within a scientific grant financed by National Science Centre, Poland under the contract UMO - 2016/22/E/HS5/00050.

NOTES ON CONTRIBUTORS

EDITORS

DR JUSTYNA NAWROT is an assistant professor in the Maritime Law Department, Faculty of Law and Administration, at the University of Gdańsk, where she teaches maritime law. In 2015 she was nominated a member of the Polish Codification Commission for Maritime Law. She is vice-president of the Polish Maritime Law Association, vice-editor of *Prawo morskie*, a scientific journal edited by the Polish Academy of Sciences, and an arbitrator in maritime disputes. Dr Nawrot was also a member of the Maritime Law Commission's board under the auspices of the Polish Academy of Sciences. She was awarded a scientific grant dedicated to the law of maritime safety. She is also main coordinator of a scientific grant addressing problems of contemporary maritime codes. She has conducted her research in the leading maritime law centres of Europe, including the Scandinavian Institute of Maritime Law at University of Oslo, the IMO International Maritime Law Institute in Malta and the IMO Maritime Knowledge Centre in London.

DR ZUZANNA PEPŁOWSKA-DĄBROWSKA is an assistant professor at the Maritime Law Unit of the Law and Administration Faculty at the Nicolaus Copernicus University in Toruń. In 2015–2019 she was a member of the Polish Codification Commission for Maritime Law. She is vice-president of the Polish Maritime Law Association, a member of the Maritime Law Commission's board of the Polish Academy of Sciences and an arbitrator in maritime disputes. In 2017 she was awarded a grant by the Polish National Science Center for research dedicated to the problems of contemporary maritime codes. She has conducted her research in numerous maritime law centers, including Tulane University Law School (as a Fulbright grantee), the Scandinavian Institute of Maritime Law, and the University of Southampton Institute of Maritime Law.

CONTRIBUTORS (in the order of their chapters)

PROFESSOR FRANCIS REYNOLDS is a Doctor of Civil Law and Emeritus Professor in the University of Oxford. He is Fellow of the British Academy, Honorary QC and barrister, as well as Honorary Bencher of the Inner Temple. Professor Reynolds is also standing consultant on English law to Ang & Partners, Singapore. He holds a Honorary Professorship at the International Maritime Law Institute of the IMO at Malta. He is Titular Member of the Comité Maritime International and Supporting Member of the London Maritime Arbitrators Association. He has held visiting professorships at the University of Auckland, Otago University, University of Sydney, University of Melbourne, Monash University, National University of Singapore, Singapore Management University and the University of Hong Kong. Professor Reynolds is author of numerous publications, including parts of *Chitty on Contracts* 24th–33rd edn 2018, *Benjamin's Sale of Goods*, 1st–9th edn 2014, *English Private Law* 1st–3rd edn 2013, and *Carver on Bills of Lading* 1st–4th edn 2017 with Professor Sir Guenter Treitel). Between 1987 and 2015 he was the editor of the *Law Quarterly Review*.

PROFESSOR DR ERIC VAN HOOYDONK is a Master of Laws (LLM, University of Antwerp, 1988), a Master of Maritime Sciences (University of Antwerp, 1988) and a Doctor of Laws (LLD, University of Antwerp, 1994). He holds a professorship at the University of Ghent. Prior to that he was a Professor of Maritime and Transport Law at the University of Antwerp and chaired the European Institute of Maritime and Transport Law. In 2007 he was appointed Chairman of the Royal Commission for the Reform of Belgian Maritime Law with the task of preparing a new Belgian Maritime Code. Professor Dr Van Hooydonk is a member of the management and editorial boards of the *Journal of International Maritime Law* (UK), *Droit Maritime Français* (France), the *Tijdschrift Vervoer & Recht* (Netherlands and Belgium) and *Antwerp Maritime Law Reports* (Belgium). He is also a titular member of the Comité Maritime International and chairman of an International Working Group of the Comité Maritime International on the Lex Maritima. Professor Dr Van Hooydonk is senior partner at Eric Van Hooydonk Lawyers. He is the author of numerous publications, including *Principles of Port Management Law* (in Dutch, 1995), *European Seaports Law* (as editor and contributor, 2003), *The Impact of EU Environmental Law on Ports and Waterways* (2006), *Soft Values of Seaports* (2006) and *Places of Refuge: International Law and the CMI Draft Convention* (2010), and *The EU Seaports Regulation* (2019).

PROFESSOR ERIK RØSÆG was formerly Director of the Scandinavian Institute of Maritime Law, University of Oslo. He is now at UiO PluriCourts – Centre for the Study of the Legitimate Roles of the Judiciary in the Global Order. He teaches and writes in the fields of the law of the sea, maritime law and third-party interests in commercial law. He has been much involved in the negotiations of liability Conventions at the IMO, chairs the Norwegian Maritime Law Commission and has chaired other committees preparing draft legislation. He has published extensively in national and international journals and books, and has been a speaker and consultant in a number of jurisdictions. He is currently involved in the Oslo Law of the Sea Forum.

PROFESSOR ANDREW SERDY is Director of the Institute of Maritime Law at the University of Southampton, where he teaches Public International Law and the International Law of the Sea, his main research interests encompassing resources and institutional aspects of the law of the sea. He is the author of *The New Entrants Problem in International Fisheries Law* (CUP, 2016). Prior to moving into academia in 2005, Andrew was at Freehill, Hollingdale & Page, Solicitors in Sydney and then spent 16 years with the Australian Government Department of Foreign Affairs and Trade, with postings in Tokyo and Warsaw before specialising in the law of the sea, including appearing for Australia in the Southern Bluefin Tuna arbitration (2000). Later he became deputy director of the Department's Sea Law, Environmental Law and Antarctic Policy Section and in this capacity drafted significant parts of Australia's 2004 submission to the Commission on the Limits of the Continental Shelf on the outer limit of the shelf beyond 200 nautical miles from the baseline.

PROFESSOR ANDREW TETTENBORN has been attached to the Institute of International Shipping and Trade Law at Swansea Law School since 2010, teaching international trade, payments and banking, and Admiralty. He has also taught at the universities of Cambridge, Exeter and Geneva and held visiting positions in Europe, Australia and the US. Professor Tettenborn is general editor of *Marsden's Collisions at Sea*, an editor of *Clerk & Lindsell on Torts* and also of the leading student textbook on commercial law (Clarke, Hooley, Munday, Sealy, Tettenborn & Turner's *Text, Cases and Materials*), He has authored numerous articles on commercial law and obligations and sits on the editorial boards of *Lloyd's Maritime & Commercial Law Quarterly* and the *Journal of International Maritime Law*.

PROFESSOR JUAN PABLO RODRÍGUEZ DELGADO is Assistant Professor of Commercial Law at Universidad Carlos III de Madrid (Spain). He has been fellow in several research stays, at, among others, Tulane University (2010), University of Southampton (2011, 2016), Fordham University (2012) and UNIDROIT (2013, 2019). Professor Rodríguez has participated as a member of the team in research projects (both national and international) financed by national entities. His publications include *El periodo de responsabilidad del porteador en el contrato de transporte marítimo* (2016) and numerous articles and book chapters, primarily in maritime law and the law of international contracts. Professor Rodríguez teaches Commercial Law (Corporate and Contract Law) and coordinates masters courses. He is also the coordinator of the Moot Madrid (http://www.mootmadrid.es/) and coach to the Carlos III University team in the International Maritime Law Arbitration Moot organised by Murdoch University (Australia).

MILAGROS VARELA CHOUCIÑO is a lawyer qualified in Spanish and Norwegian law, specializing in maritime/offshore matters. She holds two LLMs in Maritime Law from the Universities of Southampton and Oslo, and she is currently in the final year of an Executive MBA Programme at Copenhagen Business School. She is Head of Labour Relations for HR Marine at APM Moller-Maersk in Copenhagen. Before taking up this post, she was working for almost six years at the EFTA Surveillance Authority, which is an international organization tasked with the monitoring of the EEA Agreement. Her last position in the organization was Deputy Director for the Transport Unit. Before joining the EFTA Surveillance Authority she lived and worked in Norway: first, as a maritime lawyer in the Shipping and Offshore Department of Wikborg Rein and Co and thereafter as a Contract Advisor at Statoil (now, Equinor), where she dealt with the follow-up and establishment of Maintenance and Modification contracts for several offshore installations and led a tender process for the execution of EPCI contractual options.

DR JULIA CONSTANTINO CHAGAS LESSA is Assistant Professor and Academic Coordinator of the LLM Commercial and Company Law at Erasmus University Rotterdam. Before moving to Rotterdam, Dr Lessa lectured in Commercial and Maritime Law at the University of Westminster and the University of East Anglia. She has also lectured at City, University of London, where she completed her PhD in Maritime Law. Dr Lessa's research focuses essentially on the human element of shipping.

PROFESSOR RHIDIAN THOMAS is Professor Emeritus of Maritime Law and Founder Director of the Institute of International Shipping and Trade Law at Swansea University, Wales, UK. He previously held academic positions at the universities of Cardiff and East Anglia, and at universities in Europe, Scandinavia, the Far East and North America, including in 2011–2012 the Francqui Chair at the University of Leuven. He is visiting professor at Gothenburg University, World Maritime University and Bologna University. Professor Thomas is Editor-in-Chief of the *Journal of International Maritime Law*, and a member of the Comité Maritime International (and the International Standing Committee on Marine Insurance). He is an Honorary Member of the Croatian Maritime Law Association and was a member of the Departmental Advisory Committee on Arbitration Law which drafted the UK Arbitration Act 1996. His principal teaching and research interests are in the fields of maritime and shipping law, marine insurance law, international trade law and commercial arbitration. He has written, edited and contributed to many books and published widely in academic and professional journals. He has edited and contributed to two books on the Rotterdam Rules: *A New Convention for the Carriage of Goods by Sea – The Rotterdam Rules* (2009, Law Text Publishing, UK) and *The Carriage of Goods by Sea under the Rotterdam Rules* (2010, Lloyd's List Law, London, UK).

DR JINGBO ZHANG is a lecturer in commercial maritime law and a member of the Institute of Maritime Law at the University of Southampton. Her research interests are primarily in the fields of carriage of goods by sea, international sale of goods and international trade finance. Apart from teaching both undergraduate and postgraduate courses at Southampton, she is also actively involved in delivering short course training to both academic and industrial partners. Dr Zhang has published a number of journal articles in international journals, including the recent one on documentary credits in *Lloyd's Maritime and Commercial Law Quarterly*. Her edited book *Maritime law in China: Emerging Issues and Recent Developments* was published in 2016 by Informa Law from Routledge. In addition, Dr Zhang was recently invited by the House of Lords Select Committee, EU Internal Market sub-committee to provide expert evidence on the future EU-UK transport arrangements post-Brexit.

DR ELENA ORRÙ graduated in law *magna cum laude* with a thesis in transport law on 'Anticompetitive behaviours in the port and airport sectors', for which she received the 2001/2002 Paolo Cagnoni Prize and the 2001/2002 Rotary Prize for the Faculties of the University of Bologna. In 2007, she obtained her PhD in European Transport Law at the University of Bologna, with a thesis on the regime of state aids in the aviation sector. Dr Orrù is Tenured Assistant Professor of Navigation Law at the Department of Legal Studies of the University of Bologna and Adjunct Professor of 'International Contracts in Global Markets' and of 'Legal Procedures for Infrastructures and Public Works Procurement'. She has been member of several international and national research groups, on topics pertaining to navigation and transport law. She has been a researcher and Visiting Professor at foreign universities. Elena is a regular speaker at international and Italian conferences and the author of several books and articles. She is a member of scientific associations on Maritime and Transport Law and of the scientific and editorial boards of several international and national law reviews and book series.

DR DANIEL DĄBROWSKI holds a PhD at law and is an employee of the Department of Commercial Law, Transport Law and Insurance Law at the Faculty of Management and Economics of Services of the University of Szczecin. He is trained legal adviser in Poland. Dr Dąbrowski is author of numerous articles in the field of civil law, including transport law, and co-author of the following books: *Transport law. Commentary* (2014); *Convention on the Contract for the Carriage of Goods by Road (CMR). Commentary* (2015); *Contracts for passenger transport* (2018).

DR KONRAD GARNOWSKI is a trained legal adviser in Poland and an employee of the Department of Commercial Law, Transport Law and Insurance Law at the Faculty of Management and Economics of Services of the University of Szczecin. He is author of numerous articles and co-author of monographs in the field of civil law, specializing in transport law.

PATRYK CIOK is a PhD candidate at the Nicolaus Copernicus University in Toruń. He is currently a trainee attorney at law, having earlier gained experience as an insurance broker's employee. He is especially interested in the issue of carrier's liability in the transport of goods and also transport insurance. The topic of his dissertation is unimodal and multimodal cargo carrier's liability in international and domestic law.

PROFESSOR JUAN L. PULIDO BEGINES is currently Full Professor of Maritime and Commercial Law at the University of Cádiz in Spain. He is author of numerous articles and books. He holds both an LLB. and a Doctorate in Law from the Universidad de Cádiz. His current research is centered on maritime law, third-party liability, financial system law and electronic commerce law.

RICHARD COLES is dual-qualified as a solicitor in England and Wales and the Republic of Ireland. He practised as a maritime lawyer in the City of London from 1973 to 2014 with particular expertise in ship finance, shipbuilding contracts, ship sale and purchase and registration. From the mid-1990s he became increasingly involved in the world of superyachts, advising yacht owners, yacht builders, banks, yacht brokers and a leading yachting industry trade association. Upon his retirement as Partner he became a Consultant at Gateley and a Visiting Senior Research Fellow at the Institute of Maritime Law at the University of Southampton. He continues to lecture and research in his areas of expertise. He is author of *Ship Registration: Law and Practice* published in 2002, co-author (with Ed Watt) of the second edition in 2009, and a contributor and consulting editor of the third edition published in 2018. He is co-author (with Professor Filippo Lorenzon) of two editions of *The Law of Yachts and Yachting* published in 2012 and 2018. He has written a number of articles and book reviews, including 'Ship Registration and Brexit', a paper written jointly with Professor Andrew Serdy, for publication in the *Tulane Maritime Law Journal* in summer 2019.

DR OLENA BOKAREVA is Associate Senior Lecturer in private law at the Faculty of Law at Lund University. She is currently working on a postdoctoral project financed by the Ragnar Söderberg Foundation on the topic of 'Compensation and Liability for Passengers' Claims in Sea and Air Transport'. She obtained her doctoral degree from Lund University in 2015 and holds her LLM degree from the same university. Her doctoral research was based on the analysis of the Rotterdam Rules. Her academic interest lies in maritime and commercial law, carriage of goods by sea, multimodal transport and the law of the sea. She teaches maritime and transportation law at the Faculty of Law and selected topics in EU law.

PROFESSOR SOUICHIROU KOZUKA (PhD, Tokyo) is Professor of Law at Gakushuin University, Tokyo. He specialises in commercial law, corporate law and maritime, air and space law, and is editor and author of Souichirou Kozuka (ed.), *Implementation of the Cape Town Convention and the Domestic Laws on Secured Transactions* (2017, Springer). He is correspondent of UNIDROIT (the International Institute for the Unification of Private Law) and Associate Member of the International Academy of Comparative Law (IACL).

PROFESSOR JOSÉ MANUEL MARTÍN OSANTE is professor of commercial law at the Faculty of Law of the University of the Basque Country in Bilbao, Spain. Has worked for five years for the Spanish Ministry of Justice. He has lectured in commercial and maritime law at Spanish and foreign universities, including Argentina, Cape Verde, Colombia, El Salvador, France, Guatemala and Italy. He has been speaker at numerous national and international congresses of transport law and author of many publications in maritime law, on topics including collisions at sea, ship arrest, pollution and marine insurance. Professor José Manuel Martín Osante has participated in more than 20 research projects in the transport sector and is currently directing a project for the Spanish Ministry of Economy and Competitiveness: 'Transport as a Motor of Socio-Economic Development: Legal Solutions'. He is also Executive Director of the *Spanish Journal of Transport Law* and a member of the Advisory Board of the School of Maritime Administration of the Government of the Basque Country.

TABLE OF CASES

TABLE OF LEGISLATION

Conventions and Rules

European Economic Area

European Union Treaties, Directives and Regulations

National legislation

Argentina

Belgium

United Kingdom

United States

PART I

GENERAL REMARKS

CHAPTER 1

Codification

Problems of differing legal cultures

Professor Francis Reynolds

1 Introduction

This book is directed to codification of maritime law. Its topic, to some extent at least, is linked to the Comité Maritime International (CMI) project for the 'Compilation of Selected Principles of the Lex Maritima', which obviously connects with an article on the same subject published by Professor Eric Van Hooydonk in the *Journal of International Maritime Law* of 2014,[1] in which much of the same wording appears.

This first chapter starts with the general idea of codification of private law, and more specifically of contract law, where scepticism is expressed as to the possibility of achieving much in the foreseeable future. But there is no intention of being so negative on the maritime law front, so, after expanding this first point about more general codification, the chapter goes on to be cautiously optimistic about codification of maritime law, which is the subject of this book. It is not directed to domestic codification, which is a matter of rearranging a system of national law even if it uses international maritime concepts and seeks to conform with them.

2 Codification of private law in general

It is tempting to think of the idea of international codification as the result of, or at least a catalyst for, a process in which legal systems all gradually move into fusion of their private law. A codification of *international maritime* law can be seen as part of such a movement.

Indeed, a point made in support of such an exercise in Professor Van Hooydonk's article, and also in material concerning the CMI project, is that there are already, in Europe at least, several code-like compilations now available which look to the eventual prospect of amalgamating private law, or part of it, over at least the European Union. These include the Principles of European Contract Law, the UNIDROIT Principles of International Commercial Contracts, the Draft Common Frame of Reference, and the Vienna Convention on the International Sale of Goods (CISG).[2]

It is certainly true that in commercial private law the appropriate answers to a legal problem posed tend to be similar in result whatever system of law is applied to them, as all arbitrators know. This undoubted fact might tempt one to think that a single route

1 (2014) 20 *Journal of International Maritime Law* 170, containing many valuable citations to other material.
2 United Nations Convention on Contracts for the International Sale of Goods (CISG) (Vienna, 1980).

to them ought to be discoverable. And the obvious way to mark this route would be by agreeing some form of code.

But in this broad context one needs to beware. One needs to be sceptical of international codification because similarity of result may hide very considerable differences between the legal cultures used to achieve it. An example might be given of a stage on which the actors enter from different doors but meet in the centre on equal terms. But they intend to return to their own doors in due course.

I am not qualified to comment on differences among civil law countries, almost all of which have in the context of private law their own codes; but certainly the difference between civil and common law countries is very considerable; and even treating all civil law countries as one for this purpose (which it is probably not right to do), neither civil law nor common law is really going to give up its legal culture or approach to achieve uniformity in the foreseeable future, however plausible a project to achieve this may appear. It takes a long time to train as a lawyer, both as regards theory and experience, and few lawyers are going to set to acquire an armoury of completely new tricks (which perhaps they had to when the Code Napoleon came in, and perhaps again in 1900 in Germany: details of the reactions of practitioners to the transitions would be interesting).[3]

With that starting point I would like now to look at some of the existing compilations which are cited as part of the general reasons for going forward with codification.

The Principles of European Contract Law (PECL), drafted under the auspices of a Danish lawyer, and having a modest common law input, are occasionally helpful, but sometimes unfamiliar: for example, parts of them are based on the distinction between direct and indirect representation, a distinction completely unknown to most common lawyers.

The UNIDROIT Principles of International Commercial Contracts in fact make a point of avoiding that distinction; and although, like the PECL, they are largely the work of academics, they are in general obviously simpler and so more useful as a basic resource for contract drafters and arbitrators. Indeed, that is largely how they are presented.

The more recent and more elaborate Draft Common Frame of Reference (DCFR) is largely German in outlook: it would be interesting to know how a French-trained lawyer would view it, though it does not resemble the French Civil Code, at any rate before the recent changes. But although it is most interesting read from a comparative viewpoint and is presented as no more than a 'legislator's toolbox', there are not many new solutions or techniques that a common lawyer would find helpful to use and develop.

All these three are worthwhile projects. But they all – even the UNIDROIT Principles, which are the most commercial-looking in style – contain general propositions the application of which is going to require a legal culture on which to fall back for the purposes of interpretation and gap filling. This is where different legal cultures cause differences for lawyers seeking to use such codifications. This factor reduces the capacity of such codifications to solve disputes. The main genuinely international, worldwide, use of such codifications is going to be for arbitrators, who may fall back on them to find authority for obvious general propositions – for instance that, in general, failure to respond to a contractual offer does not usually import that it has been accepted. All arbitrators know that the answer to a legal problem is usually fairly easy: the problem is to reason the answer out

3 Nordic legal systems are not discussed here.

within the framework of the applicable law in a way acceptable to disputing parties. For this all lawyers know that one may need support, what common lawyers call 'authority', and the existing codes may be helpful.

There have in fact been proposals in England for a contract code: one was started for English and Scots law soon after our Law Reform Commission[4] was established in 1965. It was eventually finished (by a single senior lawyer, Mr Harvey McGregor QC) and published (surprisingly) in Italy in 1993 under the auspices of Professor Giuseppe Gandolfi. But although Prof. Gandolfi said that the draft Code 'can be compared to the landing of the Apollo 11 team on the moon . . . or the fall of the Berlin Wall', nothing has happened since and 25 years later the text already looks dated. Recently there is another draft by Professor Andrew Burrows, this time specifically presented as a restatement of existing case law, albeit in code form. This is illuminating for English common law, but I do not see it facilitating a European contract code.

The Vienna Convention on the International Sale of Goods (CISG) requires separate consideration. It is different from the above, as it is already an operative international instrument prepared with more general international consultation than the other three, though largely with theoreticians rather than practitioners – something common lawyers would regard as a disadvantage. It now operates in many countries; but it has not been adopted in the UK, and still looks unfamiliar to common lawyers even though it is sometimes claimed to use some common law solutions.

CISG could have been be adopted in the United Kingdom from the beginning; but there was no movement to do this; and now there is so much, mostly German, input already existing that for a new country to adopt it would be difficult – especially as there is no central tribunal to give a lead in official interpretation. Some other common law countries have adopted CISG (though it is often then excluded by routine contract terms in those countries): the few decisions in the US and Australia do not show much understanding when they go beyond simple matters such as quality requirements. There has been little interest in CISG in the UK; nowadays we say 'fine, but if you choose English law we will give you different rules'. In the UK we have a much older basic law called the Sale of Goods Act (which is wider than CISG because it covers the topic of property transfer): but this usually provides no more than pointers, and in fact a judgment on a commercial international sale would usually contain mostly pure common law reasoning and little reference to the Act.

On the other hand, to take a more recent example which is actually in the maritime sphere, the Rotterdam Rules could be acceptable to shipping lawyers in the UK, as they are specialised and were formulated with very extensive international participation; and, as of now, everyone would start afresh on a level playing field. Their prospects, however, seem doubtful, for reasons well known.[5]

Now we return to the overall idea of codification of commercial law or parts of it. Within Europe there may be some feeling among codifiers that common law is an odd man out – operative only in England and Ireland (Scots law is different); and that these countries ought to conform and could do so if they were willing to make a few changes.

---

4 Officially the Law Commission for England and Wales. The Scottish Law Commission was and is separate.

5 They are particularly opposed by freight forwarding interests.

So it may be tempting to say at present that as regards the EU, if the UK leaves the Union, only Ireland remains and there need be little problem (as there is not with Louisiana in the United States).

I cannot answer for the Irish, but even if this is true in the EU context, one has to remember that in the international context there is a huge range of other common law countries – the USA, Canada, Australia, New Zealand, Singapore, Hong Kong, to which we can add the countries of the Indian subcontinent (maybe excluding Myanmar), Malaysia, Anglophone Africa, parts of the West Indies, and some Pacific islands. All these use what is in some respects a rival methodology. So it is not possible to get rid of the common law approach simply by squeezing it out in Europe.

Common law systems do, of course, vary within themselves, as is the case with civil law countries. The most obviously different within them is the law of the United States. Though the US is a common law country – in some ways the nation was founded on common law values – the approach there, while readily comprehensible to a non-US common lawyer, is in substance, though not entirely in method, quite different from that elsewhere in the common law world. Commercial law is in fact dominated by a Code, the Uniform Commercial Code (UCC): but it is a Code drafted by common lawyers, and its use and interpretation require skill in US common law. To take a maritime example of this general difference, outside the UCC, Coghlin, Baker and Kenny on *Time Charters*, and Cooke on *Voyage Charters*, two very authoritative books on common law shipping law, both use American lawyers to cover the American approach to each issue as they go through. The English writers make little attempt to use the American material. An English common lawyer feels much less confident with US law than with that of other common law countries.

To revert to the EU, the best example of a partial codification genuinely operating across the Union, and hence both in civil and common law countries, is provided by the jurisdiction, enforcement of judgments and choice of law regulations (Brussels and Rome I and II). These are not codes: they do not seek to unify the substantive law, only to make uniform certain parts of procedural and conflict of laws rules in European countries. This is a more limited objective and on the whole it is achieved, though not without dissent from time to time. It is much helped by having one tribunal, the Court of Justice of the European Union, to solve disputes as to the operation of the Regulations. If the UK leaves the EU, the UK may well retain this framework. But this is a matter of basic cooperation to secure certain objectives in the effectiveness of justice internationally. It is doubtful whether a *contract code* that sought to unify the substantive law would be easily acceptable in England and Wales (I do not speak for Scotland). Drafting would require much international cooperation, and the interpretation of what was drafted would vary from country to country. If a single European tribunal were created to give authoritative interpretations, it would help, but common lawyers might doubt its commercial expertise.

In general, the common law is a perfectly valid method of solving disputes based on long experience, but like other legal systems requires quite a long apprenticeship the results of which those who practise it will not give up – and itself varies from one country to another, especially the US. Even if civil law countries are willing to smooth out their legal cultural differences, there is no way of getting rid of the common law culture in the reasonably foreseeable future.

This is something to bear in mind when thinking of codification of contract law or of civil law in general. The divide between common law and civil law, and the different methodologies of the two, are a matter of legal culture that is unlikely to go away in the foreseeable future, and one has to proceed accordingly.[6]

3 Codification of international maritime law

After this sceptical and perhaps gloomy prologue, when we turn to maritime law the situation and the prospects for at least some codification are different. This is because there really are genuine, if somewhat imprecise, international and non-domestic origins to much of maritime law. The situation is not, at any rate directly, one of seeking to reconcile different systems of private law, most but not all of which stem from the age of codification: maritime law is a separate force with different origins. Thus Article III of the Constitution of the United States designates admiralty law as a federal matter, not as ordinary private law dealt with by states.

The general point is powerfully put in our time by Chief Justice Allsop of the Federal Court of Australia in his 13th Nicholas J Healy lecture 'Comity and Unity in Maritime Law', delivered in 2016, which is printed in the CMI Yearbook for that year.[7]

It is also true that experienced and often learned practitioners seem more willing to get involved in the area of maritime law than, for example, in general commercial law such as sale of goods, let alone in the wider private law. This means that in the maritime context any codification will attract sophisticated participation that is less likely to allow it to become too theoretical; and more than that, there is likely to be much more general agreement on the outline of at any rate some of the basic principles to be formulated.

A further feature of maritime law is that it has created unique maritime institutions – ship arrest and the admiralty jurisdiction *in rem*; salvage; general average; and tonnage limitation. There is, however, a difficulty with these unique institutions. Despite great efforts by way of formulation and adoption of Conventions, without and even with Conventions they have developed differently in different countries – as indeed the codification proposals which now guide the CMI Committee themselves recognise.

An obvious example is the area of arrest of ships, the maritime lien and the admiralty action *in rem*. From the start these have been somewhat different in common law countries from their parallels in civil law countries because of the common law idea, not the same as any form of *saisie conservatoire*, of an action *in rem* against the ship, based on the notion of a maritime lien, with liability limited to the value of the ship. Then in the late-nineteenth century, in a case of 1892 called *The Dictator*[8] (the name of the ship), English and US law diverged spectacularly. English law took a completely new turn by saying that the lien was procedural, in effect a way of getting at the shipowner not the ship: it was said that what

6 The ground is extremely well-trodden, and no attempt is made to burden this chapter with references. However, an excellent explanation and justification of the common law method can be found in a recent article by Sir Philip Sales, now as Lord Sales a Justice of the Supreme Court of the United Kingdom, in 'The Common Law: Context and Method' (2019) 135 *Law Quarterly Review* 47. Also, much useful and thoughtful material and extensive citation of other articles appears in an article by Prof. Birke Haecker, 'Divergence and Convergence in the Common Law – Lessons from the *ius commune*' (2015) 131 *Law Quarterly Review* 424. See also M.A. Clarke, 'A Way with Words: Some Obstacles to Uniform Transport Law' (1998) 3 *Uniform Law Review* 351.

7 CMI Yearbook 2016, New York II, p.163.

8 [1892] p. 304. The development was authoritatively explained in F.L. Wiswall, Jr., *The development of Admiralty jurisdiction since 1800: an English study with American comparisons* (New York, 1970).

was created was not a maritime lien but a 'statutory lien'. This left true maritime liens as quite a small category in English law. Some not entirely logical features indicating that the action was against the ship remained. But these were more or less destroyed a hundred years later in another English case of 1997 called *The Indian Grace*,[9] concerning the question whether a small judgment in India barred an action *in rem* in England for a very much larger sum. Yet in 2006 the Federal Court of Australia to some extent went back on this for Australian law in a case called *Commandate v Pan Australia.*[10] But quite different overall is the position in the US, where Admiralty actions are in general conceived as based on maritime liens, treated as a much wider category than the limited maritime liens recognised in English law. Not that long ago a senior English judge caused considerable offence by saying at an international conference that in the US, maritime liens 'breed like rabbits'.[11] So despite the effect of the 1952 Arrest Convention,[12] there are quite elaborate structures of a differing nature in common law countries relating to claims brought in connection with ship operation.

There is little prospect of securing a uniform reaction on these and other matters (such as tonnage limitation) by international codification; but I stress again that the CMI proposals, and Professor Van Hooydonk in his article, do not suggest that there is.

So while I endorse the idea of study of the principles of maritime law, and affirm with Chief Justice Allsop that they exist as something separate from normal private law, what is done will have to involve navigating around the central and most obvious manifestations of those principles, which are reserved for Conventions, and which with or without Conventions may be seriously different from country to country, not only between civil law and common law but also within common law. Locating areas outside them where something is usefully to be done, and then doing it in a way that suitably reflects the international flavour, will not be easy.

Even then, one should still bear in mind my first point above, that all codifiers have to take into account differences of legal culture, and that compromise may become extremely difficult. Although in the maritime context this should be less of a problem, it is obvious that it will still exist. Where there are gaps in reasoning there will be a temptation for any lawyer to fall back on the type of reasoning familiar and indeed instinctive to him or her.

But with that caveat I endorse the terms of reference of the CMI committee, and (respectfully) of Professor Van Hooydonk's article from which they are taken. I am a bit sceptical about his reference there to the 'innermost core of maritime law', as I am about innermost cores generally. But it may be possible to find some broad general principles of the *lex maritima* on which almost everyone in the business would agree, to which to go back for very elementary propositions and guidance. They may be useful for litigators, arbitrators, legislators, and also in countries that still have only rather rudimentary rules. This last is a point made about articles 57 and 58 of the Rotterdam Rules concerning transfer of the bill of lading contract, a topic for which some countries have sophisticated rules making the

9 [1994] AC 410, [1998] 1 Lloyd's Rep 1.

10 (2006) 157 FCR 45, [2008] 1 Lloyd's Rep 119.

11 See M. Marks Cohen, 'In Defence of *The Halcyon Isle*' [1987] LMCLQ, p. 152; S. Rares, 'Ship Arrests, Maritime Liens and Cross-Border Insolvency' [2018] LMCLQ 398.

12 International Convention Relating to the Arrest of Sea-Going Ships (Brussels, 1952).

Rotterdam provisions unnecessary. Such provisions may be relevant in other countries that have less developed rules.

But there is a final reservation. Chief Justice Allsop suggests that such principles, when determined, may actually override positive law. The example he gives is of a country legislating to abolish the seafarer's lien for wages: he suggests that this may be invalid. It is questionable whether such legislation could legitimately be attacked, because it relates to insolvency, which is not an exclusively maritime subject. His other example relates to the principles behind salvage awards. Although this does seem to me a case where countries should strive to apply the same principles; it is nevertheless uncertain what will happen when they do not.

And overall the difficulty is that the interesting and big stuff is in the areas where the results, as opposed to the starting points, of the international maritime law vary considerably; so great care will need to be taken in selection of topics, and in stating generalities which carefully tiptoe round the areas which cannot easily be interfered with. Chief Justice Allsop says that international maritime law has 'utility, strength, vitality and a contemporary role in the maintenance and development of legal doctrine'. Professor Van Hooydonk says that such a codification 'could be the lubricant that smooths the path of new international and regulatory initiatives, easing contract negotiation and dispute resolution, as well as the spread of knowledge'. These are noble objectives, but not easy to attain.

So overall I suggest that international codifications of private law (or at any rate contract law) are of limited value, at any rate if the common law is to be taken in. In the maritime area, there is a much better chance, but the existing position imposes serious restrictions.

CHAPTER 2

Unification and codification of maritime law

Friends or foes?

Professor Dr Eric Van Hooydonk

1 Introduction: objective and scope

The purpose of this paper is threefold: (1) to discuss the achievements and pitfalls of unification and codification of maritime law; (2) to discuss their interaction; and (3) to suggest ways forward. For a number of reasons, these issues are of special interest to the author. To begin with, Belgium served as the cradle of the international unification of maritime law. It is also itself an important port and shipping state. In addition, the author is Chair of the Belgian Commission for the Codification of Shipping Law and also of the working group of the Comité Maritime International, which is tasked with the compilation of the principles of the *Lex Maritima*. In this dual capacity, the author of this paper is inevitably confronted with the tension between national legislation and international unification, and based on this experience an attempt will be made to formulate some useful policy-oriented suggestions.

2 Unification of maritime law, a *Belle Epoque* project

In order to understand the genesis, progress and results of the nineteenth-century movement for the international unification of maritime law, it is necessary to consider its initial objectives in their historical context. The pursuit of unification sprang up in an era of general innovation. The second Industrial Revolution brought many important technological developments, including, in the field of shipbuilding, massive increases in scale and the use of steam propulsion. Maritime communications were accelerated substantially by the introduction of the telegraph. Ports outgrew the embrace of the old city centres and took on industrial dimensions. In the political sphere, the principle of international free trade found acceptance, and was given concrete form in a large number of bilateral commerce and navigation treaties. In the economic field, these changes translated into, *inter alia*, the organisation of liner shipping. In the face of this wave of modernisation, maritime law lagged behind for a long time. Until the notion of unification took hold, maritime law remained stuck in some sort of prehistoric phase, characterised by conflicting and partly obsolete national maritime laws and practices, largely inherited from the *Ancien Régime*.

In this age of globalisation *avant la lettre*, the unification of maritime law was inevitable. One of the first, fragmented steps consisted of the drafting of the York Rules (1864), which resulted from a purely business initiative launched four years earlier in England,

and which developed into several updated versions of the York-Antwerp Rules (the first version of which was adopted in Antwerp in 1877).[1] While many other attempts were made to harmonise, for example. the rules on contract or affreightment (see the long-forgotten Sheffield Rules from 1865[2]), the first fully-fledged regulatory unification of transport rules was achieved not for sea, but for rail transport, with the adoption, in 1890, of the Bern Rules (which had in fact been in preparation since 1878).

The pursuit of a more systematic international unification of maritime law took on a more concrete shape thanks to an ambitious, today unfortunately forgotten, Belgian initiative. In 1885, with the support of the Belgian Government, the first World Commercial Law Conference was organised in Antwerp.[3] It coincided with the World Exhibition. In their report to King Leopold II, the organisers of the congress left no doubt that the global streamlining of maritime law was within easy reach:

> '[. . .] unity could be achieved without serious difficulties for some parts of the commercial law, in particular for the promissory note, the transport contract and maritime law.[4]
>
> [. . .]
>
> Maritime law, in its various aspects, has been the subject of many studies, and its uniform regulation is, so to speak, completely prepared.'[5]

The conference discussed concrete international draft provisions on, *inter alia*, the liability of shipowners and ship masters, bills of lading and carriage of goods, general average, marine insurance, bottomry, collision, salvage, ships, rights on ships, and maritime criminal law. During a second congress, in Brussels in 1888, this work was continued.[6] Not surprisingly, however, the initiators became gradually aware that the unification of the entire maritime law on a global scale was not as simple as initially thought.

However, this in no way detracts from the genuine and visionary enthusiasm of personalities such as Victor Jacobs (1838–1891). He was the Chairman of the 1885 and 1888 maritime law sections. The career of this Antwerp lawyer was as varied as it was original.

1 In our library we have a remarkable collection of pamphlets from the period 1862–1864, from the library of Edouard Van Peborgh from Antwerp, one of the founders of early harmonisation, which reflect the belief in the need for unification of maritime law.

2 See, for example, W.L.P.A. Molengraaff, 'Etude sur le Contrat d'Affrètement' (1882) 14 *Revue de droit interenational et de législation comparée*, pp. 257–284.

3 See X., *Actes du congrès international de droit commercial d'Anvers (1885). Droit maritime – Lettre de change* (Brussels/Paris, Ferdinand Larcier/G. Pedone/Lauriel, 1886), p. 441.

4 French original:

> [. . .] l'unité pourrait être obtenue sans difficultés sérieuses pour quelques-unes des parties du droit commercial, notamment pour la lettre de change, le contrat de transport et le droit maritime (X., Actes du congrès international de droit commercial d'Anvers (1885). Droit maritime – Lettre de change (Brussels/Paris, Ferdinand Larcier/G. Pedone/Lauriel, 1886), 17).

5 French original:

> Le droit maritime, dans ses divers éléments, a été l'objet de nombreuses études, et son règlement uniforme est, pour ainsi dire, tout préparé (X., Actes du congrès international de droit commercial d'Anvers (1885). Droit maritime – Lettre de change (Brussels/Paris, Ferdinand Larcier/G. Pedone/Lauriel, 1886), 17–18).

6 X., *Actes du congès international de droit commercial de Bruxelles (1888). Droit maritime – Lettre de change* (Brussels/Paris, Ferdinand Larcier/G. Pedone/Lauriel, 1889), p. 563.

A political rebel in Antwerp, as well as nationally, he became a Member of the Chamber of Representatives and also Minister of, among other matters, Public Works. He also authored, in addition to a detailed Commentary on the 1879 Belgian Maritime Code,[7] nothing short of a Draft World Maritime Code. It covered exactly 24 Articles on 13 pages.[8]

Because of these experiences, it was once again the Belgians who took the lead in arriving at a more realistic organisation of the great unification dream. In 1896 they founded the Belgian Maritime Law Association, the first of its kind. The Belgians urged maritime law practitioners in other countries to follow their example and join forces in the newly established Comité Maritime International (CMI). The first CMI Circular appeared on 2 July 1896 (i.e., before the CMI was formally established in 1897).[9] It stated that maritime trade had become essentially cosmopolitan, and that propaganda, studies, conferences and brochures were needed in order to unify maritime law. Attention also had to be paid to national legislative developments that would aim at unification.[10]

In his inaugural speech at the first meeting of the Belgian Maritime Law Association on 22 November 1896, Minister of State Auguste Beernaert, the first President of the Association and one of the founding fathers of the CMI, expressed the unification vision as follows:

> 'Is it not obvious that what is appropriate to this vast mix of interests is a single law applicable to all seas and countries, a law that would not be English, German, American or French, but would be the law, the law of all, a law elaborated with the consent of all peoples, in a day of peace and blessing[?]'[11]

The story of the pioneering days of the unification of maritime law clearly shows how the project was driven by the economic and cultural optimism and also the legal idealism of the end of the nineteenth century. Indeed, maritime law unification started as a typical *Belle Epoque* project.

Once the CMI was up and running, in the twentieth century a string of thematic international Conventions quickly came into being on matters such as collisions, salvage, maritime liens and mortgages, limitation of liability, bills of lading, etc. These were prepared by the CMI, but formalised at Diplomatic Conferences in Brussels hosted by the Belgian Government, which acted (and indeed still acts[12]) as depositary. After the Second World War,

7 V. Jacobs, *Le droit maritime belge. Commentaire de la loi du 21 août 1879*, 2 vols. (Brussels/Paris, Bruylant-Christophe/A. Maresq, 1891), pp. 565, 684.

8 V. Jacobs, *Avant-projet de loi maritime internationale* (Brussels/Paris, Ferdinand Larcier/G. Pedone-Lauriel, 1886), p. 92.

9 On this history of the CMI, see A. Lilar and C. van den Bosch, *Le Comité Maritime International 1897–1972 / International Maritime Committee 1897–1972* (*s.l.*, *s.d.*), 120 p.; F. Wiswall, *Comité Maritime International 1897 Antwerpen 1997* (Ellsworth, Maine, 1997), unpaginated.

10 (1897) *Bulletin de l'Association belge pour l'unification du droit maritime*, 1 February 1897, Iss. 1, Antwerp, J.-E. Buschmann, 1897, pp. 8–11.

11 French original:

> Ne saute-t-il pas aux yeux que ce qui convient à ce vaste mélange d'intérêts, c'est une loi unique applicable sur toutes les mers et dans tous les pays, une loi qui ne serait ni anglaise, ni allemande, ni américaine, ni française, mais qui serait la loi, la loi de tous, une loi élaborée du consentement de tous les peuples, en une journée de paix et de bénédiction [?] ((1897) *Bulletin de l'Association belge pour l'unification du droit maritime*, 1 February 1897, Iss. 1, Antwerp, J.-E. Buschmann, 1897 (12) (19).

12 See https://diplomatie.belgium.be/fr/traites/la_belgique_depositaire#1 (visited 21 August 2019).

UN-linked intergovernmental organisations such as the IMO, UNCTAD and UNCITRAL came to the fore. They, too, realised a number of unifying Conventions, taking over the leading role of the CMI.

The, all in all, quite impressive achievements of the unification movement are well known. A patchwork of Conventions on 'unifiable' themes of commercial maritime law are indeed available. Some of them, such as the 1910 Collision Convention,[13] undoubtedly reflect real uniformity. It should be stressed that the unifying treaties, as conceived by the CMI from the outset, contain deliberately unified international substantive regulations, and not merely uniform conflict of laws rules (which had been considered as an alternative solution in the early days[14]) or uniform laws, which national legislators could then transpose.[15] The IMO added a large number of important public law regulations on matters such as the safety of ships and protection of the environment. A not-to-be-overestimated result of these sustained efforts is that today it is universally accepted that maritime policy and regulation should be debated at global level, regardless of whether major politically sensitive issues or technical specificities are concerned.

On the other hand, it is important to point out the limitations and dangers of the current approach. The previously achieved, partial uniformity is weakened by an endless sequence of amendments to Conventions, each time they need to be updated. States, of course, decide voluntarily whether to follow the amendments, and this often leads to new fragmentation. The entry into force of Conventions is often delayed, and several Conventions are obviously lame ducks, because they fail ever to come into force, or, in other cases, attract only an insignificant group of States. Since the Second World War there are of course many more States, with more diverging interests, which substantially complicates decision-making. The difficulties faced by the bodies responsible for maritime law unification have led to pessimistic comments in international literature for many decades. The frustrations expressed by authorities such as Wüstendorfer (as early as 1950!),[16] Herber,[17] Griggs[18] and Tetley[19] are worth recalling.

Yet the evolution is somewhat strange. Today's globalism and technological changes are indeed not dissimilar to developments during the *Belle Epoque*. But it seems that optimism and idealism have deserted us. Patrick Griggs asked whether we are 'conventioned out'.[20] The fact is that unification is still desirable but has become more difficult to achieve.

13 Convention for the Unification of Certain Rules of Law with respect to Collisions between Vessels (Brussels, 1910).

14 Specific maritime conflicts of law rules were considered, for example, during the aforementioned 1885 and 1888 conferences.

15 On the consideration of these alternatives, see further E. Van Hooydonk, *Eerste Blauwboek over de herziening van het Belgisch scheepvaartrecht* (Antwerp/Apeldoorn, Maklu, 2011), pp. 96–98, para. 1.89 and 186–188, para. 1.229, with further references.

16 H. Wüstendörfer, *Neuzeitliches Seehandelsrecht* (Tübingen, Verlag J.C.B. Mohr, 1950), pp. 33–34.

17 R. Herber, 'German domestic and international law: lights and shadows' (1999) *Il Diritto Marittimo* (111), 111.

18 P. Griggs, 'Obstacles to uniformity of maritime law', in Comité Maritime International, *Yearbook 2002* (Antwerp, CMI, 2003), pp. 158–173.

19 W. Tetley, 'Uniformity of International Private Maritime Law – The Pros, Cons and Alternatives to International Conventions – How to Adopt an International Convention' (2000) 24 *Tulane Maritime Law Journal* 775–856.

20 P. Griggs, 'Obstacles to uniformity of maritime law', in Comité Maritime International, *Yearbook 2002* (Antwerp, CMI, 2003), (158), p. 173.

Except for politically sensitive and technical regulation, unification sometimes seems to have come to a standstill. At the time of going to press, it was still unclear what the fate of the ambitious Rotterdam Rules on the carriage of goods would be. If they do not succeed in coming into force, the question arises whether they will go down in history as the Waterloo of maritime law unification. Even more important is the observation that national legislators are increasingly re-codifying their own maritime laws. As a matter of fact, today there are probably more new national legislative activities than successful steps towards more unification. Therefore, the question arises whether we are returning to prehistory and whether one day the proponents of maritime law unification will have to start from scratch.

3 The revival of national codification

Any discussion of the evolution of the national codification of maritime law inevitably begins with the famous French Ordonnance de la Marine (1681). This masterpiece of codification was based on comparative law research and encompassed both private and public law. The Napoleonic Code of Commerce (1807) was little more than a copy-paste of the Ordonnance as far as maritime law is concerned (with the exception of public law, which was omitted).

The nineteenth century saw a worldwide codification movement. Countries where new national maritime laws or codes were introduced are Argentina, Belgium, Brazil, Chile, Colombia, Costa Rica, Denmark, Dominican Republic, Ecuador, Egypt, Finland, Germany, Greece, Guatemala, Haiti, Italy, Japan, Mexico, the Netherlands, Nicaragua, Norway, Peru, Portugal, Romania, Spain, Sweden and Turkey. These projects were largely realised in parallel with the unification movement described above. Several legislations were based on comparative law research and pronounced eclectic approaches. Not surprisingly, French law was then still very influential.

Belgium approached its late-nineteenth-century national legislation efforts, too, from a *Belle Epoque* perspective. Belgium reworked the Napoleonic provisions in 1879 and 1908 in a unifying spirit, after having studied and compared the law of various other countries. Further, it systematically adapted its national laws to the unified rules of the CMI Conventions, and the influential Belgian CMI leaders and the national legislator continuously interacted. This sometimes led to a premature adaptation of the national law (for example, to the draft CMI Convention on maritime liens and mortgages of 1906, which was in fact not finalised until 1926[21]). Belgium also influenced statute-making in other countries (such as Greece).

In recent decades, maritime law codification has undeniably experienced a revival. New maritime laws or codes have emerged, or are in preparation, in countries such as Belgium, Brazil, China, Croatia, Finland, France, Germany, Japan, Monaco, the Netherlands, Norway, Panama, Poland, Portugal, Russia, Slovenia, Spain, Sweden, United Kingdom and Vietnam. However, pressing questions are where, in these projects, the unification spirit can be found, whether comparative analysis is carried out, and whether the national legislators are devising measures intended to contribute to international unification.[22]

21 The Convention on Maritime Liens and Mortgages (Brussels 1926).

22 See E. Van Hooydonk, 'The renaissance of maritime codes – a need for international guidance?' (2015) 21 *Journal of International Maritime Law* 5–6.

In this respect it is also interesting to consider the recent Belgian codification project. This started in 2006 with a study on strengths and weaknesses of Belgian maritime law and policy.[23] The following year, an official Reform Commission was established, which carried out research and drafting work until 2016, and organised extensive public consultations.[24] Between 2017 and 2019, a political decision-making process followed (during which, unfortunately, many errors were introduced beyond the Commission's control). In 2019, the new Belgian Shipping Code was adopted by Parliament and subsequently promulgated.[25] The unifying spirit of the Belgian project is apparent from (1) thorough preparative comparative law research;[26] (2) the maximum adaptation of the national regime to international Conventions; (3) the codification of commonly used standard clauses (paraphrasing the main provisions of the most commonly applied international charter parties); (4) the reference to the York-Antwerp Rules rather than the insertion of substantive national rules on general average; and (5) an explicit reference to general principles of maritime law as an autonomous source of law. The Belgian project thus shows that, however paradoxical it may sound, a national law can contribute, to an extent, to international unity.

With a view to pending or future legislative initiatives elsewhere, we would like to make four concrete suggestions.

First, idealism should definitely be restored. The ambition to contribute to unity often seems missing in current re-codification projects. As the Belgian example has shown, national re-codification projects can, however, effectively contribute to unity in different ways.

Secondly, we consider it desirable to revive comparative law research. In the past, legal manuals contained much comparative information.[27] But few present-day codification projects seem to take account of developments and choices made elsewhere. It seems that comparative law research has been neglected, if not abandoned. The questions arise whether maybe a new language barrier is involved, or a barrier to the access to information, a new narrow-mindedness, or even a new regulatory nationalism. Ideally, comparative research should be supported by academic institutions, but unfortunately maritime law is not a prioritised branch of the law in many countries.

Thirdly, the CMI could play a more proactive role in this field. More specifically, the CMI could issue guidelines for the drafting of maritime laws (as it has done in the past for Asian and Pacific countries).[28]

Fourthly, a compilation of selected principles of the *Lex Maritima* can make a valuable contribution to the harmonisation of maritime law.[29] The CMI Working Group on the *Lex*

---

23 E. Van Hooydonk, *Schip van staat met slagzij. Sterkten en zwakten van maritiem recht en beleid in België* (Antwerp/Apeldoorn, Maklu, 2006), p. 243.

24 See www.zeerecht.be and www.droitmaritime.be (visited 21 August 2019).

25 *Belgisch Staatsblad / Moniteur belge*, 1 August 2019.

26 All the Commission's proposals were underpinned by, *inter alia*, a comparative analysis of the legislation of France, Germany, Luxembourg, the Netherlands and the United Kingdom (neighbouring countries but also maritime competitors). Where relevant, laws of other countries were also examined.

27 Suffice it to mention here the impressive multi-volume manuals of maritime law by French Professors Georges Ripert and René Rodière.

28 In the 1980s and 1990s, the CMI authored, or contributed to, three consecutive versions of the *Guidelines for maritime legislation*, which were published by the Economic and Social Commission for Asia and the Pacific (UNESCAP) in Bangkok.

29 See E. Van Hooydonk, 'Towards a worldwide restatement of the general principles of maritime law' (2014) 20 *Journal of International Maritime Law* 170–182.

Maritima[30] is preparing text proposals. Its aim is not to unify diverging rules, but to identify and 'codify' common ground, in other words, to compile shared, non-controversial principles. This would enable the promotion of uniform interpretation of underlying basic rules.

4 Concluding remarks: main findings and recommendations

The unification of maritime law was launched as a business-orientated but also quite idealistic *Belle Epoque* project. But we no longer live in the *Belle Epoque*. Unification by means of Conventions has become, to say the least, difficult owing to its inherent procedural weaknesses. But unity is under serious additional threat from the unguided missile of national re-codification. Against this background, we suggest, from our experience, four targeted policy measures: (1) restore the idealism of unification through awareness-building among proponents of national legislative projects; (2) revive comparative law research to support drafters; (3) issue CMI Guidance on national codifications; and (4) continued compilation of the *Lex Maritima*, which is still an ongoing project. All these, perhaps less conventional, measures can, in our view, usefully support efforts to further the unification of maritime law.

30 The IWG members are: CMI IWG on Lex Maritima Eric Van Hooydonk (Belgium), Chairman; Jesus Casas Robla (Spain), Rapporteur; Aybek Ahmedov (Russia); Kerim Atamer (Turkey); Tomotaka Fujita (Japan); Andrea La Mattina (Italy); Filippo Lorenzon (United Kingdom); Andreas Maurer (Germany); Mišo Mudrić (Croatia); Gustavo Omaña Pares (Venezuela); Massimiliano Rimaboschi (Italy); Frank Smeele (The Netherlands); Michael Sturley (United States); Lijun Zhao (United Kingdom/China); and Alexander von Ziegler (Switzerland).

CHAPTER 3

Unification of maritime law – a failed strategy?

Professor Erik Røsæg

1 Introduction

We pride ourselves on the long process of harmonizing commercial maritime law, which began more than a century ago. However, is this process a success story or perhaps of only limited legal substance, albeit providing a nice social club for those involved? The following will offer some reflections on this and outline an alternative strategy.

Section 2 addresses some starting points with respect to the harmonization of commercial maritime law. Section 3 discusses the relationship between harmonization and codification. In section 4, mandatory rules as a driver of harmonization will be discussed, while section 5 deals with harmonization's relationship to insurance.

2 General views on the harmonization of commercial maritime law

2.1 A health check on harmonization

In this section, the achievements of the harmonization of maritime law will be discussed on the basis of perhaps the three most successful sets of Conventions: the Conventions on oil spill compensation, the Conventions on cargo damage compensation, and the Convention on collision damage compensation.

The Conventions on oil spill compensation consist of eight Conventions[1] in three tiers of compensation, one on top of another, so that the upper layers kick in only if the lower layers do not suffice:

First tier:

- International Convention on Civil Liability for Bunker Oil Pollution Damage, 2001 (Bunker Convention)
- International Convention on Civil Liability for Oil Pollution Damage, 1992 (CLC 1992) with previous versions of 1969 and 1984)

Second tier:

- International Convention on the Establishment of an International Fund for Compensation for Oil Pollution Damage, 1992 (FUND 1992) with previous versions of 1971 and 1984)

1 There are also a few instruments around the Conventions that will be listed in the following, such as protocols, tacit amendments and clauses on the interrelation between Conventions. This complicates the picture even further.

Third tier:

- Protocol of 2003 to the International Convention on the Establishment of an International Fund for Compensation for Oil Pollution Damage, 1992 (FUND PROT 2003)

The first tier is financed by shipowners, while the second and third tiers are financed by levies on discharges of oil cargoes. This financing scheme is somewhat modified by two agreements that make shipowners contribute to the upper tiers:

- Small Tanker Oil Pollution Indemnification Agreement (STOPIA) 2006 (as amended 2017)
- Tanker Oil Pollution Indemnification Agreement (TOPIA) 2006 (as amended 2017)

Some oil spills and some effects of oil spills that are not covered by the instruments above are covered by the International Convention on Liability and Compensation for Damage in Connection with the Carriage of Hazardous and Noxious Substances by Sea, 2010 (2010 HNS Convention; with a previous version of 1996).

Although complicated, the Conventions and agreement revolve around the same concepts, and there is no doubt that this system brings harmony to the legal rules. The newer Conventions replace the older, most likely because the higher compensation amounts of the newer Conventions attract governments as legislators and creditors. The system is widespread.[2] Pollution victims get their compensation, and the polluters pay.

However, from a purely harmonization point of view, the Conventions are not very successful. First, a major country, the USA, is not a party and has its own system of pollution compensation that is conceptually quite different from the international system.[3] Second, the rules are the same, but the states differ quite significantly. For example, the likely compensation amounts to be paid vary due to cost level and latitude.[4] Formally harmonized rules do not guarantee harmonization in substance.

Also, the Conventions for damage compensation for cargo damage are numerous:

- International Convention for the Unification of Certain Rules of Law relating to Bills of Lading, Brussels, 1924 (the Hague Rules)
- Protocol to amend the International Convention for the Unification of Certain Rules of Law relating to Bills of Lading, signed at Brussels on 25th August 1924, 1968 (the Hague-Visby Rules)
- United Nations Convention on the Carriage of Goods by Sea, 1978 (the Hamburg Rules)
- United Nations Convention on International Multimodal Transport of Goods, 1980
- United Nations Convention on Contracts for the International Carriage of Goods Wholly or Partly By Sea, 2008 (the Rotterdam Rules)

2 See http://www.imo.org/en/About/Conventions/StatusOfConventions/Pages/Default.aspx (visited 27 August 2019)

3 33 USC Ch. 40.

4 IOPC Fund Document IOPC/APR19/5/2.

Here, the transition from older to newer regimes has stopped, and it is unlikely that the newer regimes will ever enter into force or get a widespread acceptance, as time has passed without significant changes. Some may still hope that the Rotterdam Rules will enter into force, but this is unlikely, as the US has run into constitutional problems,[5] and much of the ambition of the new regime was to include the US.

The resulting situation is confusing. There are several regimes around, and they are as different as such regimes can be with respect to defences, limitation amounts, and other matters. The regimes do not have clearly defined geographic scopes. Judgments in one jurisdiction are, as a rule, not recognized in other jurisdictions, regardless of whether the two jurisdictions are parties to the same Conventions. The popular Conventions – the Hague Rules and the Hague-Visby Rules – are very fragmentary. In sum, this is an ideal world for forum-shopping. Forum-shopping in cases of conflict could have been dealt with by appropriate clauses in the contracts, but even then it is the contracts and not the harmonized Conventions that save the day. The repeated and failed harmonization attempts have created more confusion rather than less.

The third example of apparently successful harmonization has other problems attached to it. This is the Collision Convention 1910,[6] which enjoys widespread acceptance (albeit not including the US) and no revision Conventions. The problem here is the substantive rules. The Convention maintains rules that have been abolished in modern law, such as the pro rata liability of joint tortfeasors and the disallowance of any kind of strict liability. Today, tortfeasors are generally jointly and severally liable. The non-strict liability causes problems in relation to the many Conventions on strict liability and is inadequate for unmanned ships.

Some of these problems can be alleviated by interpreting the Convention to deal strictly with damages to the other ship involved in the Convention (and interests related to it) but not, for example, to third parties suffering pollution damage. However, this will not eliminate the problem, for example, with respect to passengers on one ship suffering damage from pollution from another in a collision. The problem is the Convention, which was made before pollution damage and damage outside the involved ships became major issues.

There was nothing wrong with the Collision Convention in 1910. Indeed, it was quite progressive for its time, recognizing the apportionment of damages based on the degree of negligence on each side. The problem is that it has since, as a kind of bastion of harmonized law, proved difficult to alter.

The point here is not that the provisions of the Collision Convention are undesirable. (They probably are, as the solutions differ significantly from the current law in most jurisdictions.) The point is that once a harmonized solution is codified, it is difficult to change. There are no particular benefits attached to the Collision Convention that can defend the upkeep of these anomalies. Indeed, it is difficult to see any financial or practical gain from having harmonized rules in the area of law at all; the rules would better be harmonized with the ordinary law of torts.

These three examples demonstrate that the harmonized maritime law is in only apparent good health. The problems associated with the harmonized systems are legion, such as only

5 M. Sturley, 'The Rotterdam Rules and Maritime Performing Parties in the United States' (2012) 79 *Journal of Transportation Law, Logistics & Policy* 13, f. 28.

6 Convention for the Unification of Certain Rules of Law with respect to Collisions between Vessels (Brussels, 1910).

apparent harmonization, differences caused by failed harmonization attempts, and harmonization's standing in the way of progress. The story of the harmonization of maritime law is not necessarily a success story.

2.2 Gap-filling law still important

A problem often overlooked in the harmonization of commercial maritime law is the fragmentation of the rules. One tends to focus on the achievements and what has been harmonized rather than on the limited scope of harmonization. One example is the Hague and Hague-Visby Rules already mentioned. With only a couple of substantive articles, they deal with just a fraction of carriage-of-goods issues. One of the problems in getting the Rotterdam Rules into force is perhaps their much more comprehensive regulation of the issues.

An even more illustrative example is the limitation Conventions. The global limitation Conventions are mainly the following:

- International Convention for the Unification of Certain Rules relating to the Limitation of the Liability of Owners of Sea-going Vessels, 1924
- International Convention relating to the Limitation of the Liability of Owners of Seagoing Ships, 1957
- Convention on Limitation of Liability for Maritime Claims, 1976
- Protocol of 1996 to amend the Convention on Limitation of Liability for Maritime Claims, 1976, 1996

These Conventions set caps on shipowners' liabilities. The caps differ, but the amounts are of no concern here. The concern here is that, regardless of the limitation levels, this will mean different things in different jurisdictions, depending on the gap-filling law. In Norway, for example, personal injury claims in tort do not include hospitalization costs,[7] while the opposite rule is perhaps the more common. Obviously, then, the limitation amounts will have less impact in Norway than in those other countries. The harmonization by global limitation Conventions is, then, only an apparent harmonization. This would be so even if all states had been a party to the same Convention.

The differences created by the gap-filling law are important and make forum shopping attractive, regardless of Conventions. Indeed, forum shopping is facilitated, because the Conventions create a common framework that makes it easy to compare legal regimes and because at least some of the Conventions include a duty to recognize legal procedures in other States Parties.

Despite harmonization attempts, one will always use a local lawyer in maritime cases. This illustrates well the limited scope of the harmonization Conventions.

2.3 The standstill in the IMO

Unfortunately, the problems with harmonization, outlined above, are not merely temporary problems that will be resolved as the harmonization process progresses. There are no signs

7 Norwegian Torts Act, 1969, ss. 3–7.

that more extensive harmonization is in the pipeline. The golden age of the harmonization of maritime law is over, and the harmonization process is gradually coming to a halt.

The first, golden age of the harmonization of commercial maritime law started with the diplomatic conferences of 1910 and 1924, which adopted, among other things, the Collision Convention, a salvage Convention,[8] and the Hague Rules. The procedure was typically that the diplomatic conferences considered drafts developed by the Comité Maritime International (CMI), which were well founded in the shipping industry. After the Torrey Canyon oil spill of 1967, a Legal Committee was established in the International Maritime Organization (IMO). Still, the starting points were CMI drafts or industry arrangements (such as CRISTAL and TOVALOP).[9]

The second phase commenced in the 1980s and may be called the government phase. The debates were politicized. Developing countries formed their own group in the negotiations, and so did other countries. Governments forwarded agendas beyond the interests of their industry, such as environmental concerns and consumer (passenger) protection, while projects to improve commercial law, as such, did not get priority. Consequently, the Conventions proved more difficult to adopt and to put into force.

The third phase commenced in the first decade of this century. Conventions were still difficult to put into force. The HNS Convention[10] was revised, but even in its revised version, its prospects are not bright. The Legal Committee apparently considered that there were no more big projects and reduced its activity.[11] The industry and governments could no longer find harmonization projects that they both found worthwhile, and therefore neither the industry nor the governments see the IMO as a useful tool for their interests. The harmonization process has become stagnant.

The United Nations Commission on International Trade Law (UNCITRAL) constitutes an exception to this. Here, the focus on trade facilitation allows industry projects, such as the Rotterdam Rules and Judicial Sales of Ships, to flourish.[12] However, it is for governments to implement these projects. It remains to be seen whether they will get the necessary priority at the implementation stage.

It is likely that at least some harmonization projects will succeed. However, the golden age of the harmonization of commercial maritime law has ended.

2.4 The value of failed attempts

Even if the harmonization processes have not achieved anything near the harmonization of commercial maritime law, even in limited fields, the processes are not in vain. Indeed, the processes are extremely valuable, even if they do not lead to full harmonization of the law or even to a Convention in force.

8 The Convention for the Unification of Certain Rules of Law respecting Assistance and Salvage at Sea (Brussels, 1910).

9 C. de la Rue, 'TOVALOP and CRISTAL – A Purpose Fulfilled', 1996 *International Journal of Shipping Law* 285.

10 See section 2.1.

11 IMO Document LEG 106/13/1.

12 UNCITRAL Document A/CN.9/WG.VI/WP.80.

The value of the harmonization process is, above all, that states compare their systems, agree on a terminology, and are exposed to input from stakeholders. In addition, a network of personal contacts is created. Without the harmonization attempts, this would be unlikely to happen, at least outside academic circles.

An illustration of this point is the 2002 Athens Convention on liability for death and personal injury to passengers.[13] There is no ambition to harmonize the maximum liability, and States Parties may even abolish all limits on passenger claims. Still, the Convention is valuable in that there is a common insurance regime and recognition of insurance certificates and judgments as well as a new, common basis of liability against the carrier and performing carrier. A harmonized structure of thinking is perhaps more important than harmonized legal rules.

Due to the value of harmonization attempts, such attempts could very well be continued. However, if the attempts regularly fail, the processes will be of only academic interest.

2.5 Subsidiarity and democracy

Regardless of success, there is one aspect of the harmonization process that is regularly understated and that is necessary for the correct initial view of harmonization processes. This aspect is the likely effects of the negotiation processes and their results on national legislative processes and consequently on subsidiarity and democracy.[14]

When negotiations are about to commence, this is likely to influence the national debate. The international negotiations are likely to take the focus away from alternative initiatives, and no one will develop national law while an international process is ongoing.

During the negotiations, the discussions can be more or less transparent. Many states do not have the same routines for public involvement in international negotiations as in the development of national legislation. In any event, the negotiating officials are likely to be less accessible than, for example, members of parliament, and the relations to other states may be (or be said to be) an obstacle to openness. Democracy is suffering accordingly.

There is one exception to this. The interest groups that are represented in the national delegations as advisers or in the international bodies (for example, the IMO) as NGOs have a special, privileged access to the negotiators. The effect of this access is enhanced by the close relations developed when the negotiators and advisers travel together and stay together in a foreign location while the international body is in session. This is, in a way, ideal democracy – but only for the privileged lobbyists who can afford to participate and who are invited along.

After the negotiations in the international forum, the debate is brought to an end. It may be that the parliament must pass legislation to implement the deal. However, realistically, there is a take-it-or-leave-it situation. The parliament – or the stakeholders that were not represented in the international negotiations – has no chance of altering the text. Even rejection of the proposal is difficult to argue, as the proposal is the new international standard; as it has regularly been recommended as a compromise by a number of states,

13 Protocol of 2002 to the Athens Convention relating to the Carriage of Passengers and their Luggage by Sea, 1974 (London, 2002).

14 Subsidiarity is the principle that matters should be dealt with at as local a level as possible.

an international body, and industry representatives; and as the negotiators have invested months of work in the draft. Thus, nationally, the debate is over before it has even started. So much for democracy and subsidiarity.

In an alarming number of cases, international instruments for the harmonization of international law have not entered into force or have been ratified by only a very limited number of states. In addition to the failure of the harmonization attempts, this has the effect of quashing any discussions of alternative reforms. After all, one does not know whether the international instrument will one day enter into force. In this way, reforms will be impossible from the time international deliberations concerning a new instrument have started until it is clear that the instrument will not enter into force. This is a desirable situation for some and an undesirable situation for others. However, those who do not like to see reforms run the risk that the international instrument may obtain widespread acceptance after all.

2.6 Summary of initial points

The general views developed in the text above on the harmonization of commercial maritime law reveal a far from ideal picture. Clearly, international dialogue in the negotiations is very valuable (see section 2.4). However, the harmonization attempts have led to a new fragmentation caused by numerous international instruments (section 2.1). Much of the disharmony is still unresolved, and forum shopping is more attractive than ever (section 2.2). It is becoming less likely that the IMO can improve the situation (section 2.3). In any event, the harmonization processes cause problems of subsidiarity and democracy and effectively stop other reform processes (section 2.5). There is a question whether the harmonization processes are worthwhile.

3 Harmonization requires codification

3.1 Introduction

To date, no one has found a good way to harmonize maritime law without some degree of codification. Abstract, conceptual harmonization apparently does not suffice; one has to agree on concrete articles in a Convention, albeit sometimes with predefined options, or a model law. This is so despite the fact that Conventions on harmonization in maritime law are rarely, if ever, enforced in the sense that one State Party sends a *note verbale* to another State Party reminding it of its obligation under certain clauses of such Conventions. Such enforcement would indeed be difficult, because the undertakings of States Parties in the harmonization Conventions are not always well defined.

Given this historic strategy, problems of codification need to be assessed and evaluated when discussing the harmonization of commercial maritime law. First, codification of contract law will be discussed and thereafter more general codification issues.

3.2 Contract law

The problem with the codification of contract law in connection with the harmonization of commercial maritime law is that it can be, at most, supplemental to the contract. While the point in section 2.2 was that harmonization is incomplete, the point here is that supplementary codification is unhelpful.

The reason that codifications are usually only supplementary to other legal rules and to the contract between the parties may be that the codification efforts do not go further than is necessary to implement mandatory rules. The mandatory character of the rules will be discussed in section 4. Here, partial codification will be discussed, regardless of the motive for limiting the codification efforts.

One illustration of the pitfalls of supplementary codification is the Norwegian Maritime Code (NMC), s. 348(2):

> 'If the voyage carrier gives notice that the ship will arrive after the cancellation time, and states when it will be ready for loading, the voyage charterer must cancel the contract without undue delay. If the contract is not cancelled, the stated time will be the new cancellation time.'

This is a seemingly sensible rule included in some charterparties. However, in relation to charterparties already including a similar clause, it is superfluous (as it is not mandatory). In relation to charterparties not including a clause of this kind, it is confusing. Should the NMC provision be applied in the charterparty relationship, or should one assume that the parties have opted out by not including the clause in their contract, as they were entitled to? Supplementary codification adds confusion to contract interpretation.

If the codified rule is mandatory, there is no doubt that it applies between the parties. However, there will still be doubts as to which contract clauses the mandatory rule should replace. The problem has been so pressing that bills of lading occasionally state that the clauses should be upheld as far as possible if some of them should violate mandatory legislation, but general clauses obviously cannot provide clear solutions to specific problems of interpretation.

Very comprehensive codifications developed for the harmonization of commercial maritime law, such as the Rotterdam Rules, may not create doubts of this kind. However, even these rules have their limits, where uncertainty arises. In any event, experience shows that comprehensive codifications are unlikely to gain widespread acceptance. Indeed, the successful Conventions, such as the Hague-Visby Rules, are rather short.

BIMCO and other international shipping associations issue standard charterparties, bills of lading, clauses for specific purposes, and other forms. This is an example of successful codification.[15] The starting point is the contract, so that issues of supplementing the contract with the codification do not arise. Furthermore, there are different forms for various trades, so the rules do not need to be overly general. These forms apparently work well under many legal systems or include standard choices for law and jurisdiction. Such codification processes are much more successful than the codification processes that form a part of the harmonization of commercial maritime law.

3.3 Two new problems for every one resolved?

Apart from the difficult relationship between contracts and codifications made in connection with the harmonization of law, there is also another problem with codifications. They

15 https://www.bimco.org/ (visited 21 August 2019).

are necessarily a foreign element in the legal systems of which they are to form a part. This may create more problems than the codification resolves.

If the codification is implemented into national law, Scandinavian style, with some rewriting to fit into the Maritime Codes, the text of the code will fit smoothly into the local tradition. However, every time that there could be doubts about the exact meaning of a phrase or provision, one must resort to the Convention and the *travaux préparatoires* of the implementation legislation. Very often, one party or both will find support for their preferred interpretation in one place or another. The certainty of the Convention is replaced by a copious source of arguments.

The codification may also be implemented directly into the law of a State Party, either by legislation incorporating it by reference or as an effect of a monistic approach to international law. Even this kind of implementation entails a great possibility of harvesting more arguments than would have been available in a purely domestic legislation. For example, in the Swedish Tsesis case,[16] great effort was spent on the question whether the *ejusdem generis* rule of English law should be applied in the interpretation of an international Convention in English, even if that rule was not established in Swedish law.

Similarly, the *travaux préparatoires* of the codification may reduce certainty. The wording of Conventions with respect to the unification of laws is, of course, the starting point. However, it is difficult to ignore compromises actually agreed to in the negotiations, in particular when the *travaux préparatoires* are published. One example is the assurances in the *travaux préparatoires* of the Rotterdam Rules that the commercial practice of so-called merchant haulage would still be allowed, despite the wording of the Convention.[17] Whether one would rely on these promises in the final text, one does well in considering this a point of uncertainty created in the harmonization process.

3.4 Summary

Harmonization requires codification. Codification broadly clarifies the law. Many new arguments may arise, however, in the details of the interactions between the codification, on the one hand, and on the other hand the contracts, implementing legislation, and the international environment. The policy may be clearly laid out, but new uncertainties are created.

4 Mandatory rules

Few, if any, Conventions for the harmonization of maritime contract law do not include an element of mandatory law. There has been a tradition of this since the US Harter Act,[18] and in the following I will discuss mandatory rules based on liability rules for cargo damage.

Protection of a weaker party against contractual abuse enhances the chances of getting parliamentary time for the codification project. Indeed, this motive for unification projects

16 NJA 1983.1; ND 1983.1.

17 E Røsæg, 'Liability issues in respect of part performance of international carriage by cargo' (2015) 21 *Journal of International Maritime Law* 460.

18 'An Act Relating to Navigation of Vessels, Bills of Lading, and certain obligations, duties and rights in connection with the Carriage of Property', 1893.

has been so integrated into the thinking that even shipowners press for legislation to protect their customers against themselves, for example in the Rotterdam Rules.

In the following, it will first be argued that there is less need for mandatory rules now than before, and thereafter the negative effects of mandatory rules will be discussed.

4.1 A new situation

Mandatory rules may very well have been an adequate response to the UK carriers' extensive exemption clauses against US merchants and shippers some 120 years ago. However, today, much has changed.

First, extensive exemption clauses in bills of lading are rare today, even when not contrary to mandatory legislation. I base this observation both on my own experience and on the practices reflected in case law. A minimum liability has apparently become the new industry standard. Thus, there is no need for uniform, mandatory legislation to combat the ghosts of the past century.

Second, many states – and in particular states that are concerned with the protection of weaker parties in contract law – have now implemented legislation that invalidates unreasonable contract terms. The extreme example is the general unenforceability of 'unreasonable' contract clauses in the Scandinavian countries.[19] Therefore, there is less need for mandatory legislation. Indeed, mandatory legislation has the unfortunate effect that some contractors will choose the minimum liability allowed by the rules. In relation to the Hague-Visby Rules, this is particularly unfortunate, as the liability level allowed by those rules arguably would be unlikely to be upheld under general legislation on unreasonable contract terms.

Third, mandatory legislation has to some degree been rendered obsolete by competition law. If the efforts of competition law succeed in establishing a well-working market, it is likely that the more offensive abuses of freedom of contract will be avoided simply because better terms will be offered by others and preferred. Furthermore, the abuse of a dominant market position[20] to exempt liability is likely to be invalidated by competition rules. Such abuse may even trigger criminal sanctions.

A fourth development from the time of the Hague Rules is the development of the insurance industry. Both protection and indemnity (P&I) and cargo insurance are now readily available and affordable, as is other relevant insurance. The need for liability rules is thus less serious. Indeed, in some commercial relations, it makes commercial sense to abolish liability and liability insurance and rely instead on insuring one's own interest (so-called knock-for-knock). In particular, the Hague and Hague-Visby Rules are costly, because they require both liability and cargo insurance for full coverage, and because the scope of each of these insurance types is not very clearly distinguished and they are for practical purposes overlapping.

Fifth, it is now increasingly asked whether the cargo owner really is the weaker party in relation to a carrier/shipowner and, therefore, whether she needs protection by mandatory rules. The cargo side may cooperate (within the limits of competition law), consolidate,

19 Norwegian Contracts Act 1918, s. 36.
20 Treaty on the Functioning of the European Union (TFEU), Art. 102.

or grow. It would be an anomaly should the big oil companies be protected by mandatory rules in relation to independent shipowners. However, this is the current international law.

Sixth, contract practices have changed. Many sellers offer goods on delivered terms, that is, with transport included. In these cases, the transport risks can usually be agreed without any restrictions imposed by mandatory legislation and certainly not by the international maritime law regimes. Why should there be a greater need for mandatory legislation if the transport is not included in the sales contract?

Finally, the relative economic importance of cargo damage has decreased drastically over the past century. The introduction of mechanical handling, containers, and more protective packaging has reduced the number of incidents and the losses when accidents happen. In addition, various kinds of insurance for cargo damage have today been reduced to only a fraction of the total cost of the goods.[21] When the importance of cargo damage is relatively small, mandatory liability rules may no longer be necessary.

In sum, the need for mandatory rules to protect the cargo owner has decreased drastically over the past century. The need for uniform mandatory legislation has diminished accordingly.

4.2 Negative effects

The need for (uniform) mandatory legislation has decreased. In addition, there is an increasing awareness of the negative effects of mandatory rules.

In law and economics, one points out that the incentives to reduce or remove risks should encourage the party that can more inexpensively reduce or remove risks, and not the other party, to do so. If the incentives are directed towards the wrong party, the risk will be reduced or removed more expensively than necessary, to the detriment of society. This will also affect both parties in the transaction, as the cost level for each of them will affect the price, and therefore the other.

Mandatory liability rules may be an incentive with this unfortunate effect.[22] If the shipowner is made liable for cargo damage, such as theft, that will be her incentive to prevent damage. However, it may be that the cargo owner can prevent the losses more inexpensively, for example, by sending the goods without an essential part, so that they are not attractive to steal. Mandatory rules would then have the negative effect of increasing the costs to the parties and to society as a whole. This effect could be avoided, for example, by protecting the weaker party by more flexible rules (such as a reasonableness standard), so that the commercial parties could agree that the liability should be borne by the party that can more inexpensively prevent losses.

There is another negative effect of mandatory rules. The rules set the standard of reasonableness. If the mandatory rules allow the carrier to except liability for navigational errors – the core of her services – a court could hardly conclude that a similar provision is void on the grounds of unreasonableness (where there are such reasonableness rules) or

21 W. Hansen and I.B. Hovi, *En gjennomgang av ulike studier som forøker å kvantifisere logistikkostnadene*, TØI Rapport 269/2008.

22 E. Eide, Rettsøkonomiske analyser av forslaget til ny sjøtransportkonvensjon. Innlegg under seminar om 'Nye ansvarsregler for lasteskader. UNCITRALs forslag til ny konvensjon om stykkgodstransport', NOU 2010: 20, Annex 2.

construe the contract restrictively against the carrier. The mandatory rules have effects far beyond their mandatory scope.

Also, non-mandatory rules (gap-filling rules) may have a similar effect. However, the liability level of mandatory rules tends to be set lower than that of gap-filing rules, simply because they must fit all situations, as there is no possibility to contract out of them by lowering the liability. Therefore, mandatory rules have the greater negative effect.

5 Liability and insurance

The last aspect of the international processes for the harmonization of commercial maritime law that I will discuss is the complex relationship to insurance. Most of the uniform commercial maritime laws concern liability in one way or another. There is liability for loss of (or damage to) cargo as well as liability for damage caused to third parties, such as damage to other ships and pollution damage. The liabilities are generally covered by P&I insurance.

One would think that insurance is a matter for the shipowner that does not affect the right to claim liability from her or affect the harmonization of laws in this respect. However, in the negotiations of Conventions for the harmonization of commercial maritime law, insurance plays an important role. The International Group of P&I Clubs and other representatives of the insurance market play an important role and effectively limit the options that governments feel are available. This is partially a concern for the insurance market and partially a concern relating directly to compulsory insurance schemes.

5.1 Insurance market considerations

The current general P&I coverage for shipowners with respect to their liabilities totals about US$8 billion for an incident.[23] This is far more than the liability figures seen to date, and there is no rule that liability must always be insurable. Still, the uniform laws limit liability to far below these levels, mainly by reference to the insurance market.[24]

The P&I coverage is partly based on various kinds of pooling and partly on reinsurance. The reinsured losses are those in the range from US$100 million to US$3.1 billion.[25] However, the liability limits of uniform legislation do not even come close to the upper limits of the reinsured layer.

Graphically, the P&I coverage and the limits of the shipowners' liability compare as shown in Figure 3.1.

One observes that the liability levels of the international Conventions are just fractions of the insurance coverage. Still, the argument in the international negotiations was that insurance capacity necessitated the low limitation amounts in the LLMC and the HNS Convention. The argument goes that, if limits are not upheld, the overall P&I coverage

23 https://www.shipownersclub.com/the-overspill-limit/. This and the following figures apply to 2019–20 coverage. There are special limits for oil spills, passenger claims, and crew claims, which will be discussed below (see, for example, Gard Rules, 2019, Rule 53).

24 For some years, I negotiated liability treaties in the IMO Legal Committee, and have first-hand knowledge about this.

25 https://www.igpandi.org/reinsurance (visited 21 August 2019)

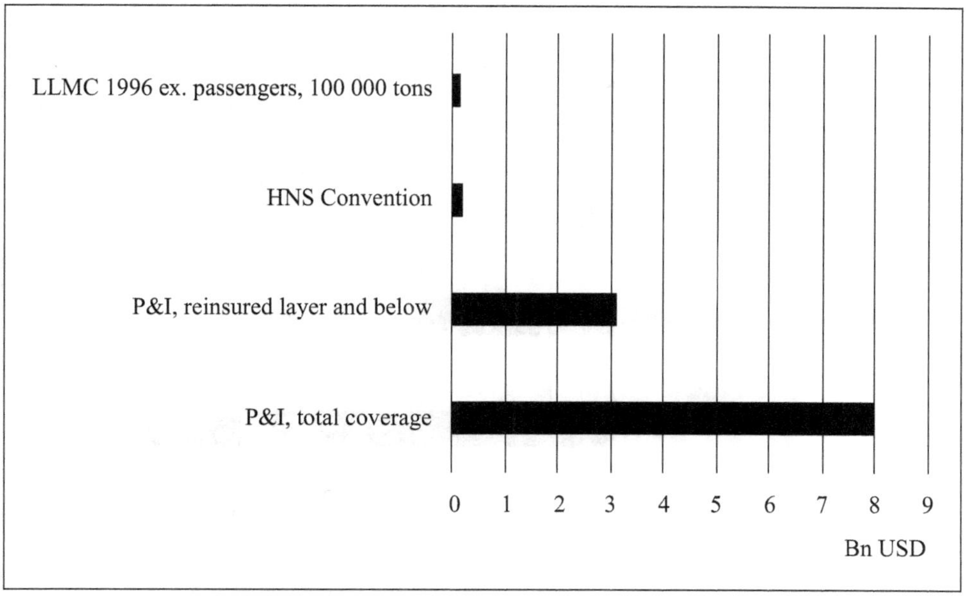

Figure 3.1 General P&I and shipowners' maximum liability levels

would have to decrease. Governments have apparently accepted this. The exception is states such as the US, which have no effective limitation, do not ratify the limitation of liability Conventions, and still benefit from the current high insurance maximums. Thus, the effect of the international harmonization process is that some states agree to limit their own and third-party claims against shipowners to fractions of the insurance coverage so that other states can benefit from the high insurance coverage and unlimited liability. In my view, this is an undesirable effect of the international harmonization process. The available insurance should be equally available to all states.

Special regimes, such as the oil spill regime, give a similar impression (Figure 3.2). The liability levels of the international regime are just a fraction of the insurance maximum. Again, the USA, for example, has no similar, effective limits and benefits from the full available insurance coverage.

In this case, the shipowners' liability is supplemented by international funds financed by levies on cargoes discharged.[26] The limits of the shipowners' liability are therefore determined by the desire to share the costs of pollution between the cargo side and the shipowners in addition to insurance considerations.

There is an extra P&I limit of US$1 billion that applies to oil spills.[27] This limits P&I exposure to oil pollution even in states that are not parties to the CLC, for example, the US. The CLC limit is low even in comparison to this limit.

Liability for death and personal injury to passengers is yet another variant of the same issue (see Figure 3.3).

26 See section 2.1.

27 See, for example, Gard Rules, 2019, Appendix III.

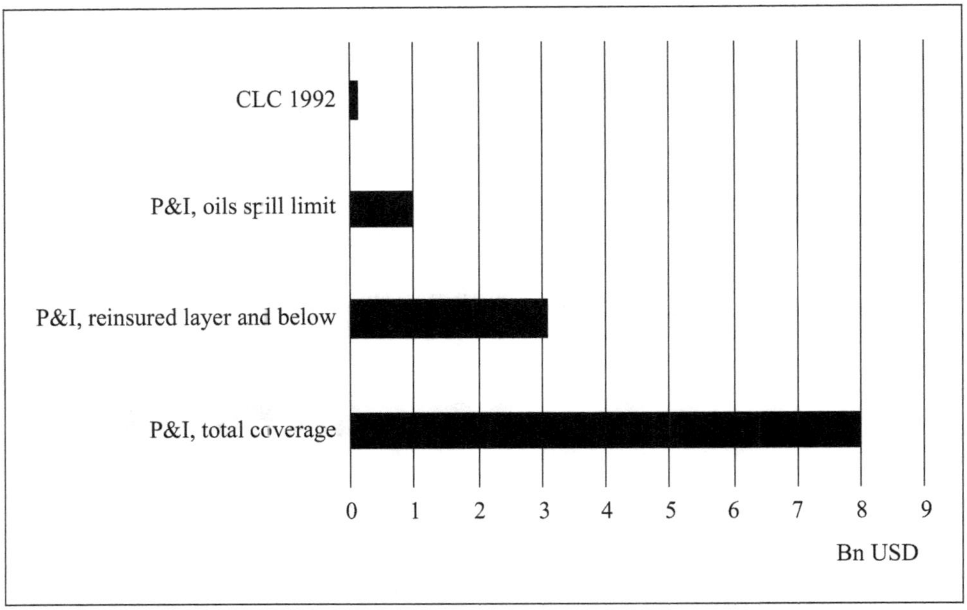

Figure 3.2 Maximum levels for oil spill claims – P&I and shipowners' liability

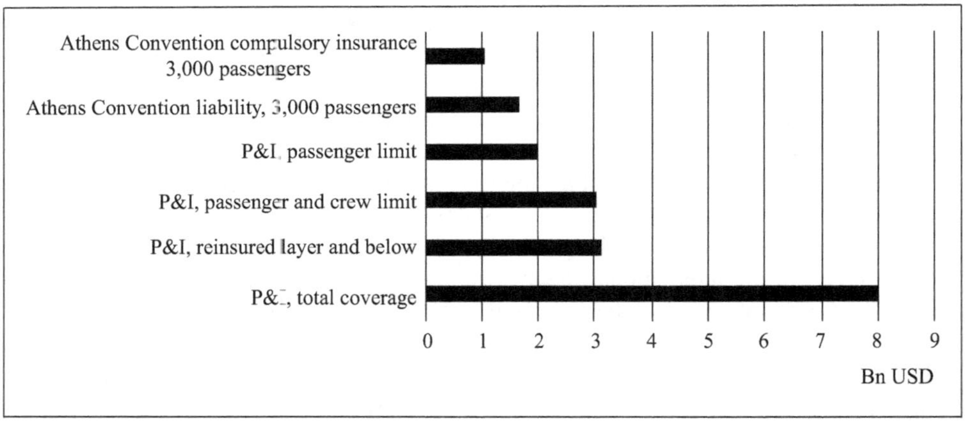

Figure 3.3 Maximum levels for passenger clams – P&I and carriers' liability

Even in this case, there are additional limits for the P&I coverage.[28] The limit of US$2 billion will apply unless there are also crew claims in the same incident (which is likely in the case of a total loss). In that case, the passenger claims will be reduced proportionally so that the sum of the passenger and crew claims does not exceed US$3 billion. Usually,

28 See, for example, Gard Rules, 2019, Appendix IV.

there are fewer crew members than passengers, but while the passengers' claims are limited, crew claims are unlimited and may even be calculated in a way that inflates the crew claims.

The Athens Convention allows claims up to and perhaps exceeding these limits. The example in the graph is for a vessel of 3,000 passengers, but there are even larger vessels. The compulsory insurance certified by the P&I Club pursuant to the Athens Convention is, however, unlikely to exceed the P&I limits.

The special P&I limits for passenger claims were established after the 2002 Athens Convention and in response to it. This is therefore not an example of an international process for the unification of maritime law that has pushed up against the insurance limits. It is, however, an example of an international Convention that is somewhat more expansive than the other Conventions. Sympathy for passengers perhaps made this easier, but claimants for pollution damage, for example, also elicit such sympathy. The passenger claims, however, had the problem that a very small percentage of the world fleet comprises passenger ships, so particularly high exposure for passenger claims will put the solidarity of shipowners in the P&I system at risk. Still, the result is that the available insurance capacity is utilized quite well by the international Convention, not leaving additional capacity to states not signed up to the international regime.

The overall impression is clearly that the international unification processes fail to utilize the available insurance fully. Because of this, the insurance limits can be maintained at a very high level. This high level of insurance coverage benefits states that do not sign up to the international Conventions and do not effectively limit shipowners' liability by national law. It does not benefit the states that sign up to the Conventions for uniform laws, as the shipowners' liability is very limited in those Conventions.

The P&I clubs have no interest in clarifying these matters. They are, for all practical purposes, owned by the shipowners and represent their views. Obviously, shipowners are interested in maintaining limited liability and maintaining full insurance coverage in the states where limited liability is not possible.

It may very well be that governments are right, in that the P&I coverage offered will be reduced if limits on the shipowners' liability are enhanced or abolished. However, the overall insured level of liability is likely to be higher than today. Furthermore, the available insurance will benefit all states, not only those that do not sign up for the international Conventions. In this way, the current concern for the insurance markets is misguided.

5.2 Cooperation with insurers required

A second aspect of the relationship between insurers and governments in the negotiations for uniform laws in the field of commercial maritime law is that governments are dependent on the insurers. There are two main reasons for this dependence. First, the government must ensure that there are available funds to pay the compensation. In shipping, where there may not be much to collect from a shipowner after a total loss, providing for liability without funding would perhaps not be worthwhile. As long as there is no interest in requiring shipowners in international shipping to maintain certain minimum financial standards, the availability of funds could most easily be arranged by means of insurance.

Second, if imposing liability on a shipowner is to seem meaningful, governments need to ensure that claims can be settled in a readily available jurisdiction where the funds are available. If action is brought against the shipowner where the damage occurs, the judgment may not be enforceable in her home jurisdiction or where her funding is. An action pursued where the funding is or in the home jurisdiction of the shipowner may, on the other hand, be inconvenient for the claimant, if even possible. Again, the solution is to revert to insurance. The insurers will accept actions at the place of the damage and will make funding available in order to continue in business.

These considerations have different weights, depending on the setting. The shipowners' commercial counterparts, such as cargo owners, can perhaps take care of themselves. Tort claimants, such as pollution victims, perhaps had no relationship to the shipowner before the claim and would need the benefits of insurance, as outlined above.

The model used in the Conventions for the harmonization of commercial maritime law (in cases where the need to integrate insurance is the greatest) is limited liability backed with compulsory insurance with direct action against the insurer. In this model, funding will be available to the claimant in a convenient jurisdiction. The liability is limited, but many states have traditionally limited the shipowners' liability anyway.

This compulsory insurance model has worked well. However, the cost of this model is that the P&I insurers have become very influential in the shaping of the system. One example is the war exemptions, which are in place because P&I does not cover war risks under its usual system. Another example is the channelling of liability and/or the duty to insure to one entity already within the scope of P&I customers. Thus, this kind of harmonization of commercial maritime law has its costs.

6 A failed strategy

It is unquestionable that the unification of commercial maritime law has brought many benefits, although it is a limited success. The ratification of Conventions rarely reaches half the jurisdictions in the world, and important maritime jurisdictions are regularly absent. The unification is piecemeal, and national law still plays a very dominant role. New replacement Conventions do not always effectively replace the old ones, so that not even the attempts at uniformity are uniform.

For governments, this means that they have lost control over a part of their legislative process. It is left to international organs for the sake of uniformity, but uniformity is not achieved. Furthermore, in particular in the Legal Committee of the IMO, attempts to develop the system further are stalled.

A part of the unification process is codification. Codifications do create a common text to be used as a starting point for conflict resolution and define common terms and problem analyses. However, the implementation efforts tend to create new uncertainties, regardless of whether the implementation is direct or by rewriting the text into national legislation. These are clear and important limitations to the harmonizing effects of the uniform maritime laws as we know them. There is no uniformity without codification, and no codification without problems of uniformity.

Traditionally, the need for mandatory legislation to protect cargo owners has been a motivation for uniform international legislation. However, the need for mandatory legislation of this kind is certainly not as strong as it used to be. In addition, the negative effects of mandatory legislation of this kind have become more apparent. Such legislation is costly, and should be avoided if possible.

Insurance has had a strong influence on the international harmonization processes in international law. Governments have been concerned with the effects of high liability limits on the insurance market. In addition, they are dependent on insurers to establish workable solutions for compulsory insurance. As long as there is virtually no control over international shipping that is relevant in this context, this is again necessary to make sure that funding is available and accessible to claimants.

The strong influence of the P&I insurers is indirectly a strong influence on their owners and customers, the shipowners. This is unfortunate and can explain why, for example, the concept of limitation of liability has been maintained for so long.

The harmonization and unification of commercial maritime law has been a mantra for more than a hundred years. It now seems like a failed strategy.

It would be outside the scope of this paper even to outline an alternative strategy. However, it is pertinent to point out the great benefits of the discussions leading up to the Conventions for uniform commercial maritime law. The problems are defined in the same way, the concepts are clarified, and the stakeholders are heard and their interests identified. Perhaps this should be the ambition, with less focus on liability limits and on preserving or strengthening positions. The model laws of UNCITRAL – or even better, their legislative guides – provide good examples.

CHAPTER 4

Codification by treaty of private maritime law from the perspective of a public international lawyer

Professor Andrew Serdy

1 Introduction

How should we refer for short to the United Nations Convention on Contracts for the International Carriage of Goods Wholly or Partly by Sea[1] – is it the Rotterdam Rules or the Rotterdam Rules Convention, and does it even matter? This contribution deliberately refrains from taking any position on whether the Rules themselves are a positive or negative development by comparison with the Hague, Hague-Visby or Hamburg Rules,[2] or on why they are not yet in force or ever will be. Instead it draws attention to some issues of drafting technique that from a public international law perspective are apt to cause confusion.

The first time it came to the author's notice that something might be amiss was not long into the new millennium, in the course of applying (unsuccessfully) for a vacancy in the Office of International Law in the Attorney-General's Department in Canberra, the Australian Government ministry that deals with maritime law, both domestic and international. This was an area of law from which the Legal Branch of the Department of Foreign Affairs and Trade, where the author was then employed, had always remained shielded – which is why, if the reader has ever been to one and wondered, it is always Attorney-General's lawyers who represent Australia at International Maritime Organization (IMO) meetings. Knowing nothing at the time about the subject apart from a dim awareness of the existence of the Hamburg Rules, it seemed prudent to bone up on them in the hope of making a good impression. Reading the Convention text, however, the author was immediately struck by the sheer oddity of what he found, nothing like any of the many other treaties which had crossed his desk in several years of professional exposure to the public international law of the sea. What follows is a similar process undertaken with the 2008 Convention, whose architecture seems to be modelled on the Hamburg Rules Convention and thus repeats the same mistakes.

2 In search of the state party's obligations

The Rotterdam Rules Convention starts like virtually all treaties with a Preamble whose essential function is to set out why states have negotiated and are now entering into

1 New York, 11 December 2008; UN doc A/RES/63/122 (22 February 2009), Annex; not yet in force.

2 Respectively contained in or annexed to the International Convention for the Unification of Certain Rules relating to Bills of Lading (Brussels, 25 August 1924), 120 *League of Nations Treaty Series* 155; Protocol to amend the International Convention for the Unification of Certain Rules relating to Bills of Lading, signed at Brussels on 25 August 1924 (Brussels, 23 February 1968), 1412 *United Nations Treaty Series* (hereinafter UNTS) 127; United Nations Convention on the Carriage of Goods by Sea (Hamburg, 31 March 1978), 1695 UNTS 3.

it,[3] a task it discharges admirably; so far, so good, therefore. Then comes Article 1 containing definitions, nothing unusual in itself, and not necessary for present purposes to quote. Moving to Article 2 on interpretation, shorn of its last few words, it reads 'In the interpretation of this Convention, regard is to be had to its international character and to the need to promote uniformity in its application . . .' – this has a potential significance to which we will return below, but again there is nothing really untoward here. For Articles 3 and 4, it suffices just to reproduce their headings: 'Form requirements' and 'Applicability of defences and limits of liability' respectively, since, as already noted, this is not a critique of their content.

By this stage, though, we have reached the end of Chapter 1, 'General Provisions', and for a public international lawyer there is cause for incipient impatience, which the reader is perhaps beginning to share. For the moment let us press on, in the hope of soon finding what we are seeking, to Chapter 2, headed Scope of Application, in which Article 5 'General scope of application' lays down to which contracts the Convention applies, while Article 6 'Specific Exclusions' is about those to which it does not apply, followed by Article 7 'Application to certain parties', which is the next one worth quoting in full:

> 'Notwithstanding article 6, this Convention applies as between the carrier and the consignee, controlling party or holder that is not an original party to the charterparty or other contract of carriage excluded from the application of this Convention. However, this Convention does not apply as between the original parties to a contract of carriage excluded pursuant to article 6.'

This is the first real clue, offered by the words 'party' and 'parties' – we are no longer talking about the parties to the Convention as a treaty, which by Articles 88 and 93 are states[4] and

---

3 The text of the Preamble reads:

> 'The States Parties to this Convention,
>
> Reaffirming their belief that international trade on the basis of equality and mutual benefit is an important element in promoting friendly relations among States,
>
> Convinced that the progressive harmonization and unification of international trade law, in reducing or removing legal obstacles to the flow of international trade, significantly contributes to universal economic cooperation among all States on a basis of equality, equity and common interest, and to the well-being of all peoples,
>
> Recognizing the significant contribution of the International Convention for the Unification of Certain Rules of Law relating to Bills of Lading, signed in Brussels on 25 August 1924, and its Protocols, and of the United Nations Convention on the Carriage of Goods by Sea, signed in Hamburg on 31 March 1978, to the harmonization of the law governing the carriage of goods by sea,
>
> Mindful of the technological and commercial developments that have taken place since the adoption of those conventions and of the need to consolidate and modernize them,
>
> Noting that shippers and carriers do not have the benefit of a binding universal regime to support the operation of contracts of maritime carriage involving other modes of transport,
>
> Believing that the adoption of uniform rules to govern international contracts of carriage wholly or partly by sea will promote legal certainty, improve the efficiency of international carriage of goods and facilitate new access opportunities for previously remote parties and markets, thus playing a fundamental role in promoting trade and economic development, both domestically and internationally,
>
> Have agreed as follows:'

4 Paraphrasing its first three paragraphs, Article 88 is in this respect fairly typical of multilateral treaties: it opens the Convention for signature 'by all States' at Rotterdam on 23 September 2009 and thereafter at the Headquarters of the United Nations in New York, but signature alone does not make the signatory state a party; for that, a second step of ratification, acceptance or approval is necessary, or alternatively, a state that has not signed the Convention can become party to it by a single step known as accession.

other international legal persons such as the European Union (EU),[5] but about the parties to contracts for the carriage of goods wholly or partly by sea, normally private companies or potentially individuals, lacking international legal personality.[6]

No doubt to the reader's relief, the fact that we have jumped forward to the final clauses signals that what lies ahead is not a tedious one-by-one recitation of the remaining articles. The next 14 chapters, encompassing Articles 8 to 81, contain the substance of the Rotterdam Rules: the detailed regulation of carriage contracts that was the parties' – perhaps one should say the States Parties' – reason for negotiating it. After this, all that is left is Chapter 17, Articles 82 to 86, Matters not governed by this Convention, which collectively set out the relationships between the Rotterdam Rules Convention and other treaties on related matters, and Chapter 18, the so-called Final clauses, which contain the standard machinery provisions found in all multilateral treaties laying down who is to be depositary of the treaty, how states become party to the treaty, what the conditions are for its entry into force, what the process is for amending it, whether or not it is possible to denounce or terminate it, and so on.

3 International legislation? Sorry, there is no such thing

All of this, though, leaves public international lawyers none the wiser as to what the rights and obligations of the parties – the States Parties, one might say the true parties, are – for up to this point there has been not even a single word about them. Remarkably for a treaty, though in this respect consistently with both the Hague Rules and Hamburg Rules Conventions and the Hague-Visby Rules Protocol, Chapters 1 to 17 are entirely devoid of the usual formulae along the lines of, or reducible in substance to, 'Each state party shall [not] do X.' Treaties are instruments in which states record agreements they have reached on their mutual rights and obligations on some subject matter, so the natural question at this juncture is whether the Rotterdam Rules Convention can truly be said to be a treaty in substance. (Clearly, as demonstrated in the foregoing, no such doubt can arise as to its treaty form, thus satisfying the definition in the Vienna Convention on the Law of Treaties:[7] 'an international agreement concluded between States in written form and governed by international law'.)

Perhaps just barely, seems to be the answer, for what we really have here is an attempt at something that in theory cannot actually exist: international legislation, even though this does not stop students, as well as others whom it is less easy to forgive for not knowing better, from commonly mischaracterising treaties this way. International law is a

5 The first two sentences of paragraph 1 of Article 93 provide that: 'A regional economic integration organization that is constituted by sovereign States and has competence over certain matters governed by this Convention may similarly sign, ratify, accept, approve or accede to this Convention. The regional economic integration organization shall in that case have the rights and obligations of a Contracting State, to the extent that that organization has competence over matters governed by this Convention.'

6 This does not mean that public bodies or states themselves cannot enter into such contracts, but when they do so they are acting commercially *iure gestionis* rather than as sovereigns *iure imperii*, and under the modern restrictive theory of immunity are no longer entitled to whatever immunity might have once have attached to them in relation to such transactions by virtue of their status. See *The I Congreso del Partido* [1983] 1 AC 244 and the United Nations Convention on Jurisdictional Immunities of States and Their Property (New York, 2 December 2004), not yet in force, UN doc A/RES/59/38 (16 December 2004), Annex, Art. 10.

7 Vienna, 23 May 1969; 1155 UNTS 331, Art. 2(1)(a).

primitive and incomplete system with very few tools at its disposal, and while treaties are the implement to hand that has to be used, for lack of anything else, to replicate the function served by legislation in domestic legal systems, in fact they are invariably contractual in nature even when they are quasi-legislative in function or intent. Legislation applies to everybody unless otherwise stated, whereas treaties under the Vienna Convention on the Law of Treaties[8] bind only their parties: *pacta tertiis nec nocent nec prosunt*. This supplies much of the explanation for why tackling complex global problems such as climate change is so difficult, as the IMO is finding it no more tractable in the narrow field of shipping than the other international bodies struggling with it in the broad. So even when the Rotterdam Rules eventually come into force, if they ever do – possibly they never will[9] and the Convention will meet the same fate as the United Nations Convention on the Conditions for the Registration of Ships[10] – their goal of unifying international shipping law will remain elusive unless the number of parties grows to something appreciably larger than the mere 20 needed as a minimum according to Article 94(1) of the Rotterdam Rules Convention.

4 The Article 94 gateway

Had we persevered with the article-by-article exposition abandoned above, it would have been necessary to reach almost the very end of the Convention text to find the substantive international legal obligation. Anomalously for an Article (94) devoted, according to its heading, to the entry into force of the Convention, in its last paragraph, and thus

8 Ibid, Art. 34. An exception is where they are merely codifying an already existing rule of customary international law (see Art. 38), but that is certainly not true of either the Rotterdam Rules Convention or any of its private shipping law precursors listed in footnote 2.

9 This is a real risk given that, a decade on from its adoption, the Rotterdam Rules Convention has only 25 signatories and four parties: Spain, Cameroon, Congo and Togo, see the relevant page on the UN depositary website https://treaties.un.org/pages/ViewDetails.aspx?src=TREATY&mtdsg_no=XI-D-8&chapter=11&clang=_en (visited 21 August 2019). This makes it otiose to discuss one other aspect of codifying regulatory treaties, namely striking the right balance with the number of ratifications or accessions required to bring a treaty into force. In more favourable circumstances this would have been an issue because on one hand it is undesirable to discourage states from becoming party, which can happen in the case of treaties creating a new regulatory regime or making an already existing one more stringent, if early ratifiers or acceders cannot be sure that a critical mass of others will follow, potentially leaving them at a disadvantage *vis-à-vis* non-parties that are subject to the old regime or to none at all. This matter received considerable attention in the Working Group entrusted with the drafting of the Convention, with proposals for the threshold number of parties ranging from three (a low number was favoured by those wishing to let the new Convention enter into force quickly among its parties) to 30 (high numbers being preferred by those states keen to avoid further fragmentation of the international legal regime of carriage of goods by sea): see UN docs A/CN.9/642 (2 November 2007), Report of [United Nations Commission on International Trade Law] Working Group III (Transport Law) on the work of its twentieth session (Vienna, 15–25 October 2007) https://undocs.org/en/A/CN.9/642 and A/CN.9/645 (30 January 2008) (visited 21 August 2019), Report of [United Nations Commission on International Trade Law] Working Group III (Transport Law) on the work of its twenty-first session (Vienna, 14–25 January 2008) https://undocs.org/en/A/CN.9/645 (both visited 21 August 2019), at 59–60 (paragraphs 265–269) and 57 (paragraph 276) respectively. A rival proposal for entry into force to occur between six and seven months after the number is reached was also under discussion (see UN doc A/CN.9/642, at 60 (paragraphs 270 and 271)), but the question was resolved in favour of the longer period now in the text: UN doc A/CN.9/645, at 57 (paragraphs 277 and 278).

10 Geneva, 7 February 1986; UN doc TD/RS/CONF/23 (13 March 1986), not in force. This phenomenon is by no means confined to treaties about maritime law, but rather affects a great many fields that states have tried to regulate by treaty: see A. Aust, 'Limping Treaties: Lessons from Multilateral Treaty-making' (2003) 50 *Netherlands International Law Review* 243–266.

perhaps no more than an afterthought if it was not even considered significant enough to warrant its own article, is found the sole link between the public international law character of the Rotterdam Rules Convention – which as a treaty can directly impose obligations only on international legal persons, i.e. states and, should it accede, the EU[11] – and the private parties to the contracts of carriage with which it is concerned. Paragraph 3 of Article 94 states:

> 'Each Contracting State shall apply this Convention to contracts of carriage concluded on or after the date of the entry into force of this Convention in respect of that State.'

It may be noted the formulation 'in respect of that State' does not have the effect of requiring the State Party to apply the Rotterdam Rules as a matter of course to contracts concluded in that state or governed by its laws as the proper law of the contract under the rules of private international law. Rather, states that become party must ensure that the substance of the Rotterdam Rules – i.e. Chapters 1 to 17 of the Convention[12] – is incorporated within their domestic law of contract. The only limitation is temporal: the obligation applies to contracts entered into once the Convention is in force for the party, though equally, if it wishes to apply the Rotterdam Rules also to pre-existing contracts, it is free to do so. And that is all: the entirety of the international legal obligation is expressible as a single sentence, and there is silence about the correlative rights of other parties which are left to be inferred from this. One might lament that the obligation had not been expressed more clearly: it is a step back from the Hague-Visby Rules Protocol, whose Article 16 is to the same effect: there the parties are to 'give effect to this Protocol either by giving it the force of law or by including in their national legislation in a form appropriate to that legislation the rules adopted under this Protocol'. Before that, the Hague Rules Convention did it the same way, though oddly there this wording is placed in the Protocol of Signature, which is less than elegant, as it thereby raises doubts over whether it applies to parties to that Convention that achieved that status by ratification or accession – although there is no sensible reason why it should not so apply.

5 Concluding remarks: a drafting suggestion for the next occasion

When the author made the preceding point rather more obliquely in his contribution on Chapter 18 to his Institute's volume of commentary on the Rotterdam Rules,[13] the late Professor Berlingieri in his review of that work noted that the Hague language was too permissive,[14] because the underlying idea of codification was that the law applied by the courts

11 It may be that indirectly the treaty can and does impose obligations and confer rights on private persons rather than relying on the states parties to act as intermediaries to this end; this depends on the relationship between international and domestic law in the constitutional dispensation of each party. In many civil law jurisdictions the constitution allows treaties to be invoked by and against private persons without the need for any implementing legislation, but such legislation is always needed in common law jurisdictions.

12 Other than Chapters 14 and 15, unless the state has opted into one or both: see Article 91.

13 Y. Baatz, Ch. Debattista, F. Lorenzon, A. Serdy, H. Staniland and M. Tsimplis, *The Rotterdam Rules: A Practical Annotation* (Informa Law, 2009), pp. 278–279.

14 F. Berlingieri, 'A review of some recent analyses of the Rotterdam Rules' (2009) CXI *Il Diritto Marittimo* 955 at 1035–1036.

of each State Party should be exactly the same, so that a litigant can be sure of achieving the same outcome no matter in which jurisdiction the suit is brought. This can be achieved only by closing off one of those avenues: the common law technique of giving the text of the treaty to parliamentary draftsmen who are then instructed to 'translate' it into the legal terminology of their own jurisdiction. Such an exercise invariably has to contend with an attendant risk of error, stemming from the fact that those at the end of the drafting chain were not present at the negotiations, do not always understand what a given provision is trying to achieve, and are hence often not in a good position to resist those instructing them who may be tempted to improve on the negotiated text by enacting what they wish had been agreed rather than what actually was.

Unlike civil law jurisdictions where it is nothing out of the ordinary and may even be constitutionally dictated, the common law does not on the whole cope well with the other avenue, which simply provides for the text of the treaty to have the force of law in the state's own legal system as though it were a legislative product of it, and there is only one other field known to the author where this is habitually what is done: treaties on the avoidance of double taxation, where litigation has exposed its disadvantages. If the revenue authorities lose a case because the court interprets the treaty differently from the executive branch which negotiated its text,[15] the latter cannot simply ask the legislature to amend the implementing legislation to reinstate its preferred interpretation, because that would be in effect to amend the treaty unilaterally.

This danger has grown with the number of languages in which the treaty text is equally authentic, from two in the Hague Convention and Visby Protocol to all six official United Nations languages in the Hamburg and Rotterdam Rules Conventions.[16] So while we must still reckon with the risk of inconsistencies among these,[17] one may concede to Professor Berlingieri that this may be the lesser evil. At all events, whether or not a choice of technique is allowed, the most logical solution not just for the Rotterdam Rules Convention but all its predecessors too would have been to have a short head treaty consisting only of the public international law part, in other words Article 94(3) and its earlier counterparts, together with the final clauses, relegating the private law remainder to a separate annex. That would be the present author's suggestion for how it should be done on the next occasion that a maritime codifying Convention is negotiated.

Returning finally to the original question, Rotterdam Rules or Rotterdam Rules Convention: if the drafters thought they were crafting international legislation, which the nature of the international legal system precludes as a category, though this and the Hamburg Rules before them surely come close, then it does not really matter how we preferentially refer to this document. Counterfactually, however, in a better designed treaty not affected by that fundamental misconception, the choice would not have been without significance.

15 As occurred for example in *Commissioner of Taxation v Lamesa Holdings BV* [1997] FCA 785.

16 See the testimonium of each of the treaties listed in footnote 2.

17 The reports of the UNCITRAL sessions at which the Convention was drafted were available in all six languages, including the annexes in which successive drafts of the text appeared, but indicate at the top of the front page that they were originally drafted in English, from which one can surmise the same would mostly if not entirely have been true of the 2008 Convention text itself.

CHAPTER 5

Codification – best left to states or to someone else?

Professor Andrew Tettenborn

1 Introduction

This paper is about the advantages, disadvantages and effectiveness of codification in private shipping law. But before launching into any discussion, there is an important preliminary point that needs to be made, which will be a theme of what appears below. Codifications, like top-quality craft vodka, come in noticeably different flavours;[1] and what may be good for one purpose may not be good for another.

Three broad varieties of codification potentially relevant to shipping law can be fairly readily distinguished. The first is the traditional state legislative codification, to be found in commercial and maritime codes. The second is supranational codification by ad hoc international Convention, as with the 1924 and 1968 Conventions setting up the Hague and Hague-Visby Rules,[2] or the 1972 Convention on the International Regulations for Preventing Collisions at Sea. To this can be added documents such as the International Safety Management Code (ISM) and International Ship and Port Facility Security Code (ISPS), produced by treaty organisations such as the IMO, which are binding codes in all but name through their incorporation by reference in domestic state law. Thirdly, there is 'soft law' codification; this is exemplified by (for example) the Principles of European Contract Law and the UNIDROIT Principles of International Commercial Contracts, and in a more formal setting by the various UNCITRAL model laws.

But all this is to forget a fifth. As any lawyer in private practice will confirm, there is an enormous standardising effect emanating from 'bottom-up' documents produced by more or less private bodies for use on a contractual basis by those who wish to employ them. There are innumerable examples; they range over the whole of commercial shipping law, from Exxon's EXXONVOY tanker charter, through BIMCO's CONGENBILL and the Lloyd's Open Form, to the Japanese Association of Shipbuilders' SAJ shipbuilding form. If anything, it is suggested that the significance of these common forms in the unification and fine-tuning of shipping law may well be greater than that of the other four combined.

1 The different forms they can take are helpfully discussed, though with particular reference to the UK, in J. Bargenda and S. Stark, 'The legal Holy Grail? German lessons on codification for a fragmented Britain' (2018) 22 *Edinburgh Law Review* 183.

2 International Convention for the Unification of Certain Rules relating to Bills of Lading (Brussels, 1924); Protocol to amend the International Convention for the Unification of Certain Rules relating to Bills of Lading, signed at Brussels on 25 August 1924 (Brussels, 1968).

2 State codes

State maritime codes are at present very much in the public eye. In the last 10 years, as one perceptive commentator has pointed out,[3] France,[4] Germany,[5] Spain[6] and Turkey[7] have produced extensive new ones (or, more accurately, new versions of old codes); Belgium, Brazil, Japan and Poland[8] are well on the way to following suit.

Such codes have been a traditional source of unified law for a long time. The impetus for their widespread use came originally from the enactment under Napoleon of the 1807 French Commercial Code (though this was by no means the first initiative,[9] and indeed itself partly reflected material going back as far as Louis XIV's 1681 *Ordonnance de la Marine* produced under Jean-Baptiste Colbert[10]). Book II of the Commercial Code (*Du Commerce Maritime*), comprising over one-third of its provisions,[11] contained much that would be familiar today: ownership, arrest, the rights of the master and mariners, time and voyage charters, bills of lading, marine insurance, general average, and time-bars. Other European codes quickly followed on the French pattern:[12] in Spain in 1829,[13] Portugal in 1833,[14] Greece in 1835,[15] the Netherlands in 1838,[16] Germany in 1861[17] and Italy in 1866.[18]

Contemporary codes continue as respects private law to reflect much the same pattern as that of 1807, though obviously there have been changes – an obvious example is the incorporation of modern Convention regimes. The French provisions are typical. Moved

3 E. Van Hooydonk, 'The renaissance of maritime codes – a need for international guidance?' (2015) 21 *Journal of International Maritime Law* 1.

4 Ordonnance n° 2010–1307 du 28 octobre 2010 relative à la partie législative du code des transports.

5 On which see S. Gahlen, 'The New German Law on Maritime Trade' (2015) 21 *Journal of International Maritime Law* 63.

6 See I. Arroyo, 'The New Spanish Maritime Navigation Act 2014, the Need for Uniformity and the International Maritime Conventions' (2014) 20 *Journal of International Maritime Law* 375.

7 New Commercial Code, promulgated on 14 February 2011 and in force from 1 July 2012.

8 J. Łopuski, *Maritime law in the second half of the 20th century. Selected articles* (Wydawnictwo Naukowe UMK, 2008), p. 87; also J. Nawrot and Z. Pepłowska-Dąbrowska, 'Maritime legislation in Poland and the proposals of the Codification Commission for Maritime Law" (2017) 23 *Journal of International Maritime Law* 220.

9 For example, Part II of the monumental 1794 Prussian *Allgemeines Landrecht für die Preußischen Staaten* devoted no fewer than 1076 articles (Arts 1389–2464) to maritime commerce, including carriage law, voyage charters, bills of lading, collisions, general average, marine insurance and bottomry.

10 Itself possibly of Dutch origin: R. Warlomont, 'Les sources néerlandaises de l'Ordonnance maritime de Colbert (1681)' (1955) 33 *Revue belge de Philologie et d'Histoire* 333. Earlier so-called codes were much more digests of decisions and laws: see generally R. Goode, 'Usage and its reception in transnational commercial law' (1997) 46 *International and Comparative Law Quarterly* 1 at 28.

11 Arts 190–436. The whole document contained 648 articles.

12 A process summed up in H. Putnam, 'The Codification of Commercial and Maritime Law' (1884) 18 *American Law Review* 427.

13 Código de Comercio, Third Book, Arts 583–1000 (pattern, though not always the wording, similar to the French production of 1807: it covered ownership, personnel, carriage, marine insurance and prescription).

14 Codigo Comercial Portuguez, Part 2 (Arts 1287–1860) (similar, but not identical, to Spain).

15 Code of Commercial Law [Κώδικας Εμπορικού Νόμου], Second Book (almost identical to the French provisions).

16 Wetboek van Koophandel, Book 2 (Arts. 309–763) (essentially the French code, with some additions).

17 The Allgemeines Deutsches Handelsgesetzbuch. Strictly, this was enacted by the German Confederation in 1861 and subsequently by the North German Confederation in 1869, and inherited from the latter when it mutated into the German Empire in 1871 (see the encyclopaedic HWB-EuP 2009, entry for Allgemeines Deutsches Handelsgesetzbuch). Book 5 (Arts 432–911) covered shipping law. The subjects covered were similar to those in the French code, plus salvage.

18 Codice di Commercio del Regno D'Italia, Second Book, Arts 284–542 (a document that closely followed the French version).

in 1967 from the Commercial Code to form Book IV of the Code des Transports[19] and most recently revised in 2016, they now cover, at least in principle, the following areas of private law: ownership; shipbuilding contracts; arrest and liens; limitation of liability; pollution liabilities; collision; salvage and general average; wreck; pilotage; towage; relations between shipowners, their servants and agents; ship management; passenger carriage; carriage of goods and bills of lading; charters (bareboat, time and voyage); fas, fob, ex ship and cif sale contracts;[20] and marine insurance.[21] The German coverage, now contained in Book 5 of the HGB[22] and heavily rewritten in 2013, is similarly fairly comprehensive. It deals in turn with owners and operators of ships; civil liability for the acts of crew and pilots; carriage of goods contracts and cargo liability; bills of lading and sea waybills; voyage charters; time and bareboat charters; passenger carriage; collisions; salvage and general average; arrest and maritime claims; and limitation of liability.[23]

In certain cases codes of this kind are very helpful. Detailed treaty regimes such as the Convention on Limitation of Liability for Marine Claims (LLMC), the International Convention on Civil Liability for Oil Pollution Damage (CLC) and the Hague-Visby Rules rely on relative uniformity of enactment and application. If there is a relevant code it is very helpful to incorporate them in it, even if not necessarily word for word[24] and even if the enacting state technically regards treaties as self-executing as a matter of internal constitutional law. Again, where third-party rights are concerned and hence a contractual regime cannot fill the gap (as with ownership issues or delictual collision liability), an accessible codification does a great deal of good, while its absence can cause considerable problems. The position of England neatly illustrates this. In that jurisdiction important matters such as ownership of vessels, collision liability, responsibility for the acts of pilots, and the proprietary and contractual effects of bills of lading are scattered far and wide in an unholy mess composed of both legislation and decisional law:[25] some things, such as the legal nature of multimodal transport documents, remain unsettled to this day.[26] The result is a nightmare for those from outside England who have to deal with it. Compare this with the logical coverage of matters of this kind in the German (HGB), where, in contrast to the position in England, the lapidary and neatly-drafted provisions in the HGB on the subject

19 Save for marine insurance, now in Title VII of the Code des Assurances.

20 See generally Code des Transports, Arts. L5000–1 to L5424–11.

21 Code des Assurances, Arts L171–1 to L173–26.

22 Handelsgesetzbuch (HGB) (Commercial Code).

23 See HGB, §§ 476–619.

24 In German law, for example, the Hague-Visby Rules are put in German legislative form in various parts of the first section of Part 2 of Book 5 of the HGB.

25 Ownership of vessels is codified, but only in part: Part II of the Merchant Shipping Act 1995 does not apply to foreign ships, unregistered vessels or equitable interests. Collision liability is entirely uncodified, save for the provisions of the 1910 Collision Convention, enacted in ss 187–190 of the same 1995 Act. Liability for pilots is dealt with by legislation as regards compulsory, but not voluntary, pilotage (Pilotage Act 1987, s. 16). The proprietary effects of bills of lading are entirely based on judicial decision; their contractual effects between carrier and cargo owner are partly, but only partly, covered by the Carriage of Goods by Sea Act 1992. And so on.

26 Multimodal transport documents involving a substantial sea leg are *probably* treated in law in the same way as solely maritime ones. But we cannot be absolutely certain. See A. Tettenborn, 'Of Bills of Lading, Multimodal Transport Documents, and Other Things', in B. Soyer & A. Tettenborn (eds), *Carriage of Goods by Sea, Land and Air: Uni-modal and Multi-modal Transport in the 21st Century* (Informa Law from Routledge, 2013), Ch. 7; and, for a sceptical view, M. Özdel, 'Multimodal transport documents in international sale of goods' (2012) 23 *International Company and Commercial Law Review* 238, 246.

of multimodal transport contracts[27] or bills of lading and sea waybills[28] are a model of comparative clarity and exactitude.

On the other hand, it is not all good news with state codes. There are problems too. A significant difficulty is that codal provisions may well over time become dead wood – there because someone feels they have to be there, but fundamentally unhelpful and uninformative – and that some subjects simply do not lend themselves to being codified. To take one example, France, Germany and Spain all continue to deal in their respective codes with one of the oldest forms of carriage contract, the voyage charter.[29] But they just state the simple default rules – the shipper's duty to come up with a cargo and load it in time or pay demurrage, the carrier's duty to provide the vessel and crew, to carry the goods, etc. etc. – which any shipping lawyer will know perfectly well anyway. This may have been sufficient in the nineteenth century when charters tended to be simple short contracts, often quickly cobbled together ad hoc. Today it is not. The charterparty law that matters these days, and which is far too complex for inclusion in any code, is contained in the detailed boilerplate to be found in standard forms such as NYPE 2015 or SHELLVOY 6. Dispositive law of the kind that will be found contained in the codes is largely sidelined and forgotten. Again, another instance of the same process at work is the French codal provision on shipbuilding contracts. Apart from demanding that they be in writing,[30] it consists of four skeletal articles[31] that say very little and leave all the details to the parties' agreement (which is almost invariably based on the carefully modulated boilerplate one of the five or so standard forms in the industry).[32]

Another difficulty with codes is that new forms of commercial arrangement may be difficult to fit into the straitjacket of a document informed by the practices of earlier years. None of the provisions in either the French or the German codes, for example, really fits a time slot charter (cross between a charter and a simple carriage contract), a time trip charter (hanging uncomfortably between a time and a voyage charter), or a cruise charter (this latter difficulty being because most of the provisions deal with vessels made available for the carriage of goods rather than people). Again, in contrast to German law,[33] the French Code des Transports has plenty to say about bills of lading but absolutely nothing about sea waybills; and so on.

Indeed, at times code provisions may be rightly felt to amount simply to a surfeit of legislation. Ever since 1807, for example, it has been felt appropriate to have a dedicated section of a code set aside for marine insurance. This tradition continues in France and Spain.[34] In Germany, by contrast, it was increasingly recognised that the marine insurance

27 HGB, §§ 452–452d.

28 HGB, §§ 513–526.

29 France: Code des Transports, Arts L5423–1 to 5423–7 and 5423–13 to 5423–14. Germany: HGB, §§ 527–535. Spain: Código de Derecho de la Navegación Marítima y Aérea, Arts 203–245.

30 Code des Transports, Art. L5113–2.

31 Code des Transports, Arts L5113–3 to L5113–6.

32 That is, the SAJ form; the AWES form; the Norwegian Shipbuilding Form; NEWBUILDCON; and the Chinese CMAC form. See A. Tettenborn, 'Contracting By Numbers: The Different Characteristics of The Main Shipbuilding Contracts', in B. Soyer & A. Tettenborn (eds), *Ship Building, Sale and Finance* (Informa Law from Routledge, 2015), Ch.1.

33 One of the few codes to deal with the subject: HGB, § 526.

34 France: Code des Assurances, Arts. L171–1 to L173–26. Spain: Código de Derecho de la Navegación Marítima y Aérea, Title VIII.

provisions in the HGB, unchanged since 1908, were essentially a museum piece, since the parties always (as they were entitled to do) contracted out of them.[35] In in 2013 the obvious step was taken; the HGB was decluttered, its provisions on marine insurance suppressed, and marine insurance subjected to the insurance code and its ordinary rules on transport insurance.[36]

3 Codification by international Convention

Turning to international codification of shipping law through Convention, in many ways this has been a discreet success story: arguably more so, indeed, than state codes. Particularly in matters where there is not a great deal of controversy, agreements of this sort can be an extremely effective way to make the law simple, uniform and accessible.

The practice essentially dates from the efforts of the Comité Maritime Internationale (CMI), set up in 1897,[37] which organised a series of conferences which gave rise to the treaties of 1910 – still in force – dealing respectively with assistance and salvage,[38] and with collisions.[39] There have been numerous examples since of successful and widely-adopted Conventions dealing with private law matters on an internationally uniform basis. One need merely mention the Conventions leading to the Hague and Hague-Visby rules; the CLC and Bunkers Conventions and their subsequent updating protocols; the 1989 Salvage Convention; the Limitation of Liability Conventions of 1957 and 1976; and most recently the Nairobi Wreck-Removal Convention 2007. The process, moreover, is an ongoing one: the CMI, for example, is currently preparing a possible Convention on the mutual recognition of judicial ship sales (the Beijing Draft).[40]

It might be thought that some of the older Conventions – for example, the 1910 Conventions mentioned above, or the two Conventions of 1952 on collision jurisdiction and arrest,[41] were no longer important, being relatively uncontroversial and having been long incorporated in legislation at the national level. In fact, however, they remain surprisingly significant. This is particularly the case in the EU, where at times they prevent established rules of maritime law being unceremoniously run down by the juggernaut of the rules of EU private international law, especially that contained in the Rome I and II and the Recast Brussels I Regulations.[42]

35 See M. Huybrechts (ed.), E. Van Hooydonk and Ch. Dieryck (co-eds), *Marine Insurance at the Turn of the Millennium*, Vol. 2 (Intersentia, 2000), p. 25. Some people in England rightly suspect the Marine Insurance Act 1906, one of the limited UK codifications of the nineteenth and twentieth centuries, of a similar irrelevance, for much the same reason.

36 See now Versicherungsvertragsgesetz (VVG), §§ 130–141.

37 See, for the history, S. Hetherington, 'The CMI and the Panacea of Uniformity – An Elusive Dream Essay' (2014) 39 *Tulane Maritime Law Journal* 159.

38 Convention for the Unification of Certain Rules with Respect to Assistance and Salvage at Sea (Brussels, 1910).

39 Convention for the Unification of Certain Rules of Law with respect to Collisions between Vessels (Brussels, 1910).

40 On which progress is described in P. Griggs, 'The Comité Maritime International (CMI) 2017 assembly and seminar' (2017) 23 *Journal of International Maritime Law* 304.

41 Formally the International Convention on Certain Rules concerning Civil Jurisdiction in Matters of Collision 1952 and the International Convention Relating to the Arrest of Sea-Going Ships (Brussels, 1952).

42 See the Regulation (EC) 593/2008 of the European Parliament and of the Council of 17 June 2008 on the law applicable to contractual obligations (Rome I) OJ L 177, 4.7.2008, pp. 6–16, Art. 25; the Regulation

There are also two further ways in which such Conventions can operate. One, very effective where complex changes are frequently required, is for a basic Convention to provide a simple means for technical matters to be kept up to date regularly and uniformly legislated by some organisation set up for the purpose. Examples include the ISM and ISPS Codes, both of which gain their force from the almost universally accepted Safety of Life at Sea (SOLAS) Convention of 1974;[43] and the Collision Regulations, which are invariably incorporated in national law but whose raw material is promulgated and kept uniform courtesy of the IMO under provisions contained in Art. VI of the 1972 London Convention on the International Regulations for Preventing Collisions at Sea. All these are of enormous importance for private law matters: in common law countries the breach of these codes by a carrier is at the very least extremely cogent evidence of negligence or, as the case may be, unseaworthiness. In civil law jurisdictions it may be of itself constitutive of fault.

Secondly, a new technique has arisen under which a basic Convention is set up as a 'framework', with further optional protocols available to deal with particular issues. The classic instance is the Cape Town Convention 2001 on the international recognition of security interests over tangible moveable assets, which lays down a framework regime that can then be supplemented by specific agreements ('protocols') for particular kinds of asset.[44] So far in force are protocols on aircraft and railway rolling stock; but there is a continuing discussion on whether a further protocol on recognition of security interests in vessels is feasible.[45] Although there are difficulties (notably connected with the creation of maritime liens and how these would relate to internationally-recognised mortgages),[46] there is some hope for a successful shipping protocol in the next few years.

Conventions are thus a fruitful source of unification. Nevertheless, they too have their limitations.[47] For one thing, the subject they deal with needs to be relatively narrow and focused: as the late Professor Tetley remarked, any attempt to agree internationally on

(EC) 864/2007 of the European Parliament and of the Council of 11 July 2007 on the law applicable to non-contractual obligations (Rome II) OJ L 199, 31.7.2007, pp. 40–49, Art. 28; and Art. 71 of the Regulation (EU) No 1215/2012 of the European Parliament and of the Council of 12 December 2012 on jurisdiction and the recognition and enforcement of judgments in civil and commercial matters (the Brussels I Regulation Recast) OJ L 351, 20.12.2012, pp. 1–32, expressly preserving the effect of existing conventions to which member States are party. Art. 28 of Rome II thus allows the 1910 rules relating to collisions to apply even where the law of the place of collision would give a different result under Art. 4 of the Regulation. Art. 71 of Brussels I Recast in similar fashion preserves the rights of courts which have arrested a vessel to exercise substantive jurisdiction over the claim notwithstanding the restrictive jurisdiction rule appearing in Art. 4. The significance of all this can be seen in the English decision in *The Po* [1991] 2 Lloyd's Rep 206 and the decision of the Rechtbank Rotterdam in the 2012 *Kaliakra case* (ECLI:NL:RBROT:2012:BV9334). The consequence of ignoring the minutiae of the rules appears neatly in another English decision, *The Deichland* [1990] 1 QB 361, and in the ECJ decision in *The Tatry* (Case C-406/92), [1994] ECR I-05439.

43 See Ch. XI-2 of that Convention.

44 See R. Goode, 'Private commercial law conventions and public and private international law: the radical approach of the Cape Town Convention 2001 and its Protocols' (2016) 65 *International & Comparative Law Quarterly* 523.

45 See in particular O. Böger, 'The Case for a New Protocol to the Cape Town Convention Covering Security over Ships' (2016) 5 *Cape Town Convention Journal* 73.

46 V. Power, 'Commentary on Assessing the Legal and Economic Case for a Shipping Protocol to the Cape Town Convention' (2016) 5 *Cape Town Convention Journal* 103.

47 Some useful pointers to what makes such conventions fail appear in W. Tetley, 'Uniformity of International Private Maritime Law – the Pros, Cons, and Alternatives to International Conventions – How to Adopt an International Convention' (2000) 24 *Tulane Maritime Law Journal* 775, 815.

some wide area, such as third-party liability as a whole, is likely to be doomed to fail.[48] But there are other drawbacks too.

For one thing, since such Conventions need to be able to be negotiated and agreed within a relatively short time, it follows that agreement is most unlikely to be reached where national approaches vary and cannot be easily reconciled. The result is often Conventions with gaps, where important matters remain unagreed and have, *faute de mieux*, to be left to the decision of national courts.

A fairly obvious instance of this process at work is provided by the otherwise helpful Arrest Conventions of 1952 and 1999. Both these Conventions lay down in detail when an arrest may be made, for what claims, and how it can be lifted; in doing this they are immensely valuable.[49] However, as often happens, what is interesting is what is not in them. Both leave at least some vital issues to be dealt with by the law of the forum. One is that of jurisdiction: if a vessel is arrested, does the arresting court automatically have jurisdiction over the substantive claim, or is this subject to the jurisdiction rules of the forum? Although the less popular 1999 Convention gives an affirmative answer,[50] the much better-adopted 1952 treaty does not, leaving the matter up to the law of the forum.[51] The other is the effect of the arrest: if made, how far does it give priority to the arresting party, and what is its effect in insolvency or where there are other creditors? In this case nothing whatever is said in either Convention;[52] it is simply accepted that this is up to the insolvency law of the *forum arresti* and any provisions it may have for giving effect to foreign insolvencies.[53] These omissions were deliberate, and forced by the existence of a fundamental difference between the common law and civil law views of arrest.[54] The common law regards ship arrest as a substantive right limited to ships, *ipso facto* giving rise to Admiralty jurisdiction and to a preferential remedy against the vessel; the civil law, by contrast, saw it as a specific example of a general right to proceed against any of the defendant's property in support of an ordinary claim, and therefore subject to all the rules, jurisdictional and otherwise, applicable to that claim.[55] The gap was simply unbridgeable: the result, an agreement that

48 Ibid, 816.

49 For a useful account of the earlier of these, see J. Kriz, 'Ship Mortgages, Maritime Liens, and Their Enforcement: The Brussels Conventions of 1926 and 1952' (1963) 12 *Duke Law Journal* 671 and (1964) 13 *Duke Law Journal* 70.

50 Art. 7(1) Jurisdiction may however be refused if another State's courts accept it (Art.7(2)).

51 Art. 7(1).

52 It is true that if the arrest is to secure a maritime lien, then other Conventions may indirectly require it to create a secured claim, by demanding that it rank ahead of a mortgage: see the International Convention For the Unification of Certain Rules of Law Relating to Maritime Liens and Mortgages (Brussels, 1926), Art. 3 and the International Convention on Maritime Liens and Mortgages (Geneva, 1993), Art. 5. But these say nothing about non-lien claims.

53 An important point within the EU, where the recast Insolvency Regulation (Regulation (EU) 2015/848) essentially requires all arresters in the EU to respect the insolvency regime in any Member State where the insolvent has its centre of main interests. Under the UNCITRAL Model Law, in force in two EU Member States (UK and Greece) and which governs the effect of insolvency in non-EU states, these matters are generally left up to the arresting state. See A. Tettenborn, 'The Arrest Conventions: an Update Needed?' in B. Soyer and A. Tettenborn (eds), *Maritime Liabilities in a Global and Regional Context* (Informa Law from Routledge, 2018), Ch. 13.

54 See W. Tetley, 'Arrest, Attachment, and Related Maritime Law Procedures' (1999) 73 *Tulane Law Review* 1895 at 1940 et seq.

55 E.g. A. Leborgne, *Droit de l'exécution*, 2e édition (Dalloz 2014), No 2953 et seq; H. Puttfarken, *Seehandelsrecht*, No 799 ('*[Dinglicher] Arrest bei uns ist ein allgemeiner Titel gegen den Schuldner, den der Gläubiger nach seiner Wahl in Gegenstände dessen gesammten Vermögens vollziehen kann*'). For an account of

both these areas had to be left effectively uncodified and up to each individual jurisdiction to decide according to its own internal law.

A further instance, less obvious, lurks in the special prescription periods which feature in almost all liability Conventions. In almost every case (except oddly enough for the Hague-Visby Rules), there is a discreet statement that any question whether the period is halted or suspended falls to be decided according to the law of the forum.[56] This matters: if there is a short prescription period of, say, two years, an extension of a year as a result of interruption is highly significant. It also reflects a long-running and intractable argument between common lawyers and civil lawyers: the former maintaining that once the limitation clock has started almost nothing short of agreement can stop it, while the latter are open to all sorts of pleas that a given state of affairs may interrupt prescription, while allowing the clock to restart once it ceases to apply.[57]

A second difficulty with international Conventions is the real possibility of differing interpretations in various jurisdictions. One way this arises is that, in the nature of things, linguistic and other difficulties make it hard for anyone to assimilate worldwide case law on a particular provision.[58] Another is that provisions may be left in a Convention that everyone accepts but no one quite understands: an understandable reaction from tired negotiators anxious to finish the business and go home, but a potent source of later trouble. Witness, for example, the enigmatic Art. IV rule 5(b) of the Hague-Visby Rules, agreed by weary delegates in 1968 without much thought as to what it meant and which some, but not other, jurisdictions have construed as limiting recovery in cargo claims to the sound arrived value of the goods and excluding all claims for consequential loss.[59]

Yet another problem can arise from a combination of imprecise wording and different legal traditions. Again, the Hague-Visby Rules provide a textbook example. It concerns Art. III rule 8, the anti-exoneration provision. English courts, with their predilection for freedom of contract, have construed this narrowly: civil law courts, traditionally more dirigiste, have often applied it more widely so as to cover (for example) identity of carrier clauses or FIOST provisions seeking to throw liability for negligent stowage back onto the shipper.[60] Limitation of liability provides another example as regards the loss of the right to limit: the LLMC wording 'recklessly and with knowledge that such loss would probably result' has fairly regularly been interpreted in England as requiring a subjective realisation

---

the difference, see A. Tettenborn, 'The Arrest Conventions: an Update Needed?' in B. Soyer and A. Tettenborn (eds), *Maritime Liabilities in a Global and Regional Context* (Informa Law from Routledge, 2018) Ch. 13 and the other authorities cited there.

56 See e.g. Art. 7 of the Convention for the Unification of Certain Rules of Law with respect to Collisions between Vessels, or Art. 16.3 of Athens Convention relating to the Carriage of Passengers and their Luggage by Sea 1974 (as amended).

57 For a useful account see the *Max Planck Encyclopedia of European Private Law*, 2nd edn, Vol II, 1309.

58 John Honnold made the point nicely in connection with the United Nations Convention on Contracts for the International Sale of Goods (CISG) (Vienna, 1980): 'Throughout the work on uniform laws, realists have told us: even if you get uniform laws you will not get uniform results.' See J. Honnold, 'The Sales Convention in Action – Uniform International Words: Uniform Application?' (1998) 8 *Journal of Law and Commerce* 207.

59 For the arguments and the details of the different interpretations, see A. Tettenborn, 'Damage, destruction and consequential loss – should carriers be different from everyone else?' (2013) 12 *Revista de Derecho del Transporte* 49.

60 The matter is described, in large detail, in W. Tetley, *Marine Cargo Claims*, 4th edn (Éditions Yvon Blais, 2008), Ch. 39. See too I. Djadjev, *The Obligations of the Carrier Regarding the Cargo: The Hague-Visby Rules* (Springer 2017), p. 106 (FIOST clauses).

that damage was likely, but in some civil law jurisdictions as satisfied by some form of gross negligence.[61]

The third difficulty with international Conventions arises from effects of later dissatisfaction. What happens when a Convention is felt to be outdated or in need of alteration? Absent universal agreement from all parties on how to improve or upgrade it (something that is never in practice forthcoming), there is no entirely satisfactory answer to this. It is obviously possible for dissatisfied parties to wipe the record clean by agreeing a new treaty in place of the old, and this on occasion happens. But then, despite the salutary practice of discouraging a plethora of very small treaty regimes by requiring a fixed number of ratifications for any Convention to come into force in the first place,[62] the result is often not unity but its precise opposite, fragmentation. The obvious example is carriage of goods by sea. This is currently, according to circumstances, subject to three possible regimes – Hague, Hague-Visby, and Hamburg (four if you add in the possibility that no treaty regime applies),[63] with another on the horizon, Rotterdam: a result that is, shall we say, not one of enviable simplicity. Again, there are now two Convention regimes for the carriage of passengers;[64] for salvage;[65] for maritime liens and mortgages;[66] and for ship arrest;[67] for limitation of liability there are no fewer than three.[68]

These problems can admittedly be mitigated. Difficulties, in particular, can be reduced by updating through protocols: that is, by negotiating and opening for signature not a new Convention but an amending agreement or protocol which progressive states can then be persuaded to adopt.[69] Examples of such updates are the updating of the CLC by various protocols, notably in 1992; and of the Athens Convention by protocol in 2002. Indeed, this

61 M. Katisvela, 'Loss of the Carrier's Limitation of Liability under the Hague-Visby Rules and the Warsaw Convention: Common Law and Civil Law Views' (2012) 26 *Australian and New Zealand Maritime Law Journal* 118; S. Gahlen, *Civil Liability for Accidents at Sea* (Springer, 2015), p. 91 et seq.

62 A practice which, for example, strangled at birth the International Convention for the Unification of Certain Rules of Law Relating to Maritime Liens and Mortgages (Brussels, 1967). Only four ratifications occurred; five were needed to bring it into force.

63 For example, transport between Brazil and Thailand with the bill of lading issued in Brazil. Although both Brazil and Thailand apply some form of Hague or Hague-Visby by local legislation, neither is party to any treaty: it follows that if carriage is subject to the law and jurisdiction of a third state such as England, no Convention is applicable unless expressly agreed.

64 The International Convention for the Unification of Certain Rules Relating to the Carriage of Passengers by Sea (Brussels, 1961) and the much better patronised Athens Convention relating to the Carriage of Passengers and their Luggage by Sea, 1974 and its Protocol of 2002.

65 The Convention for the Unification of Certain Rules of Law respecting Assistance and Salvage at Sea (Brussels, 1910), and the International Convention on Salvage (London, 1989).

66 The Convention on Maritime Liens and Mortgages (Brussels, 1926) and the International Convention on Maritime Liens and Mortgages (Geneva, 1993). A third convention, the International Convention for the Unification of Certain Rules relating to Maritime Liens and Mortgages (Brussels, 1967), was thankfully stillborn.

67 The International Convention Relating to the Arrest of Sea-Going Ships (Brussels, 1952), and the International Convention on the Arrest of Ships (Geneva, 1999).

68 The International Convention for the unification of certain rules relating to the Limitation of the liability of owners of sea-going vessels (Brussels, 1924); the International Convention relating to the Limitation of the Liability of Owners of Sea-Going Ships (Brussels, 1957); and the Convention on Limitation of Liability for Maritime Claims (London, 1976).

69 In one case, indeed, the protocol was essential to the agreement itself. The original International Convention on Liability and Compensation for Damage in Connection with the Carriage of Hazardous and Noxious Substances by Sea 1996 (HNS) gained minimal support because after the text was finalised fatal defects in it were noticed. It took an amending Protocol of 2010 to iron out these problems and give the Convention a chance of obtaining the necessary number of ratifications to bring it into force.

process can be automated through a provision for minor updates decided on by an expert group to take effect by majority vote.[70] But even here the result remains a multiplication of regimes, albeit that the variations are likely to be a good deal less violent since all will rest on the same substratum.

4 Semi-official 'soft law'

Not all proposals for international unification, even those that are official and government-sponsored, need involve a treaty regime of any kind. The drafting by (for example) UN bodies of 'model laws' which are then offered to nations or other stakeholders for possible adoption, with or without amendment, is well established. Straightforward examples are the UNCITRAL model laws on international commercial arbitration, transborder insolvency, electronic commerce and secured transactions. On a European level we have the more or less EU-sponsored Principles of European Contract Law and Common European Sales Law. Similarly, texts may be prepared not so much for adoption as for inspiration: a straightforward instance here being the UNIDROIT Principles of International Commercial Contracts.

Perhaps not surprisingly, there has been little evidence of this process affecting shipping law, save indirectly in that both commercial arbitration and transborder insolvency law are vital in practice to many shipping claims. But two sets of rules technically come in this category.

One is the York-Antwerp Rules. Although originally adopted as a purely private-enterprise initiative in 1860 in order to deal with major national variations in the law of general average, these were later taken over by public bodies, first the International Law Association in 1921 and then from 1947 the CMI, who retain today the function of producing new versions where necessary.[71] They are in form a code, but gain their legal force wholly from contractual incorporation in carriage contracts and charters.

The second, less successful, is the Lisbon Rules concerning the principles of assessment of damages in collision cases, also a production of the CMI.[72] These were deliberately produced as a non-legislative aid to the quantification and negotiation of damages in cases of collision between ships and other vessels and installations: but there is little evidence that they have had any serious influence or been at all widely used.[73]

5 Standard forms

We have left until last what is probably the most significant source of unification in shipping law: the use and development of standard contract forms of agreement drafted entirely non-governmentally by trade associations of one sort or another, and voluntarily adopted

70 As in the case of the Collision Regulations: for details see Convention on the International Regulations for Preventing Collisions at Sea (London, 1972), Art. VI.

71 For the history, see M. Cornah, 'The road to Vancouver – the development of the York-Antwerp Rules' (2004) *Journal of International Maritime Law* 155; *Lowndes & Rudolf on General Average,* 14th edn (Sweet and Maxwell, 2013), paras 00.70–00.112.

72 They are reproduced at (1987) 18 *Journal of International Maritime Law* 577, followed by a comment by Jean Warot of the CMI.

73 Though the author understands that in 2005 they were enacted as part of the statute law of Thailand.

by individual participants in the market. This is a development that has been going on for well over 100 years, at least in some areas. Thus, as regards bills of lading,[74] there is early mention in the English law reports of generic '1890 Black Sea, Azov and Danube' and a '1902 Chamber of Shipping Black Sea Berth Contract' bills.[75] Similarly, within four years of its founding in 1905, BIMCO had produced the first of its standard charters (the BALTIME 1909 form); the first NYPE time charter was approved in 1913. The UK Chamber of Shipping produced its 'River Plate Charter' (now the CENTROCON form) in 1914, and GENCON in 1922.

The result is that today there is a large number of areas where any discussion of the law is effectively a commentary on the terms of one or more standard forms of contract. The law on charters, for example, is in large part to be ascertained by reference to the structure of, standard terms to be found in, and subtle differences between, forms such as the NYPE, GENCON or ASBATANKVOY. It is by analysing these, rather than studying any general law, that we best discuss matters such as liability for bad stowage, what happens in the case of short delivery, the precise incidence of laytime and demurrage, the extent of any lien over subfreights, final voyages, liability for early or late delivery in the case of a time charter, and so on and so forth. Sometimes, indeed, multiple standard forms are involved. Thus liability as between charterer and disponent owner for third-party cargo claims is likely to be determined by a combination of the charter and the equally-standard Inter-Club Agreement produced by the P&I Clubs.

And so too with almost any other aspect of shipping law dealing wholly or largely with the liabilities *inter se* of two parties who are in contractual relation one with another. Carriage contract disputes admittedly have to start with a discussion of regimes compulsorily applicable such as Hague-Visby or, in the case of short sea traffic within the EU, the CMR:[76] but that aside, they largely turn on a reading of forms like CONGENBILL or CONLINEBILL, or (increasingly importantly) waybills such as CONWAYBILL and multimodal forms on the lines of MULTIDOCS. And the list goes on. Insurance is about the detailed analysis of the Institute Clauses; salvage about Lloyd's Open Form and similar documents; sales are governed almost exclusively by the Norwegian Saleform or some relation of it; bareboat charters by BARECON2001 or BARECON2017; towage by TOWCON. The important features of shipbuilding contracts are almost exclusively dealt with by whichever of the five or so forms in common use is being employed. And, thanks to organisations such as BIMCO, this tendency is spreading even to the more esoteric areas, such as crew management and, for that matter, liabilities arising out of the employment of armed guards in pirate-infested seas (where BIMCO in 2017 was responsible for drafting the new standard form named GUARDCON).

Why are industry forms so effective as a means of codification? An obvious answer is that they are the most likely to fit in with the needs of stakeholders, since they are drafted not by diplomatic experts or bureaucrats in the pay of state governments, but by those

74 See generally N. Gaskell, *Bills of Lading*, 2nd edn (LLP, 2005), para.1.73.

75 See *Tulloch v Cox's Shipping Agency Ltd* (1923) 14 Ll L Rep 118, 119 and *AS Peder P. Hedegaard v Handelsvertretung der UDSSR in Denmark* (1925) 22 Ll L Rep 526. A version of the latter can be found in M. Barentz, *Algemeen Nederlandsch Handelswoordenboek* (Minerva, 1916), 131.

76 Because of Art. 2 of the CMR, applying its regime with modifications to events during journeys involving short sea crossings on which the truck is not unloaded.

within the relevant industry itself whose own money is at stake. Moreover, many of these documents, dealing with all sorts of contract, from carriage of goods to shipbuilding to crew management, are produced by organisations such as BIMCO on the advice of stakeholders on both sides and specifically with the aim of drawing a proper balance between the parties' interests. For that matter, even where documents are less balanced, as with tanker voyage charters such as EXXONVOY (very much a pro-charterer document, as might be imagined given that all the oil majors are predominantly charterers), they are only default rules and can be altered in so far as one or other party has the necessary bargaining power. But there are a number of other, more specific, advantages.

5.1 Detailed vs general rules

First, there is a point about detail. Model laws, national codes or Conventions are in their nature much better suited to the laying down of fairly general rules. Legislation containing grinding, dreary detail can be difficult to persuade legislatures to pass, make intractable reading and act so as to fossilise the law and prevent the adaptation of a code to particular circumstances. But the broad-brush approach that is suited to legislation is for its part wholly inadequate for those in the shipping business. Even if a hundred years ago contracts were concluded in relatively short form with provision for specific events left up to the implications of the general law, today parties to a shipping contract prefer for good reasons to lay down their obligations in large detail.

Examples are legion: three random ones will have to suffice here. First, take a voyage charter involving liquid cargoes. The rate at which loading and discharge take place is obviously vital: tankers of all kinds are highly capital-intensive and hence the risks of immobilisation by delay fall to be carefully distributed. Any code – and for that matter the rules of a non-codified system like the common law – will simply say that loading and discharge must take place at a reasonable rate. But faced with a dispute over the matter, most parties will prefer an exact standard to argument over what is reasonable: hence numerous clauses providing for particular rates of discharge, pressures on discharge hoses, etc.[77] Secondly, in a financing bareboat charter, the owner (or rather financier) will always be concerned to know when he can cancel the charter on the basis of events throwing doubt on the long-term viability of the financing arrangement. There are always, at least in a civil law country, default rules about this contained in a maritime or commercial code. But no sane owner will wish to put his trust simply in these: instead he will rely on a precise list such as that provided in BARECON (for example, allowing insurance to lapse, or trading outside the permitted area and thus putting the vessel and her insurance cover at risk).[78] Thirdly, take the example of a ship sale. The seller must obviously under the general law hand the ship over to the buyer, together with any paperwork necessary to transfer ownership. But what else? This is not the sort of thing that can be dealt with by general provision, since circumstances vary and in any case parties' requirements change over time. Not surprisingly, one of the most important features of the Norwegian Saleform 2012, which governs ship

---

77 S. Baughen, 'Delay and Demurrage in Tanker Charters', in B. Soyer and A. Tettenborn (eds), *Charterparties: Law, Practice and Emerging Legal Issues* (Informa Law from Routledge, 2017), Ch. 10.

78 See BARECON2017, Clause 31(a).

sales largely to the exclusion of the default rules of the underlying legal system, is that it provides in detail for the documentary side of such contracts.[79]

5.2 Diversity in commercial arrangements

Secondly, there is the problem of diversity and the inveterate desire of business for flexibility in the arrangements they enter into. Within any particular kind of contract one will often find subtle variations in practice according to the desires of particular market players. It can be difficult, especially over time, for any code or Convention regime to keep up with these (other than by stating that its provisions are subject to anything to the contrary agreed by the parties, which rather defeats the object of having a code in the first place). This is a problem, however, which is very neatly through the use of standard industry forms. Three methods are widespread.

One such method, now a feature of many BIMCO contracts, consists in explicit alternative clauses, with a default in case, as often happens in the fast-moving business world, no choice is in fact made. A straightforward example is the redrafted Norwegian Saleform 2012, which comes in various flavours: 'final' or 'subject to inspection', 'buyer to drydock' or 'seller to drydock' on delivery, 'bunkers at cost' or 'bunkers at market', and so on. BARECON 2017 is another example. Where modifications to the vessel are required by law it comes in 'charterer to pay' and 'owners to share' variants: so too with the 'free of mortgage' and 'subject to mortgage', and 'owners to insure' and 'charterers to insure' varieties.

Secondly, and possibly more importantly, standard forms allow for the ready creation of 'bolt-on' additions. Sometimes these can be recondite matters of interest largely to specialist shipping lawyers. A neat but familiar example concerns the not inconsiderable risk of bad stowage by incompetent stevedores in the case of vessels let under the NYPE time charter, and who had to pay for its consequences. Clause 8 of the pre-1993 NYPE form, stating 'charterers are to load stow and trim the cargo at their expense under the supervision of the captain', was known implicitly to put this risk on the charterers.[80] But it was equally well known that the addition of the two words 'and responsibility' after 'supervision' reversed this position.[81]

This aside, however, much more important are separate standard clauses which can be inserted into a contract if required. A lot of this material is obviously kept on industry lawyers' own databases. But quite apart from that, BIMCO alone makes roughly 130 particular clauses available, which is comfortably more than its tally of complete contracts once duplicates are stripped out.[82] These deal, as one might expect, with a catholic range of topics. Some are seriously esoteric: dealing, for example, with who bears the risk of Asian gypsy moth infestation in time charters, or of Calcutta bureaucratic delays once ships on voyage charter destined for that port have reached a particular point outside its limits

79 Norwegian Saleform 2012, Cl.8.

80 See the English decision in *Court Line Ltd v Canadian Transport Co Ltd* [1940] AC 934. The post-1993 wording makes this explicit.

81 *The Shinjitsu Maru No 5* [1985] 1 Lloyd's Rep 568.

82 BIMCO's website in June 2018 made available about 130 clauses, as against roughly 150 specific contracts; but of the latter figure some 45 were outdated previous legacy versions of more modern documents.

known as the Sandheads. Others, by contrast, deal with issues of common concern, where coverage is often indeed found in many contracts anyway. Examples include the 'both to blame' clause in carriage contracts dealing with cargo's recovery from the non-carrying vessel; a cancellation clause for use in voyage charters in the event of late delivery; and the ISM and ISPS clauses, making it clear that in any charter it is the owner's responsibility to ensure that the vessel at all times complies with the requirements of the relevant Codes. Yet others deal with matters that parties may or may not, according to the background facts and their relative bargaining strengths, wish to include. A slow steaming clause, for example, may be much to the advantage of environmentally-conscious owners in a time or voyage charter; so, too, a war risks clause. Provision for issue of electronic bills of lading may benefit a time charterer; a hazardous materials inventory clause in a shipbuilding contract may save the buyer a good deal of money when it eventually comes to the disposal of the vessel; and so on.

5.3 New forms of business

In the last 50 years a number of entirely new types of contract have come into existence. The most obvious example is containerisation. This has given rise not only to specialised contracts such as container lease agreements, but also to curiosities such as the slot charter, an agreement half-way between a contract of carriage and a time charter which would be difficult to fit into any earlier codification of maritime law, but which was quickly regularised with the development of the standardised SLOTHIRE charter by BIMCO in 1993.

The most important result of containerisation, however, has been the explosive development of multimodal transport contracts. The history of this is instructive. Some European systems eventually caught up with this development, in certain cases fairly comprehensively (as with the German HGB revisions, dating ultimately from 1998 and since extensively updated),[83] in others less so (the Spanish coverage, from 2015, is patchy).[84] But none of this catching-up was swift. The UN through UNCITRAL admittedly moved a little less glacially, producing a Convention on International Multimodal Transport of Goods as early as 1980;[85] however, this was ultimately in vain, since the Convention never got sufficient support to bring it into force (a fate so far shared by UNCTAD's more recent, and far more monumental, Rotterdam Rules).

But none of these initiatives is very relevant, save possibly as regards third parties. This is because industry has had no compunction in taking over where the state has given up. Particular combined transport documents drafted within the business were well enough established by 1974 to qualify for a mention in that year's UCP300;[86] the International Chamber of Commerce (ICC) Rules for a Combined Transport Document appeared in

83 See now HGB, §§ 452–452d (Beförderung mit verschiedenartigen Beförderungsmitteln).

84 See Código de Derecho de la Navegación Marítima y Aérea, Arts 209 and 267.

85 Indeed a tentative draft convention had been produced as early as 1963: UNCTAD, *Implementation of Multimodal Transport Rules, Report prepared by the UNCTAD secretariat* (UNCTAD/SDTE/TLB/2), June 2001, paras 16–28.

86 'If the credit calls for a combined transport document, i.e. one which provides for a combined transport by at least two different modes of transport . . . banks will accept such documents as tendered.'

1975, followed by BIMCO versions such as COMBICONBILL and the Intermodal Bill of Lading, the FIATA through bill of lading, and most recently the MULTIDOC95 bill of lading and the accompanying MULTIWAYBILL. These latter documents have been in use for over 20 years with, it seems, very little difficulty.

Nor has containerisation been the only spur to development. Offshore operations, for example, have spawned a whole new class of very specialised transport contracts that would not appear in any civil code, such as HEAVYCONRECEIPT, HEAVYLIFTVOYBILL and SUPPLYTIME, dealing with the transport of heavy equipment to and from platforms and the supply of vessels to service them, not to mention the LOGIC suite of contracts dealing with the making available and operation of actual drilling equipment.

5.4 Unforeseen problems

Lastly, and most importantly, there is in practice always a problem about updating state or similar codes to deal with new problems or unexpected difficulties. It is here that industry-drafted contracts very much come into their own.

The idea that unforeseen legal complications or uncertainties could be palliated by altering shipping contract forms has a long history. At the turn of the twentieth century, for example, there was a nagging uncertainty over general average. Was a shipowner automatically barred from claiming relief against cargo if at fault, even where he was contractually or otherwise exonerated from liability for that fault?[87] US authority suggested he was:[88] English authority the opposite.[89] By mid-1904[90] the problem had been solved by the adoption of a clause providing for the English position, a solution that proved effective on a wide basis when in 1912 the clause was upheld as valid by the US Supreme Court in *The Jason.*[91] This clause subsists to this day, albeit slightly modified and now called the New Jason Clause; it, or something similar, now appears almost universally in bills of lading and charters. Again, the 'both to blame' clause referred to in passing above is another neat example. The background to this clause was the US rule that where two colliding ships were both in fault, then in contrast to the position in Europe and England,[92] cargo on either vessel could recover from the other vessel in full.[93] If the non-carrying vessel then claimed over against the carrying vessel[94] the result was a back-door nullification of the navigational fault exception, which by then was almost universal in carriage contracts.[95] Procuring legislation to suppress this anomaly was a non-starter: a Convention solution was unthinkable.

87 For detailed discussion see *General Average – Effect of Fault of the Shipmaster*, in the *Proceedings of the Twenty-First Conference of the International Law Association*, 30 September 1903, 177.

88 *The Irrawaddy*, 171 US 187 (1898). The case was not absolutely in point on contractual exoneration, since there the exoneration was statutory, contained in the US Harter Act 1893.

89 See *The Carron Park* (1890) 15 PD 203 and *Milburn v Jamaica Fruit Importing Co* [1900] 2 QB 547 (the latter a majority decision over a strong dissent).

90 The earliest mention of such a clause seems to be in *The Jason*, 225 US 32 (1912); the events giving rise to that decision happened in July 1904.

91 225 US 32 (1912).

92 See *The Milan* (1861) Lush 388.

93 See *The Atlas*, 93 US 302 (1876) and *The Chattahoochee*, 173 US 540 (1899).

94 Which it was entitled to do in both England and the US, to the extent that it had paid more than its several share: *The Giacinto Motta* [1977] 2 Lloyd's Rep 221 and *The North Star*, 106 US 17 (1882).

95 It now appears in Art. IV Rule 2(a) of the Hague-Visby Rules.

In the 1930s the solution chosen, admittedly ineffective in the US[96] but valid everywhere else, was a clause requiring cargo in such cases to indemnify the carrier.[97] And the historical list continues. Other old examples are the well-known 'Himalaya Clause', drafted in the 1950s[98] by leading English lawyer Eustace Roskill QC[99] to get over the extreme difficulty experienced by common law jurisdictions in giving effect to exoneration clauses for the benefit of third parties, and the 'Voywar 1993' clause that, among other things, dealt with the problem of closure of the Suez canal and its effect on voyage charters.[100]

Today this process is commonplace. The more commonly used standard forms are increasingly updated on a regular basis, and this development carries with it an obvious opportunity to deal with problems that have arisen meanwhile. The new NYPE 2015 form is a case in point.[101] Issues dealt with that had arisen since the previous (1993) version (or on occasion even earlier) included regulating the right to demand the issue of electronic bills of lading;[102] the machinery of delivery and redelivery;[103] the precise parameters of off-hire;[104] the vital issue of damages where a charter was terminated for non-payment;[105] the problematic lack of any right to withhold performance without putting an end to the charter;[106] technical points about bunkers aboard at the time of delivery and redelivery;[107] and so on. Again, when the ship sale contract SALEFORM 1993 was updated in 2012, the opportunity was taken to correct a number of problems that had previously had to be covered by ad hoc clauses, such as the payment procedure,[108] and a clause[109] to neutralise an alarming holding by the English courts[110] that, to everyone's surprise, a provision for sale of a vessel as is did not exclude the default terms of English sales legislation as to quality.

Nor is regular 'maintenance updating' necessarily the most important. A new difficulty may spring up that can seriously disturb the equilibrium of shipping contracts if not quickly

96 Where such clauses were upheld in charters but not bills of lading: see *American Union Transport v USA*, 1976 AMC 1480 and *US v Atlantic Mutual Insurance Co*, 343 US 246 (1952), 1952 AMC 659.

97 The date of first appearance is not entirely clear. In *US v Atlantic Mutual Insurance Co*, 343 US 246 (1952) it was implied that the clause first saw the light of day in 1937. But it had undoubtedly appeared earlier: it is mentioned in *The WW Bruce*, 14 F.Supp. 89 (1936) (rev'd on other grounds, 94 F.2d 834 (1937), cert. denied sub nom. *Pacific-Atlantic SS Co. v Weyerhauser Timber Co.*, 304 US 567 (1938)).

98 Following on from a 1952 incident in which a passenger was injured on the cruise ship *Himalaya* while the vessel was docked in Trieste. For the eventual 1954 decision see *Adler v Dickson* [1955] 1 QB 158.

99 Later the judge Lord Roskill.

100 GENCON 94, Cl.17(3).

101 See B. Soyer and T. Nikaki, 'Enhancing Standardisation and Legal Certainty through Standard Charter-party Contracts – the NYPE 2015 Experience' in B. Soyer and A. Tettenborn (eds), *Charterparties: Law, Practice and Emerging Legal Issues* (Informa Law from Routledge, 2017), Ch. 5.

102 Cl.32.

103 Cl.4.

104 See the revised off-hire clause (Cl.17).

105 Cl.11(c). Interestingly clauses like this had previously come into use ad hoc. One such had been used, and applied, in *The Astra* [2013] EWHC 865 (Comm); [2013] 1 CLC 819.

106 Clause 11(d): see too e.g. SUPPLYTIME 2005, Cl.12(f). The lack of any such right at common law (see *The Agios Giorgis* [1976] 2 Lloyd's Rep 192 and *The Aegnoussiotis* [1977] 1 Lloyd's Rep 268) is something of a scandal. Interestingly it is specifically mentioned in the German codification of charter law: HGB, § 568.

107 Cl.9.

108 See SALEFORM 2012, Cls.2 & 3.

109 Cl.18.

110 In *The Union Power* [2012] EWHC 3537 (Comm), [2013] 1 Lloyd's Rep 509. This change was very smartly introduced indeed, the arbitration award which the High Court confirmed providing the actual impetus for change.

contracted around: an explosion in piracy,[111] a judicial decision,[112] a global political development.[113] National legislation being essentially out of the question, the availability of bolt-on clauses carefully drafted to balance the parties' interests (which can later become part of the boilerplate of standard forms[114]) is vital.

A number of recent examples can make this clear. Following on from difficulties over the mechanics of pre-advices of redelivery under a time-charter and from a controversial English decision on damages for late redelivery, the result was the BIMCO 2017 time-charter redelivery clause. Increasing concern with particular countries' increased anti-corruption provisions, there came the 2015 anti-corruption clause dealing with the effects of corrupt practices. The extent to which a time charterer could justify non-compliance with orders on the basis of what might often be the national sanctions legislation of, say, the US raised difficult issues of private international law; the result was the swift appearance of a BIMCO clause to regulate the matter. Similarly exasperation with the time and effort required to sort out general average, especially where the amounts recovered were likely to be relatively small, has led in the last few years to clauses, now largely standardised in the BIMCO absorption clause of 2017, under which hull and machinery (H & M) insurers essentially pay the contribution that would have been paid by charterers or cargo interests.

6 Concluding remarks

The conclusion reached by this chapter is simple. Codification of maritime law through national commercial codes or Convention regimes continues to have some part to play. This is particularly true where insolvency, third-party rights or restrictions on the excesses of freedom of contract have a part to play. But today it is a subsidiary part. The centre of gravity has shifted. By far the most significant codificatory developments take the form of standard contract terms produced by the shipping industry or trade bodies. It is these that dictate the form of transactions; allow new forms of shipping business to flourish; and allow changes to be made easily and seamlessly when they appear to be necessary. Increasingly the books on maritime lawyers' shelves, even in civil law countries, are likely to take the form of commentaries not on national or international legislation but on privately-ordered forms of contract. This is what the industry wants, and what will allow it the full potential to develop in efficiency and productivity in the next few decades.

111 For instance, the growth in piracy spawned no less than three clauses in 2012–2013 in the BIMCO suite: the Piracy Clause for Consecutive Voyage Charter Parties and COAs 2013; the Piracy Clause for Single Voyage Charter Parties 2013; and the Piracy Clause for Time Charter Parties 2013. It also indirectly was responsible for the growth in standard clauses for the maintenance of armed personnel on board: e.g. BIMCO's GUARDCON 2012.

112 One example is *The Union Power* [2012] EWHC 3537 (Comm), [2013] 1 Lloyd's Rep 509 referred to above, giving rise to an altered SALEFORM. Another, less obvious, one is the well-known decision in *The Achilleas* [2008] UKHL 48, [2009] 1 AC 61, denying an owner recovery for loss of a lucrative (and foreseeable) follow-on fixture following late redelivery. This gave rise indirectly to BIMCO's 2017 Redelivery Clause for Time Charters, Part (b) of which carefully apportions liability for the consequences of late redelivery and takes such cases out of the ambit of the forum's general contractual rules of remoteness of loss.

113 An old example is the closure of the Suez Canal, mentioned above.

114 To give an example, Cl.32 of the NYPE 2015 form takes the form of the standalone BIMCO Electronic Bills of Lading Clause.

CHAPTER 6

Successes and failures of uniform maritime law instruments

Is there room for a new approach?

*Professor Juan Pablo Rodríguez Delgado**

1. Introduction

Since the Comité Maritime International (CMI) was began in 1897, unification of maritime law – in all its aspects – and related commercial practices have been a foundational objective (Article 1 CMI Constitution), whatever hurdles it has to overcome. To that end, the CMI has promoted the establishment of national associations of maritime law and co-operates with other international organizations (United Nations Conference on Trade and Development, UNCTAD; International Maritime Organization, IMO; International Institute for the Unification of Private Law, UNIDROIT or United Nations Commission on International Trade Law, UNCITRAL), and these international organizations are the cornerstone of this process. However, the results of those aspirations have been very uneven after 120 years. There are many advantages to achieving a uniform maritime law, but there are also many obstacles that have not been overcome (and still continue today).[1]

Many international Conventions have had few ratifications and very unequal success. Governments usually give their consent for the signing ceremony but then do not ratify the Conventions later in order to enforce them (e.g. the Rotterdam Rules).[2] Others, however, have been an unusual success (e.g., the 1910 Collision Convention,[3] the Hague-Visby Rules,[4] the Montreal Convention,[5] the 1958 New York Convention,[6] and the Cape Town Convention[7]).

* Universidad Carlos III de Madrid. This chapter has been elaborated within the framework of the Research Project DER2016–77695-P on 'Modernization of Spanish Law of Secured Transactions to Facilitate Access to Credit in an International Context', funded by the Spanish Ministry of Economy and Competitiveness.

1 Long drafting periods usually produce 'consensus' and complex norms (and even incoherent or difficult to understand and apply later), rather than 'good' law. The result too often leads to very different interpretations in the national courts in the application of the international instruments. Additionally, the reservations, declarations or opt-in or opt-out clauses produce alternative uniform criteria on the interpretation.

2 United Nations Convention on Contracts for the International Carriage of Goods Wholly or Partly by Sea (Rotterdam Rules) (New York, 2008).

3 Convention for the Unification of Certain Rules of Law with respect to Collisions between Vessels (Brussels, 1910).

4 The Hague Rules as Amended by the Brussels Protocol 1968.

5 Convention for the Unification of Certain Rules for International Carriage by Air (Montreal, 1999).

6 United Nations Convention on the Recognition and Enforcement of Foreign Arbitral Awards (New York, 1958).

7 Convention on International Interests in Mobile Equipment (Cape Town, 2001).

As so many others, more learned than I, have said, the goal of uniformity, or at least greater uniformity, is a noble one, and it should be pursued. However, uniformity may often be fleeting because trade and commerce are constantly changing, and requiring new rules and procedures. The advantages of uniformity far outweigh the disadvantages of international law, but those that exist should be mentioned.

Although maritime law is supported by a long tradition of international uniformity, it is not exclusively dependent upon the adoption of international texts and their acceptance by Contracting States. In recent years, the development of a universal maritime legal order by the adoption of unifying Conventions has slowed (despite the fact that they have continued to be elaborated). At the same time, many other tools have come into existence over the last decades (such as general non-maritime and maritime contract law) and have started to find a way to wider harmonization of international maritime law, contributing substantially to that objective and the norms governing it around the world. The use of standard forms formulated and drafted by various international agencies; model rules, guidelines or recommendations of international maritime organizations, has considerably increased in the last decades.[8] Or even the so-called 'modern lex mercatoria', or transnational commercial law, offers an alternative form of uniformity.[9]

However, not everything is light and colour in the pursued objective of maritime uniformity. There are instruments that have not achieved the expected success. The Maritime Liens and Mortgages Conventions[10] (with three in the last 90 years) or the Rotterdam Rules – on contracts for the carriage of goods by sea – are clear examples of the fact that some of the obstacles that are propagated about uniformity are a reality in the international scenario. The complexity and extension of the text, the unbalanced distribution of interests among the Contracting Parties or the excessive influence of some States that has not ratified the Rules (see here the huge influence of US),[11] have been some of the criticisms that have hampered its international adoption.

On the other hand, another recent example of legal uniformity has been the Cape Town Convention on security interests on mobile equipment. Although many of the criticisms cited for the Rotterdam Rules could be reproduced here, amazingly enough, this Convention has enjoyed public approval. Its virtues, including the scheme chosen for its development (convention/protocols), the balanced set of interests between the contractual parties, the need for a uniform regulation in market or economic incentives, among others, have made this Convention one of the most successful in the international trade scene of recent times (and certainly in record time).[12]

---

8 A quick look at the 'texts and status' webpage of UNCITRAL is good proof of that: https://uncitral.un.org/en/texts. (visited 5 May 2019).

9 Regarding the relationship between *Lex mercatoria* and *Lex maritima*, perceived as that existing between genus and species, see M. Alba Fernandez, 'Maritime Arbitration in Spain. The Delocalization of Dispute Resolution and the Shrinking Recourse to Arbitration' in L. Mistelis and M. Goldby (eds), *The Role of Arbitration in Shipping Law* (Oxford, 2017), pp. 157–166 and the authors quoted therein.

10 International Convention for the unification of certain rules relating to Maritime Liens and Mortgages (Brussels, 1926); International Convention for the Unification of Certain Rules of Law Relating to Maritime Liens and Mortgages (Brussels, 1967); International Convention on Maritime Liens and Mortgages (Geneva, 1993).

11 See in detail section 3.2.1.

12 Another recent example of a successful Convention in the area of the contracts of carriage is the Montreal Convention, 1999 (entered into force on 4 November 2003), with more than 135 Contracting States: https://www.icao.int/secretariat/legal/List%20of%20Parties/Mtl99_EN.pdf) (visited 5 May 2019).

Both instruments are a reflection of the light and shade of the international uniform panorama. Criticisms and virtues of one and the other will be, for some, justified; or lacking meaning, for others. What seems clear is that both examples of conventional/legal uniformity are examples of the necessary push that this matter requires nowadays. If the law is uniform, all participants will know that their liability (or recovery) will be the same wherever a dispute is resolved. Results will be more predictable, litigation will thus be less necessary, and the parties will be able to make their underlying business decisions in confidence, knowing what law will be applied if loss or damage occurs.[13]

2. Premises for an adequate treatment of the uniformity of maritime law

The distinction between the public and private material scope of the instruments (with the disparity in their adoption) and the international nature of maritime law will allow us to outline, as necessary premises, an adequate treatment of the uniformity of maritime law.

2.1 Need to distinguish between public and private maritime law

When referring to the uniformity of commercial law in general, and maritime law in particular, we must begin by clearly distinguishing between public and private international law. Uniformity is supported 'mainly' by public interest legislation in favour of maritime safety, environmental protection or international competencies. Thus, public law becomes a real engine of legal uniformity. Public law Conventions have had much more acceptance than those of private law, which clearly indicates the governments' greatest concern for the safety of human life, safety in navigation or environmental protection.[14]

The most successful international Conventions (independently of the drafter organization) have been, without a doubt, those dedicated to public law interest[15] such as those mentioned above (see Figure 6.1). Uniformity of the navigational rules governing the high seas is absolutely essential. As some author has exemplified, one can imagine the utter confusion that would result if the law of some flag states required a red light on the port side of a vessel and a green light on the starboard side, while under the law of others the rule was reversed.[16]

The public law Conventions have been much more accepted than those of private law in the 20th century and part of the 21st century, which indicates the governments' greatest concern for the safety of human life at sea, safety in navigation and environmental protection. The role of maritime public law seems to be indisputable nowadays. The great

13 M. Sturley, T. Fujita and G. J. Van Der Ziel, *The Rotterdam Rules* (Sweet & Maxwell, 2011), p. 3.

14 The great disasters caused by accidents involving oil spills at sea (*Exxon Valdez*, *Prestige*, etc.) produced maximum governmental awareness in favour of the uniformity of an international response (CLC 69, CLC 92, Bunker 2001 or Fund 92 reflect that concern).

15 Such as the International Convention for the Prevention of Pollution from Ships, 1973, as modified by the Protocol of 1978 (MARPOL 73/78); International Convention for the Safety of Life at Sea, SOLAS (London, 1974); UN Convention on the Law of the Sea 1982, UNCLOS; Convention for the Suppression of Unlawful Acts Against the Safety of Maritime Navigation, SUA (Rome, 1988); Convention on the International Regulations for Preventing Collisions at Sea, COLREGs (London, 1972).

16 N. Healy, 'International Uniformity in Maritime Law: The Goal and the Obstacles' (1979) *California Western International Law Journal* 494, 498.

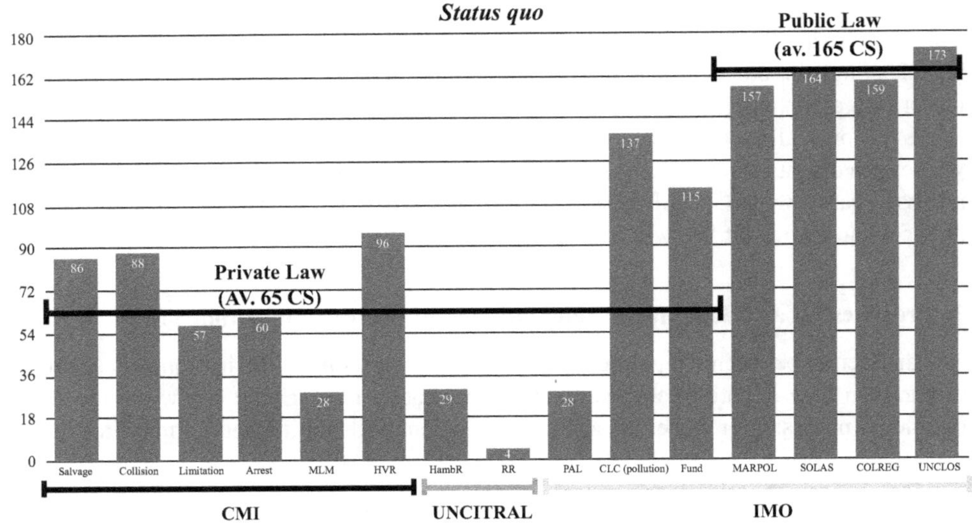

Figure 6.1

disasters caused by accidents that have occurred at sea have resulted in the concern and action of the states at the international level – from the sinking of the *Titanic* emerged the International Convention for the Safety of Life at Sea of 1974 (SOLAS);[17] from the *Torrey Canyon* arose Conventions intended to mitigate the pollution, such as the International Convention on Civil Liability for Oil Pollution Damage (CLC),[18] and from the *Prestige*, in 2002, the third supplement to the Fund 92 Convention.[19] The development of this public intervention, by means of international instruments of public law, of a deterrent, preventative and sanctioning nature has been unstoppable in the last decades and this state intervention is presented today as a guarantee of protection of human life at sea and the marine environment. This is also reflected in the principle of required international cooperation. The goals of maritime public policy would be difficult to achieve by the individual states (although a state may be very demanding, it is exposed to the consequences of what other states do). There is no way other than to agree and unify. That is the IMO's original mandate and its current mission: promote safe, secure, environmentally sound, efficient and sustainable shipping through the cooperation of states, as summarized by Article 1(a) of the IMO Convention ('to provide machinery for cooperation among Governments in the field of governmental regulation affecting shipping engaged in international trade').

On the other hand, those matters related to private law, with few exceptions, have had a different result: compared to the more than 160 ratifications (average) of treaties on issues of safety, navigation or maritime environment, those on carriage of goods, collision or arrest of ships barely achieve 65 ratifications (on average), with very striking failures such as those dedicated to mortgages and maritime liens or passenger transportation (Figure 6.1).

17 International Convention for the Safety of Life at Sea, SOLAS (London, 1974).

18 International Convention on Civil Liability for Oil Pollution Damage (Brussels, 1969).

19 Protocol of 2003 to the International Convention on the Establishment of an International Fund for Compensation for Oil Pollution Damage, 1992 (London, 2003).

A large proportion of private maritime law remains within the contractual scope under the regime of 'freedom of contract' and away from the uniformity project that is carried out by means of international Conventions.[20] It is well known that private maritime law Conventions have been intended as '*de minimis*' texts, which sought to regulate only those aspects of the contract (carriage, salvage operation, ship mortgage, arrest, etc.) in which domestic intervention was considered essential at a time when freedom of contract was given a higher prevalence (as opposed to the bulky legislation on maritime public law).

2.2 International nature of the maritime law: its origin, sources & elements

Maritime law, from its very beginnings, has been international and autonomous (admiralty lawyers and academics will remember the petition of Eudaimon of Nicomedia to the Roman Emperor Antoninus, asking for *auxilium* (Digest of Justinian): 'Lord Emperor Antoninus: Being shipwrecked in Icaria, we have been plundered by the tax-farmers who live in the Cyclades Islands.' Then, the Emperor Antoninus remarked: 'I am indeed Lord of the world, but the Law is Lord of the sea'.

But not only its origins are international. Its sources and the nature of its law, principles and purposes, are also all international:[21] (a) ships, crews and merchants have a common international science and language (or terminology), and are subject to the same seas, the same natural elements or perils; (b) most national maritime law crosses international borders; (c) the existence of international organizations to defend and promote their respective interests; (d) marine insurance forms, policies, and terms apply internationally; (e) most importantly, contracts are increasingly effected using standard forms with legal terms understood internationally (or even shipping insurance forms, policies, and terms); or (f) the jurisdiction of admiralty courts around the world (or arbitration proceedings) tends to cover the same types of maritime dispute and is often expressed in similar legal terminology.

3. The traditional use of Conventions as the principal method in order to reach maritime uniformity: advantages and obstacles

The CMI has promoted the unification of maritime law – as one of its foundational objectives – the international Conventions having been the cornerstone of this process from the beginning. Nevertheless, two centuries later, the results of those aspirations are very uneven.

3.1 Harmonization through international Conventions: advantages

The advantages of uniformity far outweigh the disadvantages of international law, but those that exist should be mentioned. If we accept the principle that uniformity in international marine law is desirable, why has it not yet been achieved?[22]

20 J.M. Alcántara, 'La uniformidad del derecho marítimo, ¿leyenda o mito?' at http://amyavigo.es/es/la-uniformidad-del-derecho-maritimo-leyenda-o-mito/ (visited 5 May 2019).

21 W. Tetley, 'Uniformity of International Private Maritime Law – The Pros, Cons and Alternatives to International Conventions – How to Adopt an International Convention' (2000) *Tulane Maritime Law Journal* 775, 782.

22 Ibid, 797.

The advantages of uniformity of international maritime law can be summarized as follows:[23] maritime law (due to its international origin) in any jurisdiction 'should be certain and predictable. Individuals and corporations, when involved in international matters, should have the right to expect laws that are clear to everyone implicated in the transaction.'[24]

If both parties work from the same legal facts – i.e., a uniform law – it can be argued that potential conflicts can be minimized and the international trade can be facilitated and stimulated. One of the principal effects is that parties in one jurisdiction are treated with the same fairness (in legal terms) as those in another jurisdiction. However, we cannot agree with some of the statements given by some authors ('the lack of uniformity of international law leads to injustice').[25] If the differences between national rights (necessarily dependent on the sovereignty and legislative jurisdiction of each state) necessarily lead to injustice, then the law as we have known it is by definition unfair. What can be said is that the differences in business law mean, under the umbrella of the international markets, obstacles to international trade and the increase of transaction costs (with the consequent result that the goods are more expensive).

The inclusion of international uniform laws will reduce the transaction costs either at court or under an arbitration proceeding when a problem arises as both parties operate under the same law and, hence, a negotiated settlement is more likely (avoiding litigation based on erroneous information about the foreign law).[26]

A systematic and organized body of substantive rules results in avoiding or reducing 'forum shopping'. It is commonly argued that increasing uniformity, ease in the determination and application of the law, result in the mitigation of forum shopping. A conflict of laws scenario (in the choice of law jurisdiction and recognition of foreign judgments) will lead to forum shopping (term used commonly pejoratively) because each litigant will seek to bring the case in the court most favourably disposed to its position (due to the fact that inexistence of uniform laws). Then, forum shopping can be problematic if it operates to disadvantage one party over another.

Many pages have been devoted to the benefits for the economic development of uniform international law, contributing substantially to creating conditions that foster both national and international economic growth. It is therefore not surprising that international organizations such as UNCITRAL, UNCTAD or UNIDROIT have directed the

23 A number of authors have pronounced on the advantages of the uniform purpose of maritime law (among others, P. Griggs, 'Uniformity of Maritime Law – An International Perspective' [1999] *Tulane Law Review* 1551; P. Griggs, 'Obstacles to Uniformity of Maritime Law' (2003) 34 *Journal of Maritime Law & Commerce* 191; N. Healy, 'International Uniformity in Maritime Law: The Goal and the Obstacles' (1979) *California Western International Law Journal* 494, 498; S. Hetherington, 'The CMI and the Panacea of Uniformity – An Elusive Dream?' (2015) 39 *Tulane Maritime Law Journal* 159; W. Tetley, 'Uniformity of International Private Maritime Law – The Pros, Cons and Alternatives to International Conventions – How to Adopt an International Convention' (2000) *Tulane Maritime Law Journal* 775, 782.

24 N. Healy, 'International Uniformity in Maritime Law: The Goal and the Obstacles' (1979) *California Western International Law Journal* 499; W. Tetley, 'Uniformity of International Private Maritime Law – The Pros, Cons and Alternatives to International Conventions – How to Adopt an International Convention' (2000) *Tulane Maritime Law Journal* 797.

25 W. Tetley, 'Uniformity of International Private Maritime Law – The Pros, Cons and Alternatives to International Conventions 'How to Adopt an International Convention' (2000) *Tulane Maritime Law Journal* 798.

26 B. Zeller, 'Uniformity of Laws: A Reality or Just a Myth?' (2008) 1–3 *International Journal of Private Law* 233.

bulk of their efforts toward establishing transnational rules in different fields related to the economic development. However, although uniform law has mainly dealt with substantive law, harmonization in procedural rules as between different states constitutes another advantage of uniform international private law. In international commercial arbitration, procedural effectiveness is facilitated by the fact that most major international arbitral institutions have uniform procedural rules, governing the details of how arbitrations are conducted.[27]

Thus, because of the greater the scope of uniformity, there will be no need to incur the trouble and expenses of proving, interpreting or analyzing foreign law (through the use of opinion's experts, witnesses, etc.). Furthermore, settlement will be facilitated if all concerned know that the law of all involving states is the same.[28]

3.2 Obstacles to uniformity of private maritime law through international Conventions

There are several obstacles standing in the way – and we list some of them below:[29]

3.2.1 Obstacles in the drafting process

LONG DRAFTING PERIODS

Creating an international instrument may take years of continuous negotiation – especially between leading and sponsoring delegations – at the headquarters of international organizations (UNCITRAL, CMI, IMO or UNIDROIT). These long drafting periods (usually more than five years) for an international Convention usually produce 'consensus' norms, rather than 'good' law (in other words, Conventions are born in adversity). In this situation, and as a consequence, states with a real need – confronted by a maritime legal problem that has affected them directly – may become fed up with waiting and decide instead on national legislation to deal with the problem.[30] Additionally, the result of that consensus is often complex and even incoherent or difficult to understand and apply later. However, there is no obvious solution to this timing problem, because speeding up the drafting process for an ill-considered instrument may be even less likely to attract support than one which has gone through the lengthy refining process.[31] However, such situations do not differ much from what happens in domestic law at the time of drafting domestic rules (except for costs, obviously).

27 W. Tetley, 'Uniformity of International Private Maritime Law – The Pros, Cons and Alternatives to International Conventions – How to Adopt an International Convention' (2000) *Tulane Maritime Law Journal* 800.

28 N. Healy, 'International Uniformity in Maritime Law: The Goal and the Obstacles' (1979) *California Western International Law Journal* 499.

29 Several authors have previously commented on the obstacles which international texts have found in order to achieve the desired uniformity: P. Griggs, 'Uniformity of Maritime Law – An International Perspective' [1999] *Tulane Law Review* 1551, 1562–1564; P. Griggs, 'Obstacles to Uniformity of Maritime Law' (2003) 34 *Journal of Maritime Law & Commerce* 191; N. Healy, 'International Uniformity in Maritime Law: The Goal and the Obstacles' (1979) *California Western International Law Journal* 500–504; W. Tetley, 'Uniformity of International Private Maritime Law – The Pros, Cons and Alternatives to International Conventions – How to Adopt an International Convention' (2000) *Tulane Maritime Law Journal* 801–811.

30 P. Griggs, 'Obstacles to Uniformity of Maritime Law' (2003) 34 *Journal of Maritime Law & Commerce* 200.

31 Ibid.

Different styles of drafting and terminology

Civil law or common law systems suppose a way of drafting which frequently prevents many states – especially those with stronger legal traditions – from accepting another system's style of drafting, interpretation, and construction of laws. And this scenario is regularly seen during the drafting process at the most important international organizations.[32] Finding a balance between those systems throughout an international text – which does not attempt to satisfy both law styles – may be very difficult to adopt internationally. The international Conventions on the carriage of goods by sea are very good examples of those difficulties. The Hague-Visby Rules were written in common law style and the Hamburg Rules[33] in the style of civil law. Is this the factor that has helped to prevent the adoption of the Hamburg Rules, or even the Rotterdam Rules?

International instruments, such as UNIDROIT Principles of International Commercial Contracts or the Vienna Convention 1980,[34] have sought to maintain a delicate balance between the contrasting attitudes and concepts of civil law and common law and are examples of such sensitive drafting.[35] Conversely, other instruments have only taken into account a specific legal system, rendering its acceptance in some countries more problematic because the importance, construction or interpretation of that concept or institution in its national maritime law are completely different (see arrest of ships Conventions[36] or maritime liens and mortgages Conventions and its difficulties of accession in common law countries).

However, does the practice differ from this way of proceeding? In other words, is this a problem or obstacle for the 'users' of uniform law? Many contracts in a jurisdiction such as Spain are drafted in Spanish and employ terminology taken from the common law or civil law, not by whim, but by real need to adapt (strategy in the elaboration of the contracts). Depending on the sector, in some the common law prevails and in others the continental or civil law. This may not be ideal, but often harmonization, by whatever means, requires convergence.

Sometimes, as a result of this complex drafting process, the treaty gives Contracting States broad latitude in deciding which particular international legal obligations they wish to be bound by – in addition to mandatory provisions. The modern system of 'declarations', known as the 'opt in' or 'opt out' provisions (see Rotterdam Rules or Cape Town Convention as recent examples), often accompany non-wide-consensus instruments. It is highly respectful of state sovereignty and legal system requirements as perceived by governments, and it permits and facilitates changes in position in accordance with changing circumstances and needs. However, it reduces its harmonizing effect and places interested in a serious state of uncertainty.

32 As Prof. Tetley mentions, the fact that the Arrest of Ships Convention 1999 takes account only of legal ownership of vessels, without including any reference to 'beneficial' ownership, may render its acceptance in the United Kingdom and other Commonwealth countries more problematic because of the importance of that common law concept in the national maritime law of those jurisdictions.

33 United Nations Convention on the Carriage of Goods by Sea (Hamburg, 1978)

34 United Nations Convention on Contracts for the International Sale of Goods (Vienna, 1980).

35 W. Tetley, 'Uniformity of International Private Maritime Law – The Pros, Cons and Alternatives to International Conventions – How to Adopt an International Convention' (2000) *Tulane Maritime Law Journal* 775, 782.

36 International Convention Relating to the Arrest of Sea-Going Ships (Brussels, 1952); International Convention on the Arrest of Ships (Geneva, 1999).

Drafting an instrument must take into account not only the laws of the sponsoring states, but also a clear knowledge of the domestic law in a large number of states. Only this firm base ensures that the resulting instrument will be compatible with the domestic law of a substantial number of states.[37]

Less is more? Over-production of international instruments

As we have seen, the lack of a real need for uniform texts has frequently led to rules based on consensus, without affecting the real needs of an often-dynamic industry. Then, when the need arises, they develop a new uniform text, producing an overelaboration of rules on the same legal issues. Examples include the Maritime Liens and Mortgages Convention (with three different instruments: 1926, 1967 and 1993), and carriage of goods Conventions (Hague Rules, Hague-Visby Rules, Hamburg Rules and Rotterdam Rules), among others.

Additionally, over-production does not refer exclusively to the number increase of international texts, but also to their extension. The 1910 Salvage Convention has 16 articles,[38] while 1989 Salvage Convention,[39] designed to replace the 1910 Convention, consists of 34 articles. HVR has 10 articles, Hamburg Rules has 34 articles; RR more than 90. This illustrates a tendency towards overelaboration of texts. Has the longer and more complex document less probability to be embraced by the states? This may explain why the Hague-Visby Rules was ratified by 96 states while the Hamburg Rules has been ratified by only 29 – at the latest count – or the Rotterdam Rules by only four states. This argument, shared by some authors,[40] decays when one observes, in the transnational scenario, other conventions that share, with those mentioned, the aforementioned over-production. An example is the 2001 Cape Town Convention on International Interests in Mobile Equipment. The text has more than 85 articles (Convention plus protocol) and more than 80 cross-references. However, the Convention has been ratified in the last 16 years by more than 77 States.

Policy reasons and US influential

During the elaboration of an international Convention, different transnational shipping interests collide (shipowners, cargo insurers, P&I Clubs, freight forwarders, cargo interests, etc.). And it is also obvious that international associations (such as the Freight Forwarders, Shipowners' Association or P&I Clubs) wield significant influence in international maritime circles, affecting international maritime legislation.[41] The interests of those shipping groups prevent some international Conventions from progressing. The Hamburg Rules and the Maritime Liens and Mortgages Conventions are – probably –very good examples of proposals which were unacceptable to many such groups.

---

37 P. Griggs, 'Obstacles to Uniformity of Maritime Law' (2003) 34 *Journal of Maritime Law & Commerce*, p. 203.

38 Convention for the Unification of Certain Rules with Respect to Assistance and Salvage at Sea (Brussels, 1910).

39 The International Convention on Salvage (London, 1989).

40 Ibid, p. 202. J.M. Alcántara, 'La uniformidad del derecho marítimo, ¿leyenda o mito?' at http://amyavigo.es/es/la-uniformidad-del-derecho-maritimo-leyenda-o-mito/> (visited 5 May 2019).

41 W. Tetley, 'Uniformity of International Private Maritime Law – The Pros, Cons and Alternatives to International Conventions – How to Adopt an International Convention' (2000) *Tulane Maritime Law Journal* 809.

Major maritime states, such as the USA, are very influential and their decisions whether or not to ratify a text are followed by some other nations. It is clear that US delegation has done a great job in the various drafting Committees (and working groups) in UNCITRAL (again, the Rotterdam Rules are a good example), proposing, through enhancement or negotiating. However, in the ratification process some of these states reject the opportunity to implement the instrument. But why this great effort during the elaboration, and the reluctance on the part of those states to ratify? Some author notes a certain 'pride of authorship' of the text or some doubts on the part of some officers of the State Department arguing that the Convention does not go far enough in some respects.[42] So, when listing obstacles to uniformity, we must include the failure of leading maritime nations to lead by example as one of the major obstacles.[43]

3.2.2 Obstacles in the interpretation/implementation of the text

Outgoings on its implementation

A state may find the financial and other benefits offered by a Convention to itself and its citizens a good reason for implementation. However, sometimes the limit of liability in the case of injury or death (under carriage of passengers Conventions) or in the case of loss of or damage to the goods can be considered unrealistically low, or high; and that will be one of the factors stopping the adoption (see the traditional discussion in this regard in the case of the Hague-Visby Rules, Hamburg Rules and Rotterdam Rules). Additionally, governments may be less excited if they discover that the Convention requires them to incur excessive expense when it comes to their implementation, or if they have to set up administrative machinery, new court processes, higher claim limits in respect of personal injury or even execution costs in case of possible breaches.[44]

High thresholds on the number of Contracting States

As a result of the elaboration of a Convention, there are usually high thresholds on the number of states that must ratify it before it comes into force internationally. When the threshold is high (unless there is a high consensus over the text), the Convention will probably never come into force internationally.

The decision on the number of states depends upon the drafters of the Convention (and the general assemblies of the promoting organizations). The Athens Convention 1974[45] had a threshold of ten states, whereas the threshold for the Rotterdam Rules Convention is 20.

Why the difference? Probably trying to avoid very reduced, specific or regional topics entering into force using international instruments rather than domestic texts (e.g. European maritime states trying to bring an international text it into force). In other words, the Convention ought to be shown to have truly universal (as opposed to merely regional)

---

42 P. Griggs, 'Obstacles to Uniformity of Maritime Law' (2003) 34 *Journal of Maritime Law & Commerce* 202.

43 Ibid., 208; N. Healy, 'International Uniformity in Maritime Law: The Goal and the Obstacles' (1979) *California Western International Law Journal* 501.

44 P. Griggs, 'Obstacles to Uniformity of Maritime Law' (2003) 34 *Journal of Maritime Law & Commerce* 206; N. Healy, 'International Uniformity in Maritime Law: The Goal and the Obstacles' [1979] *California Western International Law Journal* 501.

45 Athens Convention relating to the Carriage of Passengers and their Luggage by Sea, 1974 (Athens, 1974).

appeal before it can become operational.[46] High thresholds grant the Convention a halo of uniformity. Adversely, it may delay a Convention's entry into force.

However, it should be emphasized that this situation is not incompatible with the possibility that a favourable state, before the instrument enters into force reaching the threshold of states needed for ratifying the Convention (or even if this never happens), already incorporates it into its domestic law, especially where it concerns those issues for which there is no previous instrument already in force.

Implementation and interpretation difficulties

There is no doubt that governments do find it difficult to convert an international Convention into an accessible piece of domestic legislation. There are two methods in which the uniform rules adopted in a Convention may be incorporated into national law:[47] (a) The adopted in most civil law countries consists in the promulgation of a law that authorizes the ratification of or accession to a Convention normally annexed thereto, pursuant to which the provisions of the Convention become part of the national legal system either with the publication of the law and of the Convention in the Official Journal or at the time of entry into force of the Convention for the state, if later;[48] or (b) adopted in most common law countries, consists in the promulgation of an Act by which the force of law is given to a Convention;[49] the Act sets out necessary complementary rules, while the provisions of the Convention to which force of law is given appear in a schedule to the Act.

The difference between these two methods is that, with the civil law technique, the whole of the Convention becomes part of the national legal system, while with the common law technique force of law is given to specific provisions and the complementary legislation is incorporated in the same Act. Still, other states may 'cherry pick' parts of a Convention and incorporate in its domestic law only those aspects with which they feel comfortable.[50] A Convention may therefore actually be more successful than the statistics of ratification suggest.

Notwithstanding the efforts at uniformity, the result too often leads to very different interpretations in the national courts in the application of the international instruments.

46 P. Griggs, 'Obstacles to Uniformity of Maritime Law' (2003) 34 *Journal of Maritime Law & Commerce*, 206.

47 See F. Berlingieri, 'Implementation of Maritime Conventions: A Review of the Methods Used' (2013) *Lloyd's Maritime and Commercial Law Quarterly* 443.

48 In Spain, art. 94 of the Spanish Constitution requires the consent by the state to be bound by the treaties listed thereunder. After ratification or accession, treaties become part of the Spanish legislative system upon their publication in the Official Journal and they have primacy over domestic laws. Such publication includes the text of the instrument of ratification or accession and the full text of the Convention in the Spanish language. The Convention rules prevail over the domestic rules and consequently the scope of application of the domestic rules is restricted to situations that are outside the scope of application of the Convention.

49 In England, unlike some continental European countries, international treaties and Conventions do not have the force of law merely by reason of having been ratified by the Government. In the UK a treaty provision does not become law until it has been implemented by statute or statutory instrument (see *Attorney-General for Canada v Attorney-General for Ontario* [1937] AC 326). There are several techniques for giving the force of law to international Conventions: (a) The statute may be based on the Convention (the Convention itself not being incorporated in the statute); (b) the statute may incorporate the English text of the Convention in a schedule (e.g. the Carriage of Goods by Sea Act 1924 (now repealed) and Carriage of Goods by Sea Act 1971; Merchant Shipping Act 1995, Schs 6 and 7).

50 Additionally, some other problems arise in failure to denounce superseded Conventions. Some states ratify and implement a new Convention but fail to denounce the one that it is designed to replace.

The purpose of an international text is 'to harmonize the laws of all Contracting States on the particular topic. It is therefore very important that the interpretation of the convention should be the same, so far as possible, in all States'.[51] Nevertheless, techniques such as reservations, declarations or the previously mentioned 'opt-in' or 'opt-out' clauses produce alternative uniform criteria on the interpretation. Conflicts in the interpretation of a Convention intended to unify commercial law do not merely destroy aesthetic symmetry in the international legal order; they impose real costs on the commercial system that the Convention governs.[52]

3.2.3 Do we need uniform law? Do we need a Convention in this field?

At different instances the question has been raised whether there is actually a need for uniform law to regulate maritime contracts. Some authors and international institutions argue that the necessity of such uniform law is not felt by the industry (specially the transport one): small claims tend to be settled commercially (irrespective of the applicable law) and larger claims are referred to insurers (carriers to their liability insurers and cargo interests to their transport insurers). Such insurers handle the consequences of such claims amongst themselves (by compensation proceedings). Recourse actions between carriers are usually also handled in this way.[53] Indeed, there are sometimes reasons to prefer national law over uniform law. Domestic preferences are often better served with non-uniform rules, thus enabling the creation of better law.[54]

Often an area of law may come under review because one or two states (sponsoring states) are confronted by a maritime legal problem that has affected them directly – instead of a real and widely accepted need in the worldwide industry.[55] The result is an unwanted, unloved and therefore unratified Convention that never will come into force.[56]

---

51 Lord Collins of Mapesbury and J. Harris Dicey (gen. eds), *Dicey, Morris and Collins on the Conflict of Laws*, 15th edn (Sweet & Maxwell, 2012), p. 15. This passage was quoted with approval in *Sidhu v British Airways Plc* [1997] A.C. 430, 444.

52 M. Sturley, T. Fujita and G. J. Van Der Ziel, *The Rotterdam Rules* (Sweet & Maxwell, 2011), p. 2.

53 G.J. van der Ziel, 'The ISIC Study on intermodal liability, some comments by G.J. van der Ziel', unpublished (see in H. Hoeks, M.A.: *Multimodal Transport Law. The Law Applicable to the Multimodal Contract for the Carriage of Goods* (2009), p. 388. Additionally, FIATA is convinced that such uniform law in the form of an instrument may even have a detrimental effect on the popularity of multimodal transport. Position paper by FIATA and CLECAT, in Joint ECMT/UNECE Working Party/Group on Intermodal Transport and Logistics Paris, 3 and 4 October 2006, Informal document No. 6 (2006), 7 September 2006.

54 Ibid. However, as the author has mentioned, in the area of multimodal transport there is no room for local preferences and this is clear after more than half a century of watching the market share of multimodal transports grow, and seeing the amount of non-uniform multimodal transport law increase. The author concludes that uniform law is desirable in this area.

55 There are a series of Conventions that did not see the light of their international entry into force, probably due to this absence of a clear need: Multimodal Transport Convention (Geneva, 1980), the Convention on Responsibility of Operators of Nuclear Ships (Brussels, 1962), the Convention on Privileges and Mortgages (Brussels, 1967) (although the Convention on Maritime Liens and Mortgages of 1993 did come into force) or the Convention relating to Registration of Rights in respect of Vessels under Construction (Brussels, 1967), among others. In analyzing the success or failure of a Convention, we may be forced to conclude that the area of the law covered by the instrument was not suitable for harmonization because there was no compelling need (a fact often glossed over in the early stages of discussion of a new instrument), resulting in a waste of time and resources. See P. Griggs, 'Obstacles to Uniformity of Maritime Law' (2003) 34 *Journal of Maritime Law & Commerce* 191; 199.

56 In this sense, many international Conventions have had few ratifications and very unequal success. Governments usually give their consent for the signing ceremony but do not ratify the Conventions later in order to enforce them (e.g. the Rotterdam Rules).

However, even if the matter is not deemed necessary by the maritime industry, governments in general have a duty to extend some protection to those parties, such as small businesses, which cannot bring enough bargaining power to bear in the international commercial arena to press for sufficiently favourable contract terms.[57] Consequently, assemblies of most important organizations have directed that Conventions or other instruments designed to harmonize international maritime law should be produced only where a compelling need is established, as a precondition to starting work.[58] International laws may be unnecessary and even harmful in respect of some matters where freedom of contract is already prevalent.[59]

Once the previous question has been answered in the affirmative, another comes to mind. Have we chosen the right instrument? Is the Convention the right instrument to solve this real need? Throughout these pages I have kept to the assumption that the most important instrument of harmonization is an international Convention. In spite of the inertia among national governments when it comes to ratifying or acceding to international Conventions, the refusal of some states to give up their legislative sovereignty over some maritime matters has grown and some recent treaties have been adversely affected (are we under a Conventioned-out phenomenon?).

However, there is no wide agreement nowadays on the methods of achieving uniformity. Harmonization may result in standard rules, model laws, standard forms, recommendations or guidelines of different organizations, explanatory notes, guidelines, *lex mercatoria*, etc.), each of which has its own advantages and disadvantages and, in certain circumstances, may be more appropriate than a Convention for harmonization of law.[60] All of them can play an important role in increasing international legal uniformity.

57 H. Hoeks, M.A.: *Multimodal Transport Law. The Law Applicable to the Multimodal Contract for the Carriage of Goods* (2009) p. 389.

58 In 1990, Mr Justice Hobhouse said: 'What should no longer be tolerated is the unthinking acceptance of a goal of uniformity and its doctrinaire imposition on the commercial community. Only Conventions which demonstrably satisfy the well-proven needs of the commercial community should be ratified and legislation should only be agreed to if it is demonstrably fit to be enacted as part of the municipal law of this country'. See J.S. Hobhouse, 'International Conventions and Commercial Law: The Pursuit of Uniformity' (1991) 106 *Law Quarterly Review* 530. Cited by P. Griggs, 'Obstacles to Uniformity of Maritime Law' (2003) 34 *Journal of Maritime Law & Commerce* 202.

59 For example, an international Convention on charters would only restrict a system of contracting that is presently flexible and working well. Charters do not need to be regulated by a Convention, particularly because the parties to such contracts tend to be of relatively equal bargaining strength, and because standard charterparties are in widespread use around the world. A large territory of private maritime law remains within the contractual scope under the regime of 'freedom of contract' and away from the uniformity project that is carried out by means of international Conventions. See W. Tetley, 'Uniformity of International Private Maritime Law – The Pros, Cons and Alternatives to International Conventions – How to Adopt an International Convention' (2000) *Tulane Maritime Law Journal* 802.

60 The use of standard forms (instruments of self-regulation) or general terms formulated and drafted by various international agencies – such as BIMCO, P&I Clubs, etc. – for the use of the business world (specially in charterparties, salvage operations, towage, marine insurance policies, etc.); model rules (UCP 600, Lisbon Rules where damages are claimed following a collision, Uniform Rules for Sea Waybills, Rules for Electronic Bills of Lading, York Antwerp/Rules and Rules on General Average) has increased considerably in the last decades. Additionally, a number of clauses that are inserted in various maritime contracts have also reached a wide degree of standardization. Bills of lading are full of such clauses, whose terminology is completely standardized. When talking about *Himalaya*, New Jason, Paramount or both-to-blame collision clauses, all operators understand what they are talking about. Finally, the so-called '*modern lex mercatoria*', or transnational commercial law, which is beginning to be unofficially codified and to develop its own case law ('jurisprudence' in civilian terminology), particularly in international commercial arbitration, is an alternative form of uniformity.

4. What can we learn from the Rotterdam Rules and the Cape Town Convention?

The international legislative panorama in the field of international commercial law is full of successes and failures (the same scenario that is also reproduced in the field of maritime law). In this line, I will focus on a couple of cases that clearly exemplify how the alleged uniformity through the use of international Conventions has had very uneven success: see, for example, the failure of the International Convention on Maritime Liens and Mortgages (with three international Conventions in the last 90 years), or the recent Rotterdam Rules on the carriage of goods by sea. On the other hand, the success of Conventions, equally recent, such as the Cape Town Convention on security interests over mobile equipment, show that not everything is lost in the panorama of commercial uniformity through international Conventions.

I am aware that the analysis of a couple of Conventions is a fairly small statistical sample. However, it is not our purpose here to sample all the existing Conventions in the field of maritime law to identify the reasons for their success or failure, but only to identify and state the problem, using two of the most recent analyzed instruments.

4.1 Lack of success of the current International Conventions on Maritime Liens and Mortgages, 1926, 1967 and 1993

The need for uniform rules is increasing, with ship financing becoming more and more international.[61] While efforts have been made on an international basis to create a uniform approach (resulting in three international Conventions on maritime liens and mortgages in 1926, 1967 and 1993) no real consensus has emerged. Indeed, many of the world's leading maritime nations, including the United States and the United Kingdom, have failed to ratify any of the Conventions.

The International Convention for the unification of certain rules relating to Maritime Liens and Mortgages of 1926 attracted 28 States Parties in total,[62] but generally failed to gain support among the most important shipping nations worldwide (common law legal systems included). The International Convention for the Unification of Certain Rules of Law Relating to Maritime Liens and Mortgages of 1967 was ratified by only three states and never entered into force since it did not meet the required number of five Contracting States. The drafting and adoption of the 1993 Geneva Convention on Maritime Liens and Mortgages was motivated by what was widely regarded as a failure by the 1926 and 1967 Conventions to attract widespread support, but in the end, the 1993 Geneva Convention was even less successful with only 18 States Parties.[63] It is remarkable that,

61 F. Berlingieri, 'The 1993 Convention on Maritime Liens and Mortgages' [1995] *Lloyd's Maritime and Commercial Law Quarterly* 57; S. Harwood, *Shipping Finance*, 3rd edn (Euromoney Books, 2006), p. 131.

62 The following states are parties to the International Convention for the unification of certain rules relating to Maritime Liens and Mortgages of 1926: Algeria, Argentina, Belgium, Brazil, Cuba, Denmark, Estonia, Finland, France, Haiti, Hungary, Iran, Italy, Lebanon, Luxembourg, Madagascar, Monaco, Norway, Poland, Portugal, Romania, Spain, Sweden, Switzerland, Syria, Turkey, Uruguay, Zaire. Denmark, Finland, Norway and Sweden have declared their denunciation of the 1926 Convention.

63 The following states are parties to the 1993 Geneva Convention: Albania, Benin, Congo, Ecuador, Estonia, Lithuania, Monaco, Nigeria, Peru, Russian Federation, Serbia, Spain, St. Kitts and Nevis, St. Vincent

in a Convention on security interests or rights, no 'financier' states (the UK and the Nordic states) are party to the Convention, or 'register or flag' countries (Panama, Liberia or Marshall Islands), 'shipbuilder' countries (the Republic of Korea, China and Japan constructed 91.8% of world tonnage) and, except for Peru, there is no US state and only three European members. Of course, no common law countries, either (such as Australia, India, USA, etc.).

The purpose of listing these international instruments should be twofold: (1) on the one hand, to emphasize the absence of uniform rules regarding substantive law governing security rights in the international scenario.[64] This lack of uniformity is a serious problem for the international financing sector, especially in developing countries, limiting their access to international credit; (2) on the other hand, it shows how a future regulation[65] could offer legal mechanisms that regulate many of the substantive aspects absent in the current uniform instruments, such as the creation of international interests, validity and recognition, remedies, International Registry and their advantages, etc.

4.2 The Rotterdam Rules

The first efforts towards the worldwide harmonization of the relevant rules of law concerning carriage of goods by sea may be traced back almost 100 years. A fair balance between the ship and the cargo interests at an international level was established, at first, with the

and the Grenadines, Syria, Tunisia, Ukraine, Vanuatu. See https://treaties.un.org/Pages/ViewDetails.aspx?src=TREATY&mtdsg_no= XI-D-4&chapter=11&clang=_en. (visited 5 May 2019).

64 There are two traditional alternatives when one wants to modify something that does not work: to do it again starting from scratch, or to do it differently. The first of these, starting from scratch, would be to stumble on the same stone, not twice, but for the fourth time since we already have the experience of the International Convention for the unification of certain rules relating to Maritime Liens and Mortgages 1926, 1967 and the 1993 Geneva Convention on Maritime Liens and Mortgages. The second possible alternative that has been proposed by some authors, even me, adopting the successful Cape Town Convention system for the security interests over ships, not only for ships, but also for mobile off-shore platforms or container fleets (see, among others, O. Boger, 'The case for a new Protocol to the Cape Town Convention covering security over ships' (2016) Vol. 5, No. 1 *Cape Town Convention Journal*; R. Goode, 'Battening down your security interests: how the shipping industry can benefit from the UNIDROIT Convention on International Interests in Mobile Equipment' (2000) *Lloyd's Maritime and Commercial Law Quarterly* 161; B. Köhler, 'Heading towards Cape Town? Some remarks on the preparation of a future Protocol to the Cape Town Convention with respect to ships and maritime equipment' (2017) Vol. 22, Issue 3 *Uniform Law Review*, 507; V. Power, 'Commentary on "Assessing the legal and economic case for a shipping protocol to the Cape Town Convention"' (2016) Vol. 5, No. 1 *Cape Town Convention Journal* 103; J. P. Rodriguez-Delgado, 'Security Interests over Ships: From the Current Conventions to a Possible Shipping Protocol to the UNIDROIT Convention – Lege Data and Lege Ferenda' (2018) Vol. 49, No. 2 *Journal of Maritime Law and Commerce* 239.

65 See: J. P. Rodriguez-Delgado, 'Security Interests over Ships: From the Current Conventions to a Possible Shipping Protocol to the UNIDROIT Convention – Lege Data and Lege Ferenda' (2018) Vol. 49, No. 2 *Journal of Maritime Law and Commerce* 239. At the beginning of its elaboration, the drafters of the Cape Town Convention wondered whether the ships, or even offshore platforms and other maritime equipment, would be assets susceptible of being addressed under the Instrument. The negative answer of the shipping related international organizations (IMO, CMI and UNCTAD) was based, mainly, on the fear that the inclusion of registered ships' mortgages in an international Convention of a general nature might prove to be a cause of conflict with the newly drafted International Convention on Maritime Liens and Mortgages, and result in confusion and uncertainty. In other words, ships were excluded because of a perception (probably a misconception) that these were already catered for by existing Conventions, though in respect of consensual security interests all of these were confined to rules of recognition and none of them has been very successful (see R. Goode, 'Battening down your security interests: how the shipping industry can benefit from the UNIDROIT Convention on International Interests in Mobile Equipment' (2000) *Lloyd's Maritime and Commercial Law Quarterly* 161).

adoption of the Hague Rules in 1924.[66] However, those Rules, despite the amendments introduced by the Protocols in 1968 and 1979, did not meet the needs of the maritime traffic (even taking into account the number of states which had adopted the Hague Rules). This is reflected, among others, in the problems surrounding the scope of application (and the period of responsibility of the carrier) limited to tackle-to-tackle scope of application (and the resultant period of responsibility), the lack of specific rules for electronic communications, the exclusion of cargo on deck, multimodal transportation or the boom in containerization, etc.

With the development of international trade and shipping, the previously balanced interests would change, which would call for new rules of law to maintain.[67] The Hamburg Rules, despite constituting a significate advance with respect to the rules made in the past, were considered a new failed attempt of replacing the Hague Rules (with only 34 Contracting States representing less than the 5% of the worldwide trade). Both international regimes are manifestly insufficient to cover the needs of demanding door-to-door traffic.

The gradual loss of uniformity suffered in recent times by maritime transport law (see the Hague Rules, Hague-Visby Rules, Hamburg Rules, Multimodal Transport Convention, etc.) and with it the dissatisfaction among sectors interested in maritime transportation (especially with the increasing numbers of instruments and protocols emanating from international organizations), brought, firstly to the CMI, and secondly, to UNCITRAL, to elaborate a new international Convention on Contracts for the International Carriage of Goods, taking into account the modern transport practices.[68] The General Assembly, convinced that the adoption of uniform rules to modernize and harmonize the rules that govern the international carriage of goods would enhance legal certainty, improve efficiency and commercial predictability in the international carriage of goods and reduce legal obstacles to the flow of international trade among all states, adopted in 2008 the United Nations Convention on Contracts for the International Carriage of Goods Wholly or Partly by Sea (the Rotterdam Rules).[69] These Rules, quoting the Resolution adopted by the General Assembly, promote legal certainty, improve the efficiency of international carriage of goods and facilitate new access opportunities for previously

66 The Hague-Visby Rules were, nevertheless, under criticism from cargo interests for decades, regarded as unbalanced and too favourable for the carrier, as the exemption from liability for faults in the navigation of the vessel and the relatively low limits of liability.

67 H. Hai Li, 'The Rotterdam Rules: A Cherishable Opportunity for the Unification of the Law' (2010) *Annual of China Maritime Law* 01.

68 Among them we can mention the growing trend in the phenomenon of containerization of cargo in liner trades, the use of payment mechanisms such as letters of credit, new port technologies, the use of electronic transport documents, door-to-door transport contracts (and noting that shippers and carriers do not have the benefit of a binding and balanced universal regime to support the operation of contracts of carriage involving various modes of transport).

69 The biggest changes from the Hague-Visby Rules are probably the following: firstly, it covers not only transport by sea, as it also contains a complete set of rules that may be used for combined transports, where parts of the transportation of the cargo is performed by road or rail (from the 'tackle to tackle' to the 'door to door' approach), as long as there is an international maritime carriage leg; secondly, the mentioned exemption from liability for nautical errors has been removed; and thirdly, the limitation amounts have been increased from 667 SDR/unit or 2 SDR/kg to 875 SDR/unit or 3 SDR/kg.

remote parties and markets, thus playing a fundamental role in promoting trade and economic development, both domestically and internationally.[70]

Ten years later, the question to be asked is whether this was yet another failed attempt to promote uniformity. Since the Rotterdam Rules were opened for signing in September 2009, 25 countries have signed the Convention, including the USA, the Netherlands, Greece, France, Denmark, Sweden and Norway. Presently, only Spain, Togo, Congo and Cameroon have ratified the Convention and the Convention will not enter into force until it is ratified by 20 states. It is probably fair to say that most states have been concerned with whether the USA, and to some extent China, would ratify the Convention or not. Both expressed a great interest in developing new legislation and the US did take a leading role in the negotiation of the Convention. However, earlier optimism that the US would ratify the instrument appears to be frustrated – at least under its current administration.[71]

The Rotterdam Rules are a clear example of the fact that some of the obstacles that are preached about uniformity are a reality in the international scenario. The complexity and extension of the text, the unbalanced distribution of interests among the contracting parties (although the notorious nautical fault exoneration is abolished, making the fault which bases the carrier's liability a complete one) or the excessive influence of the common law system in its drafting process (due to the influence of the US delegation) have been some of the criticisms that have hampered its international adoption; and as a consequence its harmonizing spirit of the contract of carriage of goods by sea. However – and this is the author's opinion – the vast majority of the inconveniences that are attributed to this Convention are not based on a technical analysis of their provisions, but in a lack of certain legal analysis.

The Rotterdam Rules do not provide – in the opinion of some authors – equity and mutual benefit in international trade, constituting a very complex legal instrument, full of referrals among its provisions and tautological definitions, which leaves out of any value the international jurisprudence from 1924.[72] Nevertheless, some of these criticisms, with

70 This importance of uniformity was implicit not only in the opening clauses of the UNCITRAL Resolution, but in Art. 2 of the text (similar provisions may be found in the Vienna Convention on Sale of Goods Art. 7, the Hamburg Rules Art. 3 or the Cape Town Convention Art. 5).

71 It is disappointing that the principal reason for the United States not yet having ratified the Convention is apparently a misunderstanding on the part of an industry that will be affected only tangentially by the Convention when it eventually enters into force. Ports and terminals are reported to believe that the Rotterdam Rules would impose on them risks of potential cargo damage liability that they do not already have under the current cargo liability statute (on a 'maritime performing party'). The US Department of State recently indicated, during a presentation at the CMI/MLA Conference in New York on 2016, that the US Government Executive Branch is in favour of ratifying the Rotterdam Rules, and the State Department is exploring avenues for how to move forward to obtain Senate consent. From these comments, it seems that ratification efforts remain underway in the US, but it is not clear how or when the concerns of the ports and terminals will be satisfied. *See* www.nortonrosefulbright.com/en/knowledge/publications/aacbaf04/rotterdam-rules—-ratification-status-in-the-us-and-effectiveness-of-choosing-to-apply-them-voluntarily.

72 See 'Una respuesta Latinoamericana a la "Declaración de Montevideo"' at https://comitemaritime.org/wp-content/uploads/2018/05/Las-Reglas-de-Rotterdam-Una-respuesta-latinoamericana-a-la-Declaración-de-Montevideo-2.pdf. The 'excessive reglamentarism' that the Rotterdam Rules are accused of, stems from the need to fully regulate the field for the benefit of, precisely, the uniformity which is claimed (following the mandate of Art. 2 of the Rules and the example of other Conventions such as the Vienna Convention or the Hamburg Rules).

all due respect, cannot be valid. The Rotterdam Rules are, undoubtedly, a complex and extensive Convention, because the area that it covers is complex and extensive (the Rotterdam Rules has more than 90 articles and a number of cross-references).[73] However, there are many other international legal instruments, which are also extensive and complex, but this has not been an obstacle to its successful implementation. The Cape Town Convention has been labelled, in similar terms, as complex and too extensive (with more than 85 articles between the Convention and the Protocol and the cross-references also visible on the text).

4.3 The Cape Town Convention. Reasons for this uniformity success

The Cape Town Convention, along with the Protocols about particular assets encumbered with consensual security interests[74] – airframes, aircraft engines and helicopters; railway rolling stock and space assets, so far, has emerged as one of most successful transnational instruments in the international scene of the uniform private law.[75] The difficulties that such a topic involves –specifically those relating to the attempt to unify principles between very different legal systems in the topic of security interest and property law – have been overcome by the wide consensus that the Convention is obtaining –it currently counts more than 78 Contracting States.

The Cape Town Convention appears to have been the best way to address previous issues. The reasons may be summarized as: (a) real need in the sector; (b) economic incentives; and (c) an innovative two-instrument structure, based on a Convention and a set of Protocols.[76]

4.3.1 The existence of a real need in the sector

As we have previously shown, that lack of a real need for uniform texts has led to rules based on consensus, without affecting the real needs of an often-dynamic industry. However, this is not that situation. Since the '90s, there have been initiatives of very different scope and nature, from supranational organizations, both regionally and internationally, to address the need for harmonization of the regime of security interests in the context of

Contrary to the *de minimis* rule, intended for the Hague-Visby Rules, which sought to regulate only those aspects of the contract of carriage in which was considered essential the state intervention (and despite over 80 years having passed, the extensive case law produced still has certain issues where no express precedent can be found), the Rotterdam Rules will produce greater certainty about the interpretation and application of the Convention, as they reduce the subjects of the contract with no express regulation.

73 The presence of cross-references in a legislative text follows a valid and internationally implemented law-drafting system, which has proved effective in various international instruments currently in force (the Cape Town Convention with more than 75 – without taking into account the Protocol – or Vienna Convention with almost 70 cross-references). Besides, the cross-referencing system allows greater certainty in the application of the regime.

74 Protocol on Matters Specific to Aircraft Equipment (Cape Town, 2001); Protocol on Matters Specific to Railway Rolling Stock (Luxembourg, 2007); Protocol on Matters Specific to Space Assets (Berlin, 2012). Since 2014, a fourth Protocol on mining, agricultural and construction equipment (MAC Protocol) has been discussed by the MAC Study Group. It has also been argued that a Protocol on ship might be worth considering.

75 As of March 2019, the Convention has 79 Contracting States, and the Aircraft Protocol has 76 States Parties. See http://www.unidroit.org/status-2001capetown (visited 5 May 2019).

76 Additionally, the Cape Town Convention establishes a well-balanced mechanism between the rights of a creditor wishing to foreclose on its asset following a debtor default.

cross-border operations. This ambition is a response to a real and pressing need from the industry (*from the market to the legislator*) to fill the gaps which existed in regard to certain types of asset (namely, aircraft equipment and, to a lesser extent, railway rolling stock and space assets). The Cape Town Convention responds, on the one hand, to the need to overcome the inadequate rules on conflict-of-laws based on *res sitae* for movable property, achieving an acceptable level of substantive unification between the different legal systems, resolving legal issues caused by their mobility, i.e., conflicting rules relating to the recognition, securing and enforcement of rights in the assets as they travel across jurisdictions (*legal reasons*).

On the other hand, the system searches for and facilitates acquisition, financing and leasing of mobile assets, reduces borrowing costs and provides predictability to market participants in asset-based transactions by creating a uniform set of rules relating to the creation, perfection and priority of interests that will be universally recognized and protected.[77] In addition, the Cape Town Convention is designed to promote the financing of debtors in developing countries by improving the confidence of the financiers (*economic reasons*).[78]

4.3.2 Economic incentives for the participants

The ratification and effective implementation of the Cape Town Convention results in significant risk reduction to lenders in secured aircraft financing transactions, offering speed, certainty and cost savings. For industry, a key incentive to accede to the Cape Town Convention concerns the significant cost savings available to airlines when purchasing or leasing new aircraft.[79] In 2007 the Organization for Economic Cooperation and Development (OECD) developed a new 'Sector Understanding on Export Credits for Civil Aircraft' (ASU), providing a common framework under which Export Credit Agencies of the EU, USA, Japan or Canada (among others) can provide export credit finance for the purchase of airframes and engines. It offers a fee discount for airlines from countries that have ratified the Cape Town Convention and have made specified 'qualifying declarations' as part of this process.

The Convention and Protocol are intended to reduce risks for creditors, and consequently, the borrowing costs to debtors, through the resulting improved legal certainty. The airlines of states that adopt the Convention and the Protocol may receive a ten percent (10%) discount on export credit premiums. There is concrete evidence that the Cape Town Convention has lowered the costs of financing in connection with officially supported credits for the sale or lease of aircraft.[80]

---

77 Regarding the economic basis of the Cape Town Convention see T. Rodriguez de las Heras Ballell, *Las Garantías Mobiliarias Sobre Equipo Aeronáutico En El Comercio Internacional* (Marcial Pons, 2012), pp. 28–30.

78 However, one of the major criticisms of the Cape Town Convention system is that it considerably strengthens the position of the secured creditor *vis-à- vis* unsecured creditors, especially lienholders, depriving them of their traditional remedies for the protection of their claims. See generally T. Traschler, 'The Cape Town Convention's Remedies: Path to Harmonization' (2016) *Butterworths Journal of International Banking and Financial Law* 399.

79 Different studies concluded that the adoption and effective implementation of the Convention and Aircraft Protocol would produce estimated economic gains of several billion dollars annually between 2009 and 2030. See Ch. W. Mooney Jr. 'The Cape Town Convention's Improbable-but-Possible Progeny Part Two: Bilateral Investment Treaty-Like Enforcement Mechanism' (2014) 55 *Virginia Journal of International Law* 1, 7–8.

80 Ibid., 9.

4.3.3 Innovative two-instrument structure, based on a Convention and a set of protocols

The issue of structure was addressed at the beginning of the diplomatic conference, when it soon became clear that there was overwhelming support on the one hand for the two-instrument structure. The Convention has been drafted with the clear objective of providing an adequate response to the specific needs of each sector, which explains its dual structure Convention-Protocol.

The Cape Town system is based on an original and pragmatic multi-divisional structure[81] in order to produce a consolidated text which would integrate the provisions of the Convention and a set of 'mobile equipment' Protocols. Each Protocol deals with matters specific to different categories of asset;[82] aircraft equipment (Aircraft Protocol), railway rolling stock (Rail Protocol), space assets (Space Protocol) and, in case of adoption, mining, agricultural and construction equipment (MAC Protocol). This innovative structure operates in brilliant coordination, wisely combining equipment-specific provisions with general rules, and allowing greater flexibility in adapting the system to the different mobile equipment that will fit into the uniform text (both existing and as developed in the future).[83] Thus, it promotes uniformity across the sectors, at same time providing the above-mentioned flexibility.

The benefits of this approach bring with them certain risks. There are also a number of potential disadvantages that must be taken into account.[84] Firstly, the use of multiple protocols causes greater complexity and fragmentation of the law – and hence the cost – instead of incentivizing harmonization of commercial laws across borders. The result of this apparent complexity is not only commercial inefficiency, it also prevents some states from ratifying the multi-instrument Convention if their representatives have difficulty navigating it. Secondly, and probably the most important obstacle, the drafting of each protocol provides an opportunity to renegotiate each provision of the base Convention, which may result in a further lack of uniformity among the protocols.[85]

81 R. Goode, 'The Cape Town Convention on International Interests in Mobile Equipment: A Driving Force for International Asset-Based Financing' (2002) 7 *Uniform Law Review* 3; T. Rodriguez De Las Heras Ballell, 'The Accession by Spain to the Cape Town Convention: A First Assessment' [2014] *Uniform Law Review* 1.

82 Although it is true that the protocols allow for a divergence of rules between the various protocols, the special rules contained in accommodating the idiosyncratic needs of a particular industry should ideally be restricted only to those few rules that are necessary for the proper operation of the treaty with respect to that particular industry. See M. Sundahl, 'The "Cape Town Approach": A New Method of Making International Law' (2006) 44 *Columbia Journal of Transnational Law* 339, 360.

83 The adoption of the Cape Town Convention to other mobile equipment has another practical advantage for the states. One important aspect, and perhaps frequently forgotten in discussions on the possible elaboration of a new protocol, is that much of the work is already done. The Cape Town Convention has more than 79 ratifications, many of them belonging to countries with huge international, political and economic weight, and it is already part of their internal legal systems. These Contracting States have already taken over and internalized the proposals and the basis of the Cape Town Convention system relating to security interests or rights over movable assets, their remedies and the International Registry accession. Regarding the possible shipping protocol to the Cape Town Convention, see J.P. Rodriguez-Delgado, 'Security Interests over Ships: From the Current Conventions to a Possible Shipping Protocol to the UNIDROIT Convention – Lege Data and Lege Ferenda' (2018) Vol. 49, No 2 *Journal of Maritime Law and Commerce* 239.

84 A list of possible disadvantages may be found in M. Sundahl, 'The "Cape Town Approach": A New Method of Making International Law' (2006) 44 *Columbia Journal of Transnational Law* 364.

85 This risk arises from that provision of the Cape Town Convention – Art. 6(2) – that allows the terms of each Protocol, to the extent of any inconsistency between this Convention and the Protocol, to override any provision

5. Concluding remarks

In the study of the legal or conventional uniformity, some key points concerning two of the most recent international texts in commercial law must be examined (the Rotterdam Rules and the Cape Town Convention): [a] both texts are relatively recent: the Rotterdam Rules from 2008 and the Cape Town Convention from 2001, coming into force in 2006; [b] both Conventions have been labelled as complex and too long: the Rotterdam Rules, with more than 90 articles (and with a multitude of cross-references between articles) and the Cape Town Convention, with more than 85 articles between the Convention and the Aircraft Protocol; [c] the drafters of both texts were international organizations with huge experience in the drafting process of international Conventions (some of them very successful): the Rotterdam Rules by UNCITRAL and the Cape Town Convention by UNIDROIT; and [d] the subjects dealt with by both Conventions are traditional matters of private or commercial law: the Rotterdam Rules, related to contracts of carriage of goods, and the Cape Town Convention, regarding security interests on mobile equipment. All these elements seem to be of great importance, and from this point of view, at least at first glance, these two instruments do not differ from each other.

However, after more than 79 ratifications of the Cape Town Convention and as many ratifications of the Aircraft Protocol (necessary for the Convention to come into force) and the apparent failure of the Rotterdam Rules (with only four and without having yet come into force), several questions emerge: can we replicate the success of the Cape Town Convention in the field of maritime law? Does it make sense to replicate it? Is it possible?

We have already spoken in other forums about the reasons why a shipping protocol over ships (or shipping equipment – such as container fleets or offshore equipment) could be possible (and certainly, in view of the current texts, necessary).[86] It would now be appropriate to ask whether such a Cape Town Convention structure (convention & protocols) – and the other aforementioned reasons – would be feasible in other areas of maritime law.

The multitude of international Conventions, with a disparity of success, which currently exists in the field of carriage of goods: Hague Rules, Hague-Visby Rules, Hamburg Rules or Rotterdam Rules (for the carriage of goods by sea), Warsaw or Montreal Convention (for air), Convention on the Contract for the International Carriage of Goods by Road (CMR)[87] or the Convention concerning International Carriage by Rail (COTIF)[88] (for land) or the unsuccessful Convention for Multimodal Transport from 1980. All these texts share the contractual parties (the carrier, the shipper, the consignee, etc.), their obligations are, in broad terms, quite similar (reception, load/discharge, custody, carriage, delivery, etc.); the

of the base convention.

86 All of them share common characteristics: big-ticket mobile equipment; with similar financing techniques (secured and asset-based); uniquely identifiable assets (by its name, flag, etc.); the internationality of the asset (capable of moving from country-to-country, jurisdiction-to-jurisdiction, in a regular course of business); similar legal and credit risks for market participants (for secured creditors); or in case of default, the creditor will need to seize the asset as fast as possible in order to enforce its security interest.

87 Convention on the Contract for the International Carriage of Goods by Road (CMR) (Geneva, 1956).

88 Convention concerning International Carriage by Rail (COTIF), as amended by the Vilnius Protocol of 3 June 1999 (Berne, 1980).

document structure employed shares the same approach, in form, nature and functions (i.e. bill of lading, sea waybill, air waybill, negotiable or non-negligible instruments, electronic or non-electronic documents, etc.); and, of course, the exoneration causes, the limitation of liability or the time-bar are institutions contemplated in all the aforementioned international Conventions.

A similar approach – focused on the contract of carriage – was expressed by Professor Van der Ziel in his (unpublished) lecture at the Erasmus University. He sketched a possible future for multimodal transport law, describing a system in which only minor tweaking of each of the existing carriage Conventions:

> 'This concept enables contracting parties to choose to apply one of them to an entire multimodal contract of carriage, while thus excluding the application of all other carriage conventions. In other words, one multimodal convention with the possibility of using the multimodal regimes of the others [. . .] It would grant the industry leave to work with the rules they are most familiar with, while at the same time offering shippers the protection offered by one of the current carrier liability regimes.'[89]

Under this overview, one could imagine a single Convention on the carriage of goods, regulating common matters, which are in fact the majority, with different protocols that contemplate the singularities of each of the modes of transport. But, moving our view a little more, and almost entering the field of imagination, one could think of some other matters in which this contractual scheme would be possible (think about, e.g., matters such as the security interests previously mentioned, leasing, sales, etc.).

The reason for this 'imaginative solution' is that states will have to ratify only one Convention (thus reducing many of the obstacles mentioned above). Once the Contracting States have taken over and internalized the proposals and the basis of the base Convention (on in other words, of the proposed system) relating to the legal institution (sales, security interests, carriage, etc.) and it is already part of its internal legal system; then, the only step that would remain would be the elaboration (and then the ratification) of the new specific protocol, which could be adapted to the particular needs of maritime practice in each field. Sadly, the adjustments necessary for such a concept to become reality are unlikely to occur. Even if those settlements are made it is likely that not all of the original parties will accept the amended regime, which then creates diversity rather than uniformity.[90]

Additionally, the pessimism that comes to one when thinking about these goals is found in the traditional separation between maritime law and commercial law, as two autonomous fields of study, albeit with certain common elements. Each of them with its own principles, sources, institutions and categories, which prevent, in many cases, an adequate transmission between both areas of law. Neither have the international institutions or bodies that have dealt with one field or another (UNCITRAL or UNIDROIT, in the field of international trade law, and the CMI or the IMO in the field of maritime law), helped, in many

89 G. J. Van der Ziel, 'The ISIC Study on intermodal liability, some comments by G.J. Van der Ziel', unpublished (see an extract of the text in H. Hoeks, M.A.: *Multimodal Transport Law. The Law Applicable to the Multimodal Contract for the Carriage of Goods.* (2009) p. 387).

90 H. Hoeks, M.A.: *Multimodal Transport Law. The Law Applicable to the Multimodal Contract for the Carriage of Goods* (2009) p. 289.

cases jealous of their material scope of interest. Although we do not deny a certain autonomy of the maritime law,[91] there is a common area in which one shall work from the point of view of conventional uniformity, and we consider that the Cape Town Convention – and a possible future maritime protocol on ships – is good evidence of that. Would this mean a breach in the autonomy of maritime law or a simple means of cooperation? I leave the reader to answer this question.

91 See our opinion in J.P. Rodriguez-Delgado, 'El Derecho Marítimo Se Hace Mayor: La Avanzada Autonomía Del Derecho Marítimo Tras La Aprobación de La Ley de Navegación Marítima' [2015] XXXII *Anuario de Derecho Marítimo* 133.

CHAPTER 7

The gap between EU and EEA law

Opportunities and threats of EEA consolidation

Milagros Varela Chouciño

1 Introduction

The European Economic Area (EEA) Agreement brings together the 28 EU Member States and three of the four European Free Trade Association (EFTA) States (namely Iceland, Norway and Liechtenstein) in a single market commonly referred to as the internal market.[1] By means of the EEA Agreement, the four freedoms of the EU internal market (free movements of services, goods, persons and capitals) are applicable to these three EEA EFTA States as well as competition and state aid rules, horizontal provisions relevant to the four freedoms and certain areas of cooperation outside the four freedoms.

1.1 How does EU law become EEA law?

The institutional architecture that the EEA Agreement devises is mainly referred to as the 'two-pillar structure'.[2] The EU and the institutions are to be found in one pillar, whereas the three EEA EFTA States and their institutions constitute the other. Interactions between the pillars are conducted by the existence of joint bodies that jointly implement and develop the EEA Agreement.

The EEA institutional framework mirrors, to a great extent, the institutions of the EU in the EEA EFTA pillar. Nonetheless, the mimesis is not identical: there are many similarities but also many differences. For instance, in the EEA EFTA pillar there is both a watchdog, the EFTA Surveillance Authority (ESA), and a dispute resolution entity, the EFTA Court. They present common features with the European Commission and the European Court of Justice, respectively, but do not have exactly equal functions. Furthermore, no EEA EFTA institution serves a comparable purpose to the European Council or the External Action Service. The EEA pillar presents a stronger intergovernmental nature, and consequently more sovereignty remains with the national parliaments in Reykjavik, Vaduz and Oslo.

1 Agreement between the EFTA States on the establishment of a surveillance authority and a court of justice ('EEA Agreement') (OJ L344, 31.1.1994, p.3).

2 'The two-pillar structure of the EEA Agreement – Incorporation of new EU acts', Paper by the Subcommittee V on legal and institutional question of the Standing Committee of the EFTA States.

The EEA Agreement has its foundations in the primary legislation of the EU (namely, the Treaty in force at the time of its adoption, the EEC Treaty[3]) as well as in secondary legislation (EEA-relevant regulations, directives, decisions and certain non-binding instruments).

The EEA Agreement currently consists of 129 articles, 22 annexes, 49 protocols and a final Act (March 2019). In order to allow for the dynamism that the adoption of new legislation in the EU pillar requires, annexes and protocols are constantly updated to reflect new regulatory changes. The annexes are lists of EU secondary Acts applicable throughout the EEA. The mechanism by which EU Acts become EEA Acts is a lineal process, and two main incorporation processes are available: the standard and the fast-track procedure.

If the standard procedure is followed, once an EU Act has been adopted, an assessment needs to be conducted in order to analyse whether such Act is EEA-relevant. If the EU Act is deemed EEA-relevant, the next step is to assess whether any adaptations to it are required before its incorporation into an annex on the EEA Agreement. This incorporation is technically done by means of the drafting and approval of Joint Committee Decisions (JCD). Whenever the EEA Joint Committee adopts the JCD, the legislative Act will be incorporated in the EEA Agreement.[4] Nonetheless, it could well be that constitutional requirements must be lifted before its entry into force effectively takes place.

Another procedural mechanism for incorporation of EU legislation into the EEA is the fast-track procedure. This procedure is used for straightforward Acts that do not raise EEA horizontal challenges, call for no adaptations and do not require constitutional requirements. The rationale behind this methodology for incorporation is that some types of Act need swift incorporation in the EEA, and thus, for the well-functioning of the EEA Agreements, no delays should occur in the implementation process. Acts that are subject to this swifter procedure are found in the Annexes of the Handbook of EEA EFTA procedures.[5] Within the field of maritime transport, Acts adopted by the Committee of Safe Seas and the Maritime Security Committee can be subject to the fast-track procedure.

Simplifying things to a great extent, EU secondary Acts have to be incorporated into the Annexes or Protocols of the EEA Agreement before they become EEA law.

2 Differences between EU and EEA legal Acts: how can cracks between the pillars come to light?

There is only one Internal Market in which EU and EEA EFTA States interact, and even if the institutional framework of the EEA is often depicted as a structure of two independent pillars/columns, with the EU on one side and the EEA EFTA States on the other, using a bridge would have been a better metaphor to visualize the EEA institutional structure. Both of the two pillars support one common internal market in which homogeneity is a guiding light. If one of the pillars of the bridge were to fail, the structure would collapse, very much

3 Treaty Establishing the European Economic Community, 25 March 1957, 298 UNTS 11, hereinafter EEC Treaty.

4 Handbook of EEA EFTA procedures for incorporating EU Acts into the EEA Agreement (2016).

5 Cf. footnote 4.

like the EEA Agreement. Likewise, between the pillars, there are some joint bodies which are responsible for EEA decision-making.

On the other hand, drawing parallels with construction pillars may evoke an image of identical structures, which is far from being truthful to reality. In reality, even within the pillars there are potential gaps that, if we observe closely, can come to light. Within decision-shaping two main deviations can be recognized: (i) EU legal Acts could provide for exemptions or derogations, and (ii) EEA adaptations, instruments available only to EEA EFTA States, may be included in a JCD.

Exemptions or derogations may be embedded in the legislative text of an EU legal Act or adopted in the form of decisions by the European Commission.[6] An example of the first case is found in Article 40 of Directive (EU) 2016/1629 of the European Parliament and of the Council of 14 September 2016 laying down technical requirements for inland waterway vessels, amending Directive 2009/100/EC and repealing Directive 2006/87/EC.[7] Article 40 reads that the Directive is addressed to the Member States 'except Denmark, Estonia, Ireland, Greece, Spain, Cyprus, Latvia, Malta, Portugal, Slovenia and Finland'. If an EEA EFTA State would have liked to be part of this list, that should be included in the JCD. On the other hand, exemptions or derogations granted by means of decisions are adopted in the EU pillar by the European Commission and in the EFTA pillar by the ESA.

In the EEA EFTA pillar, there is also a further possibility. Not only may the EEA EFTA States avail themselves of derogations or exemptions, but adaptation texts may also be agreed to EU legal Acts. Those could be of a technical or substantial nature given particular circumstances of one of the States, be used to adapt a legal measure to the scope of the EEA Agreement, or they can seek to compensate for a deficit of EEA/EFTA participation in the EU legislative process.

Four main types of adaptation can be identified: (i) horizontal adaptations, that are to be found in Protocol 1 of the EEA Agreement and seek to solve recurring adaptation issues; (ii) structural adaptations due to the institutional set-up of the EEA Agreement; (iii) adaptations required to bring the scope of an act within the scope of the EEA Agreement; and (iv) other types of adaptation that need to address specific situations or concerns raised from the text of the EU legal Act in question.

In the field of transport, Annex XIII,[8] which deals with transport matters, foresees the horizontal adaptations laid down in Protocol 1 of the EEA Agreement, as well as sectoral adaptations applicable to the transport sector. In particular, and within the Acts that are EEA-relevant incorporated in Annex XIII within the field of maritime transport, currently only seven of the 103 EU legislative Acts include adaptations. Thus, even if the possibility exists to deviate, most EU legislative Acts are identical in the EU and in the EEA.

6 An example of the first case is found in OJ L 252, 16.9.2016, pp. 118–176, whereas an example of the second type of decision can be found in Article 19 of Directive 2008/106/EC of the European Parliament and of the Council of 19 November 2008 on the minimum level of training of seafarers (recast) (Text with EEA relevance) OJ L 323, 3.12.2008, pp. 33–61.

7 OJ L 252, 16.9.2016, pp. 118–176.

8 Cf. footnote 1.

3 Some thoughts on how to minimize the gap between EU–EEA law in the field of transport

Homogeneity is a key success factor in the achievement of the goals within the EEA, and thus two suggestions are hereby brought forward in order to enhance the understanding of EEA law throughout both pillars and ensure better alignment.

3.1 Legislative simplification techniques in the EU pillar: Difference between consolidation, codification and recast

As harmonization in the EU's internal market has gradually increased, the complexity of the drafting of EU legislation has followed suit. Since the early '90s, it has been understood that in order to stress the important role of the European Union and facilitate the harmonization in the Internal Market, EU legislation must be made simpler and clearer (Edinburgh declaration). Better quality and access to EU legislation would not only enable proper and harmonized implementation by the national administrations, but would also make the legal instruments readily available and more accessible to citizens and businesses.

In 1997, in the context of the Amsterdam Intergovernmental Conference, three EU institutions, the European Parliament, the Council and the European Commission, were encouraged to set out guidelines aiming at improving the quality of the drafting of EU legislation. This mandate resulted in the Interinstitutional Agreement of 22 December 1998[9] whereby those three institutions agreed on general principles to draft Community legislation and that each of them will adopt their own measures in this direction. Throughout the following years and decades, several initiatives in this context have been launched, the latest one being reflected by the 2016 Interinstitutional Agreement on Better-Law Making.[10]

In general terms, three simplification techniques can be outlined: consolidation, codification and recast.

The Legal Service of the European Commission defines consolidation as the combination in a single text of the provisions of a legal instrument and all its amendments. Legally speaking, it is deemed a mere simplification, which is of a purely declaratory nature and has no legal binding force. This exercise began in 1996 and has as its main aim making EU legislation more user-friendly and readable, enabling a more approachable access to legal instruments by having its users consult only one piece of legislation that should contain all its amendments. Typically, consolidation is used as a basis for the codified instruments.

Codification means 'the process of bringing together a legislative Act and all its amendments in a single Act'. This process can be vertical, when one original Act and its amendments are merged in a single piece of legislation, or horizontal, when two or more original

9 Interinstitutional Agreement of 20 December of 1994, Accelerated working method for official codification of legislative acts (96/C 102/02); Interinstitutional Agreement of 28 November 2001, On a more structured use of the recasting technique for legal acts (2002/C 77/01) and Interinstitutional Agreement of 13 April 2016, On Better Law-Making (L123/1).

10 Commission Staff Working Document, A review of the European Economic Area, SWD (2012) 425 final.

Acts covering subjects that are related become one single Act. No substantive changes shall be made to the Acts that are to be codified.

If substantive amendments are to be made to Acts that are to be codified, the recast technique is used. By means of the recast technique a new legal Act is adopted which incorporates the earlier Act(s), substantive amendments thereto and its formal repeal and replacement by the new Act.

Within the EEA EFTA States and between the EU/EFTA pillar, the question of codification or consolidated of EEA law has not been raised. EEA law is obscure and needs to be practised analysing not only the EU acquis in question, but also taking into account the horizontal adaptations of Protocol 1 and the adaptations envisaged in the different annexes. For example, if a port would like to understand on which legal basis maritime security inspections are carried, it will not suffice to familiarise itself with Regulation (EC) No 324/2008 of 9 April 2008 laying down revised procedures for conducting Commission inspections in the field of maritime security.[11] The port in question would need to analyse this Act in the light of Protocol 1 and read the Act in the light of the amendments suggested by point 56r of Annex XIII. It stands to reason that such a process is far from making EEA legislation readily available for citizens and businesses.

Given the complexity of EEA law, better tools should be made available for stakeholders. If, on this point, the principle of homogeneity could be invoked, it could be suggested that EEA lex, the equivalent tool for EEA EFTA States, would provide consolidated versions of EEA Acts, in which both the horizontal adaptations of Protocol 1 and the different ad hoc adaptation texts would be inserted. For obvious reasons, this would represent a significant amount of added workload in terms of EEA consolidation, but it could enhance legal certainty in the EEA and make EEA law easier to access and understand for all stakeholders.

On the other side, the costs that such a project may entail could be high and, furthermore, it would need to be understood whether consolidated versions of EEA would be granted binding or non-binding effect.

In any case, EEA legislation should be made simpler and clearer, readily available to its stakeholders and also to the EU's pillar. Simplification techniques that can be aligned with the current resources at stake should be considered in order to raise awareness on the functioning of the EEA and the potential existence of specialities within EEA law that must be borne in mind.

3.2 The increased role of EU agencies in many fields of the EU internal market

From the '90s, a series of new EU agencies started to boom, giving the EU a new dimension. These so-called 'second generation agencies' were mainly motivated by the new waves of internal market harmonization that included solving new tasks of increased technical and/or scientific nature. The majority of these agencies started their activities in 1994 or 1995, as the EEA Agreement came into force, and thus, the EEA Agreement fails to reflect this new trend.

In the field of transport, three agencies exist in the field of transport: the European Maritime Safety Agency (EMSA), the European Aviation Safety Agency (EASA) and the

11 OJ L 129, 29.4.2004, pp. 6–91.

European Rail Agency (ERA). The three agencies have been given quasi decision-making powers, i.e. they assist the European Commission or the EFTA Surveillance Authority on highly technical or scientific matters by providing advice and recommendations or draft legislative proposals. Both the European Commission and the EFTA Surveillance Authority rely heavily on the Agencies' expertise while taking decisions. Moreover, the Agencies have tasks related to research, collecting data and carrying out horizontal analysis but also sharing best practices. Last but not least, their role in providing specialized training is key to keep the specialized competence in the field of transport for staff of national administrations.

Given the fact that the EU agencies are sources of technical expertise and were set up with the final purpose of advising the European Commission, or in the case of the EFTA pillar the EFTA Surveillance Authority, in its tasks, particularly in its decision-making processes, their role in the two-pillar structure is crucial. Any gaps observed in the incorporation of agencies' founding regulations in the EEA Agreement, create *per se* a serious gap between the EU and EEA law. This gap may, in the worst cases, affect the well-functioning of the internal market. One example that can illustrate this point is the pending incorporation in the EEA Agreement of Regulation 100/2013 amending the Regulation establishing a European Maritime Safety Agency,[12] which confers new tasks to the EMSA for the EEA EFTA States. The fact that this Regulation has still not been incorporated in the EEA Agreement has meant that the EFTA Surveillance Authority cannot legally call upon EMSA for tasks that the European Commission has been receiving assistance in since 2013.

Yet another noteworthy point to make is that whenever the EU regulations establishing agencies in the transport sector were incorporated in the EEA Agreement, the EEA EFTA States sought to gain access to their management boards on equal grounds to the EU Member States and to the same level of representation as the European Commission. Currently two of the three transport agencies (EMSA and EASA) have rejected the EFTA Surveillance Authority's requests to participate in its administrative/management boards as observers. The arguments brought forward by the agencies point to the fact that there is no specific legal basis to grant such a request. This absence for the management boards causes a lack of insight into the strategic direction of the agencies, which ultimately affects the planning and strategic monitoring of the legal acquis. Furthermore, it damages the working relationship with national administrations and grants the EFTA Surveillance Authority less access to information than the States it monitors, creating an information asymmetry.

To conclude, strengthened presence in the agencies can enhance both EEA awareness and grant the EFTA pillar institutions better visibility and recognition in the EEA context. Thus, either adaptation texts should cater for a level playing field or Protocol 1 should reflect this equal standing. On the dark side, the lack of alignment may create monitoring vacuums in legislation that shall be implemented equally throughout the EEA and blind zones for its monitoring institutions that will generate undesirable outcomes.

12 OJ L 39 15/01/2013 pp. 30–40.

4 Concluding remarks

All parties in the EEA must strive to minimize the risk of an increasing gap between EU law and EEA law, since only a pragmatic and homogeneous approach between pillars will ensure that citizens and businesses are provided with a level playing field within the EEA. Delays in incorporation and implementation of EEA acquis should be minimized substantially, and EEA Acts should be consolidated in order to reflect the duties and obligations of EEA stakeholders. Equal level playing fields should be created with room in the existing framework for both EU and EEA institutions.

CHAPTER 8

The Maritime Labour Convention

A Code of minimum rights and maximum impact

Dr Julia Constantino Chagas Lessa

1 Introduction

The Maritime Labour Convention 2006 (MLC) entered into force on 20 August 2013[1] and is considered the 'fourth Pillar' of quality shipping, complementing three main International Maritime Organization (IMO) Conventions, namely the International Convention for the Life at Sea, 1974, as amended (SOLAS);[2] the International Conventions on Standards of Training, Certification and Watchkeeping 1978, as amended (STCW);[3] and the International Convention for the Prevention of Pollution from Ships 73/78 (MARPOL). The Convention is often referred to as 'super Convention', a charter of rights' and the 'seafarers' bills of rights'[4] and it is not difficult to understand why, since the Convention essentially ensures that every seafarer working on board merchant vessels involved in international trade will have guaranteed minimum rights.

The clamour surrounding the MLC is not unjustified. The Convention is the first International Labour Organization (ILO) Convention made in the mould of an IMO Convention. Thus, it possesses the best of both worlds. The ILO can inspect its proper implementation by the ratifying countries while its format allows for a network of responsibilities, which include Flag States, Port States and Labour Supplying States. Furthermore, by 2019 the number of ratifying countries represented 91% of the world ship gross tonnage, meaning that the Convention has been able to achieve what the other 68 ILO instruments failed to do – to have the ratification of the majority and most important shipping nations in the world.[5]

Although at a first sight the MLC does not bring many novelties when it comes to seafarers' rights, particularly considering that it is essentially a compilation of previous ILO instruments, by being able to finally put these ILO instruments in force, the Convention

1 Maritime Labour Convention (Geneva, 2006).

2 International Convention for the Safety of Life at Sea (London, 1974).

3 International Convention on standards of training, certification and watchkeeping for seafarers (London, 1978)

4 M. L. McConnell, 'Making Labour History and the Maritime Labour Convention: Implications for International Law-Making (and Responses to the Dynamics of Globalization)' in A. Chircop, T. McDorman and S. Rolston (eds), *The Future of Ocean Regime-Building* (Brill Online Books and Journals, 2009), pp. 349–384. See also: *ITF forms group to lobby for African offshore workers' rights, MLC is not just a tick box exercise, What's taking so long with Maritime Labour Convention?*, and *What is the Maritime Labour Convention, Seafarer rights convention will come into force from August and UK puts biometric ID for seafarers on hold*, lloydslist.com.

5 See: ILO, https://www.ilo.org/global/standards/maritime-labour-convention/lang—en/index.htm (visited 18 August 2019)

was able, particularly in its amendments, to ensure that certain mechanisms, such as the financial security schemes, were put into place in order to guarantee the full protection of seafarers' rights. The fact is that, due to its unique characteristics, the Maritime Labour Convention was able to achieve a minimum level of global harmonization still sought by most international Conventions, already serving as an example to be followed by other ILO Conventions.[6]

This chapter will seek to unveil and analyse the different aspects of the Convention since its inception, challenges until its implementation by most of the world's ship tonnage, in order to understand and seek to justify its ability to successfully achieve the codification of seafarers' minimum rights at an international level. As the MLC is an ILO Convention that mirrors IMO Conventions, being an international Convention regarding maritime law, it is expected that the analysis in this chapter will serve as guidance to future IMO Conventions as well as other international Conventions aiming to achieve similar results.

2 The MLC's inception

The MLC can be considered a work of years and it was not achieved without challenges. After all, the Convention itself is composed of no less than 68 ILO instruments, many which did not even reach the necessary number of ratifications in order to come into force.[7] In order to understand these challenges it is important to consider the origin of the Convention. Accordingly, this section will examine the international scenario prior to the MLC, what led to its creation and the obstacles overcome by the Convention drafters.

The International Labour Organization (ILO) was established in 1919, as what can simplistically be considered a result of globalization leading trade unions to realize that an international regime with common standards in the fields of labour relations and social insurance was needed in order to prevent the welfare state from failing before it had even started.[8] Within a year of the Organization establishment, three ILO Conventions addressed specific seafarers' issues: the ILO Minimum Age (Sea) Convention 1920,[9] the ILO Unemployment Indemnity (Shipwreck) Convention 1920[10] and the ILO Placing Seamen Convention 1920.[11] From the beginning, without a doubt, the Organization focused a lot of its efforts on the protection of seafarers, always aiming to reach a codification of seafarers' rights. This is evident from an extract from the Preamble of the ILO National Seamen's Code Recommendation 1920:

> 'In order that, as a result of the clear and systematic codification of the national law in each country, the seamen of the world, whether engaged on ships of their own or foreign countries, may have a better comprehension of their rights and obligations, and in order that the task of

---

6 J. Whitlow and R. Subasinghe, 'The Maritime Labour Convention, 2006: A model for other industries?' (2015) Vol. 7, Issue 1–2 *International Journal of Labour Research* 113–131.

7 A few examples are the: C007 – Minimum Age (Sea) Convention, 1920 (No. 7), C022 – Seamen's Articles of Agreement Convention, 1926 (No. 22) and C178 – Labour Inspection (Seafarers) Convention, 1996 (No. 178)

8 B. Reinalda, *Routledge history of international organizations: from 1815 to the present day* (Routledge 2009), pp. 223–224.

9 C007 – Minimum Age (Sea) Convention, 1920 (No. 7) (Genoa, 1920).

10 C008 – Unemployment Indemnity (Shipwreck) Convention, 1920 (No. 8) (Genoa, 1920).

11 C009 – Placing of Seamen Convention, 1920 (No. 9) (Genoa, 1920); B. Nelson, *Workers on the waterfront: seamen, longshoremen, and unionism in the 1930s* (University of Illinois Press, 1988), pp. 21–22.

establishing an International Seamen's Code may be advanced and facilitated, the International Labour Conference recommends that each Member of the International Labour Organisation undertake the embodiment in a seamen's code of all its laws and regulations relating to seamen in their activities as such.'[12]

As can be seen, the aim of the ILO was that, by the ratification of all its instruments, countries would develop national codes regulating the work of seafarers and guaranteeing minimum rights, creating a certain level playing field where seafarers around the globe would have similar rights, being in line with the Organization's belief that universal and lasting peace can be accomplished only if it is based on social justice.[13]

Nevertheless, prior to the MLC the Organization was never able to achieve its original goal in regard to seafarers since, preceding the Convention, out of the 72 ILO Maritime Labour instruments[14] many never entered into force for lack of ratification and others (despite the number of ratifications) were enforced by only an insignificant number of ratifying countries.[15]

It was only in 1994, during the 81st Session (1994) of the International Labour Conference, leading to the establishment at the 262nd Session of the ILO Governing Body, held in March 1995, when a working party on policy regarding the revision of standards, known as the 'Cartier Group', that the process of creation of the MLC can be said to have started. After working for seven years, the Cartier Group identified ten maritime Conventions in need of updating. This finding was followed by observations from International Transport Workers Federation (ITF) and the International Shipping Federation (ISF) that it would take a considerable period of time to update those Conventions under the usual process and that considering the significant number of maritime Conventions in need of being updated, a new mechanism should be found to facilitate their amendment to reflect changes in the shipping industry. These informal discussions led to an agreement that a new consolidated Convention was the way forward. Accordingly, in January 2001, the 29th Session of the ILO Joint Maritime Commission (a bipartite body of 20 seafarers and 20 shipowners) made a number of recommendations to be considered at the 280th Session of the ILO Governing Body held in March 2001, when a resolution concerning the review of relevant ILO maritime instruments was agreed on:

'The Commission, under this item, discussed the significance and impact of maritime labour standards. It agreed that many of the existing ILO maritime labour instruments were outdated, deficient and not reflective of modern practices; those which were up to date and pertinent were not sufficiently ratified. It concluded that the best way forward in line with the integrated approach approved by the Governing Body at its 279th Session (November 2000) was the

12 R009 – National Seamen's Codes Recommendation, 1920 (No. 9).

13 ILO, Origins and history, http://www.ilo.org/global/about-the-ilo/history/lang—en/index.htm.

14 ILO, Compendium Of Maritime Labour Instruments – Maritime Labour Convention, 2006, Seafarers' Identity Documents (Revised) Convention, 2003 Work in Fishing Convention and Recommendation, 2007, Second (Revised) edition, 2015, https://www.ilo.org/global/publications/ilo-bookstore/order-online/books/WCMS_093523/lang—en/index.htm (visited 21 August 2019).

15 A few examples are the: C007 – Minimum Age (Sea) Convention, 1920 (No. 7), C022 – Seamen's Articles of Agreement Convention, 1926 (No. 22) and C178 – Labour Inspection (Seafarers) Convention, 1996 (No. 178).

> adoption of a single "framework" instrument which would consolidate the existing body of ILO maritime Conventions and Recommendations.'[16]

The Commission followed by recommending the Governing Body to take a number of steps, including the establishment of a high-level tripartite working group on maritime labour standards to assist with the work of developing the proposed new instrument and defining the modalities of work. This working group effectively prepared the grounds for what would become the Maritime Labour Convention, 2006.[17]

The high level tripartite working group should not come as a surprise as a tripartite decision-making structure is one of ILO's unique characteristics. ILO's tripartite structure makes it a unique forum, which allows governments and the social partners of economies and Member States to freely and openly debate and devise labour standards and policies.[18] This structure is composed of governments, trade unions and employers, being the only United Nations' (UN) agency to be constituted in such a manner.[19] Accordingly, the three main ILO tripartite organs are as follows:

> 'the International Labour Conference sets the international labour standards and the broad policies of the ILO. It meets annually in Geneva. Often called an international parliament of labour, the Conference is also a forum for discussion of key social and labour questions.
>
> The Governing body is the executive council of the ILO. It meets three times a year in Geneva. It takes decisions on ILO policy and establishes the programme and the budget, which it then submits to the Conference for adoption.
>
> The International Labour Office is the permanent secretariat of the International Labour Organization. It is the focal point for International Labour Organization's overall activities, which it prepares under the scrutiny of the Governing Body and under the leadership of the Director-General.'[20]

This Tripartite decision-making process possibly made the Convention process lengthier, as between the Geneva Accord in 2001 and the final adoption of the MLC in February 2006 at the 10th Maritime Session, 94th Session of the ILC, there were six high-level tripartite consultative meetings (two of which were subgroup meetings), a preparatory technical conference, and an additional intersessional meeting. Moreover, there were several officers' meetings to resolve particular issues in the text, as well as strategic development of special procedures within the ILO framework to facilitate consideration of such a comprehensive text.[21] Nevertheless, this process undeniably managed to balance the parties'

16 Report of the 29th Session of the Joint Maritime Commission (Geneva, 22–26 January 2001), Governing Body, 28th Session, Geneva, March 2001, ILO Doc. No. GB 280/5 (Corr.).

17 For more see: M. McConnell, D. Devlin, C. Doumbia-Henry, *The Maritime Labour Convention, 2006: A Legal Primer to an Emerging international regime* (Martinus Nijhoff Publishers, 2011).

18 ILO, Tripartite constituents, http://www.ilo.org/global/about-the-ilo/who-we-are/tripartite-constituents/lang—en/index.htm (visited 21 August 2019)

19 ILO Constitution, Art. 2.

20 See https://www.ilo.org/global/about-the-ilo/how-the-ilo-works/lang--en/index.htm (visited 21 August 2019)

21 Office Commentary prepared for the International Labour Conference, 94th (Maritime) Session, 2006, *Adoption of an instrument to consolidate maritime labour standards*, Report I(1A) (Geneva: International Labour Office, 2005), pp. 1–4.

interests and achieve social justice as one of the core principles of the ILO,[22] also reflecting a shift from previous ILO practices. As noted by Professor Doumbia-Henry (by then the ILO department of standards director):

> '. . . the process of development of the text, over a period of nearly five years, by the International Labour Office under the guidance of the tripartite constituents of the Organization, reflects a shift in ILO practice in the drafting of texts for submission to the International Labour Conference. This process of more extensive consultation and international "social dialogue" led to the development of concrete tripartite solutions to address highly sensitive issues such as the provision of social security protection, employer liability and worker complaint mechanisms, before the Convention was considered for adoption. In addition, strategic approaches needed to be devised to facilitate discussion of such a comprehensive and lengthy instrument within the ILO's constitutional framework. The fact that very few amendments were submitted to the proposed text considered by the Conference and, of these, very few were controversial, testifies to the effectiveness of the tripartite process and of international social dialogue.'[23]

In fact, as M.L. McConnell points out, the role of the industry was a very important aspect of the MLC's lengthy negotiating process as international representative organizations of shipowners and seafarers negotiated solutions to many specific issues, helping to reach compromise texts in areas where some governments were having difficulty as a result of national interests. The shipowners and seafarers' representatives also attended the IMO meetings and processes, closely ensuring that labour standards were given the same profile as environmental and safety and security issues. In fact, it was truly of the pressure from these civil society representatives, far more than governments, that helped to ensure the 'cross-fertilization of ideas and cooperation to create complementary regimes'.[24]

Accordingly, the MLC can be considered the fruit of a lengthy process that actively involved many shipping industry stakeholders, but perhaps most importantly it truly embodied all the core principles of the ILO and finally making the ILO National Seamen's Code Recommendation 1920 a reality.

3 The relevance of the International Maritime Organization (IMO) to the MLC

Although the MLC is an ILO Convention, it is pertinent to highlight the importance of the IMO in promoting the Convention and supporting the endeavours of the former

22 The ILO was formed after World War I as part of the peace settlement under the Treaty of Versailles, reflecting the belief that universal and lasting peace can be accomplished only if it is based on social justice. See: ILO, Origins and history, http://www.ilo.org/global/about-the-ilo/history/lang—en/index.htm (visited 21 August 2019)

23 C. Doumbia-Henry, D. Devlin and M. L. McConnell, 'The Maritime Labour Convention, 2006 Consolidates Seafarers' Labour Instruments' *ASIL Insight* 10(23) (13 September 2006), www.asil.org/insights/2006/09/insights060913.html (visited 21 August 2019) See also J.I. Blanck Jr., Reflections in the negotiation of the Maritime Labour Convention 2006 at the International Labour Organisation (2006) 31 *Tulane Maritime Law Journal* 1 at 35–56, M. Marin and A. Charbonneau, Une convention innovante pour le travail maritime? Les apportsde la Convention du travail maritime (CTM) de 2006 (2009) XXVII *Annuaire De Droit Maritime Et Oceanique* 445–469.

24 M.L. McConnell, 'Making Labour History and the Maritime Labour Convention: Implications for International Law-Making (and Responses to the Dynamics of Globalization)' in A. Chircop, T. McDorman and S. Rolston (eds), *The Future of Ocean Regime-Building* (Brill Online Books and Journals, 2009), p. 369.

organization from its draft to its enforcement. After all, as will become clear, the Convention followed the parameters of IMO Conventions and the support of the said organization can be seen as fundamental to the overall success of the Convention.

The support of the IMO to the ILO efforts should not come as a surprise, particularly when noting that the aims of the Organization as outlined in Article 1 of its Convention[25] give a dominant emphasis to economic action for the promotion of 'freedom' and to 'end discrimination', along with references to a 'world without discrimination' and action against 'unfair restrictive practices',[26] and are thus very much in line with one of the MLC's core purposes – to provide a level playing field in the context of seafarers' living and working conditions.[27]

It is important to note that the IMO, similar to the ILO, has a consultative and advisory role.[28] Furthermore, Article 3 of the Convention clearly states that the Organization should 'provide for the drafting of conventions, agreements, or other suitable instruments, and recommend these to governments and to international organisations, and to convene such conferences as necessary', making clear that the Organization did not have the authority to adopt or amend treaties.[29]

The importance given to seafarers by IMO becomes clearer since the International Transport Workers Federation (ITF) holds a consultative status at the Organization, being a permanent representative to the organization, and monitors ITF-affiliated unions who participate in the various committees, aiming to ensure that seafarers' interests are addressed and protected when any new regulation is being considered. The ITF has always clearly highlighted the importance of IMO conventions to Seafarers, stating that 'they have a direct impact on living and working conditions',[30] always stressing the importance of their ratification, being a vital advocate of the MLC which can be recognised as a success of the Federation's restless work in promoting seafarers' rights.

In 1997, the importance of seafarers to the organization can be said to have become even clearer when the IMO started using the term 'human element'[31] in reference to a complex multi-dimensional issue affecting maritime safety, security and marine environmental protection involving the entire spectrum of human activities performed by ships' crews,

25 The IMO was formally established by the adoption of a Convention on the International Maritime Organization (Geneva, 1948) formally establishing IMO (the original name was the Inter-Governmental Maritime Consultative Organization, or IMCO, but the name was changed in 1982 to IMO) in an international conference in Geneva, http://www.imo.org/en/About/HistoryOfIMO/Pages/Default.aspx (visited 21 August 2019)

26 'It was no coincidence that all the Scandinavian countries made a statement – and an unusually strong one – to the effect that they would consider a renunciation of the Convention if IMO were to assume competence in matters of the kind mentioned in Articles 1(b) and (c). The Scandinavian countries (led by Norway), as well as Greece, have always been strong supporters of the principle of the freedom of international shipping, which according to their philosophy, should be upheld through virtually unrestricted maritime shipping regulated by nothing but free and fair competition', J.N.K. Mansell, *Flag State Responsibility: Historical Development and Contemporary Issues* (Springer-Verlag Berlin Heidelberg, 2009), p. 121, and IMO, *Brief history of IMO*, http://www.imo.org/en/About/HistoryOfIMO/Pages/Default.aspx (visited 21 August 2019)

27 MLC, Preamble.

28 IMO Convention, Art. 2.

29 The full text of the Convention at https://www.jus.uio.no/english/services/library/treaties/14/14-01/imo_consolidated.xml (visited 21 August 2019).

30 ITF, Inside the Issues – IMO and ILO, https://www.itfseafarers.org/ITI—ILO.cfm (visited 12 August 2019).

31 http://www.imo.org/ourwork/humanelement/Pages/Default.aspx (visited 12 August 2019).

shore-based management, regulatory bodies and others, adopting Resolution A.850(20).[32] The resolution referred to evoked a previous Resolution (A.680(17)) which invited governments to encourage those responsible for the management and operation of ships to develop, implement and assess safety and pollution prevention management systems and also Resolution (A.772(18)) concerning fatigue factors in manning and safety, aiming at increasing awareness of the complexity of fatigue and encouraging all parties involved in shipping operations to take these factors into account when making operational decisions.[33] Moreover, Resolution A.850(20) acknowledged the need for increased focus on human-related activities in the safe operation of ships, and the need to achieve and maintain high standards of safety and environmental protection for the purpose of significantly reducing maritime casualties.[34]

Finally, in 2001, IMO, 'noting the importance in the plan of action of the International Maritime Organization (IMO) of the human element, which is central for the promotion of quality shipping, and the core mandate of the International Labour Organization (ILO), which is to promote decent conditions of work',[35] created Resolution A.930(22). The resolution was the first international instrument offering guidelines on provision of financial security in cases of abandonment of seafarers,[36] incorporated into the MLC in 2014.[37]

Indeed, the IMO demonstrated its support and endorsement of the MLC from its draft until it came into force in 2013. This can be noted by the numerous efforts made by the organization to call attention to the human element of shipping, finally proclaiming 2010 the 'year of the seafarer', justified by the speech made by Secretary-General Mitropoulos claiming that 'the unique hazards confronting the 1.5 million seafarers of the world – including pirate attacks, unwarranted detention and abandonment – coupled with the predicted looming shortage of ships' officers, make it ever more incumbent to take immediate and effective action to forestall a situation from developing in which ships are not manned with sufficient skilled personnel'.[38]

The MLC should be perceived as a joint effort between the ILO and the IMO, together with key private shipping industry stakeholders, i.e. shipowners and seafarers' representatives. This 'group effort' was pivotal to making the Convention successful.

4 The Maritime Labour Convention's 'raison d'être' and structure

The MLC's philosophy of 'promoting decent work and a fair globalization' can be largely considered one of the reasons for its success. This philosophy is said to translate into secure

32 http://www.imo.org/OurWork/HumanElement/VisionPrinciplesGoals/Pages/Default.aspx (visited 12 August 2019).

33 http://www.imo.org/OurWork/HumanElement/VisionPrinciplesGoals/Pages/Default.aspx (visited 12 August 2019).

34 The resolution was updated by resolution A.947(23) Human element vision, principles and goals for the Organization adopted by the 23rd Assembly in November–December 2003, http://www.imo.org/OurWork/HumanElement/VisionPrinciplesGoals/Pages/Default.aspx (visited 12 August 2019).

35 Extract from the text of the IMO Resolution A.930(22)

36 IMO Resolution A.930(22)

37 http://www.ilo.org/global/standards/maritime-labour-convention/lang—en/index.htm. The financial security scheme was proposed firstly as an amendment to the Convention and only approved by the Special Tripartite Committee one year after the Convention entered into force, in 2014 at the 103rd session of the International Labour Conference.

38 http://www.imo.org/blast/mainframe.asp?topic_id=1773&doc_id=11506 (visited 12 August 2019).

decent work for seafarers and a level playing field for shipowners, since the Convention will help preventing unscrupulous ship owners and inept flag States to continue engaging in unfair competition by effectively sanctioning substandard working conditions.[39] Remarkably, the Convention:

- adopts an entirely new format for ILO conventions;
- sets out a Code that lays out the more technical and evolving dimensions governing labour conditions in the maritime transport industry.[40]
- covers close to the full gamut of socio-economic issues in the maritime sector, including the very controversial question of social security protection, ship owner's liability and repatriation; and
- sets out a new comprehensive enforcement and compliance system based on flag State inspection and certification of the requirements of the Convention complemented by port State control inspections and on board and onshore complaint handling systems.[41]

As already mentioned, the Maritime Labour Convention was born out of a necessity to update previous ILO instruments and to achieve a greater number of ratifications, hence in essence a consolidation of 68 ILO instruments. The 37 ILO Conventions revised by the MLC are the following:

- Minimum Age (Sea) Convention, 1920 (No. 7)
- Unemployment Indemnity (Shipwreck) Convention, 1920 (No. 8)
- Placing of Seamen Convention, 1920 (No. 9)
- Medical Examination of Young Persons (Sea) Convention, 1921 (No. 16)
- Seamen's Articles of Agreement Convention, 1926 (No. 22)
- Repatriation of Seamen Convention, 1926 (No. 23)
- Officers' Competency Certificates Convention, 1936 (No. 53)
- Holidays with Pay (Sea) Convention, 1936 (No. 54)
- Shipowners' Liability (Sick and Injured Seamen) Convention, 1936 (No. 55)
- Sickness Insurance (Sea) Convention, 1936 (No. 56)
- Hours of Work and Manning (Sea) Convention, 1936 (No. 57)
- Minimum Age (Sea) Convention (Revised), 1936 (No. 58)
- Food and Catering (Ships' Crews) Convention, 1946 (No. 68)
- Certification of Ships' Cooks Convention, 1946 (No. 69)
- Social Security (Seafarers) Convention, 1946 (No. 70)
- Paid Vacations (Seafarers) Convention, 1946 (No. 72)

39 J. Whitlow and R. Subasinghe, 'The Maritime Labour Convention, 2006: A model for other industries?' (2015) Vol. 7, Issue 1–2 *International Journal of Labour Research* 124.

40 This represents a novelty in ILO Convention's structure, as is the inclusion of a simplified amendment process for the Code (Article XV) via the Special Tripartite Committee (Article XIII), meaning that the Code can be amended without the need to adopt a protocol, which would require a new ratification from Member States. (See: J. Whitlow and R. Subasinghe, 'The Maritime Labour Convention, 2006: A model for other industries?' (2015) Vol. 7, Issue 1–2 *International Journal of Labour Research* 119).

41 See: J.C. Chagas Lessa, 'An Overview of the Maritime Labour Convention and its first years in force' (2016) 22 *Journal of International Maritime Law* 382.

- Medical Examination (Seafarers) Convention, 1946 (No. 73)
- Certification of Able Seamen Convention, 1946 (No. 74)
- Accommodation of Crews Convention, 1946 (No. 75)
- Wages, Hours of Work and Manning (Sea) Convention, 1946 (No. 76)
- Paid Vacations (Seafarers) Convention (Revised), 1949 (No. 91)
- Accommodation of Crews Convention (Revised), 1949 (No. 92)
- Wages, Hours of Work and Manning (Sea) Convention (Revised), 1949 (No. 93)
- Wages, Hours of Work and Manning (Sea) Convention (Revised), 1958 (No. 109)
- Accommodation of Crews (Supplementary Provisions) Convention, 1970 (No. 133)
- Prevention of Accidents (Seafarers) Convention, 1970 (No. 134)
- Continuity of Employment (Seafarers) Convention, 1976 (No. 145)
- Seafarers' Annual Leave with Pay Convention, 1976 (No. 146)
- Merchant Shipping (Minimum Standards) Convention, 1976 (No. 147)
- Protocol of 1996 to the Merchant Shipping (Minimum Standards) Convention, 1976 (No. 147)
- Seafarers' Welfare Convention, 1987 (No. 163)
- Health Protection and Medical Care (Seafarers) Convention, 1987 (No. 164)
- Social Security (Seafarers) Convention (Revised), 1987 (No. 165)
- Repatriation of Seafarers Convention (Revised), 1987 (No. 166)
- Labour Inspection (Seafarers) Convention, 1996 (No. 178)
- Recruitment and Placement of Seafarers Convention, 1996 (No. 179)
- Seafarers Hours of Work and the Manning of Ships Convention, 1996 (No. 180).[42]

The Convention also recognizes the gaps in international maritime law resulting from the evolution of the shipping industry, as for instance the proliferation of flags of convenience, which arguably has led to flag states not adequately assuming jurisdiction over social matters concerning their ships as required by international law.[43] The MLC, as will be seen later on, mitigates this problem by providing for an enforcement regime based on a network of enforcement and compliance, involving multiparties and not limited solely to flag states.

Since the main goal of the Convention was to achieve nearly universal ratification, a new strategic approach was adopted. This approach has been described as a 'blend of firmness on rights and flexibility with respects to approaches to implementation of the more technical requirements and because of the advantages it gives to ship of countries that ratify it'.[44] By removing the incentives to a regulatory race to the bottom in the shipping industry, by guaranteeing a level playing field for all, the MLC puts in practice the principles of rational institutionalist theory, where states are expected to use international institutions to improve

42 MLC, Art. X.

43 See: J.C. Chagas Lessa, 'How wide are the shoulders of a Flag of Convenience Country?' in M. Musi (ed.), *New Comparative Perspectives in Maritime, Transport and International Trade Law* (Bologna, 2014), pp. 227–252.

44 ILO, *Maritime Labour Convention, 2006, Frequently asked questions* (Geneva: ILO, 2006), 9, https://www.ilo.org/global/standards/maritime-labour-convention/what-it-does/faq/WCMS_238010/lang--en/index.htm (visited 12 August 2019).

or consolidate their preferred standards while reducing the risk of suffering competitive disadvantage in world markets.[45]

In order to achieve this flexibility without decreasing existing levels of protection to seafarers, the Convention contains several innovative approaches reflecting the development of existing ILO approaches as well as its focus on securing effective implementation and improving enforcement and encouraging social dialogue at a national level. Accordingly, there is a clear interaction of both the Convention's structure and content.[46]

As mentioned, structurally the MLC adopts an approach similar to the IMO's Conventions, which generally follow a standard design. IMO Conventions can be said:

- to comprise fairly brief articles spelling out general State obligations regarding implementation, and often, inspection, certification and port State control, scope and coverage, entry into force, amendments, and include a requirement to comply with the convention and its annex;
- to have one or more annexes containing more detailed mandatory "technical" provisions, the 'regulations';
- to often have instruments, such as codes (sometimes with both mandatory and non-mandatory provisions) and voluntary guidelines developed to complement the convention and deal in greater detail with specific elements of the regulations in the annex.
- to often the different parties of the Convention have differing amendment provisions, with the tacit acceptance procedure used to allow for more rapid updating of the technical provisions in the annexes.[47]

The Convention's structure consists of: Preamble, Articles, a Code, Regulations and Appendices. The lengthy Preamble, referring to the Law of the Sea Convention and to the IMO conventions, as well as to several core ILO Conventions (again something unusual to ILO Conventions) justifies the creation of the Convention, contextualizing the Convention provisions and serving to firmly situate it in the wider international law of the sea and international maritime law regime.[48] The ILO legal adviser, when providing an opinion about the relevance of the preamble, stated:

> 'Preambles do not contain legal obligations . . . [it] provides information as to the overall context and intention of the Convention in relation to other relevant international law and principles. In particular, it indicates a clear intention that the new Convention should, inter alia, embody the fundamental principles to be found in the ILO's "fundamental Conventions" . . . and recalls the ILO Declaration of Fundamental Principles and Rights at Work, 1998.'[49]

---

45 J. Whitlow and R. Subasinghe, The Maritime Labour Convention, 2006: A model for other industries? (2015) Vol. 7, Issue 1–2 *International Journal of Labour Research* 125.

46 M.L. McConnell, 'Making Labour History and the Maritime Labour Convention: Implications for International Law-Making (and Responses to the Dynamics of Globalization)' in A. Chircop, T. McDorman and S. Rolston (eds), *The Future of Ocean Regime-Building* (Brill Online Books and Journals, 2009), p.370

47 See for example, MARPOL, SOLAS and STCW.

48 M. McConnell, D. Devlin, C. Doumbia-Henry, *The Maritime Labour Convention, 2006: A Legal Primer to an Emerging international regim*e (Martinus Nijhoff, 2011), p. 168.

49 Note 1 (Preamble), p. 13.

The 16 Articles attempt to outline the responsibility and obligations of Contracting States, containing more general principles, obligations and rights and also provisions relating to the legal aspects of the operation and application of the Convention. An important 'Explanatory Note' can be found after the articles, which, although not officially part of the Convention text, provides further information and assistance, especially to governments, about the relationship between the parts of the Code.[50]

A claimed purpose of the Convention, as already discussed in this chapter, is to create a level playing field in the context of seafarers' living and working conditions, helping to prevent 'bad shipowners' obtaining advantages or undercutting 'good shipowners'. The 'no more favourable treatment' provision contained in Article V para. 7 of the MLC, by providing that:

> '[e]ach Member shall implement its responsibilities under this Convention in such a way as to ensure that ships that fly the flag of any State that has not ratify this Convention do not receive more favourable treatment than the ships that fly the flag of any state that has ratified it.'

aims to ensure that this purpose is achieved.

Finally, the MLC contains a two-part Code: Part A – mandatory Standards and Part B – non-mandatory Guidelines. Part B of the Code is far more extensive than part A and can be said to be what gives the Convention its flexible nature, as it essentially leaves to Member States how to implement the Convention, this being the reason why the MLC is said to be 'firm on rights but flexible on implementation',[51] as already discussed.

The Regulations and the Code provide for more specific principles and obligations, and are divided into the following five 'Titles':

- Minimum Requirements for Seafarers to work on a Ship
- Conditions of Employment
- Accommodation, Recreational Facilities, Food and Catering
- Health Protection, Medical Care, Welfare and Social Security Protection
- Compliance and Enforcement

The first four titles set out the minimum requirements to be fulfilled by the shipowner in order to guarantee minimum rights to the seafarers, setting up obligations on the Member States in order to guarantee compliance in all the ships carrying their flag. The final title confirms the responsibility of Member States to ensure the implementation of the obligations established in the Convention. It requires that compliance and further enforcement of the Convention are to take place under an effective system of inspection and certification of vessels, dividing the obligations among flag states, port states, and labour-supplying states. Note that ratifying states will often fall into at least two if not three of the categories listed.

The flexible nature of the Convention, as already stated, allows flag states to implement Part A of Titles 1 to 4 through provisions in their laws and regulations or other measures

50 M.L.McConnell, 'Making Labour History and the Maritime Labour Convention: Implications for International Law-Making (and Responses to the Dynamics of Globalization)' in A. Chircop, T. McDorman and S. Rolston (eds), *The Future of Ocean Regime-Building* (Brill Online Books and Journals, 2009), p. 371.

51 See: N. Khalid, Foster the people, *Maritime Risk International*, May 2013

which are 'substantially equivalent' to the mandatory provisions of the Code (Article VI(3) and (4)). It is important to note, however, that this 'permissiveness' is not allowed in regard to Title 5, one of the main novelties of the Convention since it follows a network system of compliance and enforcement only before seen in in IMO Conventions, more specifically SOLAS, MARPOL and STCW. Accordingly, the measures for compliance and enforcement must be followed according to the express provisions of the Convention. Nevertheless, it is up to the Member States to decide on the best way to conduct inspections on their ships and how/when to issue the compliance certificates, which will be accepted as '*prima facie*'[52] evidence of compliance, which certainly may cause problems.[53]

The MLC system of inspection and certification of vessels in order to guarantee compliance with the Convention, provided by Title 5, establishes a system based on responsibilities and obligations for flag states, port states, labour-supplying states and, to a lesser extent, to coastal states. The Convention provides for flag states to establish an inspection and certification system to ensure that the minimum standards there contained are met, and continue to be met, for ships flying the state's flag.[54] The MLC permits flag states to establish whether or not the vessel complies with the Convention, hence specific requirements may vary from state to state. As long as the obligations required by the Convention are met, such differences are allowed.[55] The Convention allows for inspections to be carried out by a 'competent authority', i.e. a national authority or by a 'recognised organisation', which are often Classification Societies.[56]

Although the Convention allows flag states to delegate their functions to these specific institutions, they will remain fully responsible for the inspection and certification of the working and living conditions of the seafarers on ships that fly their flag. In every case, national authorities may choose to undertake inspection and certification responsibilities themselves.[57]

Furthermore, vessels of 500 GT or above operating in international waters or between ports of different countries are required to carry and maintain a 'maritime labour certificate' and a 'declaration of maritime labour compliance', confirming that they have been inspected and meet the obligations of national laws that implement the Convention. The latter document should outline the measures adopted by the shipowner to ensure compliance on the ship or ships concerned.[58] The details provided in these documents are the basis of the inspection regime, as port state authorities shall assess vessels against these documents. It is important to note that the Convention limits the validity of these certificates to a period of five years. Furthermore, the validity of the certificate must be the subject of

---

52 MLC Regulation 5.2.1 §3.

53 Some countries, particularly those considered to be Flag of Convenience countries, are known for ratifying conventions and nonetheless have less strict enforcement rules. See: J.C. Chagas Lessa, MLC: Much Ado About Nothing? (2014) *European Transport Law Journal* 119–132 and J.C. Chagas Lessa, 'How wide are the shoulders of a Flag of Convenience Country?' in M. Musi (ed.), *New Comparative Perspectives in Maritime, Transport and International Trade Law* (Bologna, 2014), pp. 227–252.

54 MLC, Reg. 5.1.

55 L. McMahon, *ICS urges owners to adopt labour convention despite flag state concerns*, July 2013, Lloydslist.com.

56 For more information see: J.C. Chagas Lessa, An Overview of the Maritime Labour Convention and its first years in force (2016) 22 *Journal of International Maritime Law* 387.

57 MLC, Regs. 5.1.1.3 and 5.1.2.

58 MLC, Reg. 5.1.3.

at least one intermediate inspection within each five-year period, between the second and third year. Ships flying the flag of a Contracting State must also have a copy of the MLC available on board. Both documents must comply with the models set out in Appendix A5-II to the Convention.[59]

Regulation 5.2, providing for the port states' obligations, also requires vessels to be inspected by a Port State Control (PSC) Officer in the port of a Member State, as an additional way of determining whether the vessel is in compliance with the Convention. Standard A5.2.1 (Inspections in port) provides at paragraph 6:

> 'Where, following a more detailed inspection by an authorized officer, the ship is found not to conform to the requirements of this Convention and:
>
> (a) the conditions on board are clearly hazardous to the safety, health or security of seafarers; or
> (b) the non-conformity constitutes a serious or repeated breach of the requirements of this Convention (including seafarers' rights);
>
> the authorized officer shall take steps to ensure that the ship shall not proceed to sea until any non-conformities that fall within the scope of sub-paragraph (a) or (b) of this paragraph have been rectified, or until the authorized officer has accepted a plan of action to rectify such non-conformities and is satisfied that the plan will be implemented in an expeditious manner. If the ship is prevented from sailing, the authorized officer shall forthwith notify the flag State accordingly and invite a representative of the flag State to be present, if possible, requesting the flag State to reply within a prescribed deadline. The authorized officer shall also inform forth- with the appropriate shipowners' and seafarers' organizations in the port State in which the inspection was carried out.'

This system of enforcement and compliance, containing provisions for port state control also found in IMO Conventions, provides a powerful incentive, as non-conformity can result in ships being detained. It is important to note, however, that the necessary compliance certificates mentioned above are to be taken as *prima facie* evidence of compliance[60] by the Port Authorities in order to avoid undue delays. Accordingly, in principle, port state inspections are limited to inspection of these documents when dealing with Member State's vessels. A physical inspection of the vessel will be carried out only when the documents are not presented or the inspector believes that the documents are false, incomplete, or out of line with the actual condition of the vessel. Additionally, inspections will be carry out if the inspector believes that the ship has changed flag for the purpose of avoiding compliance with the Convention or where there has been a complaint made by a seafarer.

Due to the 'no more favourable treatment' provision, the Convention encourages fair competition, ensuring that port states treat ships of non-ratifying states in the same manner as ships of ratifying states during inspections.[61] Nevertheless, it does not seem wrong to assume that MLC certified vessels may have a small advantage during port inspections, considering that MLC's certificates can be considered '*prima facie*' evidence of compliance.

59 MLC, Standard A5.1.3.

60 It is worth mentioning that IMO Conventions, such as SOLAS, MARPOL and STCW, also provide for similar certificates of compliance.

61 MLC, Art. V(7).

Moreover, the Convention provides that Member States should cooperate whenever possible in the adoption of agreed guidelines on inspections policies, particularly those relating to the circumstances leading to the detention of the ship, in order to avoid undue delays, especially if caused by unnecessary detentions.[62]

Another novelty that the Convention brings, adding to its enforcement and compliance system, is that it also acknowledges that the welfare of seafarers is a responsibility of the labour-supplying State.[63] The Convention requires implementation of minimum standards in respect of the recruitment and placement of seafarers, and the social security protection of seafarers 'that are its nationals or are resident or are otherwise domiciled in its territory'. The MLC requires Contracting States to inspect and monitor recruitment agencies and instigate legal proceedings for breaches of licensing and other operational requirements. Every Member State shall enforce the terms of the Convention in relation to their labour-supplying responsibilities regardless of its status as maritime workforce supplier.[64]

5 The success of the Maritime Labour Convention

The Maritime Labour Convention is an undeniable success. Even before coming into force, the Convention was already considered to have made an overall positive contribution to international law and more specifically maritime law, especially when taking into consideration the capacity of the new Convention to operate as a global, comprehensive instrument with clear objectives and means of realization of such objectives, with the uneven application of maritime labour standards from one state to another reasonably expected to be remedied and finally with fair competition, which is in the interest of both shipowners and seafarers.[65] More recently, after its enforcement, the Convention has been recommended to 'be used as a model or source of inspiration for promoting decent work in other industries'.[66]

The MLC, as can be noted, includes a number of innovative features from both a structural and a broader international law perspective. From a drafting perspective, it offers a new format inspired by IMO instruments, essentially entailing a hierarchical regulatory approach with mandatory provisions and non-binding guidelines contained in a vertically integrated format. The Convention also permits national provisions implementing the rights and principles of the Convention in a manner different from those set out in the text so long as it is 'substantially equivalent' (Article VI (3) and (4)), having a flexible nature which encourages widespread ratification.

The creation of a Special Tripartite Committee under Article XIII to, among other things, carry out the simplified amendment process is another novel feature of the Convention. The Committee has already held three meetings where amendments have been proposed,

62 Ibid.

63 MLC, Reg. 5.3.

64 Julia Constantino Chagas Lessa, An Overview of the Maritime Labour Convention and its first years in force (2016) 22 *Journal of International Maritime Law* 387.

65 I. Christodoulou-Varotsi, 'Critical Review of the Consolidated Maritime Labour Convention (2006) of the International Labour Organization: Limitations and Perspectives' (2012) 43 *Journal of Maritime Law & Commerce* 467 at 489.

66 J. Whitlow and R. Subasinghe, The Maritime Labour Convention, 2006: A model for other industries? (2015) Vol. 7, Issue 1–2 *International Journal of Labour Research* 127.

discussed and accepted, with recommendations to Members being made, and has already scheduled its fourth meeting for April 2021.[67] Moreover, the committee can consult with Member States that do not have trade unions (where required by the Convention), not only allowing Member States with undeveloped industrial relations structures to ratify the Convention and ensure minimum protection for workers, but also promoting the core ILO values of tripartism and social dialogue.

As J. Whitlow and R. Subasinghe precisely stated:

> 'from an international law perspective, the MLC, 2006 can be considered a game changer. While still an international treaty binding sovereign States, its strength is that it effectively focuses on getting shipowners to change their attitude towards workers' rights. Although ratifying States are the primary target of compliance, the enforcement mechanisms are intended to influence non-State actors in the form of shipowners and ships themselves. Therefore, the primary pressure on flag States to ratify the MLC, 2006 and comply with it will ultimately come not from other governments or the ILO itself, but via the flag preferences of shipowners. The Convention's comprehensive enforcement mechanisms are crucial in this regard.'[68]

Therefore, despite some criticism regarding the weakness of the Convention,[69] the success of the Convention due to its special characteristics that led to the achievement of its ultimate goals and purposes is unquestionable. The Convention is undeniably a milestone to future international Conventions, but most importantly for maritime law instruments that often need to balance multiparty interests.

6 Concluding remarks

The MLC is without a doubt a 'game changer' in terms of international conventions, and most particularly maritime related one. The Convention's achievement as a codified guide of provisions regarding minimum welfare and standards for seafarers is undeniable. Furthermore, due to its flexible nature, which led the Convention to be ratified by no less than 91% of the world gross tonnage comprising 92 countries,[70] and enforcement system of compliance, the MLC can be said to have guaranteed that seafarers around the globe will have their minimum rights guaranteed. Finally, the frequent tripartite meeting guarantees the Convention upholds the interest of main ship industry stakeholders by constantly updating its text through amendments.

67 https://www.ilo.org/global/standards/maritime-labour-convention/events/WCMS_679152/lang—en/index.htm (visited 12 August 2019).

68 J. Whitlow and R. Subasinghe, The Maritime Labour Convention, 2006: A model for other industries? (2015) Vol.7, Issue 1–2 *International Journal of Labour Research* 125.

69 See for example: J.C. Chagas Lessa, MLC: Much Ado About Nothing? (2014) *European Transport Law Journal* 119–132 and O.O. Aguda, Maritime Labour Convention 2006: Implications for Seafarers after a Decade (2017) 8 *Nnamdi Azikiwe University Journal of International Law and Jurisprudence* 125.

70 https://www.ilo.org/dyn/normlex/en/f?p=1000:11300:0::NO::P11300_INSTRUMENT_ID:312331 (visited 12 August 2019).

PART II

CODIFICATION ISSUES IN TRANSPORT OF GOODS BY SEA

CHAPTER 9

The Rotterdam Rules and international trade

Accord or discord?

Professor Rhidian Thomas

1 Introduction

The United Nations Convention on Contracts for the International Carriage of Goods Wholly or Partly by Sea, more commonly alluded to as the Rotterdam Rules,[1] was adopted by the General Assembly of the United Nations in December 2008 and opened for signature at a conference held on 23 September 2009 at Rotterdam.[2] The proposed new Convention requires ratification or other mode of adoption by at least 20 states. To date there have been only four state ratifications, most significantly the ratification by Spain. For supporters of the Rules this must be a disappointment. This less than enthusiastic response may also suggest that the Rules to some degree or in particular regards are deficient and do not have a viable future. But whatever be their future the proposed Rules have stimulated lively debate.

The origin of the Rotterdam Rules can be traced to a call by UNCITRAL to interested organisations to develop proposals aimed at establishing a uniform law for the carriage of goods by sea. This invitation was accepted by the Comité Maritime International (CMI), which embarked on an extended period of consultation and deliberation which resulted in the formulation of draft proposals. These represented the starting point to the further deliberations by UNCITRAL over a period of some ten years and the drafting of the Rules in their final form.[3]

The underlying intention of the Rotterdam Rules is that they should replace the two existing versions of the Hague Rules of 1924 and 1968[4] and the later Hamburg Rules 1978,[5] and establish a single uniform international legal regime for the carriage of goods wholly or partly by sea. Much has been extracted from one or other of the preceding conventions, although not necessarily in identical terms, so that the new proposed convention is not wholly novel. Nonetheless, in many regards it is very different, even radically so, and may fairly be viewed as an attempt to establish a new and comprehensive legal foundation to the international carriage of goods by sea. The scale and ambition of the Rules

1 United Nations Convention on Contracts for the International Carriage of Goods Wholly or Partly by Sea (Rotterdam Rules) (New York, 2008).

2 General Assembly Resolution 63/122.

3 For an account of the history of the Rotterdam Rules, see M. Sturley, T. Fujita and G.J. Van Der Ziel, *The Rotterdam Rules* (Sweet & Maxwell 2011), Ch. I.

4 The Hague Rules as Amended by the Brussels Protocol 1968.

5 United Nations Convention on the Carriage of Goods by Sea (Hamburg, 1978).

are gargantuan, they swamp the preceding international conventions. It is also clear that the Rules are concerned with much more than the straightforward contractual relationship between carriers and shippers. It is in the nature of an international maritime and commercial code which extends to include multimodal transport with a sea leg, all transport documents and their electronic equivalents, transfer of contractual rights and matters relating to jurisdiction and arbitration.[6]

The Rotterdam Rules have many implications for international maritime trade. This is not surprising because goods carried by sea are invariably being transported in performance of an international sale contract and the attendant incidents of such contracts, such as insurance and trade finance. Rarely are goods simply in transit with shipper and consignee/receiver the same party. To the extent, therefore, that the Rotterdam Rules regulate contracts for the carriage of goods 'wholly or partly by sea', they have a role to play in traditional port-to-port trade and place-to-place multimodal trade with a sea leg. This is clearly illustrated, for example, by the standard formats of port-to-port CIF and FOB contracts, and place-to-place CPT and CIP contracts.[7]

One of the hallmarks of international maritime sales and trade is the dominant role played by transport and commercial documents. Shipping documents may be of crucial importance in providing evidence that the goods in transit correspond to the specifications in the sales contract, the manner in which the transit is being performed and further facilitate the ascertainment of the price and payment by the buyer.[8] Where the transport document is also a document of title it may be looked upon by the parties as the equivalent of the goods/cargo it records on its face and as a source of security in raising finance.[9] The transport document may also be the mechanism by which the benefit of the shipper's contract with the carrier is transferred to the buyer in circumstances when the buyer bears the transport risk.[10]

The Rotterdam Rules respond to the reality of their potential wider significance by giving considerable attention to the various relevant transport documents, their characteristics, content and legal and evidentiary significance. They will therefore often touch upon issues which are to the core of the contractual relationship between international sellers, buyers and financiers of commodities and goods transported wholly or partially by sea.

6 For Commentaries on the Rotterdam Rules, see G. Treitel, F.M. Reynolds, *Carver on Bills of Lading*, 4th edn (Sweet & Maxwell, 2017), Ch. 10; R. Thomas (ed.), *The Carriage of Goods by Sea under the Rotterdam Rules* (Lloyd's List 2010); M. Sturley, T. Fujita and G.J. Van Der Ziel, *The Rotterdam Rules* (Sweet & Maxwell 2011); R. Thomas (ed.), *A New Convention for the Carriage of Goods by Sea – The Rotterdam Rules* (Law Text Publishing 2009); Y. Baatz et al, *The Rotterdam Rules: A Practical Annotation* (Informa 2009); A. Von Ziegler, J. Schelin, S. Zunarelli (eds.), *The Rotterdam Rules 2008* (Wolters Kluwer 2009).

7 See generally, M.G. Bridge, *The International Sale of Goods* 3rd edn (Oxford University Press 2013), Chs 3 & 4; F. Lorenzon, Y. Baatz and D.M. Sassoon, *CIF and FOB Contracts* 6th edn (Sweet & Maxwell 2017), Parts II and III.

8 In international sales the price may be fixed as the market price on the date of the bill of lading, with payment to be made within a fixed period thereafter.

9 In the common law a negotiable bill of lading is recognised as a document of title, see *Lickbarrow v Mason* [1794] 5 Term Rep 683, *Sewell v Burdick* (1884) 13 Q.B.D. 159, *The Rafaela S* [2002] EWCA Civ 556; [2003] 2 Lloyd's Rep 113.

10 Most of these issues will be touched upon later in the text. For a comprehensive analysis, see G. Treitel, F.M. Reynolds, *Carver on Bills of Lading*, 4th edn (Sweet & Maxwell 2017).

In this chapter I discuss a number of provisions in the Rotterdam Rules which I have identified as having implications for international maritime trade and also identify one significant omission. I do not suggest that my list is exclusive.

2 Significance of transport documents

It has previously been suggested that maritime transport documents play a significant role in international trade contracts and trade finance arrangements, as in documentary credits.[11] What, therefore, the Rotterdam Rules have to say about maritime transport documents and their electronic counterparts is of considerable interest and potential importance.[12] The relevant provisions are set out primarily in Chapter 8, supplemented by the relevant definitions set out in Article 1.

Somewhat surprisingly, the Rotterdam Rules eschew the traditional vocabulary of international commerce with a negotiable bill of lading styled 'negotiable transport document', a straight bill of lading as a 'non-negotiable transport document that requires surrender' and a waybill as a 'non-negotiable transport document'.[13] The refusal to replicate the language of commerce appears to be indicative of an unfortunate anti-commercial perspective and ultimately it may also be unhelpful.

Much that is stipulated in Chapter 8, titled 'Transport documents and electronic transport records', will be familiar to those with experience of international trade. This includes the information to be included in the documentation, the legal effect of the documentation, the obligation or power to introduce qualifying statements and the evidentiary effect of the documentation as between carrier and shipper, and carrier and receiver.[14] The transfer of the contract evidenced by a negotiable transport document (negotiable bill of lading) is separately dealt with in Chapter 11.[15]

The law surrounding transport documentation in the context of international trade is particularly voluminous and in the present context I confine myself to two issues.

The first relates to the nature of a clean transport document in respect of which the Rotterdam Rules follow the general understanding. In international maritime trade it is predominantly the case that the seller must deliver to the buyer a clean negotiable bill of lading or other transport document.[16] The Rotterdam Rules address this issue in the following way. A transport document is required to contain a statement relating to the apparent

11 See generally M.G. Bridge, *The International Sale of Goods* 3rd edn (Oxford University Press 2013), Chs 3 & 4; J. Jack, A. Malek QC, D. Quest, *Jack: Documentary Credits* 4th edn (Tottel Publishing 2009).

12 The Rotterdam Rules provide for electronic transport documents which are treated as equivalent to their paper counterparts and labelled electronic transport records, see Chapter 3 of the Rules. In this chapter, in the interest of clarity, reference will be made predominantly to traditional paper documents but the reader should be aware that throughout the reference to a transport document includes its electronic counterpart: see generally, M. Goldby, 'Electronic alternatives to transport documents: A framework for future development?' in R. Thomas (ed.), *A New Convention for the Carriage of Goods by Sea – The Rotterdam Rules* (Law Text Publishing 2009), Ch. 9.

13 Art. 1(15) and (16), Ch. 9, Arts 45–47.

14 For a full analysis of this aspect of the Rotterdam Rules, see R. Williams, 'Transport Documentation – The New Approach', Ch. 8 in R. Thomas (ed.), *A New Convention for the Carriage of Goods by Sea – The Rotterdam Rules* (Law Text Publishing 2009).

15 See *infra* for a comment on this provision.

16 See, M.G. Bridge, *The International Sale of Goods* 3rd edn, 4.90–4.93 (Oxford University Press 2013); J. Jack, A. Malek QC, D. Quest, *Jack: Documentary Credits* 4th edn (Tottel Publishing 2009).

order and condition of the goods at the time the carrier received them for carriage.[17] If such a statement is absent the document is deemed to contain a statement that the goods were received in apparent good order and condition.[18] Most transport documents currently in use in trade contain a printed statement to this effect.[19]

The statement as to the order and condition of the goods is based on an assessment made by and incorporated in the transport document by the carrier on the basis of a 'reasonable external inspection of the goods as packaged' at the time of delivery and any additional inspection conducted by the carrier.[20] Of course, if the inspection reveals a flaw or defect or deficiency this must be stated in the document, in which case the document may be considered as 'claused' and not a clean document. As such it is capable of being rejected by the buyer.[21]

The evidentiary significance of a clean transport document is that it is prima facie evidence of the condition of the goods received by the carrier.[22] In the event that the transport document is a negotiable bill of lading or a straight bill of lading, evidence to the contrary is not permitted providing the transferee received the document in good faith[23]. The same is the case when the document is a waybill[24].

In view of the bias detectable in the Rotterdam Rules towards containerised transport it is surprising that no express provision has been made indicating how this obligation is to be discharged in the case of containerised cargo.[25] Unless the carrier has examined the contents of the container all that is visible on a reasonable external inspection is the container, which may qualify as packaging, but nonetheless it remains open to the carrier to declare that the goods are shipped in apparent good order and condition. The power to qualify under Article 40 does not appear to apply in these circumstances.[26] Obviously this will not be helpful to buyers. Different considerations would apply if the container was visibly damaged or displaying evidence that the contents might be damaged, or if the container had been stuffed by the carrier or its contents examined.

The second issue relates to the dating of the transport document. This information is of use because it will indicate whether the contract of sale is being performed within the agreed terms and may also be a mechanism to determine the price to be paid for the goods, as where the price is fixed by reference to the market price on the date the document is issued.[27] There has existed a degree of confusion about whether the date should relate to the date the document is issued or the date the goods are shipped on board or received for shipment. In principle it is the latter and the position is helped in contemporary practice by the requirement in some transport documents that both dates be included.[28]

---

17 Art. 36.2(a).

18 Art. 39.3.

19 E.g. Congenbill (2016), Conlinebill (2016).

20 Art. 36.4.

21 For the concept of a 'claused' bill of lading in English law, see *The Boukadoura* [1989] 1 Lloyd's Rep 393. Under the UCP 600, Art 27, a clean transport document is defined as 'one bearing no clause or notation expressly declaring a defective condition of the goods or their packaging'.

22 Art. 41(a).

23 Art. 41(b).

24 Art. 41(c)(iii).

25 Art. 40 does not appear to apply to the topic under consideration.

26 Ibid.

27 See M.G. Bridge, *Benjamin Sale of Goods,* 7th edn, 2–045 (Sweet & Maxwell, 2006).

28 This issue is discussed in Ch. Debattista, *Bills of Lading in Export Trade*, 3rd edn (Tottel Publishing, 2009), 9.5 *et seq*.

The Rotterdam Rules, very generally, oblige the carrier to indicate the date the goods were received or on which the goods were loaded on board or on which the transport document was issued.[29] The problem with this provision is that the indications are all in the alternative and therefore it does not provide a solution to the potential problems previously identified. There is, however, a default position. If the significance of the date is not indicated in a shipped transport document, the date is deemed to be the date of shipment. In the case of a received for shipment document, it is deemed to be the date the goods were received by the carrier.[30] This qualification assists a little but greater decisiveness would have been helpful.

3 Position of FOB sellers

The Rotterdam Rules draw a distinction between shippers and documentary shippers and impose on documentary shippers the same obligations as are borne by shippers.[31]

The relevant convention provisions are as:

> Article 1 provides –
>
> 8. 'Shipper' means a person that enters into a contract of carriage with a carrier.
> 9. 'Documentary shipper' means a person, other than the shipper, that accepts to be named as 'shipper' in the transport document or electronic transport record.
>
> Article 33 provides –
>
> 1. A documentary shipper is subject to the obligations and liabilities imposed on the shipper pursuant to this chapter and pursuant to article 55, and is entitled to the shipper's rights and defences provided by this chapter and chapter 13.
> 2. Paragraph 1 of this article does not affect the obligations, liabilities, rights or defences of the shipper.

The Rotterdam Rules on their face suggest the following. 'Shipper' alludes to the contractual shipper who by definition is in a contractual relationship with the carrier, on the terms set out in the Rotterdam Rules. The documentary shipper is not in a contractual relationship with the carrier but, nonetheless, consents to be named as shipper in the transport document or electronic transport record. This renders him subject to the obligations of the contractual carrier as set out in the Rotterdam Rules. In other words, by operation of law rather than contract he is placed in the same position as the contractual carrier. The existence of a documentary shipper, however, does not affect the contractual obligations of the contractual shipper. In the result, contractual and documentary shipper stand in a legal relationship with the carrier on similar terms.

On delivery of the goods to the carrier or performing party the shipper or, with the shipper's consent, the documentary shipper is entitled to demand delivery of a transport document.[32] In either situation if the documentary shipper 'accepts to be named as

29 Art. 36.2(c).

30 Art. 39.2.

31 These are set out mainly in Ch. 7 of the Rotterdam Rules.

32 Art. 35.

shipper'[33] he assumes the same obligations and liabilities under the Rotterdam Rules as the contractual shipper.[34] The words 'accepts to be named' in the transport document are not further defined or explained and their meaning is open to debate. The question of consent will not necessarily be attended to in advance in the contracting/booking process or during the preparation of the transport document. It may have to be declared quickly at the time of shipment. The agreement to be named as shipper in the appropriate box in the transport document would in all likelihood be strong *prima facie* evidence of consent.

The primary purpose of Article 33, it would appear, is to impose convention obligations and liabilities on FOB sellers who are not viewed as shippers in the contractual sense but documentary shippers, if named as shipper in the transport document.[35] This is not necessarily an accurate premise and the supporting analysis is suspect. It fails to appreciate the fluid nature of FOB contracts and the range of possible legal and commercial positions that may be occupied by FOB sellers. These questions may of course be analysed differently in different legal systems and the discussion below follows the analysis in English law.

The standard view of a FOB sale is that the buyer contracts for collection and carriage, and the seller delivers the goods to the carrying ship at the load port in pursuance of his contractual obligations under the sale contract.[36] This raises questions relating to the precise status of the seller and the seller's legal relationship with the carrying vessel. There are many possible variations to what may be considered the standard model. The seller may ship the goods acting as agent of the buyer. He may have engaged the carrying ship as agent for the buyer or engaged the ship nominated by the buyer as agent. In so acting, the position of the FOB seller with regard to the transport document issued on shipment may again vary significantly. The seller may receive a negotiable bill of lading which names the buyer as shipper, which the seller subsequently transfers to the buyer. Alternatively, the negotiable bill may name the FOB seller as shipper, in which case the seller negotiates the bill to the buyer. It is also possible that the seller receives a mate's receipt which is transferred to the buyer who then presents it to the carrier in return for a bill of lading naming the buyer as shipper. There may be parallel transactions, appropriately adjusted, if a straight bill of lading or waybill has been obtained by the FOB seller.[37]

Where the FOB sale relates to containerised goods it is probable that the seller will book the space and receive the transport document in his own name. If a negotiable bill of lading, it will be endorsed to the buyer. If a straight bill of lading or waybill, it will be simply delivered to the buyer. In the container trade waybills appear to be the most favoured transport document. In this kind of case the strong likelihood is that the FOB seller enters into the

33 Art. 1(9).

34 Art. 33.1.

35 M. Sturley, T. Fujita and G.J. Van Der Ziel, *The Rotterdam Rules* (Sweet & Maxwell, 2011), 6.062–6.067.

36 Under INCOTERMS FOB (2010) the broad scheme is that the buyer contracts at his own expense for the carriage of the goods except where the contract of carriage is made by the seller. The seller is not obliged to make a contract of carriage but may do so if requested by the buyer or if consistent with commercial practice, the contract being on usual terms and at the buyer's risk and expense Nonetheless the seller may decline to make a contract of carriage and in that event is obliged to promptly inform the buyer.

37 See generally M.G. Bridge, *The International Sale of Goods* 3rd edn (Oxford University Press 2013), Ch. 3.

contract of carriage, which is subsequently transferred to the buyer by simple transfer.[38] It is also possible that the shipment is to be arranged by a freight forwarder who adopts an in-house transport document, which may raise further questions.

In general under English law there is a contractual relationship between the FOB seller and carrying ship. If not express, a contract arises by implication with regard to the loading of the ship, with the contract based on the terms of the transport document issued or contemplated to the extent that they apply to the loading process. The consensual nature of the loading process and commercial necessity support the implication of such a contract.[39]

It follows that in many instances a FOB seller will be a 'shipper' within the meaning of the Rotterdam Rules, making it therefore unwise to equate generally FOB sellers with 'documentary shippers'. In each case the precise status of the FOB seller will have to be carefully analysed.

There are, however, further considerations. Under the Rotterdam Rules a shipper is a party who 'enters into a contract of carriage with the carrier'.[40] While Art 33 does not transfer the contract or create a concurrent contract, it provides that as a matter of law the documentary shipper is subject to the same obligations, liabilities and rights as shippers as specified in Chapters 7 and 13, and Art. 55. Under English law, in some cases a FOB seller may do no more (expressly or impliedly) than enter into a contract to load the ship.[41] This is a much more limited contractual engagement than the legal regime proposed by the Rotterdam Rules. In this position the FOB seller may not even be a contractual shipper as he is not entering into a contract of carriage, or even a documentary shipper.

There is a further question whether a named seller who is also identified 'as agent' in the transport document can be considered a shipper, whether contractual or documentary. The question probably remains relevant whether or not the principal is named. The Rotterdam Rules offer no solution to this unexceptional possibility. It may be postulated that a named shipper acting as agent, in the absence of the assumption of personal responsibility, would not be a contractual shipper but would not necessarily be precluded from being identified as a documentary shipper. There is, however, the surviving question whether a party who is declared to be acting 'as agent' is consenting to be named a shipper within the meaning of Art. 33.

This brief account will be sufficient to indicate that the legal status of a FOB seller in English law is various and complex. Consequently the precise potential impact of Art. 33 is difficult to assess with precision, with matters made all the more challenging by the ambiguity inherent in the article. In the final analysis the possible impact may vary with the precise way the FOB sale contract is drafted and construed. Hopefully the outcome, whatever form it may take, will not disturb the established practices of international trade by unreasonably increasing the potential responsibilities and liabilities of FOB sellers.

38 In English law the transfer of the contract is facilitated by the Carriage of Goods Act 1992, discussed *infra*.

39 *Pyrene Co Ltd v Scindia Navigation Co Ltd* [1954] 2 QB 402.

40 Art. 1.8.

41 Art. 1.8.

4 Delivery of goods against presentation of negotiable and straight bills of lading – the presentation rule

The express or implied basis of a contract of carriage of goods by sea which contemplates the issue of a bill of lading is that delivery will only be made against presentation of the bill of lading in question.[42] This is particularly the case where the bill of lading is negotiable, but equally the case when the bill is a straight bill of lading, although in this circumstance the reasons for the rule are less convincing.[43] Where a waybill is issued the transport document is of less relevance and delivery may be to the designated consignee.

This obligation is usually referred to as the presentation rule and it is probably the case that its precise application may vary in different jurisdictions. Where the rule is broken and as a consequence the carrier misdelivers the cargo, the carrier may be liable for breach of contract and/or breach of duty in bailment/tort, with the level of compensation the value of the goods lost.[44] P&I Clubs follow the presentation rule with unyielding firmness and do not provide cover for liability arising from breach of the rule.[45]

The Rotterdam Rules apply the presentation rules with similar firmness, in relation to both negotiable and straight bills of lading. In each case the carrier 'shall' deliver the goods on surrender of the transport document and 'shall' refuse delivery if the transport document is not surrendered.[46] If either transport document has been issued in sets of two or more originals only one original need be surrendered.[47]

The presentation rule is accompanied by a duty of care on the part of the carrier. Under the Rotterdam Rules the consignee or holder must 'properly identify itself' and if this duty is not sufficiently discharged the carrier 'may' refuse delivery.[48] A similar duty exists in the common law but it is difficult to formulate authoritatively the applicable standard of care. The broad theme appears to be that the carrier must act honestly and in good faith. Consequently, if the carrier knows or has reason to suspect that the presenter of the bill may not be the person with immediate right to possession or that there is another party with a superior right, delivery must be refused.[49]

In adopting this uncompromising approach the Rotterdam Rules are turning a blind eye to the realities of commercial practice, particularly in relation to negotiable bills of lading. They are, when all is said and done, documents and with their potential legal significance, particularly as documents of title, not always appreciated by those who handle them. As with documents generally they may be destroyed or go astray or be mishandled. It is frequently the case that the bill of lading is not available at the port of discharge, and this appears to be so frequently the case that it cannot be described as an exceptional occurrence. The reasons for this may be operational. The bill of lading may be stuck somewhere in the trading or banking chain, or issued long after the shipment date. It may even be

42 *The Sormovskiy 3068* [1994] 2 Lloyd's Rep 206; *The Motis* [2000] 1 Lloyd's Rep 211 (CA).

43 *The Rafaela S* [2003] 2 Lloyd's Rep 113 (CA).

44 See R. Aikens, R. Lord, M. Bools, *Bills of Lading*, 2nd edn (Informa Law from Routledge, 2016), Ch. 13.

45 E.g. North P&I Rules 2017–18, Rule 19(17)(D)(iii).

46 Arts 46 and 47.1.

47 Arts 46(a) 47(c). See also *infra*.

48 Arts 45–47.

49 *East West Corpn v DK.B.SAF 1912 A/S* [2003] QB 1509, 1537, [2003] 1 Lloyd's Rep 239, 257 [60] *per* Mance LJ.

that the bill has yet to be issued. In some trades the carrying distance is short and covered quickly so that the cargo arrives at its destination and may even have been traded before the shipment documentation has been issued.

The unavailability of the bill of lading at the port of discharge is more than a mere inconvenience to the carrier. Delay in discharging cargo may have drastic financial implications for carriers who invariably will have to bear the cost of the delay, which may be substantial. Additionally, carriers may be exposed to legal liabilities to third parties and at risk of seeing future contractual engagements validly cancelled.[50] In practice the problems about delivery against presentation of documents are resolved by reference to letters of indemnity.[51]

In English law it is possible to identify a debate as to whether the presentation rule is absolute or qualified.[52] There are judicial dicta favouring both sides of the debate. The weight of authority favours the traditional view, but there are judicial dicta which suggest that an accommodation must be made to address contingencies, as when the bill has been lost or destroyed or any similar situation has arisen, and it is possible to give a 'reasonable explanation' to account for the absence of the bill. Mr Justice Clarke (as he then was) considered that the master was justified in giving delivery without presentation of the bill of lading if 'it is proved to his reasonable satisfaction both that the person seeking delivery of the goods is entitled to possession and what has become of the bills of lading'.[53] This qualification to the rule is intentionally very narrowly and tightly drawn so that the risk of mis-delivery is virtually erased. It represents a realistic and practical approach, but nonetheless the approach was not followed in a subsequent decision of the Court of Appeal.[54]

It is disappointing that the Rotterdam Rules have failed to confront the realities of contemporary maritime commerce and recognise a limited qualification to the traditional presentation rule. If the transport document is not available at the port of discharge and this is capable of being convincingly explained so that the risk of misdelivery is virtually excluded, it is difficult to comprehend why the carrier should not be justified in giving delivery. This would represent a practical and supportable remedy, also recognising that such a position could also be achieved by express contract.[55] In the event of misdelivery it would provide protection to the carrier in contract but not necessarily for breach of a non-contractual duty in tort or bailment.

In practice the problems identified above are usually resolved by resort to a letter of indemnity.[56] This may of itself be some evidence of the impracticality of the presentation rule as currently applied and also provide a possible reason for the absence of any enthusiasm to reform the rule.

---

50 A future fixture of a charterparty will usually contain a cancellation clause.

51 Considered *infra*.

52 See *Motis Exports Ltd v Dampskibsselskabet AF 1912 Aktieselskab* [1999] 1 Lloyd's Rep 837, [2000] 1 Lloyd's Rep 211(CA).

53 *The Sormovskiy 3068* [1994] 2 Lloyd's Rep 266, 274.

54 *Motis Exports Ltd v Dampskibsselskabet AF 1912 Aktieselskab* [1999] 1 Lloyd's Rep 837; [2000] 1 Lloyd's Rep 211(CA).

55 Art. 47.2(a) recognises that a negotiable bill of lading may expressly provide that delivery may be given without presentation of the relevant bill.

56 Considered *infra*.

5 Bills of lading – multiple originals

It is one of the peculiarities of bills of lading that they are issued in sets with each bill in the set an original and, under the common law, a distinct document of title.[57] It is usual for the number of original bills issued to be stated on the face of the bill, which is useful information for a person about to trade on the basis of the bill. The reasons for this practice are far from clear and it is not easy to justify the practice in modern conditions. Nonetheless, the practice continues and also extends to straight bills of lading.[58]

The practice, particularly in relation to negotiable bills of lading, is a potential boon to wrongdoers because it facilitates fraud. It enables the holder of a set of negotiable bills of lading to sell the goods recorded on the face of the bill to as many individual buyers as there are original bills in the set. A buyer presented with a bill has no obvious means of knowing about previous or concurrent sale transactions on the basis of other bills in the set. Similarly it enables a holder to fraudulently induce a bank to advance funds against the presumed security of a bill of lading, with the bank unware that other bills in the set have been negotiated to other buyers and to other banks as security for finance.[59]

The potential problems are fully appreciated, but the practice of issuing bills of lading in sets continues. There is no system of registration which might provide protection for potential buyers and lenders, and no other method by which buyers and lenders may be given notice of previous dealings.[60] Although the opportunities for fraud are significant it has to be conceded that the amount of fraud that comes to public notice is very limited.

It is the case under the current law and practice that once a bill has been 'accomplished the others shall be void', a form of words which appears in all bills. Its object is to render the other bills in the set devoid of any legal significance, and certainly not documents of title. They are reduced to bland paper. It is, nonetheless, an ineffective and virtually useless source of protection. How is a buyer or bank to know that a bill presented has been rendered void because at an earlier point in time another bill in the same set has been the subject of a commercial or financial transaction and in that sense accomplished?

The Rotterdam Rules endorse the present practice and make no attempt to protect against the risk of fraud. They recognise that negotiable bills of lading may be issued in sets and require that the number shall be stated in the bill.[61] The Rotterdam Rules also affirm that a carrier may give delivery against the presentation of a single negotiable bill subject to the protection that thereafter 'the other originals cease to have any effect or validity'.[62] The same principles apply to straight bills of lading.[63]

The risk here identified can be avoided by contractually requiring presentation of the full set of bills. This is frequently a requirement in international sale contracts and there is nothing to preclude such a provision being introduced in contracts of carriage. The difficulty with this protective remedy is that in practice it may be difficult, if not impossible,

57 See, R. Aikens, R. Lord, M. Bools, *Bills of Lading*, 2nd edn (Informa Law from Routledge, 2016), at 3.34–3.35.

58 As recognised in the Rotterdam Rules at Art 46(a).

59 See *Barber v Meyerstein* (1870) LR 4 HL 317.

60 For judicial criticism of the practice, see *Glyn Mills v East and West India Dock Co* (1882) 7 App Cas 591.

61 Art 36.2(d).

62 Art 47.1(c).

63 Art 46(a).

to comply with the obligation because a full set may not be accessible to the relevant party. If the presentation of a single bill of lading can be troublesome in practice, it may be anticipated that the difficulties multiply when a full set must be presented. In practice these problems are again usually resolved by resort to letters of indemnity.[64]

It is suggested that the Rotterdam Rules have missed the opportunity to refashion the law and practice so as to avoid the dangers associated with bills of lading issued in sets. This could have been achieved by declaring that one is to be an original and all others copies. Such a development would not have had any noticeable adverse impact on the practice of international trade and would have been a forward step to reducing the opportunities for fraud.

6 Right of control

Chapter 10 of the Rotterdam Rules, titled 'Rights of controlling party', is concerned with the 'right of control' in connection with the contract of carriage of goods by sea.[65] This is presented as a distinct transferrable power[66] and defined at length, with the power vested in the controlling party and exercisable only during the period of responsibility of the carrier.[67] The degree of attention given to this subject appears disproportionate when compared with the relative unimportance of the concept in the modern law.[68]

The right of control is defined as a right to (i) give or modify instructions in respect of the goods that do not constitute a variation of the contract of carriage; (ii) obtain delivery of the goods at a scheduled port of call or, in respect of inland carriage, any place en route; and (iii) replace the consignee by any person including the controlling party.[69] Who initially enjoys the right and how it may be transferred will depend on the nature of the transport document.[70] In the case of a straight bill it is transferred to the consignee with the transfer of the document.[71] With regard to a negotiable bill, the right is vested in the initial or subsequent holder.[72] In each case the transfer is effected by transfer of the transport document or all the transport documents if issued in a set.[73]

The carrier is obliged to comply if the instruction is valid, can be reasonably executed when communicated to the carrier and without interfering with the normal operations of the carrier, including its delivery practices.[74] In return, the controlling party is obliged to

64 Discussed, *infra*.

65 See G.J. van der Ziel, 'Delivery of the goods, rights of the controlling party and transfer of rights', ch.10 in R. Thomas (ed.), *A New Convention for the Carriage of Goods by Sea – The Rotterdam Rules* (Law Text Publishing 2009).

66 Art. 51.

67 Arts 10.2 & 12.

68 The concept of a right to control has hardly brushed the outer skin of the common law. For a rare reference see, G. Treitel, F.M. Reynolds, *Carver on Bills of Lading*, 4th edn (Sweet & Maxwell 2017), ch. 10, paras 1-022–1-026, under the title 'Seller's Right to Redirect Goods'.

69 Art. 50.

70 Art. 51.

71 Art. 51.2(a).

72 Art. 52.3(a)–(b).

73 Arts 51.2(a) and .3(b).

74 Art. 52 (1).

reimburse expenses arising, give an indemnity in respect of third-party liabilities, or may be required to provide security for the same.[75]

There are also procedural conditions to be satisfied. The controlling party must properly identify himself and where the transfer of the right has been effected by transfer of transport document(s), the document(s) must also be produced.[76]

It is important to bear in mind that the right of control is embedded in the contract of carriage. It permits variations to the performance of that contract: it does not effect a contractual variation. This is made explicit in connection to the power to give instructions relating to the goods.[77]

For obvious practical reasons it is improbable that the right of control will have any application to the carriage of bulk dry and liquid cargoes. The right appears to be tailored to container transport, and even then it is likely to be applicable only in exceptional circumstances.

The provisions appear to ignore the obvious fact that carriage of goods by sea is rarely about transport simpliciter, with only shipper and carrier directly involved. As previously stated, cargo is predominantly in transit subject to the terms of a contract of sale, and may even be traded when in transit. The consignee may be a buyer or a first or subsequent buyer in a chain of sale contracts. In this circumstance the buyer in whatever capacity, beyond the contract of sale, may come into a contractual relationship with the carrier with regard to the contract of carriage. The carrier may also be operating under the terms of a charterparty, introducing yet a further contractual relationship, and the transport documents may have been used to provide security for trade finance.

The carrier is obliged to comply with an instruction only if it can be 'reasonably executed' when received and which 'does not interfere with the normal operations of the carrier'. In the world of contemporary international maritime trade it would be rare that a unilateral instruction relating to a change of the port of discharge or to the identity of the consignee could be complied with without placing the carrier at risk of being in breach of one or more of the contracts identified above. A carrier would be understandably reluctant to accept any instruction which placed him in breach of any related contract, and where such a risk existed it would surely be unreasonable for the carrier to comply with it. It is suggested that he would be justified in refusing on the grounds stated in the Rotterdam Rules.

One express right is to take delivery of the cargo at 'a scheduled port of call' or 'a place en route' in the case of land carriage. Quite clearly this relates to container carriage and establishes the right to take delivery at an intermediate scheduled port. Taking into account the way container vessels are loaded so as to ensure safety and efficient management of discharge at scheduled ports of call, it would seem highly unlikely that the carrier would contemplate or be in a position to assent to changing the storage and discharging plan, given the disruption and cost it would cause. Only in exceptional circumstances would such discharge be possible and reasonable to assent to. Discharge at an alternative place en route on land might be more possible to contemplate.

75 Art. 52.(2) and (3).

76 Art. 51.2(b) and .3(c).

77 Art. 50.1(a).

The right to control is an incident of the contract of carriage but a party may seek to exercise it in performance of a right or power under or relating to the contract of sale. An example would be where a contract of sale is repudiated during the course of the transit. To avoid the risk of the goods being delivered to the buyer, the seller may instruct the carrier to discharge the goods at an intermediate port or to deliver to a new consignee (which may be the seller) at the discharge port. Another example would be where goods are shipped by a seller to a buyer for delivery at a named port of destination under the terms of a way-bill, with the seller retaining the right of control. The buyer thereafter sells the goods to an on-buyer for delivery at the same port of destination. In order to discharge his delivery obligation, the buyer may request his seller to instruct the carrier to deliver to the on-buyer as the new consignee. Alternatively, the seller may transfer the right of control to the buyer who then instructs the carrier to give delivery to the on-buyer.[78]

The chapter in the Rotterdam Rules dealing with the right of control creates difficulties because it appears to be both dated and largely irrelevant. It is difficult to understand how the extensive provisions fit into the pattern of contemporary maritime trade. It again appears to be aiming more towards container transport, as evidenced by the reference to 'scheduled port of call', but there continue to be difficulties even in this context. In practice parties may elect, to the extent possible, to negotiate a variation of the contract of carriage rather than rely on the imprecise right of control. But whatever the reservations, the controlling party has been elevated to occupy a significant position in the regime of the Rotterdam Rules.[79]

7 Transfer of contractual rights

Goods carried by sea (cargo) are more often than not being transported in pursuance of an international sale contract, under which the buyer assumes the risk in the goods from the time of shipment. As a consequence the buyer may seek the benefit of the seller/shipper's contract with the carrier as protection for loss or damage in the course of transit. This may be in parallel with the protection of an insurance policy also obtained by the seller/shipper for the benefit of the buyer.[80] This position is very different from carriage per se, to which only the shipper and carrier are parties. In this case the shipper relies on the contract of carriage and any insurance he has obtained for his own benefit to obtain compensation for loss or damage to the goods in transit.

Precisely how in these circumstances rights under the contract of carriage are transferred to the buyer may vary in different legal systems. This question has caused serious difficulties in the common law because of its commitment to the doctrine of privity of contract. The position is currently governed by the Carriage of Goods by Sea Act 1992, which has streamlined and modernised the law, but not freed it from difficulty.[81]

78 Art. 51.1.

79 Art. 55.

80 This is the case under an international shipment contract, such as the CIF contract and certain forms of FOB contract.

81 For an account of the development of English law and COGSA 1992, see G. Treitel, F.M. Reynolds, *Carver on Bills of Lading*, 4th edn (Sweet & Maxwell 2017), Ch.5.

The Rotterdam Rules, by contrast to the preceding international conventions which did not reach out this far, make provision for the transfer of contractual rights in Chapter 11. This provides yet further evidence of the remarkable ambition of the Rotterdam Rules, their readiness to look beyond the precise axis of the contract of carriage of goods wholly or partly by sea.

Under the Rotterdam Rules the transfer of contractual rights and obligations is dealt with separately, following the pattern of COGSA 92. Article 57 relates to rights and Art 58 to liabilities. Incomprehensibly, the articles apply only to negotiable transport documents (negotiable bills of lading), a fact that defies commercial logic. The risk borne by a buyer under a shipment sale contract is the same whatever the transport document, whether it is a negotiable or straight bill of lading or a waybill, and the need for contractual protection exists in all instances. The buyer is not always in a position to control the precise transport document to be delivered. The choice may have been vested in the seller, and the seller in turn may have given the matter little consideration. Under the Rotterdam Rules, therefore, the contractual protection of the buyer is capable of being in the nature of a lottery. Adoption of this part of the Rotterdam Rules would also result in dual legal regimes being applicable to the transfer of contractual rights. If the transport document is a negotiable bill of lading the Rotterdam Rules apply: if is a straight bill of lading or waybill or any other kind of transport document the applicable national legal system applies. This would clearly not be a satisfactory position.

By contrast, COGSA 92 applies to all three major categories of transport documents, identified above.

Under Art. 57.1 contractual rights are transferred with the negotiation of the bill, which may be effected by endorsement and transfer or simply by transfer depending on the nature of the bill.[82] This is to connect the transfer of contractual rights with the negotiability of the bill of lading, and does so without any further restriction. There is, for example, no restriction that the issue and negotiation be in the context of a commercial or financial transaction. This is a loose approach and also potentially dangerous because it promotes speculation on negotiable bills independently of any commercial or financial interest, based on the value of bills as giving a right to receive cargo.

By contrast, under COGSA 92 the primary rule, to which there are exceptions, is that the lawful holder of a negotiable bill of lading in whom contractual rights are vested is a person who becomes holder in pursuance of a contractual or other arrangement relating to the goods and at a time when the holder thereby enjoyed the right to possession of the goods to which the bill relates.[83]

As for liabilities, Art. 58 provides that the holder of the bill assumes the liabilities only if he asserts a right under the contract.[84] Otherwise, the holder is not under any liability.[85] Again, the liabilities are those arising out of the contract evidenced on the face of the bill.

The Article does not attempt to elaborate the meaning of what it is to assert a right under the contract. It only indicates that to change the form of the bill or the negotiation of the bill

82 Art. 57.2 provides for the transfer of rights in connection with negotiable electronic transport records.

83 Section 2(1) and (2).

84 Art. 58.2.

85 Art. 58.1.

is not to be regarded as the assertion of a right.[86] This is an unfortunate omission because, as the experience under COGSA 92 has shown, many issues may arise in connection with the concept of making a claim under the contract.[87]

The underlying principle is that a transferee cannot take the benefit of a contract without at the same time assuming the obligations and potential liabilities. This is a profoundly just maxim: it is also very practical. It provides a legal position likely to find favour with financiers of international trade who resist becoming involved in the commercial dealings of borrowers. To provide finance on the security of a negotiable bill of lading as a document of title does not without more involve the assumption of commercial risks.

It is inevitable that common lawyers should be inclined to compare the provisions in the Rotterdam Rules with COGSA 92. Although both function on the basis of the division between rights and liabilities, there are many significant differences. COGSA 92 is a much more comprehensive and technical legal provision, revealing an awareness of the multiple issues that may arise. It is also more commercially oriented. The brief provisions in the Rotterdam Rules are inadequate and fail to appreciate the legal issues and difficulties.

8 Letters of indemnity – why are they absent?

A reference to letters of indemnity (LOIs) has already been made in the preceding discussion and it is clear that they have a very important role to play in international maritime commerce. Most of the difficulties surrounding transport documents and the carriage of cargo are resolved in practice by agreement to an appropriate letter of indemnity. They can be fairly perceived as the lubricant which ensures that the maritime system of trade actually works in practice. It may, therefore, be questioned why no reference is made to them in the Rotterdam Rules, which, consistent with the preceding international conventions, avoids them completely. But it may be questioned whether the omission continues to be justified.

Although not innately maritime in their legal nature, letters of indemnity occupy a prominent position in maritime commerce. Their wide adoption also gives some support to the argument that certain of the rules applicable to maritime trade, some previously considered, are impractical and call for reconsideration. Nonetheless, their availability and acceptance offer advantage to commercial parties: the security ensures that commercial operations continue without interruption and in the event that a breach of contract or duty is established the party liable has the protection of the security.

Letters of indemnity may be adopted in myriad different circumstances. To enumerate a few: when cargo is being shipped a question may arise whether the bill of lading or other transport document should be claused.[88] To facilitate matters the carrier may agree to issue a clean bill of lading if the shipper provides a letter of indemnity as protection in the event of any future liability. When a bill of lading is not available at the port or place of discharge, the owner may agree to deliver the cargo against a letter of indemnity provided by the consignee and/or another. The carrier may agree to deliver cargo at a port/place other than

86 Art. 58.3.

87 In COGSA 1982, section 3(1), conduct which triggers liabilities is defined in some detail, but nonetheless the question has attracted considerable litigation. See, G. Treitel, F.M. Reynolds, *Carver on Bills of Lading*, 4th edn (Sweet & Maxwell 2017), 5–091–5–112.

88 Considered *supra*.

the originally agreed port/place, but only if a letter of indemnity is agreed. When a seller is not in a position to deliver to his buyer all the bills of lading in an issued set, the buyer may agree to accept the proffered bills and pay the purchase price provided his position is protected by an appropriate letter of indemnity.

P&I Clubs apply the rules relating to bills of lading very rigidly and do not provide cover for liabilities which arise from any departure from what may be regarded as the standard rules relating to transport documents. Thus, for example, cover is not provided for liability arising from delivery of cargo without presentation of the relevant bill of lading, or at a port other than the port specified in the bill. Yet, in recognition of the commercial realities that confront their members, principally shipowners, they have produced standard form letters of indemnity which may be adopted by their members.[89] At the same time it is emphasised that the use of these standard formats is recommended only and not obligatory. The Clubs do not accept any liabilities arising from their adoption, nor does their availability indicate an acceptance of the insurance risk.

Notwithstanding their wide usage, letters of indemnity are often much misunderstood by parties in maritime commerce. It is consequently disappointing that the Rotterdam Rules fail to give recognition to the important function they perform and at the same time deliver a useful educational function.

9 Concluding remarks

How is the question raised in the title of this chapter to be answered? I think with a substantial degree of scepticism. The Rotterdam Rules lack the quality of commercialism. They abandon the traditional language of commerce in favour of arid terminology. Their appreciation of the potential impact of the Rotterdam Rules on the wider body of international trade that takes place around the axis of carriage of goods by sea is questionable. To the extent that there is a clear sense of commercial direction it is towards the container trade, which is far too narrow. There is a much broader hinterland. They appear to turn a blind eye to the way maritime trade actually works, the problems faced and how the difficulties are managed so as to minimise disruption. Consequently they endorse historical rules which struggle for justification in the context of contemporary trade and refuse to raise the banner of reform. They also embody strange allocations of effort, giving significant attention to an insignificant subject, the 'right to control', and are virtually dismissive of a crucially important subject, the transfer of contractual rights. The international commercial community should view them warily.

89 The Standard Form Letters of Indemnity are set out in the Rule Books of Clubs which are members of the International Group of Protection and Indemnity Clubs.

CHAPTER 10

Sea transport documents in banks' hands – bridging the UCP with commercial shipping law

Dr Jingbo Zhang

1 Introduction

International trade is the backbone of carriage of goods, while the development of carriage further facilitates international trade. Trade finance, which controls the monetary movement, is a vital segment in trade transactions. Traders, carriers and banks are mutually dependent and collectively constitute a commercial ecosystem. Commercial shipping law, therefore, should consider the interest of all the players and provide a coherent legal framework in which to operate.

This chapter aims to review the most successful unified rules in trade finance, the Uniform Customs and Practice for Documentary Credits (UCP) and to explore valuable experience that can be transferred in general commercial codification. Shipping documents, as an indispensable part of the documents tendered in documentary credit transactions, were addressed in the UCP from its very beginning and received considerable attention in each subsequent revision. However, disputes on the UCP shipping provisions have not diminished and continue to this day. Compared to current shipping law and practice, there are still gaps and deficiencies in the latest UCP revision. By revealing these problems, it is suggested that unification should be pursued across sectors for the same subject matter.

2 Commercial shipping as an integrated system

It is common for maritime law students and trainee lawyers to start their first lesson in commercial shipping law by identifying who is who. As is the case in real practice, one person can have different capacities in various contexts. For example, a person can simultaneously be the 'seller' under a c.i.f.[1] sale contract, 'charterer' under a charterparty, 'shipper' under a bill of lading, 'insurer' under a contract of insurance and 'beneficiary' under a documentary credit,[2] etc. This indicates that, to serve the backbone of international trade, various commercial sections, including carriage, insurance and banking, must co-operate with one another and participate in an integrated system. Owing to the limits of the chapter, the author focuses here on the interactions between carriage and banking only.

1 C.i.f. is a standard trade term widely used in international trade. It stands for cost, insurance and freight, which means that apart from providing the goods, the seller in this type of sales contract is responsible for making the contracts of carriage and insurance and paying for the corresponding cost.

2 The term 'documentary credit' is used interchangeably with 'letter of credit' in this chapter.

The commercial need for integrity is precisely reflected in day-to-day practice. For instance, delegates from several P&I Clubs are constantly troubled by one question:[3] Why does the shipper always request the carrier to insert the bank's documentary credit number, which has nothing to do with the carriage of goods, into a bill of lading,? It is not difficult to understand the carrier's reluctance in this scenario: the carrier is bound by statements on the bill of lading and obviously he does not want to put in writing something that he is unable to verify.[4] However, the point should be considered from the other side: Why does the shipper insist on making such a request? In short, it is a wish to ensure a smooth payment for the sale of goods transaction via the bank under a documentary credit. As we have seen in the previous example, it is very likely that the 'shipper, 'seller' and 'beneficiary' are one and the same person. Without the documentary credit number on the bill of lading, the bank may raise doubts on whether such a bill of lading belongs to the particular documentary credit transaction and therefore refuse to pay the presentation.[5] The difficulty of getting payment for the sale of goods would surely render the carriage arrangement, which is made to serve the sale transaction, pointless.

On the other hand, the buyer in a sale contract, who is also the applicant under a documentary credit, desires the bank to meticulously scrutinise the presented documents on his behalf, since he is to be parted from the money in exchange for the documents before receiving the goods. The bank, in order to obtain reimbursement from its customer (the buyer) afterwards, must follow instructions on the documentary credit to check through the documents. Apart from that, the bank may well be considering its own security, which can be generated from the shipping documents. These include contractual rights of suit[6] and proprietary rights of pledge[7] under a bill of lading.

One interesting case faced by the English courts, *The Erin Schulte*,[8] involves a confirming bank under a documentary credit suing the carrier for misdelivery and/or conversion of the goods. In an ideal world, if everything goes well, the bank will not need to concern itself with delivery of the goods or having any active engagement with the carrier, as the documentary credit provides an autonomous and independent payment mechanism based on the scrutiny of documents and documents alone. However, where the payment chain is broken, by either default in document examination or the buyer's insolvency, the bank will have to realise its security by stepping in as a cargo interest. This is exactly what happened in *The Erin Schulte*. The confirming bank had made a mistake in the chain of documentary credits and stuck with the presented documents, including the bill of lading. The confirming bank, therefore, made a cargo claim as a bill of lading holder, against the carrier, who

3 This question has been asked over years in the Southampton Institute of Maritime Law Short Course.

4 Statements on the bill of lading may trigger estoppel, which prevents the carrier denying the truth. See *Compania Naviera Vasconzada v Churchill & Sim* [1906] 1 KB 237. The Carriage of Goods by Sea Act 1992 also recognises that statements on the bill of lading constitute conclusive evidence against the carrier.

5 In *Banque de l'Indochine et de Suez SA v JH Rayner (Mincing Lane) Ltd* [1983] QB 711, p.732 Sir John Donaldson MR stated: 'however general the description [of the goods], the identification must, in my judgment, be unequivocal'. Therefore, for a bill of lading, it must be identified as belonging to the same transaction, either by adding detailed description of goods or by adding the documentary credit number to link it with the transaction.

6 The third party's right of suit under the contract of carriage is conferred by the Carriage of Goods by Sea Act 1992 under English law.

7 See *Official Assignee of Madras v Mercantile Bank of India Ltd* [1935] AC 53

8 *Standard Chartered Bank v Dorchester LNG Ltd* (*The Erin Schulte*) [2013] 2 Lloyd's Rep 338 (QB); [2013] EWHC 808 (Comm); [2014] EWCA Civ 1382; [2015] 1 Lloyd's Rep 97 (CA).

delivered the goods to someone without production of an original bill of lading. The whole incident started from an issue under a documentary credit, but unexpectedly ended up with a mysterious cargo claim under the law of carriage of goods by sea.[9]

The commercial reality draws private shipping and trade law into an integrated system. As Lord Hoffmann wisely pointed out, 'the reasonable reader would not think that the bill of lading could have been intended to mean one thing to the merchant or banker and something different to the lawyer or judge'.[10] Therefore, fragmenting the law does not achieve the needs of commercial parties or truly reflect day-to-day practice. An integral view is needed to guide the commercial parties through the hurdles. The UCP, as the most successful soft rules being used worldwide in nearly every documentary credit, has spent a considerable amount of time introducing and drafting transport provisions. From this perspective, it clearly represents the spirit of integration.

In the next part, the author presents the unification achieved by the UCP and further summarises the reasons behind the UCP's successful story.

3 UCP's unification and successful experience

There is little doubt that documentary credit has dominated trade finance for most of the twentieth century. It is fair to say that the single biggest driving force behind documentary credit's dominance is the UCP adopted by the International Chamber of Commerce (ICC). Since the first version in 1933, there have been six subsequent revisions,[11] with the progressively increasing coverage and up-to-date changes responding to the needs of practice. It is worth noting that the UCP, as codified commercial practices proposed by the non-governmental body, is not in the nature of a legal or regulatory measure. As the UCP itself states, the rules apply to any documentary credit when the credit expressly indicates that it is subject to these rules.[12] The parties can expressly modify or exclude the UCP provisions in the credit. Therefore, unless the UCP is otherwise legally recognised by the individual state, its legal force is wholly gained from contractual incorporation chosen by the commercial parties, despite its being in the form of a code.[13]

The profound impact of the UCP, however, extends way beyond a normal collection of banking practice. As Professor Kozolchyk noted:[14]

> 'No other set of international customary rules is as universally observed as the *Uniform Customs and Practice for Documentary Credits* (UCP): Banks, applicants and beneficiaries in more

9 The focal point in the cargo claim was whether and when the bank became a bill of lading holder under the Carriage of Goods by Sea Act 1992.

10 *Homburg Houtimport BV v Agrosin Private Ltd (The Starsin)* [2003] UKHL 12; [2004] 1 AC, [76]

11 These revisions took place approximately every ten years in 1951 (UCP 151), 1962 (UCP 222), 1974 (UCP 290), 1983 (UCP 400), 1993 (UCP 500) and 2006 (UCP 600). Discussion has been held regarding the next revision in 2018, but the ICC has decided to postpone the revision of UCP 600 based on the market reaction reported by the ICC national committees.

12 See, for example, UCP 600 Art. 1.

13 Established statutes which give force to the UCP under certain circumstances can be found in the US Uniform Commercial Code Revised Article 5 (1995) and the Supreme People's Court's Judicial Interpretations 'The Provisions on Some Issues Concerning the Trial of Disputes over Letters of Credit' (2006).

14 B. Kozolchyk, *Forum Für Internationales Wirtschaftsrecht*, United Nations Commission for International Trade Law (Vienna, 14 November 1991).

> than 150 nations adhere to it; carriers, freight forwarders and insurers draft their documents to comply with its specifications; legislatures model statutes after it, and courts treat it as a source of law whose misinterpretations cause quick reversal. . . . The reason why the UCP has inspired such widespread observance is not hard to surmise: it is the living law of documentary credits. By "living law" I mean the law that not only adjudicates disputes but also governs every aspect of the everyday "healthy" (unlitigated or undisputed) letter of credit transactions. The UCP, then, is a law invoked in the courtroom as well as applied in practice. As is characteristic of living law, the UCP contains didactic principles that instruct bankers on the basics of the documentary credit business.'

Given the worldwide adoption of the UCP and the benefits achieved by the uniformity of documentary credit practice, the courts have had a strong tendency to uphold the UCP regime and require the clearest wording to evidence the parties' intention of departure.[15] For example, in *Forestal Mimosa Ltd v Oriental Credit Ltd*,[16] Sir John Megaw in the English Court of Appeal held that the UCP would be overridden only in the event of an 'irreconcilable inconsistency' with the rest of the contract.

Furthermore, the UCP, as a compilation of customs of merchants, has shaped modern commercial law. One leading example of this is the US Revised Uniform Commercial Code (UCC), which put heavy reliance on standard and best practices as primary sources of commercial contract law. In terms of redrafting of the UCC Article 5 on documentary credits, it has been recognised that 'nothing else, not American common law, local practice, the law of another country, or even the UNCITRAL draft, had anything like the influence the UCP had'.[17] As a result, the UCC Revised Article 5 expressly acknowledges that when the UCP is incorporated into a documentary credit, it will generally prevail over the UCC Article 5 for any conflicts arising.[18]

The UCP's profound impact is attributed to its success in unification. There are three main reasons leading to this success. First and foremost, different from most codified work which becomes obsolete over time, the ICC runs periodic reviews and updates the UCP to reflect modern practice. For instance, with the advent of container ships and combined transport operators, the UCP added the provisions on multimodal transport document in the 1974 revision. Superior to its predecessors, the UCP 500 in 1993 comprised new provisions respecting the full range of shipping documents usually tendered under documentary credits, such as sea waybills and charterparty bills of lading. Moreover, the International Standard Banking Practice (ISBP) has been promulgated to achieve further uniformity in document checking under letters of credit. In addition, it is also key to laying down a plan for the future. The eUCP,[19] which has been introduced in anticipation of digitisation and electronic transmission of documents, effectively supplements the UCP and represents an

---

15 See also *Fortis Bank SA/NV v Indian Overseas Bank* [2011] EWCA Civ 58; [2011] 2 Lloyd's Rep 33, [29], where Thomas LJ held that courts must recognise the international nature of the UCP and approach its construction in that spirit.

16 [1986] 1 Lloyd's Rep 329; [1986] 1 WLR 631.

17 J.J. White, 'The Influence of International Practice on the Revision of Article 5 of the UCC' (1995) 16 (2) *Northwestern Journal of International Law & Business Volume* 189, 190.

18 See the UCC Revised Article 5–116(c).

19 The ICC is counting to update the eUCP, following the initial version of eUCP Version 1.0 produced in 2002. The ICC has recently approved the final text of an eUCP revision (eUCP Version 2.0) which will take effect from 1 July 2019.

attempt to keep documentary credits relevant to the new technological era. Compared to the codes which cannot easily satisfy the speed of business transformation, the UCP permits continuing expansion through timely periodic reviews to reflect modern commercial practice and the requirements of the market.

Secondly, the UCP is a 'bottom-up' work produced by private bodies for use on a contractual basis by those who wish to employ it. It is well known that commercial law was derived from the customs of merchants,[20] the original term being the '*lex mercatoria*' or 'merchant law', i.e., the law relating to the usages of markets and traders in these markets. As Devlin LJ noted, '[the law should] allow, so far as it can, commercial men to do business the way they want to do it'.[21] Even nowadays, the ability to accommodate new commercial practice and the use of custom in determining commercial contracts remain a part of modern commercial law.[22] The UCP, which adopts the 'empirical method'[23] to consolidate the existing rules and customs, fits well with the needs of stakeholders and results in a harmonious integration of additions with pre-existing commercial practice. Moreover, the UCP is drafted not by diplomatic experts or bureaucrats but by those within the relevant industries. Although the banking industry still plays a major role in the drafting process, the various UCP revisions represent a concerted and co-ordinated effort on the part of bankers, traders and lawyers, with the increasing involvement of transport and insurance experts. Being in an integrated system, 'best practices are concerned not only with the welfare of regular participants but also of third parties, such as *bona fide* purchasers/consumers and future investors and creditors and, accordingly, would also treat them reasonably'.[24]

Thirdly, the various adjudicatory mechanisms in the ICC diminish the chance of making different interpretations for the UCP provisions across jurisdictions. In the absence of any supranational judicial authority, the ICC Banking Commission has been responding to individual queries about the application of specific UCP provisions to letter of credit disputes.[25] Moreover, the ICC Banking Commission chose to issue position papers on several occasions when a perceived error in the UCP's interpretation had developed at a general level.[26] The ICC also offers a binding arbitration service (DOCDEX) for letters of credit disputes, which is conducted by experts under the auspices of the ICC and whose decisions

20 *Lickbarrow v Mason* (1787) 2 TR 63.

21 *Kum v Wah Tat Bank Ltd* [1971] 1 Lloyd's Rep 439, 444.

22 *Cunliffe-Owen v Teather and Greenwood* [1967] 1 WLR 1421.

23 P.J. Omar, 'Codifying commercial law: a project for the millennium' [1999] *International Company and Commercial Law Review* 81, in which the two traditional methods of codification, i.e. rational and empirical, are described.

24 B. Kozolchyk, 'The Modernization and Harmonization of the Commercial Law in the Twenty-first Century: the Need for A New Research and Drafting Methodology' (2016) 33 (1) *Arizona Journal of International & Comparative Law* 25, 27.

25 Some recent examples include: Gary Collyer and Ron Katz (eds), *ICC Banking Commission Opinions 2009–2011* (ICC Publication No.732E, ICC 2012); Gary Collyer (ed), *ICC Banking Commission Opinions 2012–2016* (ICC Publication No.785E, ICC 2016); Gary Collyer (ed), *ICC Banking Commission Opinions 2016* (ICC Publication No.799E, ICC 2018); Gary Collyer (ed), *ICC Banking Commission Opinions 2017* (ICC Publication No.802E, ICC 2018).

26 See, for example, ICC Commission on Banking Technique and Practice, *Position Papers Nos 1–4 on UCP 500* (1 September 1994); ICC Commission on Banking Technique and Practice, *Recommendations of the Banking Commission in respect of the Requirements for an On Board Notation* (Document No.470/1128rev final, 22 April 2010).

have been published by the ICC to produce references on the proper application of the UCP.[27] By offering the various adjudicatory mechanisms, the ICC has been able to maintain the consolidating effect of the UCP. Those opinions and decisions of the ICC have been given considerable weight by the courts in judging a letter of credit dispute, which further strengthens the unification proposed by the UCP.[28]

Learning from the UCP's successful experience, commercial shipping codification should not be expected to encounter insurmountable difficulties, as the process should also largely involve a harmonious integration of pre-existing concepts, principles and practice. The key to any codified work being effective is to keep it up to date with commercial reality. This goal could be achieved either by frequent periodic review or by intentionally leaving some flexibility for future developments.[29] It is also important to adopt the 'bottom-up' approach and let market players to shape the law according to their own practical requests. It is recognised that 'codes are no longer preferred tools of modernisation because the actual standard and best practices, instead of their reformulation or restatement by scholars and judges, are much closer to both, marketplace behaviour and market needs'.[30] Therefore, in order to keep the codes alive, reliance on standard and best practice as primary sources of law must be encouraged.[31] Furthermore, producing unified interpretations and guidelines to the rules through an open and transparent dispute resolution process would be a necessary add-on to ensure the executive power of such codified work.

4 Bridging the UCP's provisions with shipping law and practice

As the documentary credit rarely spells out all the requirements calling for a transport document, rules of practice detailing these specifics have acquired considerable importance. Since the first version of the UCP, requirements for transport documents have received considerable attention. Apart from the traditional bill of lading which forms the mainstay of transport provisions, the successive revisions of the UCP have also reacted to the increasing use of non-traditional documentation, particularly multimodal transport documents, sea waybills and charterparty bills of lading. The current UCP 600 succeeds the style under UCP 500 and enumerates the acceptable transport documents in Articles 19–27.[32]

Although UCP 600 and 500 have extended the transport provisions in UCP 400 to minimise misinterpretation and misapplication, they are still the source of confusion and

27 DOCDEX stands for Documentary Credit Dispute Resolution Expertise. For a recent example of the publication on DOCDEX's decisions, see Gary Collyer and David Meynell (eds), *Collected DOCDEX Decisions 2013–2016* (ICC Publication No.786E, ICC 2017).

28 See *Credit Industriel et Commercial v China Merchants Bank* [2002] EWHC 973 (Comm) and *Glencore International AG v Bank of China* [1996] 1 Lloyd's Rep 135.

29 A good example for this is s.1(5) in the English Carriage of Goods by Sea Act 1992, which leaves the possibility to apply the Act to the electronic communications network.

30 B. Kozolchyk, keynote speech at the Second Pacific Rim Colloquium on Economic Development and the Harmonization of Commercial Law (The National Law Center for Inter-American Free Trade, 8–10 January 2015) http://natlaw.com/event/second-pacific-rim-colloquium-on-economic-development-and-the-harmonization-of-commercial-law/ (visited on 14 August 2019).

31 The UCC 1995 revision is one of the few commercial codes to do so.

32 The provisions related to sea transport are Article 19 on multimodal transport documents, Art. 20 on bills of lading, Art. 21 on non-negotiable sea waybills, Article 22 on charterparty bills of lading, and the miscellaneous Arts 26 & 27. If a transport document called by the letter of credit does not fall into the scope of these specific provisions, the rule for general document examination in the UCP 600 Art. 14 will apply.

most disputes. It is regrettable to see that UCP 600 has left intact the most problematic issues under UCP 500. The reason is in part the lack of uniformity or standardised rules in the transport documents themselves and the industry. Furthermore, different understanding between banking and shipping practice, and the UCP's complex formulation for transport documents also generate abundant inquiries. In this part, provisions on traditional bills of lading are demonstrated as an example. Since the UCP rules for alternative forms of sea transport documentation, including sea waybills, charterparty bills of lading and multimodal transport documents, are generated from the same module, emphasis is drawn in comparison with the bill of lading only when necessary. The current UCP 600 provides:

Article 20 Bill of Lading

a A bill of lading, however named, must appear to:

i indicate the name of the carrier and be signed by:

- the carrier or a named agent for or on behalf of the carrier, or
- the master or a named agent for or on behalf of the master.

Any signature by the carrier, master or agent must be identified as that of the carrier, master or agent.

Any signature by an agent must indicate whether the agent has signed for or on behalf of the carrier or for or on behalf of the master.

ii indicate that the goods have been shipped on board a named vessel at the port of loading stated in the credit by:

- pre-printed wording, or
- an on board notation indicating the date on which the goods have been shipped on board.

The date of issuance of the bill of lading will be deemed to be the date of shipment unless the bill of lading contains an on board notation indicating the date of shipment, in which case the date stated in the on board notation will be deemed to be the date of shipment.

If the bill of lading contains the indication 'intended vessel' or similar qualification in relation to the name of the vessel, an on board notation indicating the date of shipment and the name of the actual vessel is required.

iii indicate shipment from the port of loading to the port of discharge stated in the credit.

If the bill of lading does not indicate the port of loading stated in the credit as the port of loading, or if it contains the indication 'intended' or similar qualification in relation to the port of loading, an on board notation indicating the port of loading as stated in the credit, the date of shipment and the name of the vessel is required. This provision applies even when loading on board or shipment on a named vessel is indicated by pre-printed wording on the bill of lading.

iv be the sole original bill of lading or, if issued in more than one original, be the full set as indicated on the bill of lading.

v contain terms and conditions of carriage or make reference to another source containing the terms and conditions of carriage (short form or blank back bill of lading). Contents of terms and conditions of carriage will not be examined.

vi contain no indication that it is subject to a charter party.

b For the purpose of this article, transhipment means unloading from one vessel and reloading to another vessel during the carriage from the port of loading to the port of discharge stated in the credit.

c i A bill of lading may indicate that the goods will or may be transhipped provided that the entire carriage is covered by one and the same bill of lading.

ii A bill of lading indicating that transhipment will or may take place is acceptable, even if the credit prohibits transhipment, if the goods have been shipped in a container, trailer or LASH barge as evidenced by the bill of lading.

d Clauses in a bill of lading stating that the carrier reserves the right to tranship will be disregarded.

4.1 Finding the focus

A traditional bill of lading has three classic functions, i.e., as a cargo receipt, a document of title, and evidence of the contract of carriage. Lord Hoffmann, who rejected the argument that the UCP provisions on bills of lading serve only for banks under documentary credits, held that the UCP represents the common and reasonable view of an addressee of the bill of lading:[33]

> 'It [a bill of lading] evidences a contract of carriage but it is also a document of title, drafted with a view to being transferred to third parties either absolutely or by way of security for advances to finance the underlying transaction. It is common general knowledge that such advances are frequently made by letter of credit and that the bill of lading is ordinarily one of the documents which must be presented to the bank before payment can be obtained. The reasonable reader of the bill of lading will therefore know that it is addressed not only to the shipper and consignee named on the bill but to a potentially wide class of third parties including banks which have issued letters of credit.'

By scrutinising the provisions of Article 20 above and other relevant UCP 600 provisions, it is not difficult to find that each function is more or less touched upon; however, the focus is somewhat obscure.

First, as a vital document to evidence the seller's performance on shipment and the carrier's undertaking, the UCP 600 has paid considerable attention to the function of bill of lading as a cargo receipt. The UCP 600 Article 20(a)(ii) requires a shipped bill of lading, whether by pre-printed wording or by adding an on-board notation afterwards. In absence of any contrary statement in the documentary credit, a received-for-shipment bill of lading will not be acceptable, since it may diminish the evidential effect of a bill of lading in a cargo claim. In addition, the UCP 600 Article 27 mandates banks to accept only a clean transport document, which bears 'no clause or notation expressly declaring a defective condition of the goods or their packaging'.

The UCP transport provisions do not, however, mention any specific requirements for the description of goods recorded in a bill of lading. As to the description of goods, the UCP 600 requires that, if it is stated, it may be recorded in general terms not conflicting with their description in the credit.[34] Moreover, clauses concerning the weight and quantity of goods, such as 'weight and quantity unknown', 'shipper's load and count' and 'said by shipper to contain', are acceptable.[35] This position is fit for the market expectation, since it is very common in shipping practice for the carrier to include a disclaimer clause in a bill

33 *Homburg Houtimport BV v Agrosin Private Ltd (The Starsin)* [2003] UKHL 12; [2004] 1 AC 715, [74].

34 See UCP 600 Art. 14(e).

35 See UCP 600 Art. 26(b).

of lading regarding the quantity and actual condition of the goods, but to state the apparent condition and packaging of the goods from the perspective of a reasonable observer.[36]

Secondly, regarding the function of document of title, the only provision that loosely relates to it is Article 20(a)(iv), which requires a full set of bills of lading to be tendered if more than one original is issued. As a document of title, delivery must be made against presentation of an original bill of lading, and the common rule 'the one being accomplished, the others to stand void' applies.[37] Therefore, this provision is drafted to mitigate the risk of fraud generated by the carriage practice and to protect the security interest of banks and their customers. However, there is no attempt in the UCP to address the transferability of a bill of lading. The ISBP No.745 Section E12 stipulates that when a credit requires a bill of lading to evidence that goods are consigned to a named entity, i.e. a straight bill of lading, the bill of lading should not contain the expression 'to order' preceding or following the named entity, whether typed or pre-printed.[38] This strongly indicates that bills of lading under Article 20 cover both negotiable and straight ones. It is submitted that whether a bill of lading is negotiable and how it should be endorsed are entirely left to the express agreement in the documentary credit. Therefore, the bank and the buyer who wish to strengthen their security interest in cargo delivery and potential competing claims must go one step further than the UCP set rules.

Thirdly, UCP 600 reflects the function of a bill of lading as evidence of the carriage contract by inserting Article 20(a)(v), which requires that a bill of lading must contain terms and conditions of carriage or make reference to another source containing the terms and conditions of carriage (for short form or blank back bills of lading). However, in order to reduce the bank's burden and disclaim its liability, Article 20(a)(v) further underlines that the terms and conditions of carriage will not be examined by the bank, whether they are contained in the bill of lading.[39] It is understandable that the UCP is trying to release the bank from the onerous task of reading the small print on the back of the bill of lading and to deter the bank from calling for the incorporated documents which contain the carriage terms and conditions. Nevertheless, the security interest of the bank and the buyer is the compromise to make, since the bill of lading plays a crucial role in the hands of a third party[40] during cargo claims given that it can be construed as the contract of carriage between the carrier and the bill of lading holder. For example, the 'delivery without presenting a straight bill of lading' clause has been construed as part of carriage terms and conditions and therefore would not be examined by the bank

---

36 See for example *The Mata K* [1998] 2 Lloyd's Rep 614; *The David Agmashenebeli* [2003] 1 Lloyd's Rep 92.

37 See *Glyn Mills & Co v East and West India Dock Co* (1882) 7 App Cas 591, where the carrier need not await all original bills before delivery, nor need he take further steps to ensure that the presenter is in fact the person entitled.

38 The ISBP No.745 Section E13 (b) also provides, when a credit requires a bill of lading to evidence that goods are consigned to 'order of (named entity)', a bill of lading which is only consigned to a named entity will not be acceptable.

39 The effect of Article 20(a)(v) is however not as simple as it appears to be. For the discussion on potential controversies arisen from Article 20(a)(v), see J. Zhang, 'Bills of Lading in Bankers' Hand: Does Chinese Legislation Offer Sufficient Security?' in J. Hjalmarsson & J. Zhang (eds.) *Maritime Law in China: Emerging Issues and Future Developments* (Informa Law from Routledge 2016), pp. 65–86.

40 Third party means the bill of lading holder is neither the charterer nor the shipper.

according to Article 20(a)(v).[41] In addition, as will be analysed in the next part, how to reconcile this provision with the transhipment provisions stipulated in Article 20(b)–(d) and the requirement on carrier's liability remains a puzzle.

For any piece of codified work, it is important to recognise from the beginning whom it is for and what is to be achieved. By correctly identifying the purpose of the work, it would be easy to prioritise the focus and balance the conflicting interests of various parties in the process of codification. It is submitted that most of the requirements in Article 20 focus on the evidential function of a bill of lading to reflect the performance of the seller, as to both the cargo and the contract of carriage. Article 20 is also intended to evidence the carrier's undertaking in the contract of carriage; however, the interpretation of Article 20(a)(v) can be controversial and problematic. The function of document of title has been largely ignored under the UCP and left to the parties to make an individual agreement under the framework of governing law. Based on all these elements, it is concluded that Article 20 is primarily designed to examine the parties' performance involved in a documentary credit transaction, rather than to prevent the risk generated in a potential cargo dispute or strengthen the bank's security interest in resale of the goods.

4.2 The issue of over-drafting

One of the arguments against codification is that a code, which mainly contains skeletal articles in broad-brush strokes but says very little in detail, cannot effectively guide commercial parties. However, the opposite is not necessarily good. Saying too much is sometimes as bad as too little. Over-drafting can cause unnecessary confusion and complexity, which makes the work counterproductive. One outstanding example in Article 20 is the provisions on transhipment.

Transhipment is routinely performed in the container trade where containers are often transferred between different vessels. It is also common for bills of lading to contain a clause conferring on the carrier a right of transhipment. By specifically addressing the transhipment issue in Article 20(b)–(d), UCP 600 is evidently intended to accommodate the nature of modern transportation and recognise the existing practice. The default position of the UCP 600 is that transhipment is permitted unless expressly prohibited by the letter of credit. Even though the credit has prohibited transhipment, it is still entirely possible for the goods to be transhipped.[42] However, the main problem with UCP 600 transhipment rules is that they have failed to achieve harmony either within the section itself or with other provisions in Article 20.

First, both Article 20(c) and Article 20(d) cover the situation in which the transhipment *may* happen, either by express words indicating that the transhipment may take place or by a liberty of transhipment clause in the bill of lading. The overlap causes unnecessary confusion here: should the bank disregard the possibility of transhipment according to Article 20(d), or examine it pursuant to Article 20(c)?

41 G. Collyer and R. Katz (eds), *ICC Banking Commission Opinions 2009–2011* (ICC Publication No.732E, ICC 2012) R758.

42 See Art. 20(c)(ii) and (d).

Secondly, the implication behind the words '*entire carriage* covered by one and the same bill of lading' in Article 20(c)(i) is obscure. Does this requirement simply imply that a bill of lading must show the complete physical route as stated in the documentary credit, or does it mean that the contracting carrier under a bill of lading must undertake the liability for the entire carriage? The former appears to add nothing more than what has been already stipulated under Article 20(a)(iii), i.e. the bill of lading must indicate shipment from the port of loading to the port of discharge as stated in the credit. Alternatively, for the latter, the bank needs to ensure that there is no clause disclaiming the carrier's liability before or after transhipment. However, this process will inevitably involve examination for the general carriage terms and conditions contained in a bill of lading, which are supposed to contradict Article 20(a)(v). It also sounds rather arbitrary that the bank is entitled only to examine sporadic carriage terms mentioned or related to transhipment, but not any others, even those written in the same pre-printed paragraph or on the same page.[43]

There is unfortunately no good way to eradicate the tension between the transhipment provisions in Article 20(c) and the liberty not to examine carriage terms under Article 20(a)(v), since in nature, transhipment terms are carriage terms *per se*. The best solution so far to avoid confusion and conflict is to contract out Article 20(b)–(d) entirely when incorporating UCP 600. This leads to the question on the necessity of inserting transhipment provisions in the UCP in the first place. As analysed above, the UCP appears to focus on the evidential function of a bill of lading regarding the goods and the carriage, rather than the security interest brought by the carriage contract. It should therefore stick to the focus and find the right balance between intervention and party autonomy.

4.3 Mismatch with shipping law and practice

Although the ICC Banking Commission has endeavoured to bring the shipping experts on board during various revisions, the current UCP rules still contain provisions which do not make complete sense from the perspective of shipping law and practice. For example, UCP 600 Articles 20 and 21 are identical, except the latter named itself as 'non-negotiable sea waybill'. Is it necessary to emphasise 'non-negotiable', since all the sea waybills in shipping practice are non-negotiable anyway? Moreover, does the requirement of Article 21(a)(iv), which mirrors Article 20(a)(iv) on the full set requirement, still make sense in the context of a sea waybill, as there is no need to present a sea waybill against delivery?[44] Another issue can be found in Article 22 on the charterparty bill of lading, which contains provisions nearly identical to Article 20, dividing the acceptable signatory parties into the master, owner and charterer but without further asking for an indication of the name of the carrier.[45] Based on shipping practice, either shipowner or charterer could sign a bill of

43 See G. Collyer and R. Katz (eds), *ICC Banking Commission Opinions 2009–2011* (ICC Publication No.732E, ICC 2012) R758, in which the delivery clause was stated in the same pre-printed paragraph with the status of shipment and the number of bills of lading. While the delivery clause was meant to be ignored by the bank, the statement for the latter two elements was to be examined without doubt.

44 It is understandable that banks and buyers would like to witness a sea waybill to verify the seller's carriage performance; however, receiving a full set of original sea waybills would not achieve anything more than just seeing a photocopy, since delivery is made against the proof of consignee's identity under a sea waybill.

45 UCP 600 Art. 22(a) stipulates: 'A bill of lading, however named, containing an indication that it is subject to a charter party (charter party bill of lading), must appear to be signed by the master or a named agent for or

lading in its own capacity, and the master, who normally signs a bill of lading on behalf of the shipowner, could sign for the charterer as well.[46] Without specifying the name of the carrier as requested in Article 20, the division in Article 22 is unable to provide a clear answer regarding who is the carrier and therefore loses its initial drafting purpose.

The above problems may be fixed by large-scale consultation with the relevant stakeholders to ensure that the provisions continue to match the prevailing shipping reality. However, there are other issues that cannot easily be solved, due to the lack of uniformity or standardised base rules on shipping and carriage – for instance, whether a straight bill of lading is qualified as a document of title, which needs production of an original against cargo delivery. Different jurisdictions may have different interpretations on this. Another conflict lies in the concept of clean bill of lading. The way of judging a clean bill of lading under English law depends on whether damage occurs before or after shipment;[47] while the UCP does not make a distinction on this point.

Dissatisfaction can be easily generated if an international codified work takes too much from one legal culture at the expense of others. It is difficult to balance the interest of various parties even in the same jurisdiction, not to mention reconciliation between common law and civil law systems. The UCP, which adopts the bottom-up approach in the process of codification, has achieved consensus in majority circumstances. However, for the matters that cannot be easily reconciled, gaps are left to the decision of national courts, such as recognition of fraud, available remedies and proprietary issues on a bill of lading. It is recognised that some gaps are simply unbridgeable in the process of unification and codification – they had to be left effectively uncodified and up to each individual jurisdiction to decide according to its national law, although the bottom-up drafting approach driven by commercial practice could mitigate the gap as much as possible.

5 Concluding remarks

The international dimension of commerce adds complexity to its regulation. Trade and shipping, particularly internationally, need private codification that is especially suited to its integrated feature. The UCP, as the most successful codified work provided by the ICC, recognises the needs of certainty and flexibility in the contemporary marketplace at the same time. It shapes the law of international commerce and raises commercial practices to the rank of rules of law applicable to international litigation.[48] Moreover, its valuable experience certainly benefits the future unification and codification in commercial law, including commercial shipping law.

While most of the existing codified work have fallen into disuse or disrepair, the UCP maintains its vitality by carrying out frequent periodic reviews driven from the industry. The bottom-up approach fits well with the needs of stakeholders and makes it easy to deal

on behalf of the master, or the owner or a named agent for or on behalf of the owner, or the charterer or a named agent for or on behalf of the charterer.'

46 See *Manchester Trust v Furness, Withy & Co* [1895] 2 QB 539; *Elder Dempster v Paterson* [1924] AC 522.

47 See *M Golodetz & Co Inc v Czarnikow-Rionda Co Inc (The Galatia)* [1980] 1 WLR 495, where a bill of lading could not be rendered unclean by the notation added at a later stage recording the fire damage after shipment.

48 N. Stolowy, M. Brochier, 'Reflections on the concept of norms and sources of law in commercial matters' (2018) *Journal of Business Law* 255, 276.

with new or unexpected problems. Its provisions reflect well the development of shipping practice and e-commerce, and further contribute to the development of a unified, secure legal system at the service of tradespeople all over the world.

However, in attempting to provide uniformity and reduce disputes, the shipping provisions in UCP 600 are not entirely satisfactory since some queries over interpretation continue and, in some respects, intensify. It is noted that codification should result in a harmonious integration of various sectors, rather than making isolated silos. Consultation on shipping law and practice will still need to be made at regular intervals to ensure the UCP provisions continue to match the prevailing commercial reality, and vice versa.

CHAPTER 11

The challenges of ICTs in the shipping sector among international uniform law, codification and *Lex Mercatoria*

The electronic bill of lading

Dr Elena Orrù

1 Introduction

Today, information and communications technologies (ICTs) are increasingly relevant to the shipping sector. This 'revolution' is interesting, in particular regarding the bill of lading: since the 1980s, many shipping companies and other stakeholders have been trying to develop a true electronic transport document or record performing the same functions as the paper bill of lading.

The issues arising with regard to the e-bill of lading are similar to those met by the traditional bill of lading in the past and mainly concern the applicable regime. The paper bill of lading developed before and contemporarily with its regime, which was, at the beginning, provided by the so-called *Lex Mercatoria* and only later 'codified' both in national (maritime) codes and in international conventions. On the other hand, today there is no standard e-bill of lading (or e-transport record) regularly used at international level, and therefore the lawmakers are addressing a tool that does not yet exist.

At the international and EU level, in recent years there has been a proliferation of laws on ICTs. However, no international hard law provisions in force apply specifically to e-bills of lading and deal with all the related issues.

At the domestic level, many countries have enacted or are drafting new statutes (or even codes) specifically addressing the use of ICTs or e-trade, but few provide for the shipping sector or take due account of the particular characteristics of the e-bill of lading. Moreover, due to the lack of a uniform and certain regime, the relevant international associations are adapting their model or standard contract clauses to these new instruments.

An examination of these sources is useful in order to assess whether they provide for identical or similar solutions that could be considered to express general principles and practices forming a new *Lex Mercatoria.*

This paper addresses the issue of whether a suitable regime already exists or what could be the feasible solutions in order to ensure that the e-bill of lading can lawfully perform the same functions as the paper one. Furthermore, it is necessary to ascertain whether this purpose can be achieved by a new *Lex Mercatoria* or by the interpretation of the existing law by courts or, especially in civil law systems, by revising it or enacting new statutes.

2 The paper and electronic bill of lading

2.1 The features and regime of the traditional bill of lading

In medieval times, when the bill of lading developed as a receipt for the goods loaded onboard a ship and as a document of title,[1] its regime was essentially based on the so-called *Lex Mercatoria* or – better – *Lex Maritima.*[2] The bill of lading's role as negotiable document of transport and its importance for enabling trades therefore mainly lay on the consensus on its features widely recognized at the international level, also through the development of standard models or clauses. It was only more recently that, along with the rise of nation states, a process of codification was advanced at the domestic level,[3] among the other reasons, in order to prevent some practices that did not conform to its regime as envisaged by well-established international usage.[4] In this way, however, this process contributed to hindering the degree of uniformity enabled by the above mentioned *Lex Maritima.* To counterbalance this trend and fulfil the need for uniformity and legal certainty necessary for the circulation of the bill of lading at the international level, the Hague Rules and the subsequent Hague-Visby Rules[5] were signed, under the auspices of the CMI.[6]

2.2 Issues related to the electronic bill of lading

Since the 1980s and, in particular, in recent years, the new ICTs are improving the organization and management of logistics services and international trade flows, reducing the related costs.[7] In this scenario, there have been several attempts to obtain an electronic bill

---

1 W.P. Bennet, *The history and present position of the bill of lading as a document of title to goods* (Cambridge University Press, 1914), p. 2 ff; E. Bensa, *Le forme primitive della polizza di carico: ricerche storiche con documenti inediti* (Stabilimento d'arti grafiche Caimo & C, 1925), p. 7 and 12 ss; A.P. La Rosa, *Studi sulla polizza di carico* (Giuffrè, 1958), p. 3; A.P. La Rosa, 'Polizza di carico', *Enciclopedia del diritto* (1985) vol XXXIV, p. 201, 203; G. Boi, 'Profili documentali del trasporto marittimo e brevi riflessioni sulla specialità ed autonomia della materia' (2010) *Rivista del diritto della navigazione* 45; S. Zunarelli, M.M. Comenale Pinto, *Manuale di diritto della navigazione e dei trasporti*, 2nd edn (CEDAM 2013), p. 486; R. Aikens, R. Lord, M. Bools, *Bills of Lading*, 2nd edn (Informa Law, 2016), p. 1 ff. See also *Guidon de la mer*, Ch 2, art 8. According to Bernardino Scorza, [*La polizza di carico* (Società editrice del Foro italiano 1936), vol I, p. 1], the first examples of bills of lading can be traced back to Roman times.

2 E. Van Hooydonk, 'Towards a worldwide restatement of the general principles of maritime law' (2014) 20 *Journal of International Maritime Law* 170; E. Bensa, *Le forme primitive della polizza di carico: ricerche storiche con documenti inediti, supra* note 1, p. 7. E.g., Consolato del mare, Ch 55 *passim* and 59.61.

3 Eg, 1681 Ordonnance de France, titre des connaissements; 1865 Italian commercial Code, Art. 391 ss.

4 E. Bensa, *Le forme primitive della polizza di carico: ricerche storiche con documenti inediti* (Stabilimento d'arti grafiche Caimo & C, 1925), p. 13. V 1882 Italian commercial Code, art. 555, para 5.

5 The International Convention for the Unification of Certain Rules of Law relating to Bills of Lading (Brussels, 1924), with Protocols.

6 E. Van Hooydonk, 'Towards a worldwide restatement of the general principles of maritime law' (2014) 20 *Journal of International Maritime Law* 170–171; E. Bensa, *Le forme primitive della polizza di carico: ricerche storiche con documenti inediti* (Stabilimento d'arti grafiche Caimo & C, 1925), p. 14.

7 E.K. Morlok, 'Current Trends and Perspectives on Freight Transport in North America', in L. Bianco and A. La Bella (eds), *Freight Transport Planning and Logistics* (No 317 'Lecture Notes in Economics and Mathematical Systems', Springer-Verlag Berlin Heidelberg GmbH, 1989), p. 1, 36; M.-M. Damien, 'France', in ECMT Economic Research Centre, *What Markets Are There For Transport by Inland Waterways?* (ECMT Round Tables No 108, OECD, 1999), p. 83, 121; H. Caldwell *et al*, report *Freight Transportation: the European Market* (US Department of Transportation, Federal Highway Administration, Washington, 2002), p. 10; E. Onghena,

of lading. For this purpose, it is necessary to take into consideration that the relevance of the bill of lading is not limited to the contract of carriage, but involves different contracts, in particular the contract of sale and documentary credit, where the documentary credit is agreed as method of payment between the seller and the buyer and provided that the letter of credit requires the submission of a bill of lading.

In particular, an electronic bill of lading should therefore be able to provide evidence of the existence of a contract of carriage, incorporating its terms in conformity with the relevant leading cases, of the loading onboard of the goods and their conditions, enabling the carrier to add reservations.[8] The electronic bill of lading must enable its lawful issuer to claim delivery of the goods there represented by the carrier. With specific regard to the contract of sale and documentary credit, the ICT systems enabling the issuance of an electronic bill of lading should ensure its interoperability.

As regards the advantages of an electronic bill of lading over a paper one, the former would enable an immediate transfer of the document of title, overcoming the issue of the bill of lading's arrival after the cargo and of delivery without production of the bill of lading. The main problems are, on the one hand, to obtain an electronic record that is generated, transferred and negotiated exclusively through an electronic management system, where it is kept and can be retrieved for future occurrences.[9]

On the other hand, the issue is to ensure its uniqueness and integrity through the chain of contracts and certainty of its authorship and of the identity of further holders, preventing forgeries and double transfer to different endorsees.[10] In addition, the actual construction of the ICT system and, in particular, of transmission of the electronic document should entail the autonomy of the rights and obligations represented there from the underlying relationship,[11] which many of the systems tried hitherto have not been able to do. The achievement of these goals would overcome another weakness of the paper bill of lading, that is the risk of fraud.[12]

'Integrators in a changing world', in R. Macário and E. Van de Voorde (eds), *Critical Issues in Air Transport Economics and Business* (Routledge Studies in the Modern World Economy, 2011), p. 112; H.-J. Schramm, *Freight Forwarder's Intermediary Role in Multimodal Transport Chains: A Social Network Approach* (Physica-Verlag, 2012), p. 281.

8 A. Møllmann, *Delivery of Goods under Bills of Lading* (Routledge, 2016), p. 155; E. Orrù, 'The Electronic Transport Record and Current Challenges of E-logistics and International Trade' in *2nd International Scientific Conference on Maritime Law 'Modern Challenges of Marine Navigation'* (Faculty of Law University of Split, 2018), p. 201, 205.

9 According to art. 4, let. b) and c), of the UN Convention on the Use of Electronic Communications in International Contracts, 'Electronic communication' means 'any communication that the parties make by means of data messages'. 'Data message' means 'information generated, sent, received or stored by electronic, magnetic, optical or similar means, including, but not limited to, electronic data interchange, electronic mail, telegram, telex or telecopy'.

10 A. Møllmann, *Delivery of Goods under Bills of Lading* (Routledge, 2016), p. 155; K. Takahashi, 'Blockchain technology and electronic bills of lading' (2016) 22 *Journal of International Maritime Law* 202, 203 and 207; P. Cuccuru, '*Blockchain* ed automazione contrattuale. Riflessioni sugli *smart contract*' [2017] 1 *La Nuova giurisprudenza civile commentate* 107, 108.

11 E. Orrù, 'The Electronic Transport Record and Current Challenges of E-logistics and International Trade', in *2nd International Scientific Conference on Maritime Law 'Modern Challenges of Marine Navigation'* (Faculty of Law University of Split, 2018), p. 205.

12 A. Møllmann, *Delivery of Goods under Bills of Lading* (Routledge, 2016), p. 155; K. Takahashi, 'Blockchain technology and electronic bills of lading' (2016) 22 *Journal of International Maritime Law*, p. 203; E. Orrù, 'The Electronic Transport Record and Current Challenges of E-logistics and International Trade' in *2nd International Scientific Conference on Maritime Law 'Modern Challenges of Marine Navigation'* (Faculty of Law University of Split, 2018), p. 206.

3 Past and current projects

3.1 BOLERO, essDOCS and E-title™

With regard to the different systems developed during the past more than 30 years, whereas many services consist of booking platforms for carriage or logistics services (including unimodal carriage by sea or multimodal carriage with a sea leg), where the bill of lading that can be drafted through these platforms still works as a traditional document and therefore needs to be printed,[13] other platforms have been developed for issuing a true e-bill of lading, with no great success until now.[14]

One of the first examples in order of time is Seadocs: this platform was developed in 1983 with the cooperation of Intertanko and the Chase Manhattan Bank specifically for the oil sector. Given the crucial role of bills of lading in international trade, it is not surprising that the banks participate in financing and promoting these experiments, as in the case of Blockchain technology. The certainty of authorship and security is achieved by public/private key cryptography. However, this system was not able to provide a real e-bill of lading, because the paper bills were kept by the central register that managed the platform. Another weakness of this system, which would also be found in subsequent projects, was to be limited only to subscribers and centralised. The same flaw could be found in the Bill Of Lading Electronic Registry Organization, also known as BOLERO, and CargoDocs Electronic Bills of Lading – essDOCS.[15] According to its website,[16] the latter should be able to issue a true e-bill of lading, which could be negotiated and endorsed through e-signatures.

On the other hand, the same result was not achieved with another of the first experiments, the Cargo Key Receipt system, created by Atlantic Container Line, because the e-bill of lading was not negotiable.[17]

Therefore, what these systems have in common are the issues of being closed and centralised: the main reason is that their technology was not able to create an electronic transferable record autonomously and directly enabling the identification of the lawful holder, requiring access to the central register for this purpose. Neither is it possible to avoid double spending, which was achieved only by the central administrator.[18] The central register is also intended to keep records of holdership of the electronic bill of lading for future reference.[19]

---

13 N. Gaskell, 'Bills of Lading in an electronic age' [2010] 2 *Lloyds Maritime and Commercial Law Quarterly* 233, 244 ff. This is the case, for example, of BIMCO's Idea CargoSmart, INTTRA, My Maersk.

14 M.-M. Comenale Pinto, 'I documenti elettronici del trasporto' [2012] I *Rivista del diritto della navigazione* 33, 53 ff; Nicholas Gaskell, 'Bills of Lading in an electronic age' [2010] 2 *Lloyds Maritime and Commercial Law Quarterly* 233, 260 ff.

15 Also known as essDOCS-Databridge™.

16 http://www.essdocs.com (visited 15 August 2019).

17 On this system, K. Grönfors, *Cargo Key Receipt and Transport Document Replacement* (Akademiförlaget, 1986).

18 K. Takahashi, 'Blockchain technology and electronic bills of lading (2016) 22 *Journal of International Maritime Law* 203; E. Ong, *Blockchain bills of lading* (CML working paper series, NUS Law18/07 August 2018), p. 9.

https://law.nus.edu.sg/cml/pdfs/wps/CML-WPS-1807.pdf (visited 15 August 2019).

19 J. Tan, L. Starr and Ch. Wu, UK P&I Club, 'Legal Briefing' (May 2017), p. 4.

https://www.ukpandi.com/fileadmin/uploads/uk-pi/Documents/2017/Legal_Briefing_e_bill_of_Lading_WEB.pdf (visited 15 August 2019).

Moreover, in the absence of a specific general regime, especially at international level, the equivalence between the traditional bill of lading and the e-bill of lading is based on contracts between the system operator and the user and among the users enrolled in the system.[20] The legal basis has been found on novation and attornment, which however do not perfectly fulfil the features of a bill of lading, in particular the abstractness of the relationship there incorporated from the underlying contract and the transfer of rights to third parties.[21]

On the contrary, a true e-bill of lading, like the paper one, should be potentially transferable to the order of any potential endorsee. This requires that any technology enabling its creation and transfer should be open and not restricted to the subscribers of a closed centralised system, and should allow the e-bill of lading to be accessible for its entire life.

The characteristics described above are considered the main reasons that prevented their achieving a wide success.[22]

E-title™ is a recent peer-to-peer non-centralised system, which has, as a legal basis for its operation, a multilateral contract between the company operating it and its users, called The Electronic Title User Agreement.[23] The system is based on a back-end technology provided to the single users and on digital signature in order to confirm authenticity of the electronic document. The system is, however, still based on the management of the electronic bills of lading by the system managers for maintaining secure logs and preventing fraud, but it is the E-title User Group, which is formed by all the system's members, to manage potential disputes between parties.[24]

3.2 The blockchain technology

The most recent technology to be experimented with a view to exploiting it to obtain a feasible e-transport record is blockchain. This technology was historically developed in order to enable trading with the so-called crypto-currencies,[25] but is actually experiencing

20 For example, the 1999 Bolero International Ltd Rulebook/Operating Procedures, the essDOCS' Databridge Services & User Agreement and the Electronic Title User Agreement. J. Tan, L. Starr and Ch. Wu, UK P&I Club, 'Legal Briefing' (May 2017), p. 4.

21 F. Stevens, *The Bill of Lading: Holder Rights and Liabilities* (Routledge 2017), p. 65 ff; M.A. Goldby, 'Legislating to facilitate the use of electronic transferable records: A case study. Reforming the law to facilitate the use of electronic bills of lading in the United Kingdom', p. 5.

https://www.uncitral.org/pdf/english/colloquia/EC/Legislating_to_facilitate_the_use_of_electronic_transferable_records_-_a_case_study_.pdf (visited 15 August 2019).

22 P. Mallon and A. Tomlinson, 'Bolero: electronic "bills of lading" and electronic contracts of sale' [1998] *International Trade Law Quarterly* 257; F. Stevens, *The Bill of Lading: Holder Rights and Liabilities* (Routledge 2017), p. 67; E. Orrù, 'The Electronic Transport Record and Current Challenges of E-logistics and International Trade' in *2nd International Scientific Conference on Maritime Law 'Modern Challenges of Marine Navigation'* (Faculty of Law University of Split, 2018), p. 210.

23 It has been created by E-Title Authority Pte Ltd. J. Tan, L. Starr and Ch. Wu, UK P&I Club, 'Legal Briefing' (May 2017), p. 3.

24 Unfortunately, it is not clear from its website (www.e-title.it) and other media how should it actually work, in particular whether it is based on blockchain technology, which is discussed in the following paragraph.

25 K. Takahashi, 'Blockchain technology and electronic bills of lading' (2016) 22 *Journal of International Maritime Law* 202–211; E. Orrù, 'The Electronic Transport Record and Current Challenges of E-logistics and International Trade' in *2nd International Scientific Conference on Maritime Law 'Modern Challenges of Marine Navigation'* (Faculty of Law University of Split, 2018), p. 217.

increasing interest from the banking and shipping sectors because of the great opportunities there implied for furthering the logistics flows and documentary credit.[26]

Blockchain platforms are open append-only decentralised peer-to-peer platforms, where each transaction is represented by a block holding batches of it and secured by the digital signature of the users.[27] This is obtained by synchronically recording the ledgers of the different participants. Where the economic and legal content of a block is to be transferred under a new transaction, the former block is the basis for the future transaction, giving rise to a chain of blocks, which cannot be altered. The platform grants integrity and incorruptibility of the transactions recorded on the distributed ledgers.[28] Therefore, the user can incorporate in a token an amount in bitcoins, but any other content having an economic value, such as constructive possession and title to goods, as in an electronic bill of lading. Considering specifically the creation of electronic bills of lading using blockchain technology: after having loaded the goods onboard the ship, the carrier would create a new block on the platform, incorporating the content of a traditional bill of lading, as a transaction with the shipper. The latter could transfer it as a new block built on the former one.

The flaw in blockchain platforms is that the real identity of users is not known, since the token's holders are identified by their usernames.[29] To avoid this problem, closed blockchain platforms have been developed, where prospective members are required to identify themselves. This solution, however, shares the same problem common to other closed systems.[30]

Therefore, for obtaining a true e-bill of lading it is necessary, on the one hand, to develop the proper technical infrastructure, improving blockchain technology to entirely fulfil the role of a traditional bill of lading, and the suitable legal framework.[31] If this goal were achieved, a new revolution would happen, consisting in a new dematerialization,[32] as the paper bill of lading enabled the dematerialization of the (rights into the) goods, by the incorporation of their constructive possession in the document of title.[33]

26 In particular, a e-b/l based on blockchain technology is being developed by Maersk with IBM and other stakeholders, including freight forwarder, logistics operators and port authorities: https://port.today/maersk-and-ibm-introduce-blockchain-in-shipping/ (visited 15 August 2019) and https://newsroom.ibm.com/2018-08-09-Maersk-and-IBM-Introduce-TradeLens-Blockchain-Shipping-Solution (visited 15 August 2019).

27 K. Takahashi, 'Blockchain technology and electronic bills of lading' (2016) 22 *Journal of International Maritime Law* 204; P. Cuccuru, '*Blockchain* ed automazione contrattuale. Riflessioni sugli *smart contract*', [2017] 1 *La Nuova giurisprudenza civile commentata* 107, 108.

28 K. Takahashi, 'Blockchain technology and electronic bills of lading' (2016) 22 *Journal of International Maritime Law* 202; E. Ong, *Blockchain bills of lading, Blockchain bills of lading* (CML working paper series, NUS Law18/07 August 2018), p. 10. See also, for example, https://fichtelegal.com/news/legal-considerations-blockchain-based-bills-lading/ (visited on 15 August 2019).

29 K.Takahashi, 'Blockchain technology and electronic bills of lading' (2016) 22 *Journal of International Maritime Law* 209.

30 Ibid, p. 204.

31 See para 5.

32 L. Fedi, 'La dématérialisation du connaissement maritime: utopie ou réalité du XXIe siècle?', in C. Bloch (ed.), *Mélanges en l'honneur de Christian Scapel* (Presse Universitaire d'Aix-Marseille 2013), p. 219, 227; E. Orrù, 'The Electronic Transport Record and Current Challenges of E-logistics and International Trade', in *2nd International Scientific Conference on Maritime Law 'Modern Challenges of Marine Navigation'* (Faculty of Law University of Split, 2018), p. 218.

33 'A bill of lading stands as a substitute and a symbolic representation of the goods therein described and possession symbolized by a bill of lading is the same as the actual possession', W. Parent, 'Passage of Title under Bills of Lading' [1929] *Notre Dame Law Review* 91.

The e-bill of lading would furthermore entail a dematerialization of the document of title and of performance of its delivery.

With regard to the actual application of this technology, some of the systems described in the previous paragraph explore the possibility of using blockchain technology.[34] In addition to them, it is also worth mentioning CargoX Smart B/L[35] and Wave.[36]

4 Smart contracts

The most recent issues addressed by the shipping and banking sector concern a further development of the potentialities of blockchain technology: smart contracts.[37] The first definition of a smart contract was provided, years before the advent of blockchain, by Nick Szabo:

> 'a Smart Contract is a computerized transaction protocol that executes the terms of a contract. The general objectives . . . are to satisfy common contractual conditions (such as payment terms) . . . and minimize the need for trusted intermediaries.'[38]

The simplest example of smart contracts is a vending machine, but the same author foresaw also their potentialities in the digital market.[39]

With specific regard to their use with blockchain technology, smart contracts can be described as 'self-executing digital transactions using decentralized cryptographic mechanisms for enforcement'.[40] In particular, one of their possible applications is to enable automatic enforcement of legal agreements, without the need to resort to judicial remedies,[41] including cases of supervening events.[42]

According to some scholars, smart contracts can also allow the conclusion of contracts, which are governed by the applicable (domestic or uniform) contract law, to be identified according to the nature of the parties and the place of execution of the contract.[43] Other scholars, on the contrary, rule out the conclusion of a legal agreement by

34 S. Wass, 'Bolero's electronic bill of lading service to get blockchain upgrade' (GTR 11 October 2017) https://www.gtreview.com/news/fintech/boleros-electronic-bill-of-lading-service-to-get-blockchain-upgrade/ (visited 15 August 2019); S. Wass, 'EssODCs to integrate e-bill of lading with Voltron blockchain platform' (GTR 5 April 2019) https://www.gtreview.com/news/fintech/essdocs-to-integrate-e-bill-of-lading-with-voltron-blockchain-platform/ (visited 15 August 2019).

35 https://cargox.io/solutions/Smart-BL/ (visited 15 August 2019).

36 http://wavebl.com/ (visited 15 August 2019).

37 R. O'Shields, 'Smart contracts: legal agreements for the blockchain' [2017] 21 *North Carolina Banking Institute* 177.

38 N. Szabo, 'Smart contracts' (1994, unpublished manuscript). See also N. Szabo, 'The Idea of Smart Contracts' (1997) fon.hum.uva.nl (visited 15 August 2019).

39 Ibid.

40 K. Werbach and N. Cornell, 'Contracts Ex Machina' [2017] 67 *Duke Law Journal* 313 https://ssrn.com/abstract=2936294 (visited 15 August 2019). See also R. O'Shields, 'Smart contracts: legal agreements for the blockchain' [2017] 21 *North Carolina Banking Institute* 179.

41 J.M. Sklaroff, 'Smart Contracts and the Cost of Inflexibility' [2017] 166 *University of Pennsylvania Law Review* 263, 291, https://ssrn.com/abstract=3008899 (visited 15 August 2019).

42 D. Di Sabato, 'Gli *smart contracts*: robot che gestiscono il rischio contrattuale' [2017] 2 *Contratto e impresa* 378.

43 Ibid., 393.

this instrument: its relevance under the law would not be a consequence of any agreement between the parties, but an *ex lege* effect.[44]

From an analysis of this technology and of the scholars' opinions, it seems correct to assert that smart contracts actually could not replace agreements between the parties on a legal basis, but, at least in most cases, provide for a faster and simpler execution and performance of contracts.[45] Even where the execution of a contract is obtained through smart contracts, it should be constructed as being concluded through the parties' behaviour[46] or based on the acceptance of the other party's general conditions of contract.[47] Moreover, they would not entirely rule out the risk of future disputes and the need to resort to judicial remedies.[48] The reduction of the risk of litigation would be based on the ability of the parties to envisage in detail the different possible occurrences, as in ordinary contracts. In particular, given the absence of a uniform legal framework for blockchain technology and smart contracts, it is important that the parties provide for the contract to be governed by a legal system expressly recognizing their equivalence to ordinary contracts and provide for a forum choice in favour of the courts of that country, or for arbitration. In the latter case, the choice could also be for *Lex Mercatoria* as the regime for the relationship, provided that it recognizes the equivalence of an electronic bill of lading to the traditional one.[49]

Regarding the electronic bill of lading, smart contracts could simplify and speed up the execution of the different contracts requiring its submission with one single platform. However, attention should be paid to the duties or burdens of the parties under the different contracts, in particular to their duties to examine the goods or the documents with the due diligence. As for the contract of carriage, the carrier must check the apparent conditions of the goods. With regard to documentary credits, for example, the issuing bank, the nominated bank or the confirming bank (if any) have a duty towards the principal to check the documents submitted by the beneficiary under the letter of credit. If blockchain technology could enable the incorporation of all the relevant information in the documents required by the specific letter of credit, grant their authenticity and avoid alterations and frauds, their inspection could be obtained through instructions coded in a smart contract.

5 Issues related to the applicable regime

Apart from the construction of a successful technological infrastructure, the main issue is the identification of a proper legal framework granting the equivalence of an electronic bill of lading to the paper one and providing for its regime. Moreover, this potential uncertainty is increased by the variety of technologies. In fact, whereas some of the recent state provisions or contract terms are constructed with a neutral approach towards the actual technological solutions, others limit their scope to certain specific instruments.

44 Ibid., 394.

45 Ibid., 386–387; P. Cuccuru, '*Blockchain* ed automazione contrattuale. Riflessioni sugli *smart contract*', [2017] 1 *La Nuova giurisprudenza civile commentata* 111.

46 D. Di Sabato, 'Gli *smart contracts*: robot che gestiscono il rischio contrattuale', [2017] 2 *Contratto e impresa* 395 ff.

47 Ibid.

48 Ibid., 401; J.M. Sklaroff, 'Smart Contracts and the Cost of Inflexibility', [2017] 166 *University of Pennsylvania Law Review* 291, https://ssrn.com/abstract=300889 (visited 15 August 2019).

49 See para 5.

5.1 Hard law sources

First of all, there is neither any uniform regime of electronic bills of lading nor any express provision in an international convention in force providing for the equivalence of e-bills of lading to the paper ones. In particular, bills of lading are expressly excluded from the scope of the only international convention in force, which is the UN Convention on the Use of Electronic Communications in International Contracts, signed in New York in 2005.[50]

At the regional level, within the extensive action undertaken for establishing a Digital Single Market, the EU issued the so-called eIDAS regulation,[51] which plays a significant role in the implementation and adaptation of the relevant law to new ICTs instruments and relationships. However, eIDAS does not expressly address the relevant problems relating to the role of bill of lading with regard to both the contracts of carriage and of sale, in particular as a transferable and negotiable document of title.

As for the uniform conventions dealing specifically with carriage of goods by sea, the Hague-Visby Rules[52] provide for a definition of a bill of lading as 'document of title':[53] the express reference to the word 'document' without any further specification to the means by which the document can be issued and transferred (which is coherent with the period when the convention and its protocols were drafted), does not provide a clear solution preventing any issues on their application to electronic bills of lading. The answer to the problem of the functional equivalence of an e-bill of lading to the paper one has to be found in other law sources, such as the eIDAS regulation or the domestic law.

On the other hand, the Hamburg Rules[54] allow the carrier to sign the bill of lading by different means, including electronic means, 'if not inconsistent with the law of the country where the bill of lading is issued'.[55] Under the Hamburg Rules, the regime for the equivalence between a bill of lading signed in writing on paper and one electronically signed is still left to the applicable domestic law, therefore without any uniformity of regime. Moreover, the Rules do not expressly deal with the issuance of a bill of lading by electronic means.

Finally, the 2008 Rotterdam Rules[56] move from previous experiences with e-bills of lading, in particular BOLERO, and expressly provide for the functional equivalence of the electronic transport record to bill of lading. The former is defined as 'information in one or more messages issued by electronic communication[57] under a contract of carriage by a carrier, including information logically associated with the electronic transport record by attachments or otherwise linked to the electronic transport record contemporaneously

---

50 Art. 2.2.

51 Regulation (EU) No 910/2014 of the European Parliament and of the Council of 23 July 2014 on electronic identification and trust services for electronic transactions in the internal market and repealing Directive 1999/93/EC OJ L 257, 28.8.2014, p. 73–114. The acronym stands for 'electronic Identification Authentication and Signature).

52 See note 5.

53 Art. 1, let. b).

54 The United Nations Convention on the Carriage of Goods by Sea (Hamburg, 1978).

55 Art. 14.3.

56 The UN Convention on Contracts for the International Carriage of Goods Wholly or Partly by Sea (New York, 2008).

57 According to art. 1.17, an 'Electronic communication' is an 'information generated, sent, received or stored by electronic, optical, digital or similar means with the result that the information communicated is accessible so as to be usable for subsequent reference'.

with or subsequent to its issue by the carrier, so as to become part of the electronic transport record'.[58]

Despite not being in force, the Rotterdam Rules are particularly important, because they are the first source to explicitly deal with the specific features of bills of lading, in particular issues related to the identification of its holder and its transferability.[59] The solution has the virtue of being technically neutral[60] and consists in the concept of 'exclusive control [over the e-record] from its creation until it ceases to have any effect or validity'.[61] Therefore, the endorsement of an electronic transport record is achieved by the transfer of the exclusive control over it according to the procedure outlined in art. 9.1[62] and to the requirements of a specific electronic system.

At the national level, several countries have adopted or are drafting statutes dealing with the equivalence of e-records to traditional documents. This is, for example, the case with Italy. According to art. 8-ter of the decree-law No 135 of 14 December 2018, as modified by the law No 12 of 11 February 2019, smart contracts based on distributed ledgers satisfy written form requirements under the law, provided that the parties are electronically identified. The above-mentioned decree-law, however, does not address any further issue. Moreover, contrary to the approach of technological neutrality adopted by the Rotterdam Rules, its main flaw is to demand the definition of the technical requirements that must be possessed by smart contracts to further rules and standards to be issued by the Agency for Digital Italy (AgID). This approach therefore would probably prevent uniformity at the international level and the feasibility of the Italian provisions to future technologies.

5.2 Soft law sources and contract terms

With regard to soft law instruments, an important role is played by UNCITRAL in drafting model laws on electronic communications. The first model law is the 1996 Model Law on Electronic Commerce (also known as MLEC), which was revised in 1998: like the Rotterdam Rules, the law is based on the principle of functional equivalence and technological neutrality.[63] Articles 16 and 17 MLEC, in particular, provide for the equivalence of actions undertaken in connection with, or in pursuance of, a contract of carriage by using one or more data messages, to those traditionally performed with paper documents. The non-exhaustive examples listed in art. 16 can apply also to bills of lading. Despite the express reference to 'acquiring or transferring rights and obligations under the contract' among the actions therein listed, it does not specifically address either this issue or the role of bill of lading under an international sale.[64] Another model

---

58 Art. 1.18.

59 G. Van der Ziel, 'Delivery of Goods, Rights of the Controlling Party and Transfer of Rights' (2008) 14 *Journal of International Maritime Law* 602.

60 S. Zunarelli, 'Transfer of Rights', in A. von Ziegler, J. Schelin, S. Zunarelli (eds), *The Rotterdam Rules 2008* (Kluwer Law International, 2010), p. 241.

61 Art. 1.21. J.A. Estrella Faria, 'Electronic Transport Records' in A. von Ziegler, J. Schelin, S. Zunarelli (eds), *The Rotterdam Rules 2008* (Kluwer Law International, 2010), p. 58 ff and 190 ff.

62 Arts 1.19 and 57.2 of the Rotterdam Rules.

63 A. Møllmann, *Delivery of Goods under Bills of Lading* (Routledge, 2016), p. 158.

64 J.A. Estrella Faria, 'Electronic Transport Records', in A. von Ziegler, J. Schelin, S. Zunarelli (eds), *The Rotterdam Rules 2008* (Kluwer Law International, 2010) pp. 60, 53.

law is that on Electronic Signatures, issued in 2001, which, on the contrary, do not specifically address bills of lading or transport documents.

More important is the Model Law on Electronic Transferable Records (also known as MLETR), which was adopted in July 2017. It can apply to e-bills of lading, because they fall under the definition of 'transferable document or instrument'. It consists in 'a document or instrument issued on paper that entitles the holder to claim the performance of the obligation indicated in the document or instrument and to transfer the right to performance of the obligation indicated in the document or instrument through the transfer of that document or instrument'.[65] However, the model law does not address the negotiability of an electronic transferable record, which is left to the substantive law governing the contract. However, according to the 'Explanatory note' to the MLETR drafted by the UNCITRAL itself, the definition of electronic transferable record does not include straight bills of lading and other documents whose 'transferability may be limited due to other agreements'.[66]

Like the Rotterdam Rules, the delivery of a transferable record is based on the concept of transfer of exclusive control 'as the functional equivalent of transfer of possession and thus of delivery'.[67] For this purpose, the MLETR requires the use of reliable methods for ensuring the integrity of the record, the identification of the person holding the exclusive control over the record and its accessibility further reference.[68]

However, the Model Law focuses on the transferability of the record and not on its negotiability on the understanding that negotiability relates to the underlying rights of the holder of the instrument, which fall under substantive law.

At the EU level, within the strategy *Digitising European Industry*,[69] in September 2018 the CEN-CENELEC Focus Group on Blockchain and Distributed Ledger Technologies (FG-BDLT) adopted the White Paper *Recommendations for Successful Adoption in Europe of Emerging Technical Standards on Distributed Ledger/Blockchain Technologies*. The guidelines focus on the issues concerning the compatibility of blockchain and distributed ledger technologies with the provisions of GDPR[70] and eIDAS.

With regard to contract terms, since the 1990s international organizations and associations have been drafting standard clauses. An example are the CMI's *Rules for electronic bills of lading*, which were based on the 1987 *Uniform Rules of Conduct for Interchange of Trade Data by Teletransmission* (UNCID) and could now be considered superseded by

65 Art. 2, para 3. See the UNCITRAL's *Explanatory Note to the UNCITRAL Model Law on Electronic Transferable Records* (UN publication No. E.17.V.5, 2019) para 38 http://www.uncitral.org/pdf/english/texts/electcom/MLETR_ebook.pdf (visited 15 August 2019).

66 Ibid, para 88.

67 Art. 7 and 11.2 MLETR. UNCITRAL's *Explanatory Note to the UNCITRAL Model Law on Electronic Transferable Records* (UN publication No. E.17.V.5, 2019) para 38 http://www.uncitral.org/pdf/english/texts/electcom/MLETR_ebook.pdf (visited 15 August 2019), para 121.

68 Arts 8, 10 and 11.

69 The strategy falls within the Digital Single Market package and was launched in 2016 (Communication from the Commission to the European Parliament, the Council, the European Economic and Social Committee and the Committee of the Regions, *Digitising European Industry Reaping the full benefits of a Digital Single Market*, COM(2016) 180 final).

70 The Regulation (EU) 2016/679 of the European Parliament and of the Council of 27 April 2016 on the protection of natural persons with regard to the processing of personal data and on the free movement of such data, and repealing Directive 95/46/EC (General Data Protection Regulation) OJ L 119/1, 4.5.2016, pp. 1–88.

the new ICTs described in the previous paragraphs. In May 2014, BIMCO published the 'Electronic bill of lading clause' that can be included in charterparties. The clause enables the charterer to issue, sign and transfer bills of lading, waybills and delivery orders in electronic form and provides for their equivalence to paper documents.

With regard to the other contractual relationships where the bill of lading plays a significant role, since 2002 the ICC has introduced the so-called eUCP, first as a supplement to UCP 500. Their latest version is the 2.0, supplement to UCP 600 of 2007.[71] Through a neutral approach to technological solutions, they are meant to 'permit UCP 600 terminology accommodating the electronic presentation of the equivalent of paper documents and provide necessary rules to allow both sets of rules to work together'.[72] The same aim was pursued in the 2010 edition of the ICC Incoterms® Rules, which enable the parties to use any electronic record or procedure if agreed between them or customary.

Finally, as for insurance policies, whereas traditionally the risks related to the use of ICT technologies used to fall outside the coverage, in 2010, 2013 and 2015 the International Group of P&I Clubs agreed to cover any liabilities arising in respect of the carriage of cargo under three approved electronic trading systems (BOLERO, essDOCS and E-title™), provided that such liability would also have arisen under a paper bill.[73] On the other hand, P&I coverage does not extend to other systems, including those based on distributed ledgers.

6 Concluding remarks

The different technologies experimented for the issuance of an electronic bill of lading or transport record show the actual interest of the shipping industry and trade sector. However, the current problems and uncertainties on the technological infrastructure go hand in hand with the lack of certainty as for the legal framework.

From the one side, there is intense lawmaking both at the international, European and domestic level. With regard to hard law provisions in force, however, they have mainly regional or domestic scope and do not address the issues that specifically characterise the roles and features of the bill of lading. Moreover, some of these laws are not technically neutral. As for soft law tools, UNCITRAL model laws have not been adopted by a sufficient number of countries to ensure a uniform regime.[74]

Following the analysis developed in para 5, it is also possible to conclude that some consensus is being reached on common principles concerning the functional equivalence of electronic transport records to paper bills of lading. In particular, these principles concern the equivalence of the exclusive control to the constructive possession of the document of

71 The first edition issued as supplement to UCP 600 was the 1.1. The 2.0 edition is in force since 1 July 2019.

72 Introduction to *ICC Uniform Customs and Practice for Documentary Credits – UCP 600. Supplement to UCP 600 for Electronic Presentation* (Trilingual Edn English-Italian-French, ICC Publication No. 600LE 2007) p. 94.

73 Circular 16/10 of September 2010; Circular 6/13 *Electronic (Paperless) Trading Systems – Electronic Shipping Solutions and Bolero International Ltd – updated ESSDSUA Version 2013*; Circular 12/15 *Electronic (Paperless) Trading Systems.*

74 See the UNCITRAL's *Explanatory Note to the UNCITRAL Model Law on Electronic Transferable Records* (UN publication No. E.17.V.5, 2019) para 38, http://www.uncitral.org/pdf/english/texts/electcom/MLETR_ebook.pdf (visited 15 August 2019), para. 20.

title and the transfer of this control, by the technical procedures that are specific of each system, to the delivery of the bill of lading.

However, the consensus on these principles seems far from having given rise to international usage and practices that could be considered applying *per se*, without any risk of uncertainty.

Whereas a uniform regime, based on international conventions or usage, would better grant certainty of the electronic bill of lading regime, the use of ICT solutions is therefore still based on (multi-lateral) agreements among the parties involved, which do not prevent disputes,[75] especially with regard to the technical systems that are used, since not all the provisions or contract terms opted for a neutral solution. Moreover, this contract approach is not able to fulfil the functions of bill of lading, especially with regard to third parties.

75 M.A. Goldby, 'The Rising Tide of Paperless Trade: Analysing the Legal Implications', in B. Soyer and A. Tettenborn (eds), *International Trade and Carriage of Goods* (Informa Law, 2017), p. 156 ff; J.M. Sklaroff, 'Smart Contracts and the Cost of Inflexibility', [2017] 166 *University of Pennsylvania Law Review* 299, https://ssrn.com/abstract=3008899 (visited 15 August 2018).

CHAPTER 12

The future of the regulation of the contract for the multimodal carriage of goods in the context of the Rotterdam Rules

Dr Daniel Dąbrowski and Dr Konrad Garnowski

1 Introduction

The United Nations Convention on Contracts for the International Carriage of Goods Wholly or Partly by sea was signed on 23 September 2009 in Rotterdam.[1] The entry of the Convention into force requires ratification (acceptance, approval or accession) of 20 states (Article 94(1) of the Rotterdam Rules). Although 25 states signed the Rotterdam Rules, signalling an intention to be bound by them, so far only four have ratified them.[2] Achieving the number provided for in Article 94(1) of the Rotterdam Rules does not seem to be possible in the near future. However, it is too early to proclaim a complete failure of the Rotterdam Rules. Many international conventions waited much longer for their entry into force.[3] Nonetheless, one can speak about lack of success. The Rotterdam Rules have not been widely accepted by the international community. Furthermore, even if they ultimately come into force they will not replace the Hague-Visby[4] rules, as intended, but will create another regime for the carriage of goods by sea, which will complicate the legal situation in this area.

The Rotterdam Rules are another attempt to codify the multimodal contract for carriage of goods. Such attempts have been made several times in the past, the most spectacular defeat being incurred by the multimodal convention of 1980.[5] The intention of the Rotterdam Rules is to regulate only those multimodal contracts that include an international sea leg. However, even such a cautious approach was criticised in academic writing. The question is whether the extension of the Rotterdam Rules to multimodal transport was the right solution. To what degree did this regulation affect the acceptance of the Rotterdam Rules in particular countries? It is also worth considering whether the setback of the limited regulation of the multimodal contract for the carriage of goods in

1 The Convention was adopted on 11 December 2008 during the sixty-third session of the General Assembly. The Convention is referred to as the Rotterdam Rules: United Nations Convention on Contracts for the International Carriage of Goods Wholly or Partly by Sea (Rotterdam Rules) (New York, 2008).

2 They are: Spain, Togo, Congo and Cameroon.

3 For example, the Hamburg Rules – United Nations Convention on the Carriage of Goods by Sea (Hamburg, 1978) entered into force 14 years after their adoption. Nevertheless, the process of ratification of Hamburg Rules has been more dynamic.

4 The Hague Rules as Amended by the Brussels Protocol 1968.

5 United Nations Convention on International Multimodal Transport of Goods (Multimodal Transport Convention, Geneva, 1980). This convention has been ratified by 11 countries, while it required to be ratified by 30 countries to enter into force. The last ratification (accession) took place in 2005. The Convention is referred to as the MT Convention.

the Rotterdam Rules will make it more difficult to work on an international convention that would regulate this contract to a wider extent.

2 The method of regulation of the multimodal carriage of goods in the Rotterdam Rules

From the time when work began on the new maritime convention, it was supposed to be a *maritime plus* convention,[6] thus regulating not only maritime transport, but also complementary carriage by other modes of transport. The aim was to cover the entire contractual period agreed by the parties and regulate *door-to-door* transport, the popularity of which has been growing for many years. The essence of the *maritime plus* regulation is expressed in Article 1(1) of the Rotterdam Rules defining the term 'contract of carriage'. According to this definition, a contract of carriage means 'a contract in which a carrier, against the payment of freight, undertakes to carry goods from one place to another. The contract shall provide for carriage by sea and may provide for carriage by other modes of transport in addition to the sea carriage'. It is therefore clear from this definition that the main subject of the regulation of the Rotterdam Rules is maritime transport. The regulation of carriage by other means of transport is of a supplementary nature. Due to the fact that regulation is limited to multimodal transport with a sea leg, the Rotterdam Rules cannot be regarded as a convention for a multimodal transport in the true sense of the term.[7] At the same time, however, multimodal transport frequently includes a sea leg. The Rotterdam Rules could therefore play a very important role.

As mentioned above, when regulating a multimodal carriage, the concept of a uniform system of liability adopted, *inter alia*, in the MT Convention has been abandoned. Instead, the so-called *limited network system* was adopted.[8] Under this system, the liability of a multimodal carrier for damage incurred during each stage of carriage included in a multimodal transport is regulated by the rules governing carriage by an individual mode of transport. If, however, it is not possible to determine at which stage of transport the damage occurred (*non-localized damage*), or if the damage is caused during carriage by more than one means of transport, a unified regulation of the Rotterdam Rules applies. The idea of a limited network system is expressed in Article 26. According to this article:

> 'When loss of or damage to goods, or an event or circumstance causing a delay in their delivery, occurs during the carrier's period of responsibility but solely before their loading onto the ship or solely after their discharge from the ship, the provisions of this Convention do not prevail over those provisions of another international instrument that, at the time of such loss, damage or event or circumstance causing delay:
>
> (a) Pursuant to the provisions of such international instrument would have applied to all or any of the carrier's activities if the shipper had made a separate and direct contract with

6 The term is widely used in literature. It has appeared in the work of the working group since 2003. Cf. A/CN.9/WG.III/WP.29, par. 8. See also e.g. M. Sturley, T. Fujita and G.J. Van Der Ziel, *The Rotterdam Rules* (Sweet & Maxwell 2011), pp. 60–61; F. Berlingieri, 'Multimodal aspects of the Rotterdam Rules', http://www.rotterdamrules2009.com/cms/uploads/Def.%20tekst%20F.%20Berlingieri%2013%20OKT29.pdf, pp. 1–2 (visited 16 August 2019); M. Hoeks, *Multimodal Transport Law* (Wolters Kluwer 2010), p. 23; M. Hoeks, 'Maritime Plus and the European status quo' [2010] *Scandinavian Institute of Maritime Yearbook* 157.

7 M. Sturley, T. Fujita and G.J. Van Der Ziel, *The Rotterdam Rules* (Sweet & Maxwell 2011), p. 61.

8 This system has been applied since the first draft of the Rotterdam Rules. See: Preliminary Draft Instrument WP.21 art. 4.2.1.

the carrier in respect of the particular stage of carriage where the loss of, or damage to goods, or an event or circumstance causing delay in their delivery occurred;

(b) Specifically provide for the carrier's liability, limitation of liability, or time for suit; and
(c) Cannot be departed from by contract either at all or to the detriment of the shipper under that instrument.'

This provision regulates the relationship between the Rotterdam Rules and international conventions on unimodal transport from the 'negative' side, by indicating when the Rotterdam Rules are not applicable. The time and place of the damage is of the greatest importance. The unimodal convention is applicable only if the damage occurred solely before the goods were loaded onto the ship or solely after discharging from the ship. At the same time, it must be decided whether a given transport stage taking place before loading or after discharging would be subject to the international convention regime. For example, if goods were transported to the port on a motor vehicle and there was a damage to goods during this stage, the carrier's liability would be determined based on the provisions of the CMR Convention only if the convention was applicable to a hypothetical contract of carriage which the sender would conclude with the carrier in relation to a specific transport stage.[9] If, in the example presented, the place of loading the goods onto the motor vehicle and the place of discharging from this vehicle were in the same country, then the hypothetical contract for carriage by road would not be regulated by the CMR Convention but by the relevant domestic law. In this case, the carrier would be liable for damage caused during the road stage under the Rotterdam Rules. The Rules do not prevail over the provisions of international instruments, but they prevail over the provisions of domestic law.[10] Insofar as the place of loading and the place of delivery of goods are located in two different countries, at least one of which is a contracting country of the CMR Convention (Article 1 CMR), this convention shall apply to the carrier's liability.

In addition, unimodal conventions will not be applied if the loss of or damage to goods or an event or circumstance causing a delay in delivery occurred during the period between loading onto the ship and discharging from the ship. This solution is obvious, because unimodal conventions, as a rule, do not cover carriage by sea. The carrier would then be liable under the Rotterdam Rules. Furthermore, two other situations should be considered. First of all, the Rotterdam Rules should be referred to if it is impossible to determine at which stage of the transport the damage occurred. This applies in particular to damage caused during container transport, as it is usually very difficult, if not impossible, to determine where the goods in the container have been damaged in case of such transport.[11] Secondly, the carrier will also be liable under the Rules when the event causing the damage or delay occurred during a stage other than the sea leg, but also continued during the sea leg.

9 The solution applied by the authors of the Rotterdam Rules is called 'the hypothetical contract approach' or 'hypothetical test'. See e.g. M. Sturley, T. Fujita and G.J. Van Der Ziel, *The Rotterdam Rules* (Sweet & Maxwell, 2011), pp. 65, 67; U.L. Rasmussen in A. von Ziegler, J. Schelin, S. Zunarelli (eds), *The Rotterdam Rules 2008* (Wolters Kluwer 2010), p. 148; Hoeks, *Multimodal Transport Law* (Wolters Kluwer 2010), p. 341.

10 M. Sturley, T. Fujita and G.J. Van Der Ziel, *The Rotterdam Rules* (Sweet & Maxwell, 2011), p. 68; U.L. Rasmussen in A. von Ziegler, J. Schelin, S. Zunarelli (eds), *The Rotterdam Rules 2008* (Wolters Kluwer 2010), p. 147.

11 J.M. Alcántara, 'The new regime and multimodal transport' [2002] *Lloyd's Maritime and Commercial Law Quarterly* 401; E. Eftestøl-Wilhelmsson, 'The Rotterdam Rules in a European multimodal context' (2010) *The Journal of International Maritime Law* 282.

An example of such a situation is the failure of the container cooling system, occurring at the road stage but leading to the deterioration of the goods during the sea leg.

It should be also noted that Article 26 regulates the relationship between the Rotterdam Rules and the unimodal conventions only with regard to matters relating to the carrier's liability.[12] Meanwhile, unimodal conventions also regulate other issues, such as transport documents, sender's liability, the right to dispose of goods, jurisdiction, etc. The general principle regarding the relationship between the Rotterdam Rules and unimodal conventions is expressed in Article 82 of the Rotterdam Rules. Pursuant to this article:

> 'Nothing in this Convention affects the application of any of the following international conventions in force at the time this Convention enters into force, including any future amendment to such conventions, that regulate the liability of the carrier for loss of or damage to the goods:
>
> (a) Any convention governing the carriage of goods by air to the extent that such convention according to its provisions applies to any part of the contract of carriage;
>
> (b) Any convention governing the carriage of goods by road to the extent that such convention according to its provisions applies to the carriage of goods that remain loaded on a road cargo vehicle carried on board a ship;
>
> (c) Any convention governing the carriage of goods by rail to the extent that such convention according to its provisions applies to carriage of goods by sea as a supplement to the carriage by rail; or
>
> (d) Any convention governing the carriage of goods by inland waterways to the extent that such convention according to its provisions applies to a carriage of goods without trans-shipment both by inland waterways and sea.'

It can therefore be noted that the only conflict that could arise in relation to air conventions has clearly been resolved. With regard to the conventions regulating the carriage by other modes of transport, less clear solutions have been adopted. This issue will be developed in the next section.

3 Criticism of the regulation of the multimodal carriage of goods in the Rotterdam Rules

The question arises whether the way in which multimodal carriage is regulated and the relationship between the Rotterdam Rules and the unimodal conventions are appropriate. The rejection of a uniform system of liability was the right choice. Despite some advantages of this system, it would lead to an inevitable conflict with unimodal conventions. Application of this system in the 1980 MT Convention was a main cause of failure of this convention. Bearing this in mind, the authors of the Rotterdam Rules could not follow this path. The limited network system adopted in the Rotterdam Rules solves the issue of the carrier's liability for non-localized damage. This is the problem of the greatest importance in multimodal transport and the method of its regulation must be assessed positively. It is also important that Article 26 of the Rotterdam Rules does not cause conflict with the provisions of the unimodal conventions regarding carrier's liability. According to this

12 Hoeks, *Multimodal Transport Law* (Wolters Kluwer 2010), p. 340; F. Berlingieri, 'Multimodal aspects of the Rotterdam Rules', http://www.rotterdamrules2009.com/cms/uploads/Def.%20tekst%20F.%20Berlingieri%2013%20OKT29.pdf (visited 16 August 2019), pp. 7–12; E. Røsæg, 'Conflicts of Conventions in the Rotterdam Rules' [2009] *The Journal of International Maritime Law* 242–245.

article, the Rotterdam Rules are applicable only if the provisions of the unimodal conventions could not be applied. The disadvantage of the adopted system is its unpredictability.[13] The parties to the contract of carriage will not know – at the time of its conclusion – the rules of carrier's liability for damage, loss of goods or delay, limits of carrier's liability and other matters related to the liability of the carrier. They will not be able to assess the risks associated with the concluded contract. However, this is a feature of the network system resulting from its very nature and only a unified system would ensure predictability of the effects of the concluded contract.

While Article 26 of the Rotterdam Rules is assessed rather positively, the general rule regarding relations with unimodal conventions is criticised.[14] This applies to the relation of the Rotterdam Rules to the CMR Convention, railway and inland waterway conventions. The authors of the Rotterdam Rules took the very controversial view that the unimodal convention does not apply in a situation where a contract providing for the use of more than two means of transport has been concluded. The scope of priority granted to unimodal conventions in Article 82(b), (c) and (d) of the Rotterdam Rules is therefore very narrow and concerns only those situations where unimodal conventions expressly provide for the application of their provisions to carriage by another mode of transport than that basically governed by the unimodal convention in question. Consequently, if the Rotterdam Rules enter into force, a contract of carriage providing, for example, for carriage by road and sea will be subject in its entirety to the Rotterdam Rules (with the exception of 'piggy-back' carriage). This would apply in particular to documents issued in connection with the carriage, disposal of goods, impossibility of performance, prevention of delivery, consignor's liability, etc. The CMR Convention would apply only to the regulation of the carrier's liability for damage (loss, delay) that occurred only on the road section.

It was a risky move to make a clear statement in favour of one of the views on probably the most controversial issue concerning the application of CMR and other unimodal conventions (with the exception of air conventions). The view contrary to the one adopted by the authors of the Rotterdam Rules prevails in many European countries. The acceptance of this opposite view leads inevitably to the thesis of a conflict between the unimodal conventions and the Rotterdam Rules. It can be assumed that this constitutes a significant barrier to the ratification of the Rotterdam Rules in those countries that doubt whether their ratification does not violate international obligations resulting from the previously ratified conventions. The way of regulating the contract for multimodal carriage may be one of the reasons for the failure of the convention (of course, alongside several others of even greater importance).

4 Future of the regulation of the multimodal carriage of goods

These problems lead to a question about the future of the international regulation of the multimodal transportation of goods. Is it possible to start working on a new convention that

13 See e.g. Hoeks, *Multimodal Transport Law* (Wolters Kluwer 2010), p. 16; E. Eftestøl-Wilhelmsson, 'The Rotterdam Rules in a European multimodal context' [2010] *The Journal of International Maritime Law* 277–278; B. Marten, 'Multimodal Transport Reform and the European Union: A Minimalist Approach' [2012] *European Transport Law* 133; W. Tetley, *A Summary of General Criticism of THE UNCITRAL Convention (The Rotterdam Rules)*: https://docentes.fd.unl.pt/docentes_docs/ma/wks_MA_32001.pdf (visited 16 August 2019).

14 See e.g. Hoeks, *Multimodal Transport Law* (Wolters Kluwer, 2010), pp. 368–375; E. Røsæg, 'Conflicts of Conventions in the Rotterdam Rules' [2009] *The Journal of International Maritime Law* 248.

concerns only multimodal transport? Should we return to the concept of a unified system that provides greater legal predictability?[15] It would be pointless to propose creating a new convention for the regulation of the multimodal transportation of goods. Such a convention could not provide for a carrier's unified liability system due to the inevitable conflict with unimodal conventions. Adopting a limited network system would be a partial solution. It seems that the international community should aim to create one international agreement regulating the carriage of goods in all basic modes of transport. Only the unification of the rules of carrier's liability in particular modes of transport (at least in relation to the basic issues) would allow the creation of a simple and predictable carrier's liability regime in multimodal transport. At the same time, this would eliminate the problem of recourse gaps. A multimodal carrier would be liable to the sender on the same terms that a subcontractor would be liable to him.

The idea of creating one international agreement regulating transport in various modes of transport is not new.[16] Owing to the multiplicity of stakeholders and their divergent interests, such a project is feasible within a few decades at the earliest. However, it does not seem to be impossible to achieve. Contrary to appearances, the solutions contained in individual unimodal conventions (with the exception of sea conventions) are quite similar to one another in terms of design, subject matter and scope of regulation. There are, however, many important differences regarding, for example, the basis of liability or limits on compensation. Nevertheless, the application of particular concepts in individual conventions was not determined by the specific nature of a given branch of transport, but was merely a manifestation of an arbitrary decision of the authors of the conventions. Therefore, it is not impossible to develop solutions fitting every mode of transport. It would be most difficult in relation to maritime transport, but it cannot be assumed in advance that there will be no possibility of finding a consensus. In addition, it is conceivable to leave certain distinctions between the different modes of transport, as well as to apply the right of option to join the different parts of such an international agreement. There is no doubt that the scope of regulation of such a new international agreement should be relatively narrow and concern the most important issues, so that it would be easier to obtain international acceptance of the solutions developed.

Due to the lack of international regulations, as of today, the parties to the multimodal transport contract can only specify in the contract the rules for the performance of this contract, including the principles of liability (if it is allowed under national law). The best solution is to refer to the uniform rules developed by intergovernmental organizations. However, the legal status of these rules is unclear and there is usually no certainty that they will be applied by the court in the event of a dispute.

5 The multimodal carriage of goods in national law of selected countries

Regardless of the international regulations, the regimes of national law of particular countries also provide for various solutions concerning multimodal transport. However, other

15 This is the main thesis of William Tetley: W. Tetley, *A Summary of General Criticism of THE UNCITRAL Convention (The Rotterdam Rules)*: https://docentes.fd.unl.pt/docentes_docs/ma/wks_MA_32001.pdf (visited 16 August 2019), p. 5.

16 See e.g. J. Ramberg, 'Multimodal transport. A new dimension of the law of carriage of goods?' in *Études offertes à René Rodière* (Dalloz 1981), p. 492.

countries have neglected the issue, which to this day remains unsettled (*inter alia*, Poland). Of the countries where relevant regulations may be found, attention should be drawn to Germany, Spain and the Netherlands. Each of these countries has introduced regulations which govern the multimodal transport and in each of them such contract is considered as a different type of contract of carriage.[17] The German Commercial Code (Handelsgezetzbuch, or HGB)[18] lays a general rule in § 452, which stipulates that:

> 'If the carriage of goods is performed under a uniform contract of carriage by different means of transport and if a separate contract had been concluded between the contracting parties for each part of the carriage by one means of transport and at least two of these contracts would have been subject to different legal provisions, the provisions of the first subsection shall apply to the contract, unless the following special provisions or applicable international conventions provide otherwise. This shall also apply where part of the carriage by sea is performed.'

The provision of § 452 is a consequence of the view that a multimodal transport contract is recognised as a *sui generis* contract. Therefore, as a rule, the provisions of the unimodal conventions do not apply to such a contract. They apply only by virtue of the reference in § 452a HGB, according to which:

> 'If it is established that the loss, damage or incident which caused the delivery period to be exceeded occurred during a particular part of the carriage, the liability of the carrier shall be determined, by derogation from the provisions of the first subsection, in accordance with the legal provisions which would apply to a contract of carriage on that part of carriage. The burden of proving that the loss, damage or event giving rise to a delay in delivery occurred on a particular leg of the journey shall rest with the claiming party.'

The provisions of the HGB are more versatile than the Rotterdam Rules. The requirements for application of an Act other than the HGB are not as strict as under Article 26 of the Rotterdam Rules. The HGB provides that provisions of any other Act should be applied in all situations when it is established that the loss, damage or delay occurred during a particular part of the carriage governed by the provisions of this other Act. Only if that would be impossible will the provisions of the HGB apply. This solution might seem practical, but it should be also noted that the issue of applicable law rests on the evidentiary issues. Therefore, the same problem arises as already mentioned under the Rotterdam Rules. The Regulations of the HGB also leave some degree of unpredictability and the parties to the contract of carriage will not be able to precisely assess the risk at the time of the conclusion of contract.[19]

Spanish regulations concerning multimodal carriage can be found in law 15/2009 of 11 November regulating the contract of transportation of goods.[20] Article 67 of that Act contains a definition of combined carriage which requires the goods to be carried by more than one mode of transport, but stipulates that one of them should be by land. This is a

17 M. Hoeks, *Multimodal Transport Law* (Wolters Kluwer 2010), p. 71; I. Koller, T*ransportrecht, Kommentar zu Spedition, Güttertransport und Lagergeschäft* (C.H. Beck 2013), p. 589.

18 Act of 10.5.1897 (Reichgesetzblatt I, p. 219), amended by act of 10.7.2018 (Bundesgesetzblatt I, p. 1102).

19 R. Herber, in H. Schmidt (eds), *Münchener Kommentar zum Handelsgesetzbuch* (München 2009), p. 373.

20 Ley 15/2009, de 11 de noviembre, del contrato de transporte terrestre de mercancías, BOE núm. 273 of 12.11.2009.

regulation similar to the one included in Rotterdam Rules (Article 1(1)). Subsequently, Article 68(1) of the Spanish Act stipulates that 'the multimodal transport contract shall be governed by the regulations of each mode, as if the carrier and the consignor had entered into a different contract of carriage for each stage of the carriage'. Moreover, Article 68(3) provides that if it is impossible to determine during which of the parts of carriage the damage occurred, the liability of the carrier shall be decided pursuant to the provisions of the Spanish Act. Basically, the regulations of Spanish law are similar to German law. Both Acts strive to apply the regulations that are most suitable for the part of carriage during which the damage occurred.

Provisions of the Dutch Civil Code[21] contain different solutions. In Article 8:40 a definition of a contract of combined carriage can be found. According to this provision a contract of combined carriage of goods is the contract of carriage whereby the carrier (combined carrier) engages himself under one single contract towards the consignor to perform transport in part by sea, inland waterway, road, railway, air, pipeline or by means of any other mode of transport. Contrary to the Rotterdam Rules and Spanish law, the Dutch definition of a contract of combined carriage does not require any particular mode of transport to be included. Furthermore, Article 8:41 provides that under this type of carriage each part of the transport shall be governed by the rules of law applicable to that part. In order to avoid practical problems regarding the issues common for all stages of carriage (for example, transport documents) there are also some provisions concerning these matters. Thus, Articles 8:44–8:51 govern the issue of a CT-document (combined transport document), including its contents, evidentiary value etc.

However, the most important provisions are those regulating liability of the carrier. Article 8:42 deals with the issue of non-localized damage and stipulates that the carrier is liable for the damage resulting from delay, loss or damage to the goods if it has not been established where the event causing the damage occurred. The carrier may waive liability only if he can prove that he is not liable for any of the stages of the transport where the loss, damage or delay may have occurred. At the same time, Article 8:43 provides that the liability of the carrier for a non-localized damage caused by damage, total or partial loss, delay or any other event causing damage to the goods is determined according to the rules of law applicable to the part or parts of the transport where that event may have occurred and from which the majority of the damage results.

As under other national acts, the matter at hand is determined by evidentiary issues. However, unlike German and Spanish Acts, Dutch regulations do not require proof that the damage occurred during any particular stage of carriage. Instead they assume that it is enough to prove that it may have occurred during some stages of carriage and eventually the amount of damage is the main factor determining the appropriate regime. From this perspective the German and Spanish regulations seems to be clearer and easier to apply in judicial practice. Admittedly they do not solve the issue of unpredictability of the regulations that will be applied in any given case, but it seems very difficult to avoid this problem if regimes of liability are diversified. In order to eliminate it, a particular regime would have to be determined in advance. On the other hand, this solution might lead to the situation where the applicable regulations might not correspond to the particular part of carriage

21 Nieuw Burgerlijk Wetboek Boek 8, BWBR0005034.

during which the damage occurred, even if that could be proved unequivocally. This also speaks in favour of creating a legal Act that would unify the rules of a carrier's liability in all basic modes of transport, as suggested in the previous part of this paper.

6 Concluding remarks

The future of the Rotterdam Rules is uncertain. Even if they enter into force, they will not replace the current maritime conventions. Taking into account the development of multimodal transport and the integration of carriage by different modes of transport, the efforts of the international community should be focused on creating one international agreement governing uniformly (at least to a certain extent) the carriage by different modes of transport. This would ensure predictability of the carrier's liability and eliminate the problem of the recourse gap. However, it would undoubtedly take a long time to develop such an international agreement. At present, the codification of a multimodal transport contract may and should be carried out in national law systems. From those described above, the German and Spanish regulations should be assessed positively and may be used as a basis for the works on national regulations in different countries.

CHAPTER 13

Regulation of the multimodal carrier's liability regime with a special focus of selected national maritime and transport laws[1]

Patryk Ciok

1 Introduction

1.1 A problem of unlocalized loss

One of the most important problems in the multimodal carriage is the carrier's liability regime in the case of unlocalized loss. Since the 1950s, this problem has been especially connected with the containerization[2] of transport. More precisely, the multimodal carriage of goods should be performed by at least two different modes of transport from the beginning to the end of a single carriage (for example, ship and lorry). The problem refers to the situation where a cargo carried in a container has been damaged and it is impossible to find out on which stage the loss occurred (for example, the maritime or the road stage of the carriage).

In such circumstances, it is necessary to decide which carrier's liability regime should be applied. Should it, for example, be the regime of the maritime carrier or the road carrier? Or should it perhaps be a rather different regime, suitable only for the multimodal carrier's liability?

1.2 Network system and uniform system

There are different legal solutions to the problem presented above, but they could be classified into two basic categories, i.e. into two types of legal regulation of the multimodal carrier's liability. The first of these is known as the uniform system, while the second one as the network system. In the 'pure' uniform system, it is not important to localize the place of loss. This system is applicable to a separate liability regime suitable only for the multimodal transport, even in the case of localized loss. This liability regime could be construed even on the basis of the rules which are quite different from the unimodal liability regimes.[3] In the network system, however, it is assumed that when it is known where (on which stage of the journey) the loss occurred, the liability regime applicable for each leg of transport

1 The author declares that the conducted research was funded by National Science Centre, Poland, under the contract UMO - 2016/22/E/HS5/00050 Problems of contemporary maritime codes.

2 A.P. Lisievici-Brezeanu, 'Global requirement and early praxis of multimodal transport' (2013) 5 (2) *Contemporary Readings in Law and Social Justice* 705–706.

3 R. De Vit, *Multimodal transport. Carrier liability and documentation* (LLP Professional Publishing, 1995), p. 143.

should be applied.[4] To be more precise, if it is known that the loss occurred on the road stage, for example, the regime of liability suitable for the road carrier should be applied. However, when it is not possible to establish on what stage of carriage the loss occurred, one of the regimes must be chosen. In the 'pure' network system, when the place of loss is unlocalized, the carrier is liable for organizational neglect as a rule.

It is almost impossible to find binding provisions which could be classified as the 'pure' uniform or the 'pure' network systems in the world. Therefore, there are actually various forms of both systems, which could be jointly classified as 'limited' or 'modified' uniform or network systems.[5] Such legal solutions most often include combinations of the uniform system with some rules from the network system or *vice versa.*[6] The efforts to minimize the disadvantages of both systems in their 'pure' versions result in the creation of mixed systems.[7]

1.3 International regulations

International regulations include examples of the application of both these systems (or rather their modifications). A good example of the uniform system is the regulation contained in the UN Convention on International Multimodal Transport of Goods of 1980.[8] However, the regulation contained in this Convention is not a 'pure' uniform system. According to Article 19, when the unimodal convention applicable to the leg of transport stipulates a higher carrier's liability limit, this limit (and not the limit from the 1980 Convention) should be applied. This is actually an example of the modified uniform system.[9]

Regulations based on the network system are often construed by an additional regulation contained in the normative act. This additional regulation stipulates each carrier's liability regime. It means that the unimodal regulations, i.e. land, maritime or air carriage regulations, contain additional provisions referring to the multimodal carriage. In particular, these regulations refer to the liability for loss in the case of an unlocalized place of loss.

1.4 National laws

Regulations of international conventions contain many different legal solutions, which can be classified into the same type of multimodal carrier's liability regime. Nevertheless, an even greater variety of solutions could be found in the national maritime and transport

4 Ch. Hancock, 'Multimodal transport under the Convention' in D. Rhidian Thomas (ed.), *A New Convention for the Carriage of Goods by the Sea – The Rotterdam Rules. An analysis of The UN Convention on Contracts for the International Carriage of Goods Wholly or Partly by Sea* (Lawtext Publishing Limited, 2009), p. 40.

5 P. Ciok, 'The carrier's liability for damage to cargo in multimodal transport' (2016) XIX *Studia Iuridica Toruniensia* 31–32.

6 In the uniform system, the modification is often that in the case of localized loss one should apply the limits of carrier's liability analogous to the adequate unimodal liability regime. This solution is similar to that in the United Nations Convention on International Multimodal Transport of Goods (Geneva, 24 May 1980).

7 A. Kiantou – Pampouki, 'Multimodal transport carrier liability and issues related to the bills of lading' in A. Kiantou – Pampouki (ed.), *Multimodal transport. Carrier Liability and Issues Related to the Bills of Lading* (2000), p. 27.

8 United Nations Convention on International Multimodal Transport of Goods (Geneva, 24 May 1980).

9 D.A. Glass, *Freight Forwarding and Multimodal Transport Contracts*, 2nd edn (Informa Law from Routledge, 2012), p. 327.

laws. Some of the solutions look similar to the analogical international regulations, but there are also national laws containing solutions that are unprecedented in international law. There are even circumstances in which the national regulation could not be classified into the types of liability mentioned earlier.

The author's aim in this article is to make an effort to analyze selected national regulations. The author also hopes to classify their construction in the context of the types of multimodal carrier's liability regime mentioned above.

2 National legal solutions of the multimodal carrier's liability regime

2.1 Poland

At the moment, the Polish transport law has no complex regulation of the carrier's liability in multimodal transport. However, there are a few important provisions which directly or indirectly refer to multimodal carriage.

2.1.1 The Polish Maritime Code

The Polish Maritime Code is a normative act which contains provision referring directly to multimodal carriage.[10] Article 138 of the Code stipulates that there is an opportunity to issue what some call a 'through bill of lading' (shipping bill). The carrier can issue this type of bill of lading when part of the carriage will be performed by another carrier. Of course, the carriage could be performed by a maritime carrier, but it could also be performed by another carrier by means of a different mode of transport. In the case of an unlocalized loss, the liability regime contained in the Maritime Code should be applicable.

2.1.2 The Transport Law

The Transport Law of 1984 (TL) is also an important normative act.[11] Its provisions do not refer directly to multimodal carriage, but the law regulates the multimodal carrier's liability over a limited area. According to Article 1 of the Transport Law, its scope of application contains all the legs of the transport, with the exclusion of maritime, air and horse carriage. Therefore, if the multimodal transport performed in Poland did not contain the maritime or air stage (e.g. it could contain road and rail carriage), the multimodal carrier's liability would be automatically regulated by the Transport Law.[12]

2.1.3 The Aviation Law

The provisions contained in the normative acts regulating air carriage are also important. The air carrier's liability was regulated by the Transport Law until 2002, when a new version of the statute known as the Aviation Law was enacted.[13] That Act excluded the air carrier's liability from the TL's scope of application.

---

10 Act of 18 September 2001, the Maritime Code (Journal of Laws of 2001, No 138, item 1545 as amended)

11 Act of 15th November 1984, the Transport Law (Journal of Laws of 1984 No 53, item 272, as amended).

12 D. Dąbrowski, 'The multimodal carrier's liability for non-localized loss' (2016) 4 (36) *Problemy Transportu i Logistyki* 206.

13 Act of 3rd July 2002, the Aviation Law (Journal of Laws of 2002 No 130, item 1112, as amended).

The legal solution to the carrier's general liability contained in the Aviation Law is quite different from the other Polish statutes regulating the carrier's liability regime. The Aviation Law provides that the air carrier is liable for the loss in the carriage of the passengers, luggage or goods, according to the rules of the international conventions binding on the Republic of Poland. The Aviation Law also stipulates that the international convention's regime is applicable even for domestic carriage. Additionally, there is a provision that, in a situation where more than one air convention is ratified by Poland, the carrier's liability is to be regulated by the last of the ratified conventions.[14]

That provision refers to the air conventions to which Poland is a party, in particular, the Warsaw Convention[15] and the Montreal Convention.[16] These two conventions regulate the air carrier's liability regime and both have been ratified by Poland.[17] It does not mean, however, that the former Warsaw Convention is no longer binding. The Montreal Convention contains a provision according to which, if the State Party to the Montreal Convention is also a party to the (*inter alia*) Warsaw Convention,[18] the Montreal Convention shall prevail over the rules contained there. This provision, in combination with the provision mentioned in Article 208 of the Polish Aviation Law, determines the rules of the air carrier's liability regime. It is very important because both conventions, i.e. the Warsaw Convention and the Montreal Convention, also contain a provision referring to multimodal carriage, although the regulation included in the Montreal Convention is slightly wider.

Articles 38 and 18(4) of the Montreal Convention are the two most important provisions. The first stipulates that Montreal's liability regime is applicable only to the air stage of the carriage. On the other hand, the second provision contains exceptions to this rule. Point 4 of Article 18 regulates the period of the air carrier's liability. According to this basic rule, the period does not contain any land, maritime or inland waterways stage, which would be localized outside the airport.

The meaning of the concept of 'airport', which is not regulated by the Convention, is also important. The Montreal Convention is one of the most common conventions in the world,[19] so it is possible to interpret this concept with the support of the judiciary in many countries. For example, in the USA the meaning of 'airport' is rather strictly interpreted. In the case known as *Victoria Sales v Emery*,[20] the court judged that the cargo localized on the outside of the airport's fence and used by the airport's staff was not part of the airport. It could be said that according to the US judiciary the area of the airport is strictly limited by the fence.[21]

---

14 Art. 208 of the Aviation Law.

15 Convention for the unification of certain rules relating to international carriage by air (Warsaw, 1929).

16 Convention for the Unification of Certain Rules for International Carriage by Air (Montreal, 1999).

17 Actually, the Montreal Convention was ratified by Poland in 2005 (the statute of 17 June 2005, regarding binding force of the Convention for the Unification of Certain Rules for International Carriage by Air, opened for Signature in Montreal on 28 May 1999 (Journal of Laws nr 150, item 1237); the Montreal Convention has also been ratified by the European Community – EC (today European Union) became a party to the Montreal Convention on 28 June 2004. The Republic of Poland has been a member of the EU since 2004.

18 The same provision also refers to such legal acts as the Guadalajara Convention of 1961 or the Protocols amending the Warsaw Convention.

19 At the moment, there are the 133 parties to the Convention, i.e. 132 states in the World and one international organization, i.e. the European Union.

20 *Victoria Sales v Emery* [1990] 917 F 2d 705, 2 Cir.

21 M.A. Clarke, *Contracts of carriage by air*, 2nd edn (Informa, 2010), pp. 116–118.

There are two exceptions to the rule referring to the airport's area, however. The first exception is analogous to the one in the Warsaw Convention, but the second one is contained only in the Montreal Convention.

The first exception refers to the loading and unloading goods onto or off a plane. It refers to the use of means of transport other than a plane as a support to the loading of goods onto or unloading of goods off a plane. In such a case, the Convention says that there is a presumption that the possible loss was caused by an incident which occurred during the air carriage. Another words, if the goods were transported on a truck to the plane within the area of an airport (but it cannot be stated that the loss during the whole carriage had not occurred on the plane), the carrier would be liable according to the air carrier's liability regime. However, some practical problems could arise. A good example is the case of *Quantum Corporation Ltd v Plane Trucking Ltd*,[22] which could also be considered on Polish grounds. In this case, goods had already been unloaded off the plane and loaded onto a truck which was already moving on the road, but had not physically left the airport area. Technically, since the process of unloading the plane had been finished, doubts could arise as to whether the air carrier's liability regime could be still applicable.[23]

The second exception refers to the situation in which the carrier (without the consent of the goods sender) uses a means of transport other than the plane to carry goods on the route (or even on part of the route only). For example, if a loss occurred when the goods were carried on a lorry (although, according to the contract, the carrier should have transported the goods by plane), the air carrier's liability regime would be binding, regardless of whether or not the loss had been localized.

This regulation prevents the carrier from benefiting from a breach of the contract. Firstly, additional loading and unloading causes a bigger risk of damage to the cargo. Secondly, another unimodal liability regime would be more beneficial for the carrier (especially if the other liability regime could be based on the lower limits of liability[24]). It would be unfair if the carrier should cause a loss of the cargo due to a change in the means of transport and be liable according to the rules of the less strict liability regime.

2.2 Spain

2.2.1 Basic normative acts

The basic normative acts of the Spanish transport law include, in particular, the Third Book of the Spanish Commercial Code[25] as well as statutes such as the Maritime Navigation Act (Ley de Navegación Marítima, LNM),[26] Ley de Navigación Aérea of 21 July 1960,[27] and the Ley del contrato de transporte terrestre de mercancías of 12 November

22 *Quantum Corporation Ltd v Plane Trucking Ltd* [2002] EWCA Civ 350, [2002] 1 WLR 2678 [28].

23 B. Soyer, A. Tettenborn, *Carriage of goods by sea, land, and air. Unimodal and multimodal transport in the 21st century*, 1st edn (New York, Informa Law from Routledge 2014), p. 95.

24 M. Hoeks, *Multimodal transport law* (Proefschriftmaken, 2009), p. 204.

25 *El Código de Comercio de 1885 es el código de derecho mercantil vigente en España desde el 22 de agosto de 1885* – The Commercial Code of 1885 is the code of commercial law in force in Spain since 22 August 1885.

26 Ley 14/2014, de 24 de julio, de Navegación Marítima – the LNM came into force 27 May 2015.

27 Ley 48/1960, de 21 de julio, de Navegación Aérea – came into force 12 September 1960.

2009 (LCTTM)[28] (previously Ley de Ordenanción del Transporte Terrestre of 30 July 1987, LOTT). However, most regulations referring to multimodal carriage are contained in the last of these normative acts.

2.2.2 Types of multimodal carriage in the former Spanish regulations

The LOTT contained its own definition of multimodal carriage. According to this former Spanish regulation, multimodal carriage was defined as a combined or successive carriage with a few carriers engaged on the basis of one contract of carriage. Each carrier could participate in the carriage during one of the stages only. The regulation also stipulated that at least two or more means of transport should be used.[29] It was also possible to carry goods on the basis of a contract known as the contract for 'uniform' carriage. It is not, however, a reference to the 'uniform system' of the multimodal carrier's liability regime mentioned earlier. The uniformity of the contract, in this case, means that the contract for carriage is concluded only with a carrier who eventually uses other carriers to perform the contract. However, the other carriers are not parties to the first 'uniform' contract, contrary to the contract for multimodal carriage described earlier.

The legal relationship between the carriers is independent of the contractual relationship between the first carrier and the goods sender. The Spanish transport law also includes regulation of the contract known as *transporte con reexpedición.* In a way, this type of contract is a mixed form of the two types of multimodal carriage contract described below. In this type of contract, the goods sender also concludes the contract with only one carrier, who then concludes the contract for carriage with another carrier. Their relationship, i.e. the contractual relationship between the first carrier and the carriers who perform carriage on each stage of the carriage, is not independent of the contract concluded with the goods sender. In this situation, the first carrier is some kind of an agent, whose task is to conclude a contract with another carrier on behalf of the goods sender.

2.2.3 Current regulations

The regulations referred to above show us how original the regulations contained in the Spanish transport law were. Nevertheless, the regulation changed slightly in 2009, when the new normative act regulating land transport, i.e. the above-mentioned Ley del contrato de transporte terrestre de mercancías, was enacted. This Act introduced a different regulation of multimodal carriage. In this Act, the multimodal contract of carriage is defined as:

> 'contract of carriage entered into by the shipper and the carrier to move goods by more than one mode of transport, being one of them, regardless of the number of carriers involved in its execution'.[30]

The LCTTM is another regulation containing a provision referring to the multimodal carrier's liability. The provision stipulates that in a basic standard situation, one should

---

28 Ley 15/2009, de 11 de noviembre, del contrato de transporte terrestre de mercancías – came into force 12 Februar 2010.

29 Art. 28 LOTT.

30 Art. 68(1) – translation from the website: https://www.global-regulation.com/translation/spain/1441778/law-15-2009-of-11-november%252c-the-contract-of-transportation-of-goods.html (visited on 16 August 2019).

apply the liability regime suitable for the mode of transport being carried out. However, in a situation where it is impossible to determine the phase of the journey during which the damage occurred, the liability of the carrier shall be decided pursuant to the provisions of the LCTTM. This solution resembles the analogical provision of the Rotterdam Rules (despite the fact that the Spanish normative act refers to the land carriage and not to the maritime carriage). Similar solutions can be found in German law[31] and in the law of some Latin American countries,[32] for example. Of course, there are differences between those legal solutions, but it is possible to claim that they share some common basic concept.[33]

Although it seems that these changes in the Spanish law were enacted by coincidence in 2009, it is not the case. The Rotterdam Rules[34] have not yet come into force. To become binding, the Rotterdam Rules must be ratified by a minimum of 20 countries.[35] Although the Rotterdam Rules were signed by over 20 states, only four counties have so far ratified this Convention. Spain was the first country to ratify it, adopting the Convention in January 2011.[36] The concept of multimodal carrier's liability contained in the Rotterdam Rules seems to be an inspiration for the Spanish lawmakers. Moreover, it should be emphasised that, in Spanish transport law, the Rotterdam Rules are mentioned by name. Spanish statute LNM contains at the moment a reference to the Convention of 1924, but the Spanish lawmakers also included provision referring to the Rotterdam Rules. One of the final provisions of the LNM stipulates, that in the case of coming into force the RR, the Spanish government will be obliged to inform the Spanish Cortes Generales[37] about the necessity of the LNM changes.

It is a good example of the scope of the changes which could be necessary for states intending to adopt the Rotterdam Rules as binding law and become parties to the Convention in the future.

2.3 China

It is worth comparing the regulations mentioned earlier with national laws in other parts of the world. The national law of China is a good example.

2.3.1 Basic normative acts

Contrary to Polish law (which could be taken as an example), Chinese law contains quite complex regulations on the multimodal carrier's liability regime. There are two basic

31 In the German Commercial Code, to be more precise: §452 Handelsgesetzbuch, enacted 10 May 1897.

32 E.g. separate regulation of the multimodal carriage enacted in Brazil (Law 9611 of 19 February 1998 on Multimodal Transport of Goods) or Argentina (Law 24921: Multimodal Transport of Goods, Official Gazette 12 January 1998): A.P. Alleone Luksevicius, L.C. Santana Montenegro, M. Vinaud Prado, F.G. Ferreira Da Silva, Multimodal transportation – efforts to make it happen in Brazil, *International Journal of Business Tourism Applied Sciences*, http://www.ijbts-journal.com/images/main_1366796758/0081-Anna.pdf (visited on 18 August 2019).

33 D. Dąbrowski, 'The multimodal carrier's liability for non-localized loss' (2016) 4 (36) *Problemy Transportu i Logistyki* 205.

34 United Nations Convention on Contracts for the International Carriage of Goods Wholly or Partly by Sea (Rotterdam Rules) (New York, 2008).

35 Art. 94(1) of the Rotterdam Rules: 'This Convention enters into force on the first day of the month following the expiration of one year after the date of deposit of the twentieth instrument of ratification, acceptance, approval or accession.'

36 http://www.unis.unvienna.org/unis/pressrels/2011/unisl149.html (visited 18 August 2019)

37 i.e. the Spanish Parliament.

normative acts which regulate multimodal carriage – the Chinese Maritime Code[38] (ChMC) and the Contract Law.[39] The Maritime Code refers to the carriage which includes the maritime leg of the route.

2.3.2 The Chinese solution

China has adopted a network system (or rather a modified network system), but the system is construed in a slightly different way from the Rotterdam Rules. To some extent, it resembles the Rotterdam Rules in that the ChMC contains provisions on the applicability of the maritime regime to situations of unlocalized loss. However, there is a big difference, because this provision is applicable only to carriage governed by the Maritime Code. Also, the ChMC does not contain a provision analogous to the Rotterdam Rules' provision referring to the relations with the other modes of transport.

It is worth adding that the Chinese system of the multimodal carrier's liability regime is rather complex, especially in comparison with the Japanese system, for example. As mentioned above, the two normative acts have the basic meaning. Therefore, it is possible to divide them into two basic types. The first contains the maritime stage of the carriage, while the second contains no maritime stage at all. The first one is regulated by the Chinese Maritime Code, while the second is regulated by Contract Law.

2.3.3 'Hybrid' regulations

The Chinese Maritime Code is a good example of what some call 'hybrid' regulations. It means that the legal solutions contained in the ChMC are construed as a mix of the solutions found in conventions such as the Hague–Visby[40] rules and the Hamburg rules,[41] but not only these. For example, none of these conventions regulates the maritime carrier's liability period with the use of the *door-to-door* formula, although the formula is used in the ChMC. The distinction between the two types of carrier, ie the 'contractual carrier' and the 'actual carrier',[42] is another interesting solution contained in this normative act. However, the regulations referring to multimodal carriage mention the 'multimodal transport operator'[43] (the ChMC) or 'multi-modal carriage operator' (the Contract Law).

In multimodal carriage which also includes the maritime stage, the ChMC stipulates that in the case of the localised loss one should apply the regime of liability suitable to the stage of the carriage route including the place of loss. However, in the case of unlocalised

38 The Maritime Code of the People's Republic of China (Adopted at the 28th Meeting of the Standing Committee of the Seventh National People's Congress on 7 November 1992, promulgated by Order No. 64 of the President of the People's Republic of China on 7 November 1992, and effective as of 1 July 1993).

39 The Contract Law of the People's Republic of China (Adopted and Promulgated by the Second Session of the Ninth National People's Congress 15 March 1999).

40 International Convention for the Unification of Certain Rules relating to Bills of Lading; amended by the Protocol to amend the International Convention for the Unification of Certain Rules relating to Bills of Lading, signed at Brussels on 25 August 1924 (Brussels, 1968) and the Protocol to amend the International Convention for the Unification of Certain Rules of Law relating to Bills of Lading as modified by the Amending Protocol of 23 February 1968 (SDR Protocol) (Brussels, 1979).

41 United Nations International Convention on the Carriage of Goods by Sea (Hamburg, 1978).

42 The 'contractual carrier' is the subject which concluded a contract of carriage and the 'actual carrier' is the carrier which actually carries the shipment: D. Song, 'Identification of Carrier under Carriage of Goods by Sea in China' (2008) 48 *Asian Business Law* 49.

43 Analogical wording contained in the Convention of 1980.

loss, the rules contained in the Maritime Code[44] should be applied. An analogous situation could be observed in the case of carriage which does not contain a maritime stage. Of course, the difference is that in unlocalised loss the rules from the Chinese Contract Law are applicable.[45]

2.4 USA

2.4.1 Basic normative acts

In the USA, there is yet another situation. There is no complex or clear regulation of the multimodal carrier's liability regime. The most important normative acts are the Carriage of Goods by Sea Act 1936 (US COGSA) and the Interstate Commerce Act of 1887 with the amendment passed in 1935 and known as the Carmack Amendment. The American system of liability in multimodal transport is characteristic of the network system, but is somewhat complicated. There are some very specific regulations which regulate this matter in a more particularised way. The period of maritime carrier's liability is regulated in a different way from the Rotterdam Rules, too. There are also quite a large number of precedences referring to the multimodal carrier's liability regime.

2.4.2 *A network* system in the USA

In the USA the term 'network system' has several meanings. One meaning is similar to that in Europe, i.e. this meaning refers to the situation where the carrier is liable for losses on each stage of the carriage on the ground of the liability regime binding for each leg of the transport. Another meaning, however, refers to the situation where the carrier is liable for the loss only if he physically carries the goods.[46]

2.4.3 Scope of application

As mentioned above, the most important normative acts are US COGSA 1936 (which regulates maritime transport) and the Interstate Commerce Act of 1887 with the 1935 amendment (known as the Carmack amendment). This second Act regulates land transport. Initially, the scope of this Act included railway transport only. However, since 1935 the Act has also been binding for road transport. In many cases, it can be rather difficult to find out to which liability regime the multimodal carrier is liable.

Section 10501(a) of the Interstate Commerce Act says that this Act could be binding for a leg of transport other than the land carriage when the carriage on the maritime stage, for example, is only a continuation of the transport on land and the whole carriage is under the

44 Art. 106: 'If the section of transport in which the loss of or damage to the goods occurred could not be ascertained, the multimodal transport operator shall be liable for compensation in accordance with the stipulations regarding the carrier's liability and the limitation thereof as set out in this Chapter.'

45 Art. 321: 'Where damage to or loss of the cargo occurred within a particular segment of the course of a multi-modal carriage, the multi-modal carriage operator's liability for damages and any limitation thereon are governed by the applicable transportation law of the jurisdiction which such segment is under. Where the segment in which the cargo was damaged or lost cannot be determined, the liability for damages shall be borne in accordance with this Chapter.'

46 L. Zhu, M. Deniz Guner-Ozbek, H. Yan, 'Carrier's Liability in Multimodal Carriage Contracts in China and its Comparison with US and EU' in '*International Forum on Shipping, Ports and Airports*', Conference Paper (Chengdu, 2010), p. 114.

control of the land carriage. This is a basic rule. However, in many cases the interpretation depends on specific precedents. For example, in *Norfolk Southern Railway Company v James N. Kirby*[47] and *Kawasaki Kisen Kaisha Ltd, et.al v Regal-Beloit Corp*[48] the US Supreme Court ruled that the seaway bill of lading is a very important factor. If the maritime stage of carriage has the seaway bill of lading, the whole carriage does not lose the maritime character only because the goods are carried partly on land.

There is another complication which has to be considered. In addition to nationwide statutes or precedents, statutes or precedents binding only in each state could be very important.

2.5 Japan

2.5.1 The earlier situation in Japanese transport law

In Japan, multimodal carriage was not regulated for a very long time. This lack of regulation referred not only to the multimodal carrier's liability but multimodal carriage in general. For example, the normative acts which regulate maritime carriage in Japan were based on the Hague Rules (with its lack of multimodal carriage regulation) and the US COGSA statute.[49] The Japanese normative act, however, was not a copy of this regulation and it had its own solutions. In the context of multimodal transport, the liability period of the carrier had special importance. According to Article 3 of the Japanese Act equivalent to US COGSA,[50] the carrier's liability period includes the receipt, loading, stowage, carriage, custody, discharge and delivery of such goods. Actually, this is another example of the 'hybrid regulation'. The Japanese statute has been based on the Hague Rules since 1924 and its additional Protocol was added in 1968, but the regulation of the carrier's liability period is more characteristic of the Hamburg Rules of 1978.

2.5.2 Changes in the Japanese transport law

The regulations mentioned in the section above referred to the multimodal carrier's liability in a very limited area. However, this situation has recently changed. Japanese transport law (especially maritime law) has undergone extensive reforms.

In addition to the above regulations, Japanese transport law included the Japanese Commercial Code of 1899, in particular. This Code was based on the model of the German Commercial Code, i.e. the Handelsgezetzbuch.[51] Many issues (such as multimodal carriage, for example) were not regulated. Therefore, work on the reform of Japanese transport law was initiated in 2011. The goal was to reform such areas as bills of lading and the charter or regulation of domestic air transport, too. Japanese transport law until then had actually included hardly any regulations referring to this kind of carriage.[52]

The reform of the regulations referring to multimodal carriage also included multimodal carrier's liability. According to the earlier plans, the regulation based on the network

---

47 *Norfolk Southern R. Co. v James N. Kirby, Pty Ltd.* [2004] 543 U.S. 14.

48 *Kawasaki Kisen Kaisha Ltd. v Regal-Beloit Corp.* [2010] 561 U.S. 89.

49 The Carriage of Goods by Sea Act 1936.

50 The Japanese Carriage of Goods by Sea Act 1992, translated by Prof. Kazuo Iwasaki, the Nagoya Keizai University: http://www.jseinc.org/en/laws/japanese_cogsa.html (visited on 18 August 2019).

51 Handelgesetzbuch, 10 May 1897 – Book Four: 'Maritime Tade' was of special importance.

52 M. Sasaoka, 'Reform of transport law in Japan' (2013) 35 *Zeitschrift für Japanisches Recht/Journal of Japanese Law* 41.

system. In the case of localized loss, the carrier should be liable on the grounds of the regime adequate to the stage of the carriage[53]. However, a party to the contract of carriage should be free to shape the legal relations in cases when there ane no *ius cogens* regulations in Japanese transport law or international conventions binding on Japan. Moreover, it is worth mentioning that the pattern of the bill of lading with the network system created by the JIFFA organization[54] has been used in Japanese trade. However, it had also contained a provision with a presumption that unlocalised loss occurred on the maritime stage of the carriage. This means that when this pattern was applied the carrier was liable for unlocalised loss as the maritime carrier[55].

2.6 India

2.6.1 Regulation of the multimodal transport law

Regulations binding on India are another interesting example of the solutions contained in the national law. This is one of the countries which have separate normative acts with more or less complex regulation of multimodal carriage. In India, it is the Multimodal Transportation of Goods Act enacted in 1993.[56] Other states with similar normative acts include Mexico, Argentina and Brazil.[57] Of course, there are differences between such normative acts. Although the statutes are often based on the Multimodal Convention of 1980 or on International Chamber of Commerce Rules, the results are not the same.[58]

2.6.2 Amendments to the Multimodal Transportation of Goods Act of 1993 (MTGA)

When the Indian statute came into force, its legal solutions to some extent resembled the provisions contained in the Convention of 1980. As far as the carrier's liability is concerned, the MTGA of 1993 includes important new provisions creating the separate carrier's liability regime different from unimodal carriers' liability regimes. In the case of localised loss with the localised place of occurrence, the limit of liability for such a loss or damage borne by the multimodal transport operator shall be determined in accordance with the provisions of the relevant law applicable to that mode of transport during the course of which the loss or damage occurred.[59] The provisions contained in the Act of 1993 allowed the system in India to be classified as a modified uniform system similar to the Convention of 1980. The amendments enacted later (i.e. in 2000[60]) changed this situation slightly and

53 M. Amemiya, *Reform of Commercial Code (Transport Law) in Japan*, http://www.maritimelaw.jp/pdf/ICML2018.pdf (visited 23 August 2019), p. 6.

54 Japan International Freight Forwarders Association.

55 Japan Internationalal Freight Forwarders Association Inc. (JIFFA) Multimodal Transport Bill of Lading, 9(5), https://www.ecl.co.jp/carriage/mtbl.pdf (visited 18 August 2019).

56 No. 28 of 1993. It is also worth remembering the statute of 2000, known as the Multimodal Transportation of Goods (Amendment) Act 2000, dated 5 December 2000, Act No. 44 of 2000.

57 Mexico: Regulation on International Multimodal Transport, 6 July 1989; Argentina: Law No. 24.921: Multimodal Transport of Goods, Official Bulletin 12 January 1998; Brazil: Law No. 9.61 of 19 February 1998 on Multimodal Transport of Goods.

58 M. Hoeks, *Multimodal transport law* (Proefschriftmaken, 2009), p. 8.

59 Chapter IV, point 15 of the MTGA 1993.

60 Amendment of section 15.9 contains the provision:'Provided that the multimodal transport operator shall not be liable for any loss, damage or delay in delivery due to a cause for which the carrier is exempted from liability in accordance with the applicable law.'

currently it is hard to determine unambiguously whether the MTGA system is still a uniform system or whether it has already become a modified network system.

However, it is worth saying that the provisions contained in the transport law in India are the closest to the uniform system, in contrast to the national laws analyzed earlier.

2.7 New Zealand

There is a different situation in other parts of the world, for example New Zealand. New Zealand is one of the states belonging to the common law system. However, their legal solution to the carrier's liability is original not only in comparison with civil law states but also with the systems in countries such as the UK or USA.

2.7.1 New Zealand's Carriage of Goods Act of 1979

The normative act of 1979, known as the Carriage of Goods Act[61] (CGA), is important for transport law in New Zealand. The uniqueness of New Zealand's solution stems from the fact that the CGA applies to:

> 'every carriage of goods, not being international carriage, performed or to be performed by a carrier pursuant to a contract entered into after the commencement of this Act, whether the carriage is by land, water, or air, or by more than one of those modes.'[62]

This scope of the CGA's applicability means that the act (of course only in the domestic area) regulates the multimodal carriage,[63] too. However, it has to be said that in the case of New Zealand it is hard to talk about any classification of its law as a uniform or network system. This classification is based on the situation when it is necessary to choose which system should be applied, especially in the case of unlocalized loss. But in New Zealand (regardless of a few exceptions) there is no difference between the liability regimes of land, air or water carriage. This means that there is no problem with choosing the adequate liability regime because all of them are actually the same. It seems that the New Zealand legislator followed similar considerations to the Polish legislator in the 1980s, when the Polish normative act (the Transport Law of 1984) was enacted. In those days, the trends were quite important, especially the German trends regarding the uniformity of the transport law referring to each mode of transport. The Polish TL combined the regulations for road, railway and air carriage.[64] However, even when the TL came into force, maritime carriage was regulated separately by the earlier Polish Maritime Code.[65]

61 Carriage of Goods Act 1979, 14 November 1979, Public Act 1979 no 43 http://www.legislation.govt.nz/act/public/1979/0043/latest/DLM33495.html (visited 18 August 2019).

62 Section 5(1) CGA 1979.

63 B. Marten, *Maritime Law in New Zealand* (Thomson Reuters, 2016), p. 178.

64 As mentioned earlier, this situation changed in 2002, when another normative act, i.e. the Aviation Law, came into force. This statute regulated aircraft carriage separately: P. Ciok, 'Regulacja odpowiedzialności przewoźnika towarowego w prawie polskim – od II Rzeczypospolitej Polskiej do dnia dzisiejszego', *Polska Niepodległa 1918–2018* (2018), p. 163.

65 In those days, the Maritime Code of 1 December 1961 (Journal of Laws 1961, nr 58, item 318 as amended) was binding. It had regulated maritime carriage before the actual Maritime Code of 2001 (mentioned before).

2.7.2 CGA's scope of application

New Zealand's legislator went further than the Polish legislator because the CGA of 1979 also regulates carriage on water. It means that, in the area of the domestic carriage, the CGA regulates maritime and inland waterways carriage.[66] This normative act regulates the carrier's liability for damage to cargo separately for the contractual carrier and the actual carrier (which resembles the Chinese regulation to some degree), but the basic rule is that the carrier is liable for the loss from the moment the goods are accepted for carriage. Nevertheless, as mentioned above, the New Zealand solution actually eliminates the problem with the multimodal carriage (especially as regards unlocalized loss). If the unimodal liability regimes were construed in the same way, the multimodal carrier's liability would be based on the same principles.

3 Concluding remarks

To sum up, it is clear and obvious that each country in the world has its own legal solution to the multimodal carrier's liability regulation. The maritime leg and the other types of transport are regulated differently and usually in quite a different way from in the Rotterdam Rules. Each country has construed its own legal solutions which are usually (but not exclusively) based on the network system. One can also observe various levels of significance of the maritime law in regulating the multimodal carrier's liability. There are countries where the maritime law is of primary importance in the regulation of this type of liability. There are also countries where the local national maritime law regulates multimodal carriage in combination with the transport law binding on land (China). There are also situations where the maritime law is excluded from the multimodal transport's regulation because it is regulated only by the transport law for land (Spain). There are even regulations where multimodal transport is regulated separately from the unimodal regimes (India). Finally, there are countries with no separate unimodal regimes (New Zealand).

All these examples demonstrate that the national maritime law often plays a significant role in regulating multimodal transport, but it is not a basic rule. Perhaps this situation will change, when (or if) the Rotterdam Rules finally come into force. If the countries amended their provisions to make them similar to the Rotterdam Rules solutions, the significance of the national maritime laws in regulating the multimodal carrier's liability might grow. Currently, however, it cannot be stated that, in this area, national maritime laws in each country dominate other branches of transport law.

66 B. Marten, *Maritime Law in New Zealand* (Thomson Reuters, 2016), p. 178.

PART III

CODIFICATION IN THE AREA OF CARRIAGE OF PASSENGERS AND LEISURE NAVIGATION

CHAPTER 14

The role of sailing and leisure navigation in the codification process of maritime law (in the framework of the Spanish Maritime Navigation Law of 2014)

Professor Juan L. Pulido Begines

1 Introduction

I think it is generally accepted that we are at a time when the law of leisure navigation does not fit easily into any particular category within the law. When a process of codification of maritime law is approached, many doubts arise on what to do with this area of the law: is it part of maritime law? Is it something else? Is it completely independent? What is the relationship between that branch of law and the general law of navigation? Should this area be framed in consumer law, or common law?[1]

The reason for this can be found in the fact that the law of leisure navigation does not fit 'comfortably' within maritime law, because the latter has been built on foundations that are alien to the former.

In the classical or pre-industrial era, maritime law rested on maritime trade (navigation was carried out always and exclusively for trade). This explains why a good part of the content of the first Commercial Codes, was for the regulation of nautical trade (Code de commerce of 1807, in which 250 of the 648 articles were devoted to Maritime Law, Book II). To a large extent, this view continues to prevail in some countries.[2] The codification of maritime law has traditionally been based on merchant shipping regulations.

If we turn our attention to the current situation, we find that this sector of the legal system is built on parameters of public law, linked to safety in navigation and the prevention of pollution, which have to do with 'industrial risk'.

In civil law states, the codification of maritime law raises the question of the role of the law of leisure navigation in that process. Many questions arise: should all vessels must comply with the same regulation? Which factors determine which of the regulations a vessel must comply with: the size of a vessel, the number of passengers it carries on board, or how the vessel is used? Should the regulation of vessels in commercial use for sport or pleasure be considered as merchant shipping?

1 On Consumer Law and navigation, see M. Zubiri de Salinas, 'La protección del consumidor en la Ley de Navegación Marítima: los contratos de pasaje, crucero y arrendamiento náutico' in J. L. García-Pita and A. Díaz de la Rosa (eds), *El Derecho marítimo de los nuevos tiempos* (Madrid, 2018), pp. 789–818.

2 We can find a good example of this issue in the Spanish Ley de Navegación Marítima, 14/2014, de 24 de julio 2014 (LNM): the stay of a foreign vessel in a Spanish port requires a *shipping agent*, under the terms set out in art. 10.2 LNM, *with the exception of pleasure boats*, which may be directly represented by their registered owner or captain.

Two trends can be identified: on the one hand, those who consider that sporting navigation is part of maritime law; on the other, those who maintain that sailing and leisure navigation needs specific regulation.

From this starting point, this paper will address three main issues.

First of all, the specific distortions (specific problems or particularly problematic issues) that this situation poses within the concrete framework of Spanish law.

Next, and on a more general basis, the problems that this raises when the process of codification of maritime law is carried out. For this purpose, the recent Italian experience in this field will be analysed.

Finally, we will consider some possible remedies and, in particular, proposals for the future.

2 Leisure navigation in the Spanish Maritime Navigation Law of 2014 (LNM): distortions posed by the current situation

2.1 Pleasure boat charters

We must start with a question: for what reason has the legislator included the regulation of *nautical charters* in the LNM? This question is relevant, especially taking into account that successive drafts of the LNM did not include this issue,[3] which was introduced in the parliamentary process.

This is not the place, nor is there enough space in this work, to make an exhaustive analysis of the parliamentary procedure of the LNM.[4] Suffice it to say that in principle a non-compulsory regulation was proposed: this proposal was rejected. In the end, an incomplete and mandatory regulation was introduced, which the legislator recognised as being alien to that framework.[5] This follows from the Preamble or Statement of Purpose of the said Act.[6]

We can only conclude that the legislator, possibly owing to pressure from the industry itself, introduced into the LNM the lease of sports boats as a matter of pure opportunity: there was a gap that urgently needed to be filled, in answer to the constant criticism from the sporting nautical sector, and he took advantage of the occasion of the LNM to address the issue.

But the result was unsatisfactory, for many reasons. First of all, the main question is not adequately solved; besides, the new regulation introduces new problems: the delimitation between the various figures of the contracts of operation of the ship. This denotes, in short, a lack of maturity of the very concept of maritime law used by the legislator.

3 See, Memoria del Anteproyecto LNM, published by the Ministerio de Justicia: http://www.mjusticia.gob.es/cs/Satellite/Portal/1292427518642?blobheader=application%2Fpdf&blobheadername1=Content-Disposition&blobheadername2=Grupo&blobheadervalue1=attachment%3B+filename%3DAnteproyecto_de_ley_general_de_la_navegacion_maritima_(Memoria)..PDF&blobheadervalue2=Docs_CGC_Secciones+especializadas

4 http://www.congreso.es/public_oficiales/L9/CONG/BOCG/A/A_014-01.PDF (visited 27 August 2019).

5 This negative assessment is not shared by other scholars, as is the case of M. Zubiri de Salinas, 'Los contratos de pasaje, remolque y arrendamiento náutico', in A. Emparanza Sobejano and J. M. Martín Osante (eds) *Comentarios sobre la Ley de Navegación Marítima* (Madrid, 2015), p. 422.

6 Literally: 'el arrendamiento náutico, conocido comúnmente como chárter y que goza de particularidades propias'.

This inadequate regulation has brought out relevant and more general issues on the subject, which affect not only the specific regulation of nautical charters, but also some core issues of maritime law.

Among the most complex problems raised by this issue is to determine the meaning and scope of the expression 'absence of profit', that is, the problem of commercial employment of recreational craft. The Spanish doctrine has already had to address the fact that the owner of a sports boat does not navigate it for his own use, but to hire it out to third parties in exchange for a price. It seems evident, then, that what the legislator intends is that the *ultimate purpose* of the contract must always be recreational and not commercial.[7] The aim sought by the end user of the vessel must be recreational, and this despite the fact that there may be intermediate legal relationships of commercial purpose, ordered to fulfil that main purpose. In other words: the objective of leisure that qualifies the contract operates with respect to the lessee, but for the lessor it can be a profitable economic activity.[8] In fact, the LNM regulates the relationship between those who have the ship by any title and the final renters; the relations between the owners and the managers of the ship, or other interposed figures, will be subject to their own discipline, depending on the obligations assumed by the parties.

Linked to this, it is also difficult to discern the boundary between the nautical charter contract and the passenger contract, or the 'tourist cruise'.[9] The drafting of the LNM inferred an important consequence for the determination of the legal nature of the contract: the obligation of the lessor consists, simply, in making the ship available to the lessee, not in navigating or carrying out a transport of persons.[10] In other words, the lessor of the ship never assumes the obligations of the carrier in the passenger contract and, if he does, we are dealing with a contract of a different legal nature to the nautical lease.[11]

7 The same requirement operates in other systems, such as Italian Maritime Law. See A. Mignone, 'L'utilizzo commerciale delle unità da diporto tra regolamenti e prassi operativa' (2016) GIURETA XIV, *Rivista di Diritto dell'Economia, dei Trasporti e dell'Ambiente* 146.

8 M. Zubiri de Salinas, 'Los contratos de pasaje, remolque y arrendamiento náutico', in Alberto Emparanza Sobejano and J. M. Martín Osante (eds) *Comentarios sobre la Ley de Navegación Marítima* (Madrid, 2015), pp. 422–423; R. Coles and F. Lorenzon, *The Law of Yachts and Yachting* (London, 2012), p. 171. According to F. Pellegrino, 'Charter di unità da diporto', in A. Antonini (ed.) *Trattato breve di diritto marittimo*, 4th edn (Milano, 2013), p. 134; this business is articulated through a commercial contract. However, in Spanish law the qualification of this contract as commercial is at the least dubious.

9 It should be borne in mind that in practice it is not uncommon to find cases that could be qualified as 'sport cruises', in the sense that an operator offers a package of pleasure services for a pleasure craft, which includes accommodation, maintenance, a fixed itinerary – more or less detailed – with stopovers, and accessory services on board and on land (lessons in navigation, fishing, diving, excursions, etc.). In Italy this modality has been called 'Noleggio unitario per finalità di crociera', and is characterised because the leisure purpose of the tourist cruise coincides with the recreational purpose of the nautical lease, which makes the separation between both modalities difficult. G. Benelli, 'L'utilizzazione commerciale delle unità da diporto tra noleggio e crociera turistica' in (2015) *Rivista Italiana di Diritto del Turismo* 129–145.

10 M. Zubiri de Salinas is of the same opinion: 'Los contratos de pasaje, remolque y arrendamiento náutico', in A. Emparanza Sobejano and J.M. Martín Osante (eds) *Comentarios sobre la Ley de Navegación Marítima* (Madrid, 2015), p. 423. An identical thesis holds, in the field of Italian law: F. Pellegrino, 'Charter di unità da diporto' in A. Antonini (ed.) *Trattato breve di diritto marittimo*, 4th edn (Milano, 2013), p. 127.

11 An in-depth study of the doctrinal construction of the concept of passage and the meaning of 'transportation' or 'displacement' in it can be seen in E. Olmedo Peralta, *Régimen jurídico del transporte de pasajeros. Contratos de pasaje y crucero* (Madrid, 2014), pp. 117 et seq, where it is emphasised that not every operation of maritime transport of people is a passenger contract.

Finally, a question of systematic order arises: is the nautical lease one of the contracts for the use of the ship?[12] It seems clear to me that the leasing of pleasure craft needs a special regulation, different from that contained in contracts for the use of the craft. In other words: this contract cannot be considered as one of the contracts of use of the vessel, since the counterpart of the contract and the cause thereof differ.

These are just three examples of the many doubts that this issue raises. Therefore, it can be concluded that the introduction of the leasing of sports boats in the LNM is a bad idea that should be reviewed. The result is unsatisfactory in many ways, but, above all, because as well as not solving the main issue (the lease), this discipline introduces into the LNM problems of the boundaries between the various types of contract for the use of the ship.

2.2 The insurance of recreational boats

Perhaps it is in the regulation of the insurance of recreational boats that the purpose of the legislator in 'separating' this area of law (leisure navigation) from the common frame of maritime law is more clearly revealed, with the aim of protecting the insured person in this type of contract, as consumer.

Because, indeed, it cannot be said that, as is generally the case in *ordinary* maritime business, the insurance of pleasure boats used without the aim of making a profit is a '*contract between equals*', since in these cases there is no balance between the bargaining power of the parties.[13] Rather, the insured person can be compared to the consumer who adheres to the contract set by the insurance company and, therefore, needs protection.[14]

Under the provisions of Article 406 LNM, insurance contracts that are intended to compensate for damage caused by the risks inherent in maritime navigation are subject to this law. In what is not foreseen in the LNM, the common Insurance Contract Law[15] (LCS) will apply. However, paragraph 2 of that Article provides that compulsory insurance of recreational boats will be governed by the provisions of the Insurance Contract Law, and clauses to the contrary will be considered null. This legislative option, which has been criticised

12 This issue has always raised doubts, in most jurisdictions. See, for example, in Italian law, M. Riguzzi, 'La locazione e il noleggio di unutà da diporto', in A. Antonini and F. Morandi (eds), *La navigazione da diporto* (Milano, 1999), pp. 69–70.

13 A. Mestre, 'El seguro de embarcaciones deportivas y de recreo' (2002) XIX *Anuario de Derecho Marítimo* 259 (see also, from the same scholar, 'Problemas del aseguramiento de embarcaciones deportivas y de recreo' (2007) *V Jornadas de Derecho marítimo de San Sebastián* 111–137); and J. M. Martín Osante, 'Régimen jurídico español de la navegación marítima de recreo y deportiva' in U. La Torre and A. L. Melania Sia (eds), *Diporto e Turismo tra autonomía e specialità. Un'occasione per un incontro interdisciplinare* (Roma, 2014), pp. 92–94; M. L. Chiarella, 'Recesso del consumatore e navigazione da diporto' in U. La Torre and A. L. Melania Sia (eds), *Diporto e Turismo tra autonomía e specialità. Un'occasione per un incontro interdisciplinare* (Roma, 2014), pp. 214 et seq.

14 A. Zurimendi Isla, 'El seguro de embarcaciones de recreo en España' in U. La Torre and A. L. Melania Sia (eds), *Diporto e Turismo tra autonomía e specialità. Un'occasione per un incontro interdisciplinare* (Roma, 2014), p. 197; P. Bonassies, C. Capel, *Droit maritime*, 2nd edn (Paris, 2010), p. 886. For the passenger as a consumer, see E. Olmedo Peralta, *Régimen jurídico del transporte de pasajeros* (Madrid, 2014), pp. 155 et seq. See also M.T. Gómez Prieto, 'Consideraciones críticas sobre la sentencia del Tribunal Supremo 119/2013, de 12 de marzo de 2013' (2014) XXX *Anuario de Derecho Marítimo* 357.

15 Ley 50/1980, de 8 de octubre, de Contrato de Seguro.

by the doctrine,[16] has been confirmed by jurisprudence.[17] On the same interpretative line, and consistently with it, the Supreme Court[18] has established that the specialist competence to rule cases of compulsory insurance of pleasure craft corresponds to the Courts of First Instance, and not to the Mercantile Courts (the specialized judges competent in cases related to maritime law).[19]

Therefore, compulsory insurance of boats dedicated to sports or recreation is governed by the provisions of the LCS, and excluded from the LNM, without any valid agreement to the contrary (Article 406.2). From this categorical statement it is inferred that the compulsory insurance of pleasure craft *is not marine insurance*,[20] with the important consequences that this entails in terms of the applicable legal sources.[21] The legal solution is based on the assumption, well founded, that in this field of law the insured does require special protection, and therefore submits the contract to the mandatory discipline of the LCS.[22] However, *sensu contrario*, it should be understood that non-compulsory insurance of recreational boats is, indeed, marine insurance, although in this case there are important peculiarities, especially when it comes to defining risks.[23]

---

16 See M. Clavero Ternero, 'La limitación de responsabilidad del armador del buque de recreo en la Ley de Navegación Marítima y en la jurisprudencia del Tribunal Supremo' in P. J. Baena Baena and N. López Santana (eds), *Estudios sobre la responsabilidad de los operadores de transporte en la Ley de Navegación Marítima* (Cizur Menor, 2017), p. 353.

The question whether or not recreational craft insurance should be subject to the rules of maritime insurance has long been the subject of Spanish doctrine, with the majority of scholars arguing that this insurance is a maritime insurance, subject to the principle of universality of risks. However there are also those scholars who maintain that the rule of complete autonomy of the will of the parties should not operate in the field of recreational navigation, given the diverse negotiating power of insurer and insured. See J. M. Martín Osante, 'Régimen jurídico español de la navegación marítima de recreo y deportiva' in U. La Torre and A. L. Melania Sia (eds), *Diporto e Turismo tra autonomía e specialità. Un'occasione per un incontro interdisciplinare* (Roma, 2014), pp. 92 et seq.

17 Ruling of the Supreme Court of Spain (STS) of 16th December 2011 (890/2011, RJ 2012, 296) and STS 6 May 2015 (241/2015, RJ 2015/2234). The same interpretation has been applied in France, by virtue of the provisions of art. L-110–2 Code de Commerce. Cfr. P. Bonassies, C. Capel, *Droit maritime*, 2nd edn (Paris, 2010), pp. 82–83.

18 STS 16 December 2011 (890/2011, RJ 2012, 296).

19 And this despite the fact that, as M. Clavero Ternero underlines in 'La limitación de responsabilidad del armador del buque de recreo en la Ley de Navegación Marítima y en la jurisprudencia del Tribunal Supremo' in P.J. Baena Baena and N. López Santana (eds), *Estudios sobre la responsabilidad de los operadores de transporte en la Ley de Navegación Marítima* (Cizur Menor, 2017), p. 353, the jurisdiction of the mercantile courts seems the most appropriate for this type of litigation, taking into account that art. 86.ter of the LOPJ confers on that jurisdiction the knowledge of the claims relating to the application of Maritime law.

20 The same rule operates in Italian law, although the matter is not peaceful, in which the insurance of recreational craft can be equated to that of automobiles. In this sense, for example, S. Ferrarini, *Le assicurazioni marittime*, 3rd edn (Milano, 1981), p. 108; M.M. Comenale Pinto and E. Rosafio, *Il Diporto come fenomeno diffuso, Problemi e prospettive del diritto della navigazione, Quaderni della rivista del Diritto della Navigazione*, 4, 2015, p. XXI. Nevertheless, this solution has been criticised by relevant scholars, for example U. La Torre, 'Unità da diporto ed assicurazione r.c.' en U. La Torre and A.L. Melania Sia (eds), *Diporto e Turismo tra autonomía e specialità. Un'occasione per un incontro interdisciplinare* (Roma, 2014), p. 169.

21 The different modalities of the insurance contract, in the absence of any applicable law, will be governed by this law, whose precepts are mandatory, unless they are otherwise provided for. However, contractual clauses that are more beneficial to the insured will be considered valid (Art. 2 LCS).

22 A. Zurimendi Isla, 'El seguro de embarcaciones de recreo en España', in U. La Torre and A. L. Melania Sia (eds), *Diporto e Turismo tra autonomía e specialità. Un'occasione per un incontro interdisciplinare* (Roma, 2014), p. 198.

23 Regarding hull insurance, in the English business market a series of *Named Perils* operates, while in other markets, such as Italy, a full risk scheme is in operation. See G. Boi, 'Profili evolutivi delle assicurazioni

Regardless of the criticism that that article deserves and its interpretation by the Supreme Court, it seems evident that this discussion reflects the doubts that exist on the matter. Is pleasure boat insurance a maritime insurance? In all its modalities? If so, what is the rationale for subjecting mandatory liability insurance to one regulation and non-compulsory for another?

2.3 Limitation of liability of recreational vessel owners

This is a classic issue of discussion among maritime scholars, which has raised doubts in many legal systems. The positions are polarised in two very clear extremes: on the one hand, those who maintain that the regime of limitation is applicable to recreational vessels, and, on the other, those who hold the contrary view.

Does the non-recognition of the right to limit liability of the owner of the recreational vessel make sense? Is this solution not a better way for compensation of damages?

In the important judgment of the Spanish Supreme Court of 6 May 2015 (no. 241/2015), the court established the rules on the matter clearly and correctly, in my opinion. According to the High Court, the owners of a recreational vessel cannot limit their liability based on Art. 2 of the Limitation of Liability Convention 1976 (LLMC 1976).

The basis of this decision is that the application of the Convention requires commercial, mercantile, profit-making or business activity, which is completely incompatible with the recreational and non-lucrative character of the yacht in the case examined. And this on the assumption that the limitation of liability is a *privilege* justified by the exposure of business assets to maritime risks; in other words, it is a privileged regime with respect to the full compensation for the damages that constitute the general rule of our Law of Damage, and, therefore, its application to a recreational craft used for a purely private use is not justified.

To rationalise that exclusion, the court argues that the LLMC 1976 (Art. 2) requires that the damage be related to the 'operation' of the ship. The term 'operation' has been translated into Spanish as 'explotación', a concept firmly linked to the idea of business. That translation might not be the best. Nevertheless, as regards this question, in Spanish law the key issue currently is the construction of the concept of 'operation' of the ship, also embodied in Art. 396.1.a LNM. According to the court, it is inferred from the wording of the Article that the application of the limitation of liability regime requires that the vessel be used for commercial purposes. And that requirement is incompatible with the private or recreational use of the boat.

Ultimately, the key to the issue is not the *nature of the ship*, but the *nature of the claim*: maritime-commercial claims are subject to the rules of the Convention, but not claims of a purely civil or private nature. The court considers that the limitation of liability embodied in LLMC76 is a benefit that is only justified in the development of a lucrative activity as a means of privileging and promoting the maritime business.

This interpretation, which was also initially followed in neighbouring countries, was refuted; for example, in France.[24] However, it is defended by a sector of the doctrine in

corpi nella náutica da diporto' in M.M. Comenale Pinto and E. Rosafio (eds), *Il Diporto come fenomeno diffuso, Problemi e prospettive del diritto della navigazione, Quaderni della rivista del Diritto della Navigazione* 4, 2015, pp. 21 et seq.

24 P. Bonassies, C. Capel, *Droit maritime*, 2nd edn (Paris, 2010), p. 284.

Italy, under the argument that a different solution could even be considered unconstitutional.[25] In common law, a similar opinion has been defended by some authors.[26]

In Spain, the arguments of the High Court have also been refuted by scholars[27] who understand that the term 'explotación' is an inadequate translation of the term 'operation' of the original English version. It is also argued that the Convention itself allows States Parties to exclude vessels of less than 300 tons from the scope of application. Seen in this light, it is understood that the criterion used by the Convention to allow the non-application of its rules is the size of the vessel, not the type of navigation for which it will be used.

In any case, the very discussion about whether or not the limitation of liability should be applied to recreational vessels is a good symptom of the problems we are discussing in this work: the doubts regarding the applicable law to legal conflicts arising from the use of recreational boats.

In particular, as far as the regime of limitation of liability is concerned, the Spanish High Court does not exclude the limitation of liability *per se*, in a generalised manner, when the cause of the damage is a recreational vessel. Rather, what is excluded is the operation of this system of limitation of liability when the use of the craft is recreational or 'private'. Obviously, this complicates the issue and forces us to examine the legal impact of the profit-making use of recreational boats.

2.4 Other examples

Many other issues could be analysed in relation to the these distortions. But such in-depth analysis would be too long for a book of this kind. Therefore, I will limit myself to mentioning them briefly.

Regarding the regime of responsibility for damages caused to third parties by the use of recreational boats: does the common civil liability regime apply, or, rather, the special rules on collision? This issue has always raised doubts, but has acquired renewed interest, due to the fact that, in Italy, Art. 40 of the Codice della Nautica da Diporto refers the issue of civil liability to third parties arising from the use of the vessel to Art. 2054 C.c. (dedicated to the circulation of vehicles),[28] and establishes a mandatory insurance regime

25 A. Antonini, 'L'autonomia del diritto della navigazione, il ruolo del diritto comune e la posizione sistematica della legislazione sulla navigazione da diporto' in U. La Torre and A.L. Melania Sia (eds), *Diporto e Turismo tra autonomía e specialità. Un'occasione per un incontro interdisciplinare* (Roma, 2014), pp. 15–61.

26 G. Gilmore and C. L. Black, *The Law of Admiralty*, 2nd edn (Foundation Press, 1975), pp. 880–884.

27 M. Clavero Ternero, 'La limitación de responsabilidad del armador del buque de recreo en la Ley de Navegación Marítima y en la jurisprudencia del Tribunal Supremo' in P.J. Baena Baena and N. López Santana (eds), *Estudios sobre la responsabilidad de los operadores de transporte en la Ley de Navegación Marítima* (Cizur Menor, 2017), pp. 352 et seq; J.M. Martín Osante, 'Régimen jurídico español de la navegación marítima de recreo y deportiva' in U. La Torre and A.L. Melania Sia (eds), *Diporto e Turismo tra autonomía e specialità. Un'occasione per un incontro interdisciplinare* (Roma, 2014), pp. 90–91; A. Mestre, 'Limitación de responsabilidad de las embarcaciones de recreo: Un debate abierto (comentario y revisión de la sentencia del Tribunal Supremo 241/2015, de 6 de mayo de 2015)' (2015) XXXII *Anuario de Derecho Marítimo* 287–293; and B. de la Vega Justribó, *La limitación de responsabilidad por créditos marítimos* (Madrid, 2008), pp. 65–67.

28 Decreto legislativo, 18/07/2005 n° 171, art. 40: '*La responsabilità civile verso i terzi derivante dalla circolazione delle unità da diporto, come definite dall'articolo 3, è regolata dall'articolo 2054 del codice civile e si applica la prescrizione stabilita dall'articolo 2947, comma 2, dello stesso codice*'.

(Art. 41).[29] Specifically: are injuries and damages caused in the context of a nautical sports competition subject to compensation?[30]

What is the position of guests on board? Is the guest a third party to the contract?

Is maritime mediation is to be placed in the framework of consumer law? Is it necessary to introduce a specific discipline about it? In Italy, there is an Associazione Italiana del mediatori marittimi.

Regarding the territorial scope of the law of recreational navigation, should the same rules apply to navigation both in inland waters and in the sea?[31]

Can the owner of a recreational boat be distinguished from the registered owner? It seems evident that the figure of the shipowner is unusual in the field of sports navigation, where there is rarely a split between fitting out and *property*.

It seems evident that the figure of the shipowner is strange in the field of sports navigation, where there is rarely a split between armament and property. But what about the megayachts business? In Italy, some scholars maintain that the owner of a sports boat can be distinguished from the registered owners.[32]

3 The codification of maritime law

3.1 General problem: the codification of maritime law

Both from its content and from its Explanatory Memorandum, it is clear that the Spanish LNM does not attempt to regulate recreational navigation, on the assumption that this is not its purpose.

But that is not really so: it is evident that a legal text whose purpose is to regulate 'navigation', widely considered,[33] must necessarily entail recreational navigation.

For this reason, despite the general statement, the LNM regulates some aspects such as the registration of ships, inspections and safety, navigation accidents, etc., whose rules apply to all types of ship, regardless of their use.

The legislator's decision is understandable. The essential purpose of the LNM is to regulate commercial navigation, a business carried out by entrepreneurs who have traditionally had a wide margin of autonomy to order the content of their agreements. Hence the desire of the LNM to respect as far as possible the principle of autonomy of the will of the contracting parties.

29 M.M. Comenale Pinto, 'Impiego del mezzo náutico e profili di responsabilità' in U. La Torre and A.L. Melania Sia (eds), *Diporto e Turismo tra autonomía e specialità. Un'occasione per un incontro interdisciplinare* (Roma, 2014), pp. 111 et seq.

30 G. Camarda, 'La responsabilità per danni a terzi nel corso dell'attività náutica ricreativa e sportiva' in A. Antonini and F. Morandi (eds), *La navigazione da diporto* (Milano, 1999), pp. 87–116; B. Casado Andrés, *Responsabilidad civil deportiva* (Madrid, 2015).

31 A. Claroni, A. Romangoli, 'Il diporto nelle acque interne' in *Quaderni della rivista del diritto della navigazione*, 2015, pp. 95 et seq.

32 A. Antonini, 'L'autonomia del diritto della navigazione, il ruolo del diritto comune e la posizione sistematica della legislazione sulla navigazione da diporto' in U. La Torre and A. L. Melania Sia (eds), *Diporto e Turismo tra autonomía e specialità. Un'occasione per un incontro interdisciplinare* (Roma, 2014), p. 59.

33 I. Arroyo Martínez, *Curso de Derecho marítimo*, 3th edn (Cizur Menor, 2015) pp. 95–96; J.L. Gabaldón García, *Compendio de Derecho marítimo* (Madrid, 2016), pp. 17 et seq.

However, it seems evident that leisure navigation requires a special and different regime in most of its aspects. In many jurisdictions, the law of recreational navigation is considered part of consumer law and, therefore, must be regulated outside the scope of maritime law.[34]

To a large extent, the model embodied in the Spanish LNM also complies with the requirements of European law, given that Community legislation has a similar impact on the two sectors, *consumption* and *sports navigation*, promoting its harmonisation within the framework of a *Recreational craft industry*, subject to common rules that guarantee the proper functioning of an internal market.[35]

In this way, it can be seen how *the law of sports navigation is dragged by centripetal forces, which bring it closer to the core of Maritime law, and by centrifugal forces that move it away from it.*

So in Spain we are at the same point as we were before the LNM 2014. There is a large normative dispersion, with rules prior to 2014, lacking adequate coordination. This raises a complex panorama, with superposition of norms of diverse nature that are difficult to interpret and apply.

We find ourselves, therefore, facing an important crossroads; we must decide what to do with the law of leisure navigation. And, basically, there are two options: either to leave it in the broader field of maritime law, endowed with a greater or lesser specialty, or to exclude it from maritime law and submit it to its own autonomous regulations.

3.2 The Italian experience: between autonomy and specialty

Before analysing the possible advantages and disadvantages of these solutions, it is a good moment to look at the recent Italian experience.

In Italian law, leisure navigation has traditionally been placed in the common field of maritime law (Codice della navigazione 1942, Title VIII, book I, Navigazione da diporto[36]). But recently, new legislation creating a new branch of law was approved: Codice della nautica da diporto 2005).[37]

This legislative option has both defenders[38] and detractors[39] and their actual scope and effects are doubtful. The most immediate consequence of the Italian legislative option has

34 P. Delebeque, 'Le commerce maritime' in P. Le Cannu (ed.), *D'un Code à l'autre: le droit comercial en mouvement* (Paris, 2008), p. 303. See also, M.L. Chiarella, 'Recesso del consumatore e navigazione da diporto' in U. La Torre and A.L. Melania Sia (eds), *Diporto e Turismo tra autonomía e specialità. Un'occasione per un incontro interdisciplinare* (Roma, 2014), pp. 213–231.

35 M. L. Chiarella, 'Recesso del consumatore e navigazione da diporto' in U. La Torre and A. L. Melania Sia (eds), *Diporto e Turismo tra autonomía e specialità. Un'occasione per un incontro interdisciplinare* (Roma, 2014), pp. 215–216.

36 Codice della navigazione (R.D. 30 marzo 1942, n. 327).

37 Gazzetta Ufficiale N. 202, 31 August 2005. Enabling reform by Ley nº. 167, 7th October 2015. See, E. Romagnoli, 'la reforma del Codice della Nautica: prime osservazioni sulla l. 167/15' (2015) *Il Diritto Marittimo* 768.

38 A. Antonini, 'L'autonomia del diritto della navigazione, il ruolo del diritto comune e la posizione sistematica della legislazione sulla navigazione da diporto' in U. La Torre and A.L. Melania Sia (eds), *Diporto e Turismo tra autonomía e specialità. Un'occasione per un incontro interdisciplinare* (Roma, 2014), pp. 15–16; and F.A. Querci, 'La questione dell'autonomia della náutica da diporto' in A. Antonini and F. Morandi (eds), La *navigazione da diporto* (Milano, 1999), pp. 179–185. The latter emphasises that: '. . . l'autonomia del suo sistema normativo, della sua disciplina, o meglio di un vero e proprio corpus iuris precostituito'.

39 In this sense, most of the Italian doctrine. For example, in addition to the opinions that will be developed in the following pages, the theses expressed in the collective work by M.M. Comenale Pinto and E. Rosafio (eds),

been the appearance of a large number of doubts and problems related to the applicable law. In other words, the problem of defining the boundaries between the new law of leisure navigation and the old maritime law arises.

That is why the experience of the Italian law, probably the most advanced in terms of sports navigation, highlights that this issue still requires further study and maturation. This explains why the new regulation of 2005 is already undergoing reforms, reforms aimed at adapting their content to the changing circumstances of a sector that, without doubt, is maritime, but *which refuses to fit into the traditional legal schemes of the of maritime law.*

What conclusions can we draw from the Italian experience?

First, it is evident that the Leisure Navigation Law has undergone a process of progressive specialisation. There is general agreement on this and today there is no discussion. In any case, it is clear that, since leisure navigation in Italy has become a mass phenomenon, it requires a specific response.

The second and main point is that, starting from that basis is necessary to extract some practical consequences that are not yet clear. In other words, has specialisation culminated in the configuration of an *autonomous* branch of law? The answer to this question is controversial in Italy, where the recent reform has been criticised.[40] In fact, most Italian scholars consider that, despite the use of the denomination of *codice*, it cannot be said that such autonomy exists.[41]

However, the refusal to accept that in Italy there is currently an autonomous leisure navigation law faces two resounding obstacles.

First of all, the *primacy of its own sources*. Art.1 Codice della nautica da diporto clearly establishes, in my opinion, the autonomy of its own sources of law with respect to those of Diritto della Navigazione, although this is a subordinate source. Art.1.3 Codice della nautica da diporto establishes that for what is not foreseen in it, it will be necessary to apply *le leggi, i regolamenti e gli usi di riferimento overo, in mancanza, le disposizioni del codice della navigazione*. Therefore, the special rules on leisure navigation will have preference of application with respect to the general maritime law. As has already been pointed out, this supposes a derogation of the hierarchy of applicable rules, which privileges subordinate sources such as regulations and uses over the Codice della navigazione.[42]

Despite the clarity of the precept, most of the Italian doctrine considers that the discipline of sports navigation in Italy continues to be a special but not autonomous law.[43] And to reach this point they have had, in my opinion, to force the arguments too far, making the facts fit their desires. Because it is not easy to make this thesis compatible with the system of sources contained in the laws examined, which has led to qualifications such as the

Il diporto come fenomeno diffuso: problemi e prospettive del diritto della navigazione, Quaderni della rivista del Diritto della Navigazione, 4, 2015.

40 A. Antonini, 'La responsabilità nella circolazione delle unità da diporto', 2007 Dir.Trasp. 74 et seq.

41 See M.M. Comenale Pinto, 'La locazione delle unità di diporto' 2007 *Il Diritto Marittimo, Fasc. I*, 104; M. Deiana, Il nolleggio delle unità da diporto at http://www.giureta.unipa.it/phpfusion/readarticle.php?article_id=194 (visited 27 August 2019), p. 4.

42 M. Deiana, Il nolleggio delle unità da diporto at http://www.giureta.unipa.it/phpfusion/readarticle.php?article_id=194 (visited 27 August 2019), p. 4. However, in the opinion of this author, the system does not yet have complete autonomy.

43 L. Tullio (Lefebvre d'Ovidio-Pescatore-Tullio), *Manuale di diritto della navigazione*, 13th edn (Milano, 2013), p. 230.

existence of '*una sorta di autonomía speciale della materia della navigazione da diporto nel più generale contesto della navigazione marittima*'.[44] It would be an internal subsystem, within the framework of the law of navigation, endowed with special autonomy or *second degree*, which is explained only in the internal framework of the law of navigation.

And, secondly, the very name used: *Code*. Why is the word code used by the national legislator? Is this denomination trivial or frivolous? What does it mean? Obviously, if you did not want to set up an autonomous system of law, the word *Code* should not have been used.

In short, I think there are reasons to defend the view that the Codice della nautica da diporto contains a true autonomous system of law, both for the mentioned autonomy of sources and for the use of the very word '*codice*'.[45]

4 Possible remedies, future perspectives

It has been discussed for years whether the law of leisure navigation is a completely autonomous system or simply a special sector within the framework of maritime law. It can be said that, until now, there has not been a satisfactory answer to this question.

Based on the considerations outlined above, two main issues are raised.

First, *what is the essence of that specialty*? That is, what is the criterion that should be used to set the boundary between the general (maritime law) and the particular (leisure navigation law).

Second, *is that specialty of such a degree as to make it necessary to configure a specific and differentiated legal regime for sports navigation*?

The answers to both questions are necessarily linked.

4.1 The reasons or the essence of the specialty of the law of leisure navigation

Regarding the former, the various legislations do not follow a clear criterion. In some cases, the specialty falls on the different cause or purpose with which navigation is carried out: leisure in our case, compared to the commercial purpose of common maritime law.[46] With this thesis, we face the problem of the qualification and regulation of leisure navigation carried out with a commercial purpose. That is to say, we must determine which rules apply to leisure navigation carried out for profit.

If anything has drawn attention to the experience of comparative law in recent years, it is the fact that *the profit motive has ceased to be a valid criterion to distinguish between leisure navigation law and general maritime law*. Some arguments in favour of this thesis have been made in the previous pages, when dealing with the applicability of the Convention on Limitation of Liability to non-merchant boats; and also in section 2.2 on the marine insurance of leisure boats.

44 L. Tullio (Lefebvre d'Ovidio-Pescatore-Tullio), *Manuale di diritto della navigazione*, 13th edn (Milano, 2013), p. 11, 231.

45 A. Antonini, 'L'autonomia del diritto della navigazione, il ruolo del diritto comune e la posizione sistematica della legislazione sulla navigazione da diporto' in U. La Torre and A.L. Melania Sia (eds), *Diporto e Turismo tra autonomía e specialità. Un'occasione per un incontro interdisciplinare* (Roma, 2014), p. 18.

46 Ibid, pp. 15–16.

Now, we must analyse the matter again, this time with more general scope. In Italian law, Art. 1.1. Codice della nautica da diporto, in its original wording, established that recreational navigation is a process that takes place in maritime or internal waters for recreational or sporting purposes and not for profit (*Ai fini del presente codice si intende per navigazione da diporto quella effettuata in acque marittime ed interne a scopi sportivi o ricreativi e senza fine di lucro*).

However, in 2011 the definition was reformed (which denotes a lack of maturity of the concept used), to replace the mention '*and without profit-making intention*', by the following phrase: '*as well as that exercised for commercial purposes, including through the vessels referred to in article 3 of the Law of July 8, 2003, n. 172, without prejudice to the discipline envisaged therein*'.[47]

In view of this legislative change, the most recent Italian doctrine has formulated an interpretation of the meaning of the reform that seems correct to me. According to M. Deiana,[48] in its new wording, the Codice della nautica da diporto fully recognizes the commercial use of pleasure craft, distinguishing two figures or models:

1.- '*Neat*' or '*Pure*' Leisure Navigation.
2.- Commercial Leisure Navigation.

For the purposes that concern us in this book, what is relevant is that, once again, the nature of leisure navigation carried out for profit is debatable.

From the systematic and conceptual point of view, the problem that this presents is the following: *if the leisure navigation can be done with profit motive (a causal element), the absence of profit can no longer be a determining element to qualify the navigation as recreational.*

Therefore, it is necessary to use another criterion to distinguish between leisure and ordinary navigation. The limiting criterion could be that of the vessel itself, an objective element. This more objective criterion, based on the nature of the ship or its dimensions, may be the most reasonable, for the future. However, at present, it is not sufficiently developed in any jurisdiction. Therefore, for the time being, it is not operational.

In addition, it leads us to a new conceptual problem: what is a sports boat? This is an issue for which we do not have a clear answer either. Because, what is the determining factor for these purposes: the shape of the ship, its means of navigation, the intention of the parties, regardless of the purpose with which it is used? Should the recreational vessel be used exclusively for this purpose or can other uses be attributed to it without changing its nature? The enormous variety in this type of ship must be kept in mind. And also the fact that fishing boats or commercial vessels can occasionally be used for recreational purposes.[49]

47 '*Ai fini del presente codice si intende per navigazione da diporto quella effettuata in acque marittime ed interne a scopi sportivi o ricreativi e senza fine di lucro, nonche' quella esercitata a scopi commerciali, anche mediante le navi di cui all'articolo 3 della legge 8 luglio 2003, n. 172, ferma restando la disciplina ivi prevista*'.

48 M. Deiana, Il nolleggio delle unità da diporto at http://www.giureta.unipa.it/phpfusion/readarticle.php?article_id=194 (visited 27 August 2019), p. 4.

49 M. Grigoli, *La navigazione da turismo* (Bari, 2007), pp. 39 et seq.

In short, and to conclude this point: the key issue to the future is, in my opinion, to find a way of determining where the essence of maritime law lies: whether in the organizational aspects of navigation or in the private law aspects of sailing.

From the point of view of private law, it is very difficult, if not impossible, to build a valid maritime law for all situations that occur in real life. For this reason, I consider it necessary to restrict the *common* maritime law to navigation, and to distinguish sectoral regulations for the different activities: commercial, recreational, fishing, etc. This does not prevent the rules of commercial maritime law being applied to other sectors, in certain cases and whenever necessary, either by analogy or by their own expansive force.

4.2 Autonomy or specialty?

As regards the second point, autonomy, the uncertainty surrounding this issue is even greater. If we analyse the recent Italian experience, we see that all solutions have drawbacks.

On this matter we find two clearly divergent positions.

On the one hand, most scholars, both in Spain and Italy, based on a broad concept of maritime law, consider that leisure maritime law is a special part of it. For this reason, the full incorporation of leisure maritime law within the framework of general maritime law is defended, on the understanding that the same generic principles can be applied to all types of navigation, under a unitary treatment.

However, operators in the sector demand a greater autonomy or specialty of the law of leisure navigation with respect to the regime of maritime law, and even an independent regulation of this area of the law.[50] And for this purpose, they argue that the demands of the leisure navigation sector and those of the merchant marine segment are different.

There are good arguments in favour of this last thesis: autonomy is a characteristic feature of a specific area of law, when the principles of this sector imply a derogation from the general principles. Therefore, autonomy is the consequence when a specific sector of reality presents its own and peculiar demands, that cannot find an adequate solution through the application of general regulations. And this is precisely what happens with the law of leisure navigation.

In this regard, it should be borne in mind that the necessary protection of the consumer should not lead to excessively rigid regulation, which would be a hindrance to the industry.[51] Otherwise, this could lead to changing the country's flag to other more favourable flags.

In my opinion, the law of leisure navigation can and should be largely autonomous. This branch of economic activity requires a well-defined, simpler and less formalistic regulation, allowing for adequate growth and development of the sector, an *ad hoc* discipline, adapted to the demands of recreational navigation. The law of leisure navigation must have its own rules, different from those provided for merchant shipping, to guarantee operators accessibility and intelligibility.

50 A. Mestre, 'El seguro de embarcaciones deportivas y de recreo' (2002) XIX *Anuario de Derecho Marítimo* 247–264.

51 M.M. Comenale Pinto, 'La locazione delle unità di diporto' 2007 *Il Diritto Marittimo, Fasc. I*, 108.

Now, whether or not that legal system should be considered completely autonomous within the field of the general maritime law is a minor issue, which depends largely on the meaning we give to concepts such as *autonomy*, *sources of law*, *code*, etc. . . ., matters that are not conceptually clear in the field of the general theory of law.

On the other hand, to achieve this high level of autonomy, it is not necessary to write a specific '*code*' on the matter. For this purpose, the instrument of *consolidated text* may be valid. It should not be forgotten that at present there are reasonable doubts about the convenience of codifying the law, at least in the sense that the *codification of law* had in the nineteenth and twentieth centuries. This issue has always been the subject of debate, but it acquired renewed interest on the occasion of the commemoration of the second centenary of the Code de commerce of 1807.

The idea of codification comes largely from Jeremy Bentham, who defends in his great work the idea that the law must be complete[52] and originate from sovereign power.[53] In the framework of the liberal revolution, codification was the method used by liberals to carry out a much-needed legal homogenisation, which overcame medieval particularities.

This task was developed in France with remarkable success, thanks to the genius, authority and organisational capacity of Napoleon. But in other countries, such as Spain, there was never a comparable period of reformist impetus. For that reason, the codifying work was prolonged and became bogged down in the turbulence of the liberal revolution.

The question is to determine whether the idea of codifying law is still valid in the twenty-first century. In particular, in the case of maritime law: is it possible to codify it? It is convenient?[54] These are among the issues most discussed today by the legal-scientific doctrine.

At present, the claim that the law in general, and the maritime law in particular, can be framed in a very broad and stable body of rules is unrealistic. For the following reasons.

On the one hand, technological innovations are constant and remarkable. And the process of codification of the law requires a certain stability in the reality regulated by the codified norms, which should not be subject to constant alterations.

Likewise, business exploitation models are currently changing: new players appear, globalisation takes place, etc . . .

On the other hand, before starting the task of codifying maritime law, we must define its limits: maritime commercial law, transport law,[55] criminal law, etc . . . And we must not forget that the profiles of maritime law are changeable and always diffuse.

Last but not least, the international character of maritime law, which is becoming more and more pronounced, should not be forgotten, to the point that it can be said that, at present, its sources are not found within the national framework, but rather in the international arena.

52 J. Bentham, *Principles of Legislation* in J.H. Burns (general ed.), *The Collected Works of Jeremy Bentham* (London, 1970), pp. 156 et seq.

53 Ibid, pp. 18 et seq.

54 Mª. P. García Rubio, 'Sociedad líquida y codificación' (2016) Vol. 69, nº 3 *Anuario de derecho civil* 744 et seq; P. Rescigno, 'Le prospettive di un diritto europeo ed uniforme dei contratti' in *Codicie. Storia e geografía di un'idea* (Roma, 2013), pp. 235–244.

55 Many scholars defend the configuration of a broad transportation law, codified, with a general part, and various special parties, among which would be the maritime navigation. M.A. Huybrechts, 'The *bicentennial* of the Code of Commerce of 1807', in A. Bruyneel and J.P. Buyle et al (eds), *Bicentenaire du Code de commerce* (Bruxelles, 2007), pp. 343–350.

This has led some scholars to propose that the modern codifications of maritime law should become '*deposits*' or '*warehouses*' of international treaties.[56] To a large extent, this is what the Spanish legislator has done in the LNM of 2014.

These difficulties, and others that are removed, make the codification of maritime law very difficult, although not impossible. There are those who propose to obviate the problems indicated, what has been called a *codification à droit constant*,[57] according to the terminology of the French doctrine, or *Consolidation-Codes*[58] In Italy, that is *an open model*, in the manner of the 1992 Dutch Code (which, with a numbering formula for their articles depending on their location, allows for constant legislative reforms without affecting its structure). But it must be borne in mind that, whatever it is called, this phenomenon constitutes a simple legislative technique that seeks to order and clarify the existing rules; in other words, it is a different approach, more modest in its ambitions, than the codifying idea, which is to create something new, a brand new regulation, subject to common principles and with an idea of stability.

5 Concluding remarks

It is doubtful whether we in Spain should copy the recent Italian experience: a decoding process and subsequent recoding procedure, which indicates that there is a lack of clear thinking on what to do with leisure navigation law.

In my opinion, as regards leisure navigation law, the result expressed in the LNM is unsatisfactory in many ways. In addition to not adequately solving the main issue (creating an adequate regulation for the subject), a new problem is produced, which is the delimitation between the various figures of the contracts of operation of the ship and nautical charter contracts. This is a symptom, in short, of a lack of maturity of the very concept of maritime law used by the legislator. Only on the basis of a very broad concept of maritime law, different from that contained in the LNM, can a leisure navigation law be considered a special part of it.

This broad concept of maritime law, defended by a good number of Spanish and European scholars, would allow a clarification of leisure navigation's role in the general framework of maritime law, without having to force the legal institutions. Because, although it is true that a good part of maritime commercial regulations can be applied to sports navigation,[59] there is no doubt that certain subjects require a specific solution, depending on the purpose of the navigation and the status of the people participating in it.

---

56 Ibid, p. 349: '. . . *the Code of Commerce ought to become a depository of international treaties or, if one wishes, a "storage facility" or a "warehouse" for international treaties relating to transport and shipping*'.

57 P. Delebeque, 'Le commerce maritime' in P. Le Cannu (ed.), *D'un Code à l'autre: le droit comercial en mouvement* (Paris, 2008), pp. 297–305: '. . . *il serait dommage de ceder à certaines sirènes. Du reste, les vrais plaisenciers ne souhaitent pas être assimilés à de simples consommateurs*'.

58 N. Irti, 'Consolidazioni e codificazioni delle leggi civil' in *Codice civile e società política* (Roma, 2007), pp. 71–83.

59 In Spain, see for example: A. Mestre, 'Problemas del aseguramiento de embarcaciones deportivas y de recreo' (2007) *V Jornadas de Derecho marítimo de San Sebastián* 114. Solution also defended by the principal authors in many other nations, for example, in France (E. du Pontavice, *Droit maritime*, 12th edn (Paris, 1997); M. Remond-Gouilloud, *Droit maritime*, 2nd edn (Paris, 1993), and Germany (D. Rabe, *Seehandelsrecht*, 4th edn (München, 2000).

In any case, the debate on the role that the regime of leisure navigation should occupy in the broader field of maritime law remains open.[60] It cannot be said that there are consolidated and generally accepted ideas about it. Sports navigation is tinged with consumer law, and today few things are clear about the nature and position of this branch of the law. There are states where it is codified separately (a Consumer Code distinct from general private law, as in France, Italy or Austria), while others integrate it in the Civil or Civil/Mercantile Code (Netherlands, Argentina, Germany, Czech Republic).

In short, the law of leisure navigation is an obstacle to the codification and ordering of maritime law, as the law of consumption is an obstacle for the codification of private law. It is the manifestation of the same problem, and as yet we do not have generally accepted and acceptable solutions for this.

60 P. Delebeque, 'Le commerce maritime' in P. Le Cannu (ed.), *D'un Code à l'autre: le droit commercial en mouvement* (Paris, 2008), p. 303.

CHAPTER 15

Yacht Codes – a solution to the problem of equivalent safety standards for large yachts

Richard Coles

1 Introduction

The commercial yacht charter industry was in its infancy when the Safety of Life at Sea,[1] Load Line[2] and Standards of Training, Certification and Watchkeeping[3] Conventions came into being. Because of the fragmented nature of the industry at that time, there was no single body in the UK available to represent the views of the industry to the wider shipping industry represented by the Chamber of Shipping and the seafarers' trade unions.[4] During the late 1980s and early 1990s, there was a rapid growth in the number and size of large pleasure yachts engaged in commercial charter activity and it became increasingly evident that certain aspects of merchant ship safety standards were incompatible with the safety needs of large yachts. There are currently an estimated 6,200 yachts in existence worldwide between 24 and 200 metres in length engaged in commercial, or purely private, use. The larger yachts are usually semi-custom built, or constructed and fitted out by a specialist builder to the owner's exclusive design and specification.[5] The manner in which they are operated is thus very different from that of passenger or cruise ships.

2 The solution and its legal framework

Amending any international convention is a slow process, notwithstanding the IMO tacit acceptance procedure that can be used to amend annexes to SOLAS and STCW, but not the main body of these conventions, the amendment of which will require the cooperation and support of all of the states that are party to the relevant convention. The tacit acceptance procedure does not apply at all to the LL Convention. Since large commercial yachts tend

1 The International Convention for the Safety of Life at Sea, as amended, referred as SOLAS (London, 1974).

2 The International Convention on Load Lines, referred as LL (London, 1966).

3 The International Convention on Standards of Training, Certification and Watchkeeping of Seafarers, as amended, referred as STCW (London, 1978).

4 MYBA – the Worldwide Yachting Association (formerly the Mediterranean Yacht Brokers' Association) represents yacht brokers and managers of professionally crewed yachts. It was not formed until 1984. The Professional Yachtsmen's Association represents crew members and was formed in 1991. Both organisations are based in the South of France. Superyacht UK, a division of the British Maritime Federation, was formed in 2003 to represent and promote the interests of the superyacht industry in the United Kingdom.

5 Typically in Italy, the Netherlands, the United Kingdom, Germany, Turkey or the United States, in that order.

to be flagged in a small number of flag states, the regulatory problems facing their owners was unlikely to be a priority for many delegates at the IMO.

Fortunately, a solution was available within the 'equivalent arrangement' provisions in each of the three conventions.[6] After widespread consultation within the yachting industry in the UK and abroad, the Marine Safety Agency ('MSA'), now the Maritime and Coastguard Agency ('the MCA'), published in 1997 a set of equivalent arrangements, the Code of Practice for Safety of Large Commercial Sailing and Motor Vessels ('LY1').[7] LY1 was notified to the IMO by the UK Government as an equivalent arrangement under the three relevant IMO Conventions. As State Party to the Conventions the notification was given not only on behalf of the United Kingdom but also on behalf of those UK Crown Possessions and relevant Overseas Territories having their own shipping registries. At that time Bermuda, the Cayman Islands and the Isle of Man were the only jurisdictions permitted to accept for registration pleasure yachts of 150 gross tons or more, being designated as Category 1 registers able to register any size or type of vessel.[8]

To give the Code the force of law in the UK, the Secretary of State[9] enacted[10] a piece of delegated legislation known as the Merchant Shipping (Vessels in Commercial Use for Sport or Pleasure) Regulations 1998 ('the Regulations').[11] Similar legislation was enacted in the three other jurisdictions mentioned above.

3 The scope of the LY1

The Code applied to vessels in commercial use for sport or leisure (being pleasure vessels 'engaged in trade' for the purpose of Article 5 of the ICLL) which were 24 metres in load line length and over or, if built before 21 July 1968, 150 gross tons and over and which did not carry cargo and did not carry more than 12 passengers.[12] There was also an effective upper tonnage limit of 3,000 gross tons.

The Regulations required that all commercially operated large vessels to which the Code is applicable shall comply with the Code and not proceed to sea unless a certificate of compliance with the Code is in force,[13] issued, in the case of the UK, by the MSA (now the MCA), or a classification society acting on its behalf. Although not mandatory for pleasure vessels, the Code recommended that pleasure vessels should comply with the standards of the Code on a voluntary basis.[14]

---

6 Article 8 of LL, Regs 1–5 of SOLAS and Art. 9 of STCW, as amended, permit a State Party to notify to the IMO an alternative safety standard that it considers to be at least equivalent to that required under the relevant international convention.

7 See generally, F. Lorenzon, 'Yacht Codes: Safety and Compliance for Superyachts' in F. Lorenzon and R. Coles, *The Law of Yachts and Yachting*, 2nd edn (Abingdon, Informa Law from Routledge, 2018).

8 Merchant Shipping (Categorisation of Registries of Overseas Territories) Order 1992, SI 1992/ 1736. Gibraltar and the British Virgin Islands joined the list of Category 1 registers at a later date.

9 For the Department of the Environment, Transport and the Regions, now the Department for Transport.

10 By virtue of ss 85–86 of the Merchant Shipping Act 1995.

11 SI 1998/2771, as amended.

12 For vessels of less than 24 metres in load line length four separate small vessel codes were published by the MSA pursuant to Reg. 5, for which see MGN 280 (M).

13 Regulation 4(4).

14 Section 1.11 of LY1.

4 The contents of the Code

LY1 was published by the MSA in the form of a Merchant Shipping Notice[15] intended to be read in conjunction with the Regulations. It consisted of 98 pages of rules covering such issues as structural strength, watertight integrity and bulkheads, rigging and sails, windows and skylights, stability, lifeboats and rescue boats, storage of petrol and other fuels (including aviation), manning and crew certification, including recognition of commercially endorsed RYA[16] Yachtmaster and Coastal Skipper certificates, as well as certain engineer qualifications where appropriate, passenger and crew accommodation issues, to name only a few of many subjects where there are obvious difference between the needs of the commercial luxury yacht sector and those pertaining in the merchant shipping environment. LY1 and later editions of the Code take into account the various IMO convention 'milestones' that mark the point at which particular surveys and certification are required.[17] The Code provided that it should be reviewed and if necessarily updated within five years of its coming into force by the standing committee representing the industry-wide working group responsible for developing the Code.[18]

5 Subsequent developments: LY2 and LY3

After widespread consultation within the large yacht industry, an enlarged working group produced the first major revision of the Code published by the MCA in August 2005. For the sake of simplicity, the new Code was entitled the Large Commercial Yacht Code or LY2. Among a number of improvements, additional chapters were added to take into account the new obligations imposed on ship operators by the International Ship Management Code[19] and the International Ship and Port Facility Code,[20] neither of which had been implemented when LY1 came into force.[21] Within less than two years, the working group recommended the addition of an additional Annex 6 dealing with technical standards for helicopter landing areas. The new annex and a number of minor changes to the text were included in LY2 (Edition 2) published in September 2007.

The Maritime Labour Convention 2006 ('MLC')[22] presented a major challenge to the designers, builders and owners of yachts constructed after the coming into force of the MLC,[23] particularly Regulation 3.1 that deals with the accommodation and recreational

15 MSN 1792.

16 The Royal Yachting Association.

17 24 metres load line length, 300, 400, 500 and 3,000 gross tons.

18 Section 3.4, LY1.

19 The International Management Code for the Safe Operation of Ships and for Pollution Prevention (ISM Code) adopted on 4 November 1993 by resolution A.741 (18).

20 The International Ship and Port Facility Code (ISPS) adopted on 12 December 2002 by resolution 2 of the Conference of Contracting Governments to SOLAS 1974, as may be amended.

21 Interestingly, Annex 2 of LY2 provides guidance and recommendations on the implementation of safety management systems for vessels under 500 gross tons for which full certification under the ISM Code is not mandatory ('sometimes referred to as Mini ISM').

22 The Maritime Labour Convention (Geneva, 2006).

23 Article VIII(3) of the MLC provided that the Convention would come into force 12 months after the date on which 30 members of the ILO with a total share of 33 per cent of the world gross tonnage of ships had ratified the Convention, which occurred on 20 August 2013.

facilities of seafarers.[24] Clearly, the mandatory minimum dimensions of crew cabins and rest areas that may be easily accommodated within a merchant ship may be impossible to achieve in a pleasure yacht, particularly a sailing yacht. After extensive consultation, the working group produced two additional paragraphs containing equivalent provisions relating to crew accommodation, distinguishing between yachts above and below 200 gross tons. These new sections,[25] along with a large number of other improvements, were published in August 2012 prior to the coming into force of the MLC. Significantly, the new edition of the Code, LY3, removed the upper limit of 3,000 gross tons, thus permitting a megayacht of any size to be coded as a commercial yacht provided the number of passengers did not exceed 12, the limit above which SOLAS requires a vessel to be certificated as a passenger ship.

6 Passenger yachts

While the majority of owners of large yachts were content with a limit of 12 passengers, there arose a demand ten or more years ago for a means of increasing the number of passengers without the necessity of converting the vessel into a fully SOLAS-compliant passenger ship, assuming that such a conversion was financially viable. Since the Cayman Islands flag was by far the most popular jurisdiction for large yachts at that time,[26] the Red Ensign Group of registries ('REG') in 2008 supported an initiative by the Cayman Islands Shipping Registry ('CISR') to develop on behalf of the whole Group a code of practice containing equivalent standards to enable between 13 and 36 passengers to be carried on a large yacht, whether operating as a pleasure yacht or a commercial vessel.

The initiative resulted in the publication of the Red Ensign Group 13–36 Passenger Yacht Code in November 2010, generally known as the Passenger Yacht Code, or simply 'PYC'. In order to keep abreast of the frequent changes to IMO Conventions affecting passenger ships, it was necessary to update the PYC on an annual basis until 2016, no mean effort bearing in mind the small number of PYC vessels in service or in build.

7 The Red Ensign Group Yacht Code

During the course of 2016, it was decided that, for marketing and other reasons, future editions of the LYC and the PYC would be combined and published by the REG, rather than the MCA and the CISR respectively.[27] The new Code would be known as the Red Ensign Group Yacht Code, abbreviated to REG-YC. REG-YC was launched in November

24 See generally, M. Bek, Chapter 4, *Yachting and the Maritime Labour Convention 2006* in J. Lavelle (ed) *The Maritime Labour Convention 2006: International Labour Law Redefined* (Abingdon, Informa Law from Routledge, 2013).

25 Sections 21A and 21B.

26 By 2015 the number of pleasure and commercial yachts over 24 metres load line length registered in the leading five jurisdictions was as follows: Cayman Islands 1,104, United Kingdom 528, Malta 486, Marshall Islands 312 and St Vincent and the Grenadines 257. Source: the statistics were supplied to the author by each of the flag state administrations concerned in September 2015.

27 The detailed arrangements for reviewing the existing codes were announced to the Industry in a meeting of the REG-YC Industry Working Group held during the London Boat Show on 13 January 2017. The writer is indebted to the REG Code Secretariat for providing a copy of the minutes of that meeting.

2017. However, to give the yachting industry sufficient time to adapt to the new Code, REG-YC would not come into effect for another 25 months. It is made up of three parts; Part A (The Large Yacht Code), Part B (The Passenger Yacht Code) and the Common Annexes containing material common to both Parts.[28] REG-YC came into full force for vessels with keels laid on or after 1 January 2019.[29] In the meantime, existing vessels that were currently coded under LY1, LY2 or LY3, or earlier editions of the PYC, remained subject to the standards in force at the time of their initial survey. However, at their first annual survey after 1 January 2019 they will be expected to comply with certain specified sections of REG-YC.[30]

8 The adoption or use of yacht codes in other EU jurisdictions

The use of yacht codes is not unique to the United Kingdom, its Crown Possessions and Overseas Territories. Italy is consistently the country building the largest number of superyachts.[31] A new law, No 172 of 8 July 2003, authorised the issue of delegated legislation, the *Codice della Nautica da Diporto*, the Yachting Code.[32] While the Yachting Code makes a distinction between the commercial and private use of pleasure craft, the writer has been advised by Avv. Alberto Pasino[33] that the Code and subsequent Italian legislation[34] do not contain any equivalent arrangements for Italian-flagged yachts as an alternative to the safety standards required under SOLAS, LL and STCW Conventions. This may in part explain the popularity of the UK flag among Italian yacht owners.

Malta[35] followed the United Kingdom in adopting its own Commercial Yacht Code in 2007 after consultation with industry stakeholders. The Code was deposited with the IMO as an equivalent standard under the Conventions.[36] The third edition was published in 2015 and the layout and general content are in many respects similar to LY3.[37] The latest version

28 There are Annexes dealing with Certification and Hours of Work, Helicopter Landings Areas and Application of International Conventions and National Legislation as well as 12 other subjects.

29 The REG-YC (January 2019 Edition) is available at http://www.redensigngroup.org/publications/ (visited 18 August 2019).

30 Part A Paragraph 1.6 (2) or Part B Paragraph 1.7 (1). For a list of those requirements of the REG-YC that are retrospectively applied to existing vessels, see the Cayman Maritime Guidance Note 01/2019 (Rev 1.0) dated 11 February 2019, available at http://www.cishipping.com/policy-advice/guidance-notes/ (visited 18 August 2019).

31 In an article by Caroline White entitled *Slow is the New Fast* it was reported that of the 23 yachts of between 24 and 40 metres in length that were launched in May 2018, 12 were built in Italy. It is not known how many of these were built for export or in which jurisdiction they will be registered. C. White, 'Slow is the New Fast' *Boat International*, August 2018, pp. 28–29.

32 Legislative Decree of 18 July 2005 No 171, about which see generally A. Pasino, *The Reform of the Italian Yachting Code* in *The Book of Proceedings of the 2nd Adriatic Maritime Law Conference on Comparative Maritime Law, 25–27 May 2017* (Zagreb, Hrvatska Akademija Znanosti Umjetnosti I Jadranski Zavod, 2018) pp. 47–56.

33 Senior Partner in the Trieste office of Zunarelli Studio Legale Associato.

34 Law 7 October 2015, No. 167.

35 According to Table 2.8, *Review of Maritime Transport* (UNCTAD, 2018) ('UNCTD'), Malta ranked fifth in the world and first in Europe in 2018 by deadweight tonnage of merchant ships registered, but with fewer yachts registered than in the UK in 2015: see fn.24 and https://unctad.org/en/pages/PublicationWebflyer.aspx?publicationid=2245 (visited 18 August 2019).

36 See IMO LL3/Circ 172 of 7 November 2007 and IMO SLS.14/Circ.298 of 8 November 2007.

37 Malta Commercial Yacht Code 2015 is available at http://www.transport.gov.mt/admin/uploads/media-library/filesCYC%202015pdf (visited 18 August 2019).

applies to vessels whose keels were laid after 1 October 2015 and existing vessels built under previous versions of the Code were required to comply with the new Code not later than their first periodic survey after 1 October 2015. Unlike the UK and Red Ensign Group Codes, the Malta Code applies to vessels of between 15 and 24 metres in length as well as vessels above that size. Paragraph 20.2.2 of the Malta Commercial Code provides that yachts that are already certified in accordance with the MCA LY2/LY3 or by the Italian *Regolamento di Sicurezza per il Noleggio* will be entitled to a three-month Certificate of Compliance (with the same navigational range as the existing certification) pending completion of an initial survey by the Malta administration.

9 Yacht codes in jurisdictions outside the European Union

As has already been seen, the Red Ensign Group of Registries includes jurisdictions within and outside of the EU, with the Cayman Islands having the largest number of superyachts of any non-EU register.[38]

The second most popular non-EU flag-state is the Marshall Islands, which has the third-largest merchant fleet in the world[39] and a growing number of superyachts. The Republic of the Marshall Islands (RMI) adopted its first Commercial Yacht Code in October 2008, ten years after LY1 came into force. The original code was replaced in 2013 by a new RMI Yacht Code which addressed the changes that had taken place since the 2008. The 2013 edition was subsequently revised in April 2017.[40]

The RMI Yacht Code requires that, regardless of gross tonnage, all Marshall Islands registered commercial yachts shall comply with the relevant chapters of the code applicable to such yachts. It further requires that any vessel of any tonnage seeking to be coded as a passenger yacht carrying more than 12 passengers but no more than 36 shall comply with the chapters of the code applicable to a passenger yacht (PAXY).

Controversially, the Code contains a chapter permitting the coding of private yachts of 18 metres or more in length overall and less than 500 gross tons, enabling them to engage in limited chartering for no more than 84 days per calendar year and restricted to no more than 12 passengers, referred to as a Private Yacht Limited Charter (PYLC). The hybrid nature of the PYLC programme is inappropriate for a yacht cruising in EU waters for Customs and fiscal reasons.

Finally, there is a fourth category of vessel – a Yacht Engaged in Trade (YET). A YET is a private yacht of over 24 metres in length that, subject to meeting certain documentary requirements, is entitled to obtain a Temporary Certificate of Registry allowing the vessel to undertake temporary chartering of up to 84 days a year in EU waters (currently limited to French and Monegasque Waters). There is the usual limit of no more than 12 passengers.[41]

---

38 On 31 December 2017 there were 1,018 yachts (pleasure, commercial and passenger yachts) registered at CISR as opposed to 210 merchant ships over 100 tons. Source: Information provided to the writer by Mr John-Kaare Aune, Deputy Director of CISR on 2 February 2018.

39 3,419 vessels with a deadweight tonnage of 237 million. Source: Table 2.8 of UNCTAD referred to in fn.35.

40 The 2013 RMI Yacht Code MI-103 rev.04/17 is available at http://www.register-iri.com/forms/upload/MI-103.pdf (visited 18 August 2019).

41 The CISR has introduced a similar YET programme by means of Shipping Notice 03/2017 (rev 1.1) rather than by inclusion in the REG-YC.

This programme has clearly been introduced with the agreement of the French and Monegasque Governments to give greater flexibility to yacht owners in the heart of the West Mediterranean cruising area.

Like the Marshall Islands, the Bahamas has one of the largest merchant fleets in the world.[42] It has been particularly successful in attracting cruise ships to its register. Coupled with the islands' close proximity to both the Caribbean and Florida, it came as no surprise that the Bahamas Maritime Administration ('BMA') should seek to expand into the large yacht sector. In 2008 the BMA published a guide to the registration of yachts in which it was stipulated that vessels over 24 metres in length seeking registration in the Bahamas should not only be in class with a member of the International Society of Classification Societies but also comply with the UK Large Yacht Code (LY2). Although a former British colony, the Bahamas is an independent country and it is therefore somewhat surprising that a UK code should be adopted in this way.

This anomaly was resolved by the introduction in March 2011 of the Bahamas Yacht Code,[43] essentially a 'cut and paste' version of LY2 published by agreement with the MCA. The Code remains in force to the present day. Because it predates LY3, the upper limit of 3,000 gross tons has not been removed and the other changes introduced by LY3, in particular those relating to the Maritime Labour Convention, are not included. There is no separate provision for passenger yachts as is possible in the REG-YC and the RMI Yacht Code. The number of large yachts registered in the Bahamas remains small when compared with the Marshall Islands and the REG member states outside the European Union.

Barbados is a country with a much smaller registered fleet that, nevertheless, appears on the Paris MOU Port State Control White list.[44] Barbados has very few yachts on its register and does not publish its own yacht code for commercial yachts. Since 2014, the Barbados Maritime Registry has however required such yachts to comply with LY2 or LY3 and to undergo annual inspection by a Barbados authorised surveyor. Compliance with LY2/LY3 is coupled with recognition of the UK RYA/DTp Yachtmaster and Coastal Skipper qualifications for certain categories of yachtmaster and chief officer; a good example of the adoption of UK/REG codes and safety standards outside the Red Ensign Group of registries.

The St Vincent and the Grenadines (SVG) register is a well-known open register with a significant number of yachts registered.[45] The Administration published in 2008 a Safety Code of Practice for Pleasure Yachts Engaged in Commercial Trade.[46] The Code applies to yachts of 10 metres or over in length and less than 500 gross tons, that are engaged in commercial trade, carrying no cargo and up to 12 passengers. While the SVG register may attract tonnage because of possible savings in registration and survey fees, the writer

42 1,418 vessels with a dead-weight tonnage of 76 million. Source: Table 2.8 of UNCTAD referred to in fn 35.

43 The Bahamas Yacht Code for Commercial Yachts 2011 is available at https://www.bahamasmaritime.com/wp-content/uploads/2015/08/133bulltn.pdf#targetText=Bahamas%20Safety%20Inspection&targetText=least%20once%20during%20the%20five,Bahamas%20Yacht%20Code%20(BYC) (visited 18 August 2019).

44 See generally, Chapter 8, E. Watt and R. Coles (Ed.) *Ship Registration: Law and Practice*, 3rd edn (Abingdon, Informa Law from Routledge, 2018).

45 See fn.24.

46 SVG Code Yachts Engaged in Commercial Trade-Edition 2008-Rev 4 is available at http://svg-marad.com/Downloads/Law%20and%20Directives/Shipping%20Acts/Commercial%20Yacht%20Code%20%28july%2008%29.pdf (accessed 18 August 2019).

believes and that the owners of charter yachts, and potential charterers, may be deterred by the detention record of SVG-flagged vessels between 2016 and 2018 as evidenced by the country's presence in the latest Paris MOU on Port State Control Grey List published in August 2019.[47]

The Cook Islands, a self-governing nation in free association with New Zealand, is a less well-known flag state that has adopted yacht codes for large commercial and private yachts of 24 metres and above in length.[48] However, the presence of that country on the Paris MOU Black List[49] may be an even greater deterrent to yacht owners considering a choice of registry.

10 Concluding remarks

Compared to the number of commercial vessels in the world fleet,[50] the number of large yachts is very small. This may in part explain the mismatch between the requirements of the large yacht industry and the mainstream shipping world in the major IMO Conventions.[51]

The solution to the problem was made possible by the equivalent arrangement provisions in the relevant conventions.[52] The UK Government on behalf of itself and the other Red Ensign jurisdictions was the first to consult the international yachting community as a prerequisite to launching the first commercial yacht code, LY1. With approximately 30% of the world's large yacht fleet now registered in REG jurisdictions,[53] the Code, and its subsequent editions now consolidated into the REG-YC, has become a safety benchmark within the international yachting industry.[54]

The two other major players in the large yacht registration market, The Marshall Islands and Malta, have successfully introduced their own yacht codes with the Marshall Islands' containing hybrid arrangements enabling private pleasure yachts to undertake limited chartering, assuming this is permissible on a local basis.

In the writer's view, the key to the success of yacht codes is the ability of flag state administrations to review and update the codes in order to address the relentless flow of amendments to the IMO Conventions, in particular SOLAS, and to provide an appropriate level of technical support to meet the exacting needs of yacht owners, builders and other stakeholders within the large yacht world. The UK/Red Ensign Group and the Marshall Islands administration have until now risen to the challenge, but for flag states with fewer

47 See p 28 Paris MOU Annual Report 2018 available at http:www.parismou.org/sites/default/files/2018-%20WGB%20.listst.pdf (visited on 20August 2019).

48 Available at http:www.maritimecookislands.com/wp-content/uploads/2015/12cook-islands-large-yacht-code-v4 (visited on 20 August 2019).

49 See p 31 Paris MOU Annual Report 2018 referred to in fn 47.

50 50,732 seagoing vessels over 1,000GT, see Table 2.3 UNCTAD referred to in fn.35.

51 See fnn 2 to 4.

52 See para 2.

53 See an article by G. Howorth, *What now for the Red Ensign?* in *Superyacht Business*, Issue 56, February 2017.

54 The adoption of LY2 as an equivalent safety standard by the Bahamas and Barbados maritime administrations is clear evidence of this point. Furthermore, in yacht sale transactions the widely used MYBA MOA 2008 Addendum One lists an MCA Code compliance document as one of the key documents required to be produced on completion of a yacht purchase.

resources or a limited ability to engage with the yachting industry, the task may be more difficult. For this reason it seems unlikely that few jurisdictions other that the UK and the other British territories comprising the Red Ensign Group, Malta and the Marshall Islands will feel it necessary or appropriate to introduce and keep up to date their own yacht codes. The writer believes that this is particularly so in the case of passenger yacht codes that are necessary to satisfy the small demand for this option at the very top end of the superyacht market.

CHATPER 16

Claims for personal injuries by cruise ship passengers under international and EU regimes

Dr Olena Bokareva

1 Introduction

This chapter analyses the international regime providing compensation for personal injuries for passengers travelling on a cruise ship. The cruise shipping companies offer passengers the top facilities of a holiday resort in addition to travelling to virtually all destinations in the world. The risks associated with cruising can be of both a maritime and land (hotel) nature since the passengers move freely on board ship and participate a variety of activities during the cruise. Additionally, while at sea the ship is exposed to all the dangers pertinent to any ship. Thus, in certain cases the carrier is entitled to exclude or limit its liability for certain types of loss or damage.

The main goal of the chapter is to examine liability and compensation in relation to international sea passengers, focusing mainly on sea cruise passengers. Notably, these claims are more complex than those for ordinary passenger carriage, owing to the nature of cruising. The current international regime pertaining to passengers is embodied in the Athens Convention 2002.[1] There are also various instruments at EU level which need to be examined, including EU Regulation 392/2009,[2] which implements the Athens Convention 2002, and the new Directive (EU) 2015/2302 on package travel and linked travel arrangements.[3]

2 International aspects of cruises

It is alleged that the origin of the word 'cruise' comes from the French word '*croiser*' which literally means wandering the seas from one coast to another, which is different from regular transport.[4] In the *Dictionary of Nautical Words and Terms*, 'cruising' is defined as sailing in different directions for the purpose of search, or for visiting different places.[5]

1 Athens Convention relating to the Carriage of Passengers and their Luggage by Sea, 2002 (London, 2002).

2 Regulation (EC) No 392/2009 of the European Parliament and of the Council of 23 April 2009 on the liability of carriers of passengers by sea in the event of accidents OJ L 131, 28.5.2009, pp. 24–46.

3 Directive (EU) 2015/2302 of the European Parliament and of the Council of 25 November 2015 on package travel and linked travel arrangements, amending Regulation (EC) No 2006/2004 and Directive 2011/83/EU of the European Parliament and of the Council and repealing Council Directive 90/314/EEC OJ L 326, 11.12.2015, pp. 1–33.

4 J.L. Pulido Begines, 'Cruise Ship Law', in J. Basedow et al (eds), *The Hamburg Lectures on Maritime Affairs 2011–2013* (Springer, 2014), p. 211.

5 C.W.T. Layton, *Dictionary of Nautical Words and Terms*, 4th edn (Brown, Son & Ferguson, Ltd, Nautical Publishers 1994), p. 114.

Tracing the history of cruise shipping, one can mention the historical overview of British shipping. It is noted that the P&O shipping company proposed the first cruise ship in the late 1830s, which encouraged British passengers to take holidays at sea.[6] The modern carriage of passengers started in the early twentieth century, mainly as a transportation service between Europe and the United States. Later on, the airline industry almost completely replaced it after Pan American Airways inaugurated the trans-Pacific service and the Atlantic service in 1936.[7] It is contended that in the nineteenth century sea voyages were mainly undertaken by people trying to escape oppressive regimes or poverty at home and were eager to start a new life in countries, such as the US, offering more opportunities. Therefore, such voyages were considered more as a necessity than as holidays or relaxation.[8]

At present, the carriage of passengers by sea has a different purpose, focusing more on offering customers all-inclusive resort facilities than providing a pure transportation service. On some short ferry routes there are still passengers who need to be transported from one place to another, sometimes together with their vehicles. However, the main thrust is on the development and growth of cruise shipping that provides passengers with an opportunity to visit all resort destinations in the world and enjoy a vacation similar to one they might have at land-based resort hotels.

As observed by one commentator: '. . . [cruising] is the fastest growing segment of the leisure travel industry and continues to grow.'[9] It is evident that the global cruise industry is experiencing a substantial increase in the number of cruise passengers. The Caribbean region remains the most popular cruise destination. According to statistical data, 28.2 million passengers took cruises in 2018 and the projection for 2019 is 30 million.[10] More than 50 per cent of all cruise passengers originate from the US.[11]

With hindsight, the first cruise liner was the *Prinzessin Viktoria Luise*, which was built by the Hamburg America Line in 1901 and could carry 200 passengers.[12] At present, the biggest cruise ship is the *Symphony of the Seas*, built by Royal Caribbean in 2017. She can accommodate 6,680 passengers and provide luxury facilities such as numerous restaurants, bars, theatres, an ice rink, various pools and even robot bartenders.[13] Apart from luxury holidays, cruise lines can accommodate various demands by offering specialised cruises for business customers, for a particular age group or for educational programmes.

In analysing the cruise shipping business, a notable commentator postulates that its framework is very complex, since there are no specific rules governing conflicts arising from legal relationships in cruising.[14] The major difficulty lies in the nature of cruising,

---

6 N. Robins, *The Cruise Ship: A Very British Institution*, The History Press (Reprint edition 2008).

7 C.H. Whitehurst Jr, 'Is the legal definition of a passenger ship obsolete?' (1979–1980) 11 *Journal of Maritime Law and Commerce* 527, 529.

8 C. Hill, *Maritime Law*, 6th edn (Informa Lawfrom Routledge, 2003), p. 455.

9 J.L. Pulido Begines, 'Cruise Ship Law', p. 200.

10 V.P. Nanda, 'U.S. Perspective on the Legal Aspects of Cruises' (2018) 66 *The American Journal of Comparative Law* 66, Issue suppl_1, 213–242; see also CLIA, '2019 Cruise Industry Outlook', www.cruising.org/news-and-research/research (visited 19 August 2019).

11 J. L. Pulido Begines, 'Cruise Ship Law', p. 213.

12 www.cruiselinehistory.com/albert-ballin-inventor-and-father-of-the-pleasure-cruise (visited 19 August 2019).

13 www.ship-technology.com/projects/symphony-seas-cruise-ship (visited 19 August 2019).

14 J.L. Pulido Begines, 'Cruise Ship Law', pp. 201–202.

since cruises provide transportation services, covered by a contract of carriage, and it is evident that transport plays a vital role in any kind of passenger carriage. In this manner, the legal regime applicable to the carriage of passengers by sea will obviously apply.[15] At the same time, since the purpose of the cruise contract is to provide not solely transport, but also holiday and relaxation, the regime of carriage of passengers does not cover all the aspects of cruise shipping and package travel. Therefore, one should also consider the legislation relevant to customer protection and package travel. As was rightly observed, '[T]he cruise industry is very peculiar, staying between "two worlds": consumer law and maritime law, each one with its own rationale and demands.'[16]

In the view of one author, general contract law applies to contracts for passengers' carriage. Previously, it was common practice to include a clause in passengers' contracts, excluding the carrier's liability for any personal injury suffered in the course of passage. Such clauses were considered onerous by the courts of some countries.[17] One example is the case of *Adler v Dickson*[18] which later gave rise to the so-called *Himalaya* clauses in contracts of carriage.

Although maritime transport in general is considered to be a relatively safe mode of transport, accidents do occur. The sinking of the *Titanic* in 1912 is perhaps the worst passenger ship accident. This disaster initiated international action by the shipping community to develop a legal regime of safety standards for passenger ships. However, there were other dramatic accidents in the first half of the twentieth century, leading to the loss of passenger ships such as the *Lusitania, Empress of Ireland, Britannic* and *Andrea Doria*, to name a few.[19]

As a response to the *Titanic* tragedy, the first international instrument devoted to the safety of ships was the International Convention for the Safety of Life at Sea (SOLAS). SOLAS was initially adopted in 1914, and then amended in 1929, 1948 and 1960. The version which is in force at present is SOLAS 1974, as amended.[20] The necessity for international action was self-evident due to the global character of shipping and the need for protection of life and property on the high seas, which is in the interest of many nations.[21] Although these are very important instruments, their analysis is beyond the scope of this chapter, which mainly focuses on the carrier's liability arising from personal injuries on cruise ships. Despite international and regional standards related to safety implemented in many countries, incidents involving passenger ships still occur, which are dealt with in the next few paragraphs. In this respect, one can recall a statement made by a notable author: '[N]o one, however, will argue that an unsinkable or disaster-proof ship can be built.'[22]

15 Ibid, p. 204.

16 Ibid, pp. 207–208.

17 C. Hill, *Maritime Law*, pp. 446–447.

18 *Adler v Dickson* (*The Himalaya*) [1954] 2 Lloyd's Rep 267.

19 www.pbs.org/lostliners/chart.html (visited 19 August 2019).

20 www.imo.org/en/about/conventions/listofconventions/pages/international-convention-for-the-safety-of-life-at-sea-(solas),-1974.aspx (visited 19 August 2019).

21 A.K. Kuhn, 'International Aspects of the Titanic Case' (1915) 9(2) *American Journal of International Law* 336–351, 349.

22 C.H. Whitehurst Jr, 'Is the legal definition of a passenger ship obsolete?' (1979–1980) 11 *Journal of Maritime Law and Commerce* 527, 529.

The *Costa Concordia*, which grounded off the coast of Giglio Island in 2012, is considered to be the largest passenger ship in history to be in distress. Thirty-two people died as a result of the accident and many passengers suffered injuries during the salvage operations. The passengers' claims were brought in different countries, some of them still pending. Costa Cruises offered a settlement of about US$14,400 to each uninjured passenger. The master of the ship was convicted of multiple counts of manslaughter, causing a maritime accident and abandoning ship before all passengers and crew had been evacuated; he was sentenced to 16 years' imprisonment. The Court of Cassation, Italy's highest criminal tribunal, upheld this decision in 2017.[23]

A recent incident involving the cruise ship *Viking Sky* demonstrated the vulnerability of cruise ships and rescue operations in rough weather. A two-year-old ship carrying 1,373 passengers and crew was on a two-week cruise 'In Search of the Northern Lights' – the first winter cruise on Viking Cruises' itinerary.[24] Heading towards Stavanger, Norway, the ship encountered extreme weather and lost its power in a very dangerous area close to rocks. Since it was impossible to carry out evacuation by lifeboats in rough weather, helicopters airlifted 479 people off the ship. As a result of the incident, 36 people sustained various kinds of injury.[25] According to the Coast Guard the ship could have become a disaster shortly before one engine was finally restarted. The company announced that all passengers would be reimbursed after the accident, the costs for the return journey and a personal invitation to travel on a new cruise as compensation. It remains to be seen whether any of the passengers will bring a claim against the company.[26]

In the sections to follow, international and EU regimes will be considered and discussed on their adequacy for cruise passengers' claims and the interplay between the two relevant regimes.

3 International regime

It should be noted that the legal regime pertaining to passengers is substantially different from that for the carriage of goods. It is not easy to state precisely which law will apply to a particular passenger claim; however, this can be determined from the ticket incorporating standard terms and conditions. Thus, it is vital to know whether the state of the court considering the claim is a party to an international convention governing passenger carriage. Personal injury claims is a broad category and may include a variety of different claims for damage suffered because of shipping or non-shipping incidents. Some of these include loss of life and serious injuries as a result of a shipping incident, others relate to incidents

23 www.independent.co.uk/news/world/europe/costa-concordia-captain-francesco-schettino-jailed-a7733611.html (visited 19 August 2019).

24 J. Walker, 'Viking Sky Loses Power, Starts Evacuation of Passengers' (*Cruise Law News*, 23 March 2019) www.cruiselawnews.com/2019/03/articles/power-loss/viking-sky-loses-power-starts-evacuation-of-passengers/ (visited 19 August 2019).

25 J. Stacey, 'Cruise Ship Viking Sky Loses Power, 479 Passengers Airlifted' (*Maritime Injury Lawyers blog*, 26 March 2019) www.maritimeinjurylawyersblog.com/cruise-ship-viking-sky-loses-power-479-passengers-airlifted/(visited 19 August 2019).

26 S.F. Faull, 'Viking Sky passengers get their money back – and offer of a new cruise' (*Norway Today*, 26 March 2019) norwaytoday.info/travel/viking-sky-passengers-get-their-money-back-and-offer-of-a-new-cruise/ (visited 19 August 2019).

similar to those in land-based hotels. There is also a category of claims for non-economic loss such as psychological trauma, disappointment and ruined holidays. Some of these cases will be discussed in the following sections.

3.1 Athens Convention 1974

The closest international regime relevant to cruise passengers is the Athens Convention relating to Carriage of Passengers and their Luggage by Sea, 1974 as amended by Protocol 2002, which establishes international minimum standards for the carrier's obligations and liabilities. However, it should be noted that not all states are parties to either the 1974 or the 2002 version of the Convention. Some states apply their national law to passengers' claims, which might differ substantially from the international regime and can create unexpected results for the claimant or its descendants.

Before the original Athens Convention 1974, which entered into force in 1987,[27] the international shipping community undertook several attempts to develop a regime pertaining to the protection of passengers travelling by sea; but without any major success.[28] The basis of the carrier's liability for death and personal injury to passengers as well as for loss of or damage to luggage is based on fault under the Athens Convention 1974. The burden of proof rests with the claimant unless the accident arose from or in connection with shipwreck, collision, stranding, explosion or fire, or defect in the ship. The limits of liability constituted 700,000 francs[29] for death and personal injury. Later on, Special Drawing Rights ('SDRs') were substituted for Poincaré francs by Protocol 1979, and the limit of liability for death and personal injury was accordingly changed to 46,666 SDRs.[30] In addition to official ratifications and accessions, a number of states have incorporated the Athens Convention 1974 into their domestic legislation. One criticism directed towards the Convention was its low level of compensation, especially after several incidents involving ferries; thus it became necessary to amend the limits.

The result of these amendments became a Protocol to the Athens Convention adopted in 2002, which entered into force in 2014. The text of the Protocol was consolidated with the main Convention and will be further referred to as the Athens Convention 2002. It establishes the carrier's liability for death and personal injury due to shipping incidents, as well as non-shipping incidents. The Convention may also apply through contractual incorporation, especially in cruise contracts.

The Convention entered into force after more than ten years because of certain difficulties concerning compulsory insurance. With the help of the IMO and supporting instruments facilitating ratification, these difficulties were overcome. It is true to say that

27 The number of Contracting States was 25, but some later denounced the Convention and joined the Protocol of 2002.

28 See e.g. The International Convention for the Unification of Certain Rules relating to the Carriage of Passengers by Sea, 1961, entered into force in 1965 and ratified by a small number of states; the International Convention for the Unification of Certain Rules relating to the Carriage of Passengers' Luggage by Sea, 1967 (not in force); F. Berlingieri, *International Maritime Conventions, Volume I: The Carriage of Goods and Passengers by Sea*, 1st edn (Informa Law, 2014), Ch. 4.

29 Units consisting of 65.5 milligrams of gold of millesimal fineness 900.

30 See the opinions and criticism of the liability limits in B. Soyer and G. Leloudas, 'Carriage of Passengers by Sea: A Critical Analysis of the International Regime' (2018) 26 *Michigan State International Law Review* 483.

it achieved more success and acceptance than its predecessor. This is apparent from the number of participating countries, some 30 Contracting States, including the EU which joined the Convention along with its Member States. However, it is conspicuous that in a number of countries the original Athens Convention 1974 remains in force, which can potentially lead to conflict of conventions in situations where both conventions apply to one claim. It must be noted that the two regimes in force create a situation in which it is not easy for the claimant or his lawyer to assess in advance the applicable regime, as this can largely depend on the chosen forum.

Analysing the status and role of the Convention internationally, Hobhouse, J. gives a very clear description in *The Lion* case.[31] Even though it concerned the Athens Convention 1974, it is also relevant to the Athens Convention 2002. He postulates that:

> 'The Convention, unlike other conventions, has no documentary requirement . . . That is not the scheme of this Convention, although it does clearly contemplate that documents may come into existence. All this Convention does is provide a regime and lay down a code which is to apply to govern the rights and liabilities of carriers and passengers. It is that type of scheme. It is not one which is contractually dependent. So it is not a scheme which depends upon the incorporation of particular provisions into a contract. It is a scheme which imposes its provisions as a matter of law upon the parties.'[32]

In *Warner v Scapa Flow Charters*, a recent case concerning the time limits for actions for damages arising out of the death of or personal injuries to a passenger, an issue relating to interpretation was highlighted. In particular, references were made to the leading decision related to the Montreal Convention 1999, *Fothergill v Monarch Airlines Ltd.*[33] It was recalled that while interpreting an international convention, national courts must look at the objective meaning of the words used and the purpose of the convention as a whole.[34] It was further stated that:

> 'The Athens Convention, like many international conventions concerning international carriage and transport, aims within its scope to create an international code which replaces the differing domestic rules of the states which have acceded to it by uniform international rules.'[35]

Another decision is *South West Strategic Health Authority v Bay Island Voyages*[36] concerning claims against a carrier for contribution. It was clearly stated there that the Athens Convention does not cover these claims, since its aim is to govern passengers' claims against carriers. As pointed out:

> 'The Convention is a convention for the unification of certain rules relating to the carriage by sea of passengers and their luggage – it does not purport to be a complete code governing all liability of sea carriers to whomsoever owed in respect of the carriage of passengers and their luggage.'[37]

31 *R.G. Mayor v P&O Ferries Ltd and Others (The Lion)* [1990] 2 QB 144 (Com. Ct.).
32 Ibid, at 153.
33 *Fothergill v Monarch Airlines Ltd* [1981] AC 251.
34 *Warner v Scapa Flow Charters* [2019] UKSC 52, [14].
35 Ibid, [13].
36 *South West Strategic Health Authority v Bay Island Voyages* [2015] EWCA Civ 708.
37 Ibid, [15].

These are important statements which reiterate the significance of achieving uniformity in application and interpretation of the international Convention relating to passengers, especially since the Convention would be applied by domestic courts in various countries.

3.2 Overview of the Athens Convention 2002 and its salient features

In a similar manner to its predecessor, the Athens Convention 2002 provides an international regime for civil liability of carriers, limitation of liability and compensation to passengers for losses suffered during the carriage. Such losses include loss of life or personal injury or loss of, or damage to, their property/luggage. Both instruments bear certain similarities but also distinctive features in terms of the liability regime, insurance and compensation available to the passengers. Unlike the Athens Convention 1974, the new Convention establishes strict and fault-based liability for the carrier, two tiers of limitation amounts and compulsory insurance. A distinction between a shipping and non-shipping incident implies different levels of liability and compensation.

Notably, the Athens Convention 2002 does not apply to *all* passenger carriage by sea. It does not deal with liability arising out of a ruined holiday that is covered by relevant domestic law or EU legislation on package travel. Also, according to Article 22 there is a possibility for a State Party to exclude the application of the Convention in cases where the carrier and the passenger are nationals of that state, and therefore there is no presence of a foreign element.

Another important feature of the Athens Convention is that it has mandatory application in contrast to soft-law instruments or contractual provision. Thus, in case of a conflict it will prevail over any conflicting contractual terms and make them invalid if they relieve any person liable under the Convention of liability or lessen the liability.[38]

In the Convention, 'carrier' means a person by or on behalf of whom a contract of carriage has been concluded, whether the carriage is actually performed by that person or by a performing carrier. The notion of 'performing carrier' is also provided and separated from the 'carrier' and can comprise owner, charterer or operator of a ship, who actually performs the whole or part of the carriage. Additionally, the liability of the performing carrier is governed by a separate article.[39]

The Convention defines categories of passengers who fall within the scope of the Convention. In particular, Article 1(4) states that a 'passenger' means 'any person carried in a ship, (a) under a contract of carriage, or (b) who, with the consent of the carrier, is accompanying a vehicle or live animals which are covered by a contract for the carriage of goods not governed by this Convention'. It is apparent that the crew members are excluded from the scope since their contracts are contracts of employment and not contracts of carriage.

According to the Convention, 'ship' means only a seagoing vessel and excludes an air-cushion vehicle. *The Sea Eagle* case[40] is a good illustration of this. While examining the notions of 'a ship or vessel', the court concluded that *Sea Eagle* was a ship capable of being used, and actually used, in navigation.[41] In terms of whether she was a 'seagoing'

38 Art. 18.
39 Art. 4.
40 *Michael v Musgrave (The Sea Eagle)* [2012] EWHC 1438 (Admlty).
41 Ibid, [28]–[30].

ship, the important issue was not whether a ship *could* go to sea but whether she *did* go to sea. Thus, *Sea Eagle* was a ship or vessel which was 'seagoing' for the purpose of the Athens Convention.[42]

Another important definition provided in the Convention is a 'contract of carriage'. According to Article 1(2) it is not necessary that the passenger himself enters into a contract of carriage. It is enough that he is covered by a contract of carriage that was concluded on his behalf. 'Carriage' is also defined as:

> 'a period during which the passenger and/or his cabin luggage are on board the ship or in the course of embarkation or disembarkation, and the period during which the passenger and his cabin luggage are transported by water from land to the ship or vice-versa, if the cost of such transport is included in the fare or if the vessel used for this purpose of auxiliary transport has been put at the disposal of the passenger by the carrier.'[43]

Notably, the period when the passenger is in a marine terminal or station or on a quay or in or on any other port installation is not considered as carriage. In the same manner, shore excursions from cruise ships are beyond the scope of the Convention.

The issue of embarkation/disembarkation was raised in the next two cases mentioned below. One of them concerned injuries suffered during the claimant's stepping onto a large wet plywood board that had been placed on the shingle at the foot of the steps.[44] The main question was whether the accident occurred in the course of disembarkation from the boat within the meaning of the Athens Convention 1974. In the view of Hamblen LJ:

> '. . . the process of disembarkation covers the whole period of moving from the vessel to a safe position on the shore and whilst a person was still using equipment which facilitates disembarkation, such as the steps and board in this case, he is still in the process of disembarking.'[45]

Furthermore, it was decided that the steps were not part of the boat since they were a semi-permanent structure on the beach. An analogy was made with the Warsaw/ Montreal Conventions which govern carriage of passengers and luggage by air. Finally, it was decided that the accident occurred while the claimant was still disembarking from the boat, and thus triggered the application of the Athens Convention.

In another case, *The Norwegian Jade*,[46] the claimant boarded the tender for the purpose of transportation from the ship to the shore at Santorini and sustained injury after tripping over a hazardous step while aboard a tender boat. It was alleged that the incident occurred during the course of international carriage and that the Athens Convention 1974 applied. The carrier objected that the incident occurred in the course of 'carriage'. In particular, the defendant suggested that the wording of the Athens Convention is different in relation to disembarkation at port (when the carrier is responsible for the passenger and/or his cabin luggage) and where the passenger is being transported from the ship to port by water

42 Ibid, [31]–[33].
43 Art. 1(8).
44 *Collins v Lawrence* [2017] EWCA Civ 2268.
45 Ibid, [18].
46 *Lawrence v NCL (Bahamas) Ltd (The Norwegian Jade)* [2017] EWCA Civ 2222.

transportation.[47] This submission was rejected by the judge as being contrary to a purposive construction of the Convention since it would limit disembarkation to the beginning and end of the voyage.[48] The judge also noted that many cruise passengers are elderly and therefore less fit to look after themselves. Thus, the carriers should exercise due care towards these passengers.[49]

Another important requirement for the application of the Convention is that the carriage itself must be 'international' according to Article 1(9). It is stated that the contract of carriage should provide that the place of departure and the place of destination be situated in two different states. However, it is also clarified that these two places might also be located in one state in cases when, according to the contract of carriage or the scheduled itinerary, there is an intermediate port of call in another state. The latter obviously refers to the cruise contracts, which usually provide for departure from one port and calling at different intermediate ports before the ship returns to the same port.

The claimant has an option to bring a claim before one of the courts, if the court is located in a State Party to this Convention, and subject to the domestic law of each State Party governing the proper venue within those states with multiple possible forums.[50] The rules on the time-bar provide that actions for damages due to death or personal injury or for loss of or damage to luggage is two years.[51]

3.3 Carrier's liability and limitation of liability for passengers' claims

It is important to note that the drafters of the Athens Convention 2002 have chosen the notion of 'personal injury' in respect of liability of the carrier. Comparing the terminology with that employed by the Montreal Convention 1999, it can be observed that the term 'personal injury' is broader than 'bodily injury',[52] and apparently may include compensation for non-material damage.[53] The difference in terminology can be explained by the fact that during air transportation passengers must fasten their seatbelts and cannot easily move in the aircraft during take-off and landing. In contrast, sea passengers are invited to explore the ship during the voyage and can be subject to different risks and injuries unrelated to transportation. It is less clear, though, how this notion will be interpreted by a particular court in each case. Comparing the cause of action under both sea and air regimes, it is evident that Article 29 of the Montreal Convention is more restrictive than Article 14 of the Athens Convention. In particular, the wording of the Montreal Convention is as follows:

> 'In the carriage of passengers, baggage and cargo, any action for damages, however founded, whether under this Convention or in contract or in tort or otherwise, can only be brought subject to the conditions and such limits of liability as are set out in this Convention without prejudice to the question as to who are the persons who have the right to bring suit and what are their

47 Ibid, [23].
48 Ibid, [24].
49 Ibid, [28].
50 Art. 17.
51 Art. 16(3) provides a maximum 3- or 5-year limit in certain cases but not more.
52 Convention on the Unification of Certain Rules for International Carriage by Air, Montreal 1999.
53 It was explicitly explained by the draftsmen and the leading cases from several jurisdictions.

> respective rights. In any such action, punitive, exemplary or any other non-compensatory damages shall not be recoverable;'

whereas Article 14 of the Athens Convention provides that:

> 'No action for damages for the death of or personal injury to a passenger, or for the loss of or damage to luggage, shall be brought against a carrier or performing carrier otherwise than in accordance with this Convention.'

Thus, it can be concluded that the claimant may bring claims for so-called ruined holiday or for loss of enjoyment, which are beyond the scope of the Athens Convention.[54]

The liability regime established under the Athens Convention 2002 is provided in Article 3. It states that in the case of loss suffered as a result of death or personal injury to a passenger caused by a shipping incident, the carrier's liability should not exceed 250,000 units of account in respect of that passenger on each distinct occasion, unless the carrier proves that the incident occurred as a result of war, hostilities, civil war, insurrection or a natural phenomenon of an exceptional, inevitable and irresistible character; or was caused by a third party with the intent to cause the incident. The Convention defines 'shipping incident' as shipwreck, capsizing, collision or stranding of the ship, explosion or fire in the ship, or defect in the ship.[55] Non-shipping incidents may include so-called hotel land-based incidents, such as food poisoning, falling from the stairs, accidents in the swimming pool, falling overboard, and medical maltreatment.[56] Accidents occurring during shore excursions are excluded from carrier's liability in the cruise contracts.[57]

In cases where the loss is higher than 250,000 units of account, the carrier shall be further liable unless he proves that the incident which caused the loss occurred without the fault or neglect of the carrier. Where the loss occurred because of a non-shipping incident, the carrier is liable if the incident was attributable to the fault or neglect of the carrier and the claimant bears the burden of proof.[58] In any case, the liability of the carrier for the death of or personal injury to a passenger under Article 3 shall in no case exceed 400,000 units of account per passenger on each distinct occasion.[59] Notably, the carrier might lose its right to limit liability in case the damage resulted from an act or omission of the carrier done with the intent to cause such damage, or recklessly and with knowledge that such damage would probably result.[60]

The provisions on compulsory insurance were seen as obstacles for joining the Convention and raised concerns among the insurance sector, especially P&I Clubs offering third-party liability insurance. To overcome this difficulty and attract more participation, the IMO drafted a provision on reservation and Guidelines which address the issues related

54 A. Saggerson, *Package Holiday Law: Cases and Materials* (XPL Publishing, 2008), p. 562.

55 Art. 3(5)(a).

56 T.A. Dickerson, 'The Cruise Passenger's Dilemma: Twenty-First-Century Ships, Nineteenth-Century Rights' (2003–2004) 28 *Tulane Maritime Law Journal* 447.

57 See e.g. the clause in Carnival Terms and Conditions: 'Carnival is not responsible for any losses, damage, death, injuries, or claims . . . while off Carnival's ships or tenders in any port of call . . . Guests engage in all such activities off the ship at their own risk.'

58 Art. 3(2).

59 Art. 7(1). Note that Art. 23 allows future amendments of limits regarding the limits set in Arts 3(1), 4 bis (1), 7(1) and 8 through a special procedure.

60 Art. 13.

to war and non-war insurance. The limits of the compulsory insurance or other financial security should be not less than 250,000 units of account per passenger on each distinct occasion. The carrier must obtain insurance or financial security to cover its liability under the Convention regarding death and personal injury to passengers.[61]

It is a point of observation that the liability of the carrier stated in Article 3(6) relates only to loss arising from incidents that occurred in the course of the carriage, which resembles the wording in the Athens Convention 1974. The claimant in turn bears the burden of proof that the incident took place in the course of the carriage, and of the extent of the loss.

The notion of 'in the course of the carriage' in relation to the Athens Convention 1974 was examined in *Davis v Stena Line Limited.*[62] In this case a passenger fell overboard from the ferry *Koningin Beatrix* during the passage from the Irish Republic to Wales. Due to the prolonged and unsuccessful rescue plan employed by the master and the bridge team, the passenger died before he was rescued.[63] In the court it was concluded that even though a passenger was in the sea and not on board a ship when he died, the parties agreed that he died during the course of carriage within the meaning of the Convention, and thus the Convention applied.

One of the most common non-shipping incidents is gastroenteritis, in particular norovirus which is a very common illness in closed communities, *inter alia*, schools and cruise ships. One recent case related to this issue is *Nolan and Others v TUI UK Ltd.*[64] In this case at least 217 passengers and crew members were affected by gastroenteritis. Among them 28 passengers sued the carrier for personal injury and 15 sued for damage and disappointment as a breach of contract, alleging fault or neglect of the defendant under Article 3(1) of the Athens Convention 1974. The claimants alleged that the defendant did not warn that there was norovirus on the previous cruise and that the necessary clean-up operations were not undertaken prior to the current cruise. However, the claimants could not succeed in their claims since the expert medical and scientific evidence demonstrated that the defendant was not at fault and carefully followed the policy regarding cleaning and food handling.[65] Finally, it was concluded that there was no link between the outbreak of norovirus on a previous cruise and that on the current cruise. Apparently, this might have been caused by one or more passengers on the new cruise.[66]

Another common incident on cruise ships is slipping and falling. In *Dawkins v Carnival Plc*[67] the claimant while walking through the restaurant fell and injured her knees and wrists. The claim was governed by the Athens Convention 1974. The defendant demonstrated that the inspection system was operating effectively at the time of the accident and that the water could not have remained on the floor for a long time. However, the claimant appealed, pointing out that it was not enough to show that the inspection system was proper; it had to be demonstrated that the system was properly implemented at the time of the accident. The Court of Appeal allowed the appeal and concluded that a high standard of

61 Art. 4 bis. Similar legislation was adopted in the EU reflected in Directive 2009/20/EC of 23 April 2009 on the insurance of shipowners for maritime claims.

62 *Davis v Stena Line Ltd* [2005] EWHC 420 (QB).

63 Ibid, [60].

64 *Nolan and Others v TUI UK Ltd* [2016] 1 Lloyd's Rep 211.

65 Ibid, [85]–[91].

66 Ibid, [90].

67 *Dawkins v Carnival Plc (T/A P&O Cruises)* [2012] 1 EWCA Civ 1237.

care is expected from the carrier, in particular as regards the floor in the restaurant, which was under the management of the carrier. Since the hazard was present on the floor, it led to the negligence of the defendants.[68]

Article 19 of the Athens Convention 2002 refers to other conventions dealing with limitations of liability of owners of seagoing ships. It is evident that the relevant convention would be the Convention on Limitation of Liability for Maritime Claims 1976,[69] amended by a 1996 Protocol, generally known as LLMC 1996.[70] It provides the limits of liability for passenger claims in Article 7(1) as follows:

> 'In respect of claims arising on any distinct occasion for loss of life or personal injury to passengers of a ship, the limit of liability of the shipowner thereof shall be an amount of 175,000 Units of Account multiplied by the number of passengers which the ship is authorized to carry according to the ship's certificate.'

Under the 1996 Protocol the amount of compensation payable in the event of an incident was increased. Also, a 'tacit acceptance' procedure was introduced with the aim of updating the amounts in the future. The 1996 Protocol was amended in 2012 and has been in force since 8 June 2015. The limits were further raised so that the limit of liability for claims for loss of life or personal injury on ships not exceeding 2,000 gross tonnage is 3.02 million SDRs. For larger ships, the additional amounts were calculated; all of them were increased.

4 EU law relating to passengers and travellers

Passenger transport plays an important role in the mobility of EU citizens, since 23 Member States are coastal countries, including several island states. It is also estimated that more than 400 million people pass through EU ports every year. Also, 120 million passengers are transported by domestic passenger ships, within the same Member State.[71] The EU has also developed a sophisticated regime covering all modes of passenger carriage, including carriage by sea and a separate regime for those who buy holiday packages.[72]

EU legislation on passenger ship safety has been put in place following accidents such as the sinking of the *Herald of Free Enterprise* in 1987 and the *Estonia* in 1994, which resulted in the loss of 193 and 852 lives respectively.[73] It complements international and national standards, provides for safer ships and more efficient handling of ship accidents. A number of legislative texts that improve the common rules on safety of ships carrying passengers in EU waters was adopted in 2017 and will be applicable within the EU from

68 Ibid, [18], [28].

69 Convention on Limitation of Liability for Maritime Claims (LLMC) (London, 19 November 1976).

70 Protocol of 1996 to amend the Convention on Limitation of Liability for Maritime Claims of 19 November 1976 (London, 2 May 1996).

71 *Adjusting Course: EU Passenger Ship Safety Legislation Fitness Check Brussels*, COM (2015) 508 final (Report from the Commission to the European Parliament and the Council), 2.

72 Regulation (EC) No 392/2009 of the European Parliament and of the Council of 23 April 2009 on the liability of carriers of passengers by sea in the event of accidents (Athens Regulation) OJ L 131, 28.5.2009, pp. 24–46. See also Regulation (EU) No 1177/2010 of the European Parliament and of the Council of 24 November 2010 concerning the rights of passengers when travelling by sea and inland waterway and amending Regulation (EC) No 2006/2004 (Sea Passengers Rights Regulation) OJ L 334, 17.12.2010, pp. 1–16.

73 'Safety of passenger ships', www.ec.europa.eu/transport/modes/maritime/safety-and-environment/safety-passenger-ships_en (visited 19 March 2019).

21 December 2019. It is notable that on 23 May 2018, the European Commission adopted a proposal relating to a common safety framework for small passenger ships (length less than 24 metres). These rules will concern ship design, fire hazards and emergencies.[74] Also, with the participation of the EU within the IMO, an international agreement was adopted, which sets out more stringent rules on the safety of passenger ships. When the amendments enter into force in 2020, all new passenger ships will have to be designed to remain afloat for longer following damage to the hull. This corresponds to the EU goals of maintaining high safety standards, especially for passenger ships.[75]

Tourism is recognised as a major economic activity in the EU, having a positive impact on economic growth and employment in Europe. It is also an increasingly important aspect of the life of European citizens, who are travelling for either leisure or business.[76] With regard to cruises, a European branch of the Cruise Lines International Association (CLIA)[77] or CLIA Europe comprises 29 cruise members and 42 associate members, representing nearly 100 per cent of the industry operating in Europe.

EU harmonisation of passenger and travel law needs to be discussed because in part it applies to cruise shipping. The framework for cruise shipping within the EU needs to be placed in proper legal context. The major question is whether it will fall under transport or tourism activities. On the one hand, the rules of tourism law can cover cruise shipping since most of the cruises are bought as part of a package. However, on the other hand, transport is a vital element of cruising and thus leads to the application of transport law. Thus, the question is which regime will prevail in case of a conflict – package travel legislation or the Athens Convention 2002?[78]

With the entry into force of the Treaty on the Functioning of the European Union (TFEU) in 2009, the importance of tourism is recognised; the EU now has powers in this field to support, coordinate and complement action by the Member States. The competence to participate in transport agreements, especially in the area of sea and air transport, is granted explicitly in Article 100(2) of the TFEU and falls under the shared competence, while tourism is placed under a supporting competence of the EU pursuant to Article 6(d) and 195 of the TFEU.

4.1 Athens Convention 2002 within the EU: salient features of Regulation (EC) No 392/2009

The EU's involvement in the regional implementation of the Athens Convention 2002 is significant, also because the EU joined the Convention along with its Member States.[79]

74 Ibid.

75 'Maritime Transport: Commission welcomes international agreement to increase the safety of passenger ships', 16 June 2017', ec.europa.eu/transport/modes/maritime/news/2017-06-16-maritime-transport-commission-welcomes-international-agreement_en (visited 19 August 2019).

76 *Europe, the world's No 1 tourist destination – a new political framework for tourism in Europe*, COM(2010) 352 final (Communication from the Commission), 2.

77 CLIA is the world's largest cruise industry trade association representing the interests of cruise lines, travel agents etc. before regulatory and legislative policy-makers.

78 J.L. Pulido Begines, 'Cruise Ship Law', p. 209; J.M. Bech Serrat, 'Consumer Travel Law' in Christian Twigg-Flesner (ed.) *Research Handbook on EU Consumer and Contract Law* (Edward Elgar, 2016), pp. 361–362.

79 The Athens Protocol of 2002 allows participation of a Regional Economic Organisation. Some elements of the Convention, i.e. relating to the jurisdiction, recognition and enforcement of judgments, belong to the exclusive competence of the EU; thus the EU needed to become a Party to the Convention.

The EU ratified the Athens Convention 2002 in December 2011 and adopted Regulation (EC) No 392/2009 to implement the Athens Convention 2002 (Athens Regulation) within the Union. This Regulation governs the liability regime based on the Athens Convention 2002 and the IMO Reservation and Guidelines for the Implementation of the Athens Convention (IMO Guidelines).[80] The Athens Regulation is broader than the Athens Convention 2002 and applies to both international and national transport within the EU. Additionally, it encompasses new provisions, such as compensation for the mobility equipment of disabled passengers, and immediate compensation in the event of death of €21,000. It also contains an obligation to inform the passengers of their rights.

With regard to liability, Article 3 of the Athens Regulation contains provisions on liability and compulsory insurance and refers to the corresponding provisions of the Athens Convention and the IMO Guidelines. Article 5 also refers to LLMC 1996 regarding further limitation available for the carrier. A novelty of the Athens Regulation – provision on advance payment indicated in Article 6(1) states that it should cover immediate economic needs proportionate to the damage suffered within 15 days of the identification of the person entitled to damages. In the case of death, such payment shall be not less than €21,000. However, such payment is not viewed as recognition of liability by the carrier and may be offset against any subsequent sums paid based on this Regulation.

In examining the role of the EU implementation of the Athens Convention 2002 one can appreciate that this participation and the subsequent implementation triggered the faster application of the Convention within the EU even before its official entry into force. Moreover, it speeded up the entry into force of the Convention globally by attracting a sufficient number of ratifications. It is now a part of EU legislation and falls under the jurisdiction of the Court of Justice of the EU (CJEU) to interpret it. At present, there is no CJEU case law regarding the interplay between the Athens Convention and EU legislation. However, potential difficulties can be envisaged, especially in respect of conflict with international regimes and how it will be applied and interpreted in non-EU States Parties to the Convention.[81] In such a scenario, the EU Member States will be facing dubious obligations under international law and EU law. It is not easy to predict how these conflicts will be resolved.

4.2 Legislation on passengers' rights and package travel

Another relevant regulation related to sea passengers is Regulation (EC) No 1177/2010 Concerning the Rights of Passengers when Travelling by Sea and Inland Waterway,[82] which mainly deals with delays and cancellations. The Regulation covers passenger services not only between ports located in Member States but also outside the Union. It covers

80 IMO Ref. A1/P/5.01, Circular letter No. 2758, 20 November 2006.

81 B. Soyer, 'Emergence of EU Maritime Law' in D. Patterson and A. Södersten (eds), *A Companion to European Union Law and International Law*, 1st edn (John Wiley & Sons, Inc., 2016).

82 Regulation (EU) No 1177/2010 of the European Parliament and of the Council of 24 November 2010 concerning the rights of passengers when travelling by sea and inland waterway and amending Regulation (EC) No 2006/2004 (Sea Passengers Rights Regulation) OJ L 334, 17.12.2010, pp. 1–16.

passenger services where the port of embarkation is located outside a Member State if a Union carrier operates it.[83] This Regulation also defines a cruise as:

> '[a] transport service by sea or inland waterway, operated exclusively for the purpose of pleasure or recreation, supplemented by accommodation and other facilities, exceeding two overnight stays on board.'

Apart from transport legislation, there is also a regime created to accommodate package travel within the EU. A recently adopted Directive (EU) 2015/2302 on package travel and linked travel arrangements[84] had amended the Directive on EU on Package Travel, Package Holidays and Package Tours 90/314/EEC (Directive 90/314/EEC).[85] Cases decided by the national courts and the CJEU demonstrated a number of problems with regard to interpretation of the Directive, including liability and limitation of liability, the definition of 'package' and the notion of non-material compensation.[86] As a response to certain grey areas in the Directive 90/314/EEC, a new Directive was adopted in 2015 and Member States were under obligation to transpose it into their national legislation by 1 January 2018. The Directive is now applicable as from 1 July 2018.[87] It is stressed in the Directive that Member States should abstain from introducing into their national law provisions diverging from those set in the Directive in order to achieve the necessary level of harmonisation. Directive (EU) 2015/2302 extends protection of the 1990 EU Package Travel Directive to those who book other forms of combined travel, e.g. a self-chosen combination on a website, or a flight plus hotel or car rental. It applies to three types of package, such as pre-arranged packages, customised packages and linked travel arrangements. The package should include at least two different types of travel service, including services such as carriage, accommodation, rental cars and any other service. However, if the packages and linked travel arrangements last for less than 24 hours unless overnight accommodation is included, the Directive does not apply.[88] It also does not apply when offered occasionally and on a not-for-profit basis to a limited group of travellers and those that are purchased based on a general agreement for the arrangement of business travel.

Even though the Directive does not strictly apply to carriage by sea it can nevertheless apply if the cruise is a part of a package. Therefore, to what extent the new regime might be in conflict with the Athens Convention 2002 and the Athens Regulation warrants further

83 'Union carrier' means a carrier established within the territory of a Member State or offering transport by passenger services operated to or from the territory of a Member State.

84 Directive (EU) 2015/2302 of the European Parliament and of the Council of 25 November 2015 on package travel and linked travel arrangements, amending Regulation (EC) No 2006/2004 and Directive 2011/83/EU of the European Parliament and of the Council and repealing Council Directive 90/314/EEC OJ L 326, 11.12.2015, pp. 1–33.

85 *Report on the Implementation of Directive 90/314/EEC on Package Travel and Holiday Tours in the Domestic Legislation of EC Member States*, SEC(1999) 1800 final (EU Commission),

86 *Milner v Carnival Plc* [2010] 3 All ER 701 (damages for a ruined holiday), Case C-168/00 *Simone Leitner v TUI* [2002] ECLI:EU:C:2002:163; Case C-400/00 *Club Tour* [2002] ECLI:EU:C:2002:272, see also Saggerson (2008).

87 Note that the European Commission referred Ireland to the CJEU for failing to transpose the Directive into national law by 1 January 2018 and called the Court to impose financial sanctions for the breach, referring to Art. 260(3) TFEU, europa.eu/rapid/press-release_IP-19–1478_en.htm (visited 19 August 2019).

88 Art. 1(2).

discussion. The topic of cruises was underlined by CLIA Europe in its position paper regarding the new Directive. It was suggested that it has to be clarified that a cruise (whether fly/cruise or cruise only) is a 'package' as defined by the Directive since it is not always recognised in some Member States' jurisdictions.[89] However, in the final text there is still no definition of a cruise and the explicit provision that a cruise is a package is missing; reference to cruises is only mentioned in several places in the Preamble and the main text. One must observe that even Regulation (EC) No 1177/2010 is clearer with regard to the cruise definition.[90]

The provision regarding compensation for damages in Article 14 warrants examination. The traveller is entitled to compensation from the organizer for any damage sustained by the traveller for any lack of conformity. It is notable that the notion of 'any damage' chosen by the legislators is rather broad and can be given various interpretations in different EU Member States and also the CJEU, and may also comprise compensation for non-material damage. As a result, this unpredictability can lead to conflicts with other mandatory conventions, in particular the Montreal Convention 1999, which excludes any compensation for non-material damage. The implications of the new Directive provoke further discussion and it is now too early to say firmly to what extent it will create conflicts with the existing international regime on passengers or respective EU legislation.[91] A positive observation in this respect is that the legislators made an attempt to govern possible conflicts by including a provision regarding existing international conventions or EU Regulations. It states that the Directive will not affect the rights of travellers provided under these instruments and that any overcompensation should be avoided. Even though this attempt to cope with conflict of conventions deserves positive appreciation, it may not resolve conflicts in all cases. It remains to be seen in what manner the CJEU will interpret these provisions. There is a hope that the CJEU will be consistent in its judgments and establish a common EU position with regard to different instruments.

So far, there is no case law dealing with either Directive (EU) 2015/2302 or the Athens Regulation. However, for illustrating possible conflicts two cases will be examined in the concluding part of this section on the EU regime. Two decisions stemming from English courts are of interest. Even though both cases concern Directive 90/314/EEC implemented in the form of the Travel, Holiday and Package Tours Regulations 1992 (Regulations 1992) and the Athens Convention 1974, it is interesting how the courts approached and resolved the conflicts between two instruments. In *Lee and Another v Airtours Holidays Ltd*[92] the claimants brought an action against the defendants Airtours Holidays Ltd and Airtours Plc for personal injury, including psychological damage, loss of possessions and loss of their holiday due to the sinking of *Sun Vista* as a result of fire. The passengers were rescued by

---

89 CLIA Europe, *Proposal for a Directive of the European Parliament and of The Council on package travel and assisted travel arrangements, amending Regulation (EC) No 2006/2004, Directive 2011/83/EU and repealing Council Directive 90/314/EEC* (CLIA Europe Position Paper, 2013), www.cliaeurope.eu/images/downloads/tourism/CLIA%20Europe%20position%20-%20Revision%20of%20the%20Package%20Travel%20Directive_FINAL.pdf (visited 19 August 2019).

90 O. Bokareva, 'Directive (EU) 2015/2302 on Package Travel and Linked Travel Arrangements – Application to Cruises' (2018) Editorial to 24 *Journal of International Maritime Law* 337.

91 The European Travel Agents' and Tour Operators' Associations, *The Revision of the Package Travel Directive* (ECTAA's Position Paper, Ref. BC13-086/4400, 2013).

92 *Lee and Another v Airtours Holidays Ltd and Another* [2004] 1 Lloyd's Rep 683.

lifeboats, but their belongings were lost. The claim was brought under reg. 15 of the Regulations 1992. Reg.15(3) provides that:

> 'In the case of damage arising from the non-performance or improper performance of the services involved in the package, the contract may provide for compensation to be limited in accordance with the international conventions which govern such services.'

However, the defendants argued that the Athens Convention having the force of law should apply save to the extent that it was expressly overridden by the Regulations. At the same time, they relied on the terms of the Directive which prompted the Regulations. The claimants objected that the defendants could rely on the Athens Convention 1974 since no contract was ever issued, and especially not a contract which referred to compensation being limited in accordance with any international convention.

One of the issues raised was whether the limitation of liability provisions under the Athens Convention applied to claims under the Regulations 1992. In the view of the judge, the Regulations represent an alternative regime which must prevail according to EU law. One of the differences is that under the Regulations the fire would qualify as 'improper performance' of the contract in accordance with reg. 15(2). By contrast, under Article 3(1) of the Convention, the relevant test would be 'fault or neglect'. Answering a question whether an operator, sued under reg. 15, could claim the protection of Articles 5, 7 or 8 of the Convention, the judge replied in the negative. Once the liability provisions of the Convention are overridden by the Regulations, limitation of liability provisions or other provisions of the Convention could not apply.[93]

Another case pertinent to the relationship between the two instruments is *Norfolk v My Travel Group Plc* case.[94] The package holiday comprised flights to and from Bristol and a sea cruise starting at Palma. The claimant was injured in an accident on the vessel by slipping on water on the floor of a lift, and brought the claim under the 1992 Regulations for damages for consequential losses, including pain, suffering and loss of amenity, and including loss of enjoyment of the rest of her holiday. The claimant submitted that pursuant to the Directive the Athens Convention should apply only if it is brought expressly to the notice of the consumer, whose protection was covered by the Regulations. It was also alleged that the claim was not a claim for damages for personal injury but a statutory claim for damages for improper performance of the contract. The judge pointed out that if there was an intention on the part of the draftsmen to apply the Convention 'only in circumstances where there had been an express reference in the contract involving a carrier, rather than the Convention applying as a matter of law', it should have been clearly stated.[95]

The judge postulated that by accepting the allegation that this was not a claim for damages for personal injury but a statutory claim for damages for improper performance of the contract, the international scheme of the Athens Convention could be undermined, and further held that:

> 'The fact that the regulations flow from a directive, which emanated from the Council of Europe, in my judgment does not affect the standing of the international Convention. True it

93 Ibid, [40].
94 *Norfolk v My Travel Group Plc* [2004] 1 Lloyd's Rep 106.
95 Ibid, [13]–[14].

is that the aim of the international Convention is harmonization as is the expressed aim of the council directive. But be that as it may the reality remains that one group's harmony may be another group's distortion.'[96]

It must be reiterated that these two cases decided by the English courts were based on the previous Directive 90/314/EEC as implemented in the UK and the Athens Convention 1974. At present, the EU legislation has been transformed both by international instrument – the Athens Convention 2002 which is now part of EU legal order (unlike the Athens Convention 1974) and the new Directive (EU) 2015/2302 on package travel. These novelties might also change the approach of the domestic courts and the CJEU, who will have to consider both instruments as EU law and interpret them based on EU methods of interpretation.

5 Concluding remarks

This chapter demonstrates that the existing regime applicable to cruise shipping is complex and multifaceted and combines various aspects of transport and consumer law. This is especially evident in the context of EU legislation pertinent to passengers and travel which includes various instruments based on international and EU law. Although granting a broad scope of protection to EU passengers and travellers, it must be recognised that the conflicts between these instruments might be inevitable. Thus it presents difficulties for sea cruise passengers who will be faced with several regimes and it may be difficult for the passenger claimant to determine which is the best forum.

As was stressed elsewhere, the CJEU may play a significant role in solving this uneasy exercise in applying a proper regime to passengers' claims and at the same time maintaining a reasonable balance between international and regional instruments which should ideally complement each other for the benefit of passengers instead of creating undesirable conflicts.

With respect to international legal regimes applicable to cruises, it was underscored that there is no special convention dealing solely with cruises. Therefore, the Athens Convention 2002 will probably remain the closest instrument dealing with this type of passenger carriage and will achieve its goal in unifying the liability regime related to passenger carriage internationally. Hopefully, more states will join the Convention in the future and apply it to passengers' claims.

96 Ibid, [15].

PART IV

NATIONAL CODIFICATIONS OF MARITIME LAW

CHAPTER 17

Maritime law codification in Japan

Elements considered and those not considered

Professor Souichirou Kozuka[1]

1 Maritime law in the Commercial Code

1.1 Introduction

The transport law of Japan went through a total reform in 2018, after having largely maintained the original text since 1899. The resulting amendments to the Commercial Code and relevant laws entered into force on 1 April 2019.

The reform raised several important issues regarding the codification of maritime law. These include: (1) the relationship of maritime law to the law on other modes of transport, (2) the uniqueness of maritime and transport law as compared with the general contract law, (3) the policy towards the globally formed rules, in particular international conventions, and (4) the role of codification in responding to the practice developed through the modern practice. This chapter visits these issues in turn.

The reform process was commenced officially by the Minister of Justice's consultation about the modernisation of transport and maritime law in February 2014. Two months later, the Legislative Council established the Committee on Commercial Law (Transport and Maritime Law) in response. In fact, the private study group, made up of academics, practitioners and the staff of the Ministry of Justice, conducted extensive research and examination of the issues prior to this official process, which prepared the basis of the deliberations. The Legislative Council approved the 'Outline of the Reform' in February 2016, based on the conclusions of the Committee.[2] A bill to amend the Commercial Code and related laws was drafted based on the Outline, and introduced before the Diet in October 2016, which the Diet approved in May 2018 and the Government then published as Law no.29 of 2018.

---

1 This chapter partly derives from the author's research funded by the Japan Society for the Promotion of Science (JSPS), grant identifier 15H01917.

2 As a detailed examination of the law after the reform, see T. Fujita (ed.), *Modernizing the Transport and Maritime law: the 2018 Revision of Japanese Commercial Code* (Yuhikaku, forthcoming). For the reform process and issues discussed, see M. Sasaoka, 'Reform of Transport Law in Japan' (2013) 35 *Zeitschrift für Japanisches Recht* 39 (on the preparatory works of the private study group); T. Fujita, 'Maritime Law Reform in Japan' [2014] *CMI Yearbook* 413 (on the concluded work of the private study group); M. Sasaoka & G. Goto, 'Reform of Transport Law and Maritime Law in Japan' (2015) 50 (4/5) *European Transport Law* 471 (on the Interim Report published by the Committee in 2015); S. Kozuka, 'Japan's Maritime Law Reform in an International and Regional Context' (2016) 30 *Australian and New Zealand Maritime Law Journal* 125 (on the Outline of Reform approved by the Legislative Council).

1.2 Transport industry in Japan

When considering the transport law in Japan, the unique features of its transport industry must be recognised. Japan consists of four major islands and many smaller islands, entirely surrounded by sea. It has no land frontiers. It has exceptional ferry lines with Korea that can carry cars, but there is no connection by car or train with other countries. As a result, maritime transport is a major industry sector in Japan. While there are major shipping companies for international maritime transport of goods, the domestic maritime transport of goods is dominated by numerous small shipping companies. Most of these have only one or a few vessels. As of 2017, the number of commercial ships operated by Japanese shipping companies is 2,456, of which only 177 are registered in Japan.[3] Many other ships are registered in offshore registries, most notably in Panama.

A recent development is the booming demand for cruise ships, in particular between China and Japan. Many Chinese tourists visit the southern part of Japan, namely Kyushu and Okinawa islands, by cruise ship.

1.3 Commercial Code before the reform

The Japanese Commercial Code was codified in 1899, based on a draft prepared by a German lawyer, Carl Friedrich Hermann Roesler.[4] The original Commercial Code had five Books, containing provisions on the General Rules, Companies, Commercial Transactions (*Handelsgeshäft*), Bills of Exchange and Maritime (*Seehandel*), respectively. After Japan ratified the Geneva Convention Providing a Uniform Law for Bills of Exchange and Promissory Notes and the Geneva Convention Providing a Uniform Law for Cheques in 1933, Book IV on the Bills of Exchange was deleted and replaced by independent statutes, the Act on Bills of Exchange and Promissory Notes[5] and the Act on Cheques.[6] The other Books remained for decades. While Book II on Companies was amended frequently, other Books have not been much changed, except on the occasion of the ratification of the International Convention Relating to the Limitation of Liability of Owners of Sea-going Ships of 1957, when the provision providing for abandonment was removed and replaced by the Act on Limitation of Liability of Shipowners (ALLS).[7]

However, the Commercial Code was rapidly 'decodified' in the early 2000s.[8] The Companies Act,[9] enacted in 2005, deprived the Code of its Book II with more than 400 provisions. The Insurance Act of 2008[10] followed, which again removed dozens of provisions

3 The Japanese Shipowners' Association, *Kaiun Toukei Youran 2018* (Summary of Maritime Statistics 2018), Table IV-1 (in Japanese) https://www.jsanet.or.jp/data/pdf/2018data40-1.pdf (visited 20 August 2019).

4 On the history of the Commercial Code of Japan, H. Baum and E. Takahashi, 'Commercial and Corporate Law in Japan: Legal and Economic Developments After 1868' in W. Röhl (ed.), *History of Law in Japan Since 1868* (Brill 2005), 330.

5 Law no.20 of 1932.

6 Law no.57 of 1933.

7 Law no.94 of 1975.

8 On the developments in the twentieth century, see T. Fujita, 'The Commercial Code in Japan' in W.-Y. Wang (ed), *Codification in Asia* (Springer 2014), p. 121; M. Sasaoka, 'Reform of Transport Law in Japan' (2013) 35 *Zeitschrift für Japanisches Recht* 48–50.

9 Law no.86 of 2005.

10 Law no.56 of 2008.

from Book III (Commercial Transactions). Thus, when the reform of transport and maritime law began, there was a possibility that the relevant provisions would be made into an independent statute, further removing dozens of provisions from the Code, or even dismantling the Code altogether. This path was not taken, however, and the provisions on the transport and maritime law have remained in the Commercial Code.

1.4 Transport law and maritime law

Following the tradition of the European codification in the nineteenth century, whose origin dates back to the parallel codification of the Ordinance of the Terrestrial Commerce and the Ordinance of Maritime by Louis XIV of France, the original Commercial Code contained the rules on transport contracts in Book III (Commercial Transactions), and the provisions belonging to 'maritime law', which included the rules on maritime transport contracts, in Book V (Maritime). The Commercial Code before the reform applied the transport law provisions and not maritime law provisions to transport over inland water by providing that the term 'carrier' meant 'a person who performs carriage of goods or passengers on land, lake, river or port' (Art. 569 of the Commercial Code prior to 2018. The provisions of the Commercial Code are hereinafter cited only by the article number). The provisions in Book V were drafted as self-contained. In other words, no provision in Book III was applicable to maritime transport, though Book V before the reform incorporated some provisions in Book III by reference (Arts 766 and 776 prior to 2018). After the Books on Bills of Exchange and Companies were removed from the Code, 'Commercial Transactions' became Book II and 'Maritime' became Book III, but the traditional structure remained.

The reform of 2018 changed this structure. The new Art. 569, no.1, of the Commercial Code provides that the term 'carrier' in the Code means 'a person that undertakes land transport, maritime transport or air transport'. Given that this provision is in Book II (Commercial Transactions), it means that the transport law rules in Book II apply also to maritime transport, and the provisions in Book III (Maritime) modify the rules in Book II when special rules are necessary with regard to maritime transport. Thus, the Japanese Commercial Code has finally parted with the historical parallelism of (land) transport law and maritime law, and adopted a hierarchical approach. As a result, there is no longer a provision in Book III on the maritime carrier's duty of care in cargo-handling, because the provision on the carrier's duty of care (new Art. 575) in Book II applies to the maritime carrier. Book III still contains a provision on the maritime carrier's duty of care to make the ship seaworthy (new Art. 739), as this is relevant only to the maritime carrier and not to carriers of any other mode of transport.

1.5 Law on inland water transport

A minor change relating to the relationship of transport and maritime law is made to the rules on transport over inland water. As already noted, the Commercial Code before the reform governed transport on inland water by Book II, as a kind of land transport. This has been changed by the new Commercial Code, which introduces the concept of the 'non-seagoing ship' (Art. 747). Under the new Code, maritime carriage as a defined term means carriage of goods or passengers by either a seagoing or non-seagoing ship (Art. 569, no.3). Therefore, the provisions on contracts of maritime carriage apply to carriage by both

Figure 17.1 Major islands of Japan and the Seto Inland Sea

seagoing and non-seagoing ships. Still, other provisions in Book II (Maritime), such as those on the shipowner's liability or bills of lading, apply only to seagoing ships (Art. 684). As the background, 'inland water' under the Japanese law includes Seto Inland Sea, which is indeed surrounded by the main islands but extends to almost 20,000 square metres (see Figure 17.1). It would be strange if the duty to make the ship seaworthy did not apply to a carrier which carries goods over such a large 'inland water'.[11]

11 M. Sasaoka & G. Goto, 'Reform of Transport Law and Maritime Law in Japan' (2015) 50 (4/5) *European Transport Law* 502.

2 Transport and maritime law as special rules to the Civil Code

2.1 The relationship to the Civil Code

The reform of transport and maritime law coincided with the last phase of the reform of the Civil Code, which was approved by the Diet in 2017 after decade-long controversies.[12] Because the focus of the Civil Code reform was on the law of obligations, covering mainly contract law, there was a cross-over in the subjects of two big reforms.

It is obvious that the rules on contract of carriage are special rules to the general contract law in the Civil Code. Among the contract types in the Civil Code, the contract of carriage is considered a special type of contract of work (*Werkvertrag*), the subject of which is to complete a work that the obligor undertakes to perform. This understanding is reflected in the definitional provision for the carriage of goods (Art. 570):

> '[a] contract of carriage of goods becomes effective when the carrier receives goods from the shipper and undertakes to transport and deliver the goods to the consignee, and the shipper promises to pay the freight against the performance.'

The text is drafted to closely follow the definitional provision of the contract of work in the Civil Code, which reads:

> '[a] contract of work becomes effective when one party undertakes to complete a certain work and the other party promises to pay the remuneration against the performance of the work' (Art. 632, the Civil Code).

As the Civil Code was modernised at almost the same time, the new Commercial Code removed provisions on issues that do not derogate from the general rules of contract law, implying that the relevant provisions of the Civil Code apply. As with the relationship of the transport law and maritime law, a hierarchical approach is again adopted here. Duplication of provisions is excluded, and only the special rules are codified in the Commercial Code, which is ranked as the special Code to the Civil Code.

2.2 The fault of servants and agents

As a result of this hierarchical approach, reference to servants and agents has been dropped from the new provision on carrier's liability. The relevant provision before the reform provided that the carrier was liable for damages arising from the loss of, damage to, or delay in carriage of goods unless *the carrier itself, forwarder and its employees as well as others employed for carriage* did not fail to use due care in receiving, delivering, storing and carrying the goods (emphasis added) (Art. 577 prior to 2018). The reference to the forwarder implied that 'others employed for carriage' included independent contractors. The provision was based on the doctrine of liability due to the fault of servants and agents (*Erfüllungsgehilfe*) applied to the contract of carriage. According to the hierarchical approach,

12 On Japanese contract law under the revised Civil Code, see H. Sono, L. Nottage, A. Pardieck and K. Saigusa, *Contract Law in Japan* (Kluwer Law International 2018).

the reference is not needed if it simply reiterates the general doctrine applicable to any type of contract.[13] As a result, the new provision provides as follows:

> 'When the goods are lost or damaged, or the cause of loss or damage arises, during the period between the time when goods are received and the time when they are delivered, or the goods arrived in delay, the carrier is liable to compensate damages arising therefrom. However, this does not apply if the carrier proves that *it* did not fail to use due care in receiving, carrying, storing and delivering the goods.' (Art. 575, emphasis added)

The provisions on the liability for carriage of passengers (Art. 590 for personal damages and Art. 592 for damages to luggage) are drafted in the same manner in this respect.

An interesting finding is that the Civil Code after the reform does not have an explicit provision on the liability due to the fault of servants and agents. The absence of such a provision, however, does not mean that the fault of servants and agents is irrelevant. The general rules of liability for non-performance in the Civil Code provide that the obligee (creditor) is not entitled to claim compensation for damages if the obligor's non-performance cannot be attributed to the obligor in light of the 'contract or other basis of obligation and the general understanding concerning the transaction'. The intention of the drafter is that the 'contract' may specify whether, and to what extent, the fault of servants and agents is attributable to the obligor. Applying this general rule, a contract of carriage usually assumes that the carrier employs various servants and agents as well as independent contractors in the course of transport. Therefore, subject to specific arrangements between the parties, the carrier is held liable for damage caused by the fault of its servant or agent.

2.3 Relationship of contract law liability and tort liability

2.3.1 The case law

In contrast to the issue of fault by servants and agents, the new Commercial Code introduced a solution limited to transport and maritime law on the issue of the concurrent existence of contractual and tort liability, where the Civil Code refrained from providing for a generally applicable rule. Interestingly, the adopted solution is similar to Article IV bis of the Hague-Visby Rules, but not entirely identical.

The case law in Japan holds that the contractual claim arising from the contract of carriage coexists with the tort claim based on the ownership (or any other title, if applicable) to the carried goods against the carrier (*Anspruchskonkurrenz*).[14] The consignee may choose either of the claims when demanding compensation from the carrier. Though the Supreme Court pronounced it as a general rule, the case related to a dispute over the loss (wrongful delivery) of goods in carriage. Furthermore, the courts have held that the provisions included in the Commercial Code apply only to the contractual claim arising from the contract of carriage.[15] These provisions include the rule on the amount of

13 M. Sasaoka & G. Goto, 'Reform of Transport Law and Maritime Law in Japan' (2015) 50 (4/5) *European Transport Law* 481, note 35.

14 Supreme Court, 5 Nov. 1963, *Minshû* Vol.17, no.11, p. 1510.

15 On the provision concerning the amount recoverable, Great Court of Judicature, 15 February 1932, *Hôgaku* Vol.1B, p. 113; on the provision concerning the valuable goods, Appeals Court of Tokyo, 25 March 1985, *Hanrei Taimuzu* no.553, p. 238; Kobe District Court, 24 July 1990, *Hanrei Jihô* no.1381, p. 81.

damages recoverable in case of loss of, or damage to, the goods, which shall be calculated by reference to the market value of such goods at the place and time at which the goods should have been delivered (Art. 576 (1)). Also included is the rule on valuable goods, which exempt the carrier from any liability if the shipper fails to declare the kind and value of the goods at the time of consignment (Art. 577 (1)). Based on the case law and the lower court decisions, these provisions, which are apparently in favour of the carrier, are not applicable if the tort claim is raised against the carrier. Such can be the case when the shipper is the owner of the goods carried, or is a contractual carrier vis-à-vis the owner of the goods and subrogates to the owner's interest through compensating him. It is also possible that a cargo insurer subrogates to the owner by indemnifying him and raises a tort claim.

2.3.2 The Civil Code reform

The Civil Code reform failed to address the coexistence of contractual and tort liability in general, because it was considered too complicated to govern by a generally drafted rule. However, in the context of transport and maritime law, the provisions exempting and limiting the liability of the carrier can be circumvented by choosing to pursue the tort liability. The nature of the transport service is considered to justify these provisions, as in the course of business the carrier deals with massive amounts of goods without knowing their details. If it is not a purely technical issue but a policy issue, it would be unreasonable not to address circumvention of these provisions by way of the coexisting tort liability claim. Therefore, the new Commercial Code has introduced a provision to apply specific provisions regulating the liability of the carrier to a liability claim in tort against the latter (Art. 587 for liability from a carriage of goods contract, also applied to liability for luggage in a carriage of passenger contract by way of Art. 593 (2)). The provisions applicable to tort claims include, besides those on the amount of damages and liability for valuable goods, those on the extinction and time-bar of the carrier's liability (Art. 584 and 585, respectively). To the extent that the carrier's liability is limited or exempted, the liability of the carrier's employee against the shipper or consignee is also limited or exempted (Art. 588, applied to liability for luggage in a carriage of passenger contract by way of Art. 593 (2)).

2.3.4 Comparison with the international rule

The newly introduced rules appear similar to Art. IV bis of the Hague-Visby Rules, which provides that the defences and limits of liability of the carrier are applicable whether the liability is founded in contract or tort and that such defences and limits are also available to a servant or agent of the carrier, with the exception of independent contractors. However, in the course of debates over the reform, a question was raised about applying the provisions to govern the contract liability to a tort claim if the claimant is a consignee. The consignee acquires the same rights as those of the shipper once the goods arrive at the destination or the goods are totally lost (Art. 581 (1)). However, it does not mean that the interests of the consignee are identical to those of the shipper. The Supreme Court case of 1998 reveals the problem. In that case, the shipper chose to send valuable goods (processed diamond) by courier without declaration. If it had been declared to be valuable goods, the carrier would have rejected carriage by ordinary courier but urged the use of the special service for sending valuable goods. When the diamond was lost, the consignee (subrogating to the owner of the diamond) sued the carrier based on the tort claim, alleging that a clause in the standard contract for courier service does not affect the rights of the consignee, who is not a party to the contract. The Supreme Court refused the claim by holding that such an argument is barred by the principle of good faith and fair dealing (as codified in Art. 1 (2) of the Civil Code) because the consignee had sent to and received from the shipper valuable goods (jewellery) by ordinary courier many times without complaining, apparently admitting the use of an ordinary courier for the sake of saving expenses. The decision implies that applying provisions governing the contractual claim would not be justified, where there are no special facts indicating that the consignee admitted or engaged in the conditions of the carriage contract.

With this case in mind, the new Commercial Code provides that the provisions on contract liability do not apply to tort liability of the carrier against the consignee when the consignee had objected to the carriage arranged by the shipper (Art. 587 proviso). Nor does it apply to the tort liability against the holder of the bill of lading, if issued under the contract. In these respects, the new provision has diverged from Article IV bis of the Hague-Visby Rules. As a result, the International Carriage of Goods by Sea Act (ICOGSA)[16] has maintained the provision (renumbered as Art.16, ICOGSA) implementing Article IV bis of the Hague-Visby Rules, despite the newly introduced provision in the Commercial Code.

3 Codification and international rules

3.1 Japan's ratification of international maritime law conventions

The codification of maritime law cannot be discussed without considering the impact of international instruments. In fact, however, Japan has been rather selective in the reception of international conventions. Among the maritime (private) law conventions, Japan is a party to the following conventions:[17]

- Protocol to amend the International Convention for the Unification of Certain Rules Relating to Bills of Lading as modified by the Amending Protocol of 23 February 1968, 1979 (SDR Protocol, incorporating the Visby Amendments)
- Protocol of 1996 to Amend the Convention on Limitation of Liability for Maritime Claims of 19 November 1976 (LLMC 96)
- Protocol of 1992 to amend the International Convention on Civil Liability for Oil Pollution Damage, 1969 (CLC 92)
- Protocol to the International Convention on Civil Liability for Oil Pollution Damage 1976
- Protocol of 1992 to amend the International Convention on the Establishment of an International Fund for Compensation for Oil Pollution Damage of 1971 (FUND 92)

16 Law no.172 of 1957.

17 On the overview of uniform law conventions to which Japan is a party, see H. Sono, 'Going Forward with Uniform Private Law Treaties: A Study in Japan's Behavioral Pattern' (2017) 60 *Japanese Yearbook of International Law* 10.

- Protocol to the International Convention on the Establishment of an International Fund for Compensation for Oil Pollution Damage 1976
- Protocol of 2003 to the International Convention on the Establishment of an International Fund for Compensation for Oil Pollution Damage 1992 (FUND PROT 2003)
- Convention for the Unification of Certain Rules of Law with respect to Collisions between Vessels, 1910
- Convention for the Unification of Certain Rules of Law with Respect to Assistance and Salvage at Sea, 1910

Japan always denounces the older instruments (such as the International Convention for the Unification of Certain Rules of Law relating to Bills of Lading (Hague Rules) (Brussels, 1924) and International Convention relating to the Limitation of Liability of Owners of Sea-Going Ships (LLMC 1957) (Brussels, 1957) when ratifying a more recent protocol amending the convention.

3.2 Implementation of international conventions

These conventions must, of course, be implemented appropriately. However, when Japan ratified the SDR Protocol to the Hague Rules and amended the ICOGSA to implement it in 1992, a mistake occurred. The provision on limitation of liability was drafted to read that the qualification of 'per package or unit' applied to both the limitation amount of 666.67 Special Drawing Rights (SDRs) and 2 SDRs per kilo of gross weight of the goods lost or damaged, instead of limitation up to 666.67 SDRs 'per package or unit' and limitation up to 2 SDRs 'per kilo'. On the occasion of reform this time, this mistake in implementation has been corrected to be accurately in line with the text of the Convention (Art. 13 of the ICOGSA).

Interestingly, none of the above conventions ratified by Japan has been merged into the general law on the subject, but they have been implemented by separate statutes. The Hague-Visby Rules (originally the Hague Rules) are implemented by enacting the ICOGSA, which provides for a self-contained set of provisions applicable to international carriage by sea. Curiously, the scope of application of the ICOGSA is broader than the scope of application of the Hague/Hague-Visby Rules and includes any carriage of goods by a ship of which either the port of loading or port of destination is outside of Japan. As a result, the provisions on maritime carriage in the Commercial Code are applicable only to domestic carriage, of which both the port of loading and port of destination are in Japan. The LLMC is implemented by ALLS, while the CLC and FC are consolidated into one statute titled Act on Ship's Civil Liability and Compensation for Oil Pollution (LCOP).[18] The 1910 Collision Convention and the 1910 Salvage Convention are not implemented through domestic legislation but are directly applicable.

Such persistent refusal to accept international conventions into the Commercial Code has not changed through the reform of this time. The ICOGSA has remained a self-contained statute, and the Commercial Code does not apply to international carriage by

18 Law no.95 of 1975.

sea (as defined above). The provisions in the Commercial Code that govern the issues of carriage of goods but are not addressed by the ICOGSA apply to international carriage by sea except certain listed provisions (Art. 15 of the ICOGSA).

3.3 Extension of policy under international conventions

The refusal to accept international conventions in the Commercial Code is a matter of the drafting style. It may imply, however, that the policy adopted by the international convention is not easily extended to transactions outside the scope of the convention. The Commercial Code, which is applicable to domestic maritime carriage, does not provide for limitation of liability of the carrier to a certain amount.[19] Neither is the exemption for nautical fault and fire, though strongly demanded by the industry, extended to domestic maritime carriage. It is possible to provide for such exemptions by an agreement. The standard form widely used for domestic maritime carriage in Japan stipulates a clause to exempt the carrier against damages due to nautical fault.[20]

3.4 Influence of the conventions not ratified and privately made rules

Ratification of a convention is not the only way that a state's law is influenced by international rules. An international convention could be the source of inspiration for the reform. There are also international rules other than conventions, in particular privately made rules.[21] As an example of the former, the new Commercial Code has introduced the special compensation right of the salvor when the salvage operation included preventative measures against threatened environmental pollution (Art. 805). Apparently, the provision is inspired by the International Convention on Salvage of 1989, to which Japan has not yet become a party. Similarly, some amendments to the collision law are extension of the rules in the 1910 Collision Convention (to which Japan is a party) to incidents with no international elements, in which case the Convention does not apply.[22] To be specific, the new Commercial Code extends the provisions on the collision of ships to 'quasi-collision', an incident where a ship comes too close to another ship either by her navigation or manoeuvre or by the non-observance of the regulations and causes damages to the latter ship, or to goods or persons on board the ship (Art. 790). Another provision added to the Commercial Code extends the provisions on the collision and quasi-collision to a collision of a seagoing ship and non-seagoing ship (Art.791). These provisions apparently derive from Articles 13 and 1 of the 1910 Collision Convention, respectively.

---

19 On the reasons for not introducing the limitation by amount, see G. Goto, 'Carriage of Goods: Carrier's Liability' in T. Fujita (ed.), *Modernizing the Transport and Maritime law: the 2018 Revision of Japanese Commercial Code* (Yuhikaku, forthcoming), pp. 37–38.

20 M. Sasaoka & G. Goto, 'Reform of Transport Law and Maritime Law in Japan' (2015) 50 (4/5) *European Transport Law* 492.

21 For detailed analysis of the impact of international rules on the reform, see S. Kozuka, 'Japan's Maritime Law Reform in an International and Regional Context' (2016) 30 *Australian and New Zealand Maritime Law Journal* 125.

22 Article 12 of the 1910 Collision Convention.

Less saliently, the provisions on general average have been redrafted to be in line with the York Antwerp Rules – the drafter appears to have consulted the 1994 Rules, most widely used in practice. Amending the provision on the definition of general average that required 'damages and costs caused by the action *of the master* with regard to the ship or cargo' (emphasis added), the new definition provision is drafted '[w]hen an action is taken to avoid common risk to the ship, cargo and other property, . . .' (Art. 808). It has deleted reference to the action by the master to reflect current practice that the costs arising from arrangements made by the shipowner, instead of the master, is also included in the general average, such as in the case of a salvage agreement. It further adds reference to 'other property', which is defined as property on board the ship other than cargo (Art. 792 (1)), as current practice affirms general average even when there is no cargo on the ship but risk exists with regard to bunkers or empty containers. These practices are based on the York Antwerp Rules 1994.

However, the new Commercial Code has been selective in adopting inspiration from international rules. An example is seen in how the rules on maritime liens have been changed.[23] The lien for procedural costs of auctioning the ship and her accessories was ranked first under the Commercial Code before the reform, while the lien for costs of preserving the ship and her accessories ranked second. The new Commercial Code has deleted these liens (Art. 842), which appears to be in line with the International Convention on Maritime Liens and Mortgages of 1993. However, the lien for claims concerning costs necessary to continue navigation has been maintained (Art. 842, no.4), which diverges from the 1993 Convention. Furthermore, the reform is unlikely to affect the Supreme Court decision of 2002 that affirmed a lien under the Civil Code to accrue on the ship.[24] In that case, the lien arose from the ship repairers' claim for its work as a 'lien for a claim to preserve a mobile property' under Art. 311, no.4, of the Civil Code. A lien under the Civil Code ranks after the maritime mortgage on the ship (Art. 848 (2)) but lasts as long as the secured claim exists, as opposed to extinguishing in one year in the case of a maritime lien (Art. 846). The lien under the Civil Code is, in some respects, similar to 'other maritime liens' under the 1993 Convention, but not identical.

The new Commercial Code has introduced a provision about the sea waybill (Art. 770), which was not addressed at all before the reform. The new provision explicitly admits that the sea waybill can be issued electronically. However, as opposed to the bill of lading, no rules are provided with regard to rights of the relevant parties. It is well recognised that the sea waybill in practice often incorporates the CMI Uniform Rules for Sea Waybills. Still, the Commercial Code has not adopted rules inspired by the CMI Rules but instead left it to the parties to decide whether or not to incorporate them.

3.5 Selective reception of international rules

It was outside the scope of the reform of the transport and maritime law to consider ratifying any maritime law convention that Japan has not yet ratified. In fact, the Japanese

23 See M. Sasaoka & G. Goto, 'Reform of Transport Law and Maritime Law in Japan' (2015) 50 (4/5) *European Transport Law* 523.

24 Supreme Court 5 February 2002, *Hanrei Jihô* no.1787, p. 157.

Government decided to ratify the International Convention on Civil Liability for Bunker Oil Pollution Damage (Bunker Convention) and Nairobi International Convention on the Removal of Wrecks 2007 (Nairobi Wreck Removal Convention) just after the reform. The two conventions will be implemented by amending the LCOP, and the bill to amend the Act was submitted to the Diet in March 2019. The next issue will be ratification of the International Convention on Liability and Compensation for Damage in Connection with the Carriage of Hazardous and Noxious Substances by Sea, 1996 (HNS Convention), followed possibly by the Salvage Convention of 1989.

A further question is whether Japan will become a party to the Athens Convention relating to the Carriage of Passengers and their Luggage by Sea. The original Athens Convention of 1974 was not acceptable as it provided for limitation of liability for the death and injury of passengers. Japan's policy in this respect has been consistent, as shown in its exclusion of passenger claims from the global limitation of liability (Art. 3 (4), ALLS) by making use of Article 15, paragraph 3bis, added by the 1996 Protocol to the LLMC. However, the Athens Convention amended by 2002 Protocol is different. Under the amended Convention, the carrier can no longer benefit from the cap on liability, but is subject to the two-tier liability: the carrier is not liable exceeding 250,000 SDRs if it successfully proves that the incident which caused the loss occurred without the fault or neglect of the carrier. This is the same as the 1999 Montreal Convention (Convention for the Unification of Certain Rules for International Carriage by Air), to which Japan is a party. There seems no strong reason for Japan to reject 2002 Athens Convention.[25]

For the moment, the liability rules for passenger carriage under the new Commercial Code is different from PAL. The carrier is liable for damage incurred by the passenger unless the carrier proves that it has not failed to use due care in the carriage (Art. 590). The liability concerning luggage of which the possession is transferred to the carrier (i.e. checked-in luggage) is governed by the same rules as liability for goods under the carriage of goods (Art. 592), while the carrier is not liable for loss of, or damage to, luggage of which the possession is not transferred to the carrier (i.e. cabin luggage) unless the carrier caused the loss or damage intentionally or through negligence (Art. 593 (1)). These provisions have not been changed in the reform, except in some minor points.

One significant amendment made by the reform is that the new Commercial Code prohibits an agreement to exempt or limit the liability of the carrier for death or injury of the passenger. Such an agreement shall be null and void (Art. 591 (1)). The provision is placed in Book II (Commercial Transactions) and, therefore, is applicable to any mode of transport. As the new Book III (Maritime) totally deleted special rules on carriage of passengers by sea, the maritime carrier cannot claim the specificity of maritime transport. The passenger's damage mainly caused by delay is not included in the scope of the prohibition. Furthermore, the prohibition does not apply to the emergency carriage in case of a disaster such as fire or earthquake or to the carriage of a person whose life could be endangered by the ordinary turbulence entailed by the carriage (for example, a seriously ill person) (Art. 591 (2)). Consistent with Japan's policy towards international conventions concerning

25 See T. Fujita, 'When does Japan not Conclude Uniform Private Law Conventions?' (2017) 60 *Japanese Yearbook of International Law* 59.

liability for death and personal injury, the new Commercial Code requires that the liability for death or personal injury shall be fully compensated.

4 Various issues raised by modern practice

4.1 Time charter

The codification always faces the question to what extent the code should adapt to the development in practice. The new Commercial Code is, after all, rather conservative and has not addressed many types of new practice. The only addition is the rules on time charter and multimodal transport.

Time charter was a problematic issue before the reform. The Commercial Code used to have no specific provision, and the old highest court decision (by the Great Court of Judicature before the Second World War) held that it was a combination of a demise charter and a labour supply agreement.[26] Such an interpretation led to the conclusion that the time charterer, as a demise charterer supplying labour at the same time, was liable to a cargo claim arising from the time charter. In a more recent case, however, the Supreme Court held that the party to be liable for a claim for cargo damages shall be determined by the description in the bill of lading, because the holder of the bill of lading may not know other facts concerning the charter, and held the shipowner liable under the bill of lading in the case.[27] As regards the liability for collision, the Tokyo District Court applied the provision on the liability of the demise charterer 'by analogy' and held the time charterer liable in a case where the shipowner was a Liberian company without any substantial business.[28]

Given these complications, the new Commercial Code has introduced a section on time charter, consisting of four provisions. The first provision defines time charter as an agreement under which 'one party undertakes to make a ship with the crew on board available to the other party for a certain period of time and the other party promises to pay hire against it' (Art. 704). The time charterer has the right to give directions to the master about the route of navigation and other matters necessary to employ the ship (Art. 705), while being responsible for the ordinary expenses entailed in the employment of the ship, such as costs of bunkers, pilotage and port charge (Art. 706).

Then the new Commercial Code provides that some provisions stipulated elsewhere in the Code also apply to the time charterer (Art. 707). They include the duty (of the carrier) to make the ship seaworthy (Art. 739 (1)) and the accrual of liens by the acts of the demise charterer concerning the employment of the ship (Art. 703 (2)). The liability of the demise charterer against a third party (Art. 703 (1)) is not included in the provisions applicable to the time charter, which means that the time charterer, as a general rule, is not liable for collision. Depending on the facts of the case, the court may still have power to qualify the

26 Great Court of Judicature, 28 June 1928, *Minshû* Vol.7, p. 519. On this and other old cases, see generally, H. Yoshimoto, 'The Time Charter in Japan: A Comparison' (1988) 1 *Transnational Law* 449.

27 Supreme Court, 27 March 1998, *Minshû* Vol.52, no.2, p. 527. See Časlav Pejović, 'The Identity of Carrier Problem under Time-Charters: Diversity despite Unification of Law' (2000) 41 *Journal of Maritime Law and Commerce* 379.

28 Tokyo District Court, 17 June 1974, *Hanrei Jihô* no.748, p. 77.

'time charter' in a specific case to be an agreement of a different nature (such as the demise charter) in fact and hold the alleged 'time charterer' liable.

4.2 Multimodal transport

Another evolution in the reform is the introduction of one provision on liability of the carrier in the case of multimodal transport. The provision adopts the so-called network system. The liability of the carrier in multimodal transport for loss of, damage to or delay in delivery of the goods is subject to the Japanese law or the international convention to which Japan is a party that should apply to the mode of the transport employed for the segment under which the cause of the loss, damage or delay occurred (Art. 578). The relevant law is not the law or convention that actually applies to the segment (which may be another state's law or the convention to which Japan is not a party), but the law or convention hypothetically applicable if the governing law of the relevant segment were the Japanese law.

The reason for adopting the network liability system is obvious. Given the geographical nature of Japan, any international multimodal transport includes a maritime or air transport segment. Therefore, the multimodal operator usually wishes to benefit from the application of the Hague-Visby Rules (ICOGSA) or 1999 Montreal Convention, *inter alia* the limitation of liability under them. The desire is all the more relevant, because the statutory limitation of liability is absent in the general liability rules for carriage of goods. Therefore, the multimodal transport operator has provided for network liability through their conditions of carriage in practice.[29] The reform this time has codified such practice into a Code provision.

However, the new Commercial Code has not accepted the contractual arrangements in full. As regards the problem of concealed damage, the standard contracts in practice apply the law of international maritime carriage (i.e. the Hague-Visby Rules or ICOGSA), which apparently provides for the lowest limitation of liability. This was not accepted. Under the new Commercial Code, if the carrier cannot specify the mode of transport employed in the segment in which the cause of loss, damage or delay occurred, the carrier cannot invoke this provision, but is subject to the general rules on the liability for carriage of goods. Thus, the concealed damage case is, though not addressed as such, solved in favour of the cargo owner through the burden of proof.

5 Concluding remarks

The maritime codification in Japan was conducted as part of the transport and maritime law reform. To a larger context, it forms a part of the country's efforts to modernise its basic Codes. By examining the manner in which the codification developed, it is possible to observe the features of the current Japanese approach towards codification.

The first feature is the conservativism. Despite the 'decodification' of the Commercial Code that took place in early 2000s, the transport and maritime law reform did not take

29 S. Kozuka, 'Japan' in Aliki Kiantou-Pampouki (ed), *Multimodal Transport: Carrier Liability and Issues related to the Bills of Lading* (Bruylant, 2000), p. 149.

out the relevant provisions from the Code, which could have resulted in totally dismantling the Code. Furthermore, the parallel existence of the transport law in Book II (Commercial transactions) and maritime law in Book III (Maritime) has also remained. As regards the substantive revisions, modern practice has been addressed, but only the most notable, such as time charter and multimodal transport. Many known issues, such as the liability of the actual carrier or limitation of liability of the carrier by a certain amount, were not codified. As this author noted on another subject, Japanese law reform is basically minimalist, and leaves many issues to the arrangement of private parties.[30]

Secondly, notwithstanding the apparent conservatism, the reform took on the ahistorical radicalism. No attention is paid to the historical background of having the Civil and Commercial Codes, and transport law in Book II of the Commercial Code is hierarchically placed as special rules to general contract law in the Civil Code. In a similar manner, maritime transport law in Book III of the Commercial Code is again hierarchically placed as special rules to the (general) transport law, abandoning the historical independence of maritime law vis-à-vis (land) transport law. This has, as a result, saved duplication of some provisions codified in two Codes, or in two Books of the Commercial Code.

Thirdly, with regard to the international rules, the Japanese codification of maritime law has been cautiously selective. There are several provisions inspired by international rules, or extended beyond the scope of application of international conventions. However, in many respects the new Commercial Code of Japan rejects the rules of the international conventions. As a matter of form, international conventions, when ratified, are implemented in a self-contained separate statute and never merged into the Commercial Code. Furthermore, Japan has failed to be a party to some of the conventions that many states in the world have ratified.

30 S. Kozuka and J. Lee, 'The New Japanese Insurance Act: Comparisons with Europe and Korea' (2009) 28 *Zeitschrift für japanisches Recht* 73.

CHAPTER 18

Codification of maritime law

The experience of Spain[1]

Professor José Manuel Martín Osante

1 Introduction: Spanish Maritime Navigation Law (Act 14/2014) – general characteristics

The main source of Spanish private maritime law is the Spanish Maritime Navigation Law (Act 14/2014 of 24 July 2014, referred to hereafter as the LNM). This is a single piece of legislation that, among other provisions, supersedes and repeals Book III of the Spanish Code of Commerce of 1885, and regulates the various aspects of maritime navigation under a new structure.[2] Specifically, the LNM comprises the following sections: Preliminary Title 'General provisions'; Title I 'On administrative organisation of navigation'; Title II 'On vehicles for navigation'; Title III 'On the subjects for navigation'; Title IV 'On contracts for use of ships'; Title V 'On ancillary navigation contracts'; Title VI 'On navigation accidents'; Title VII 'On limitation of liability'; Title VIII 'On maritime insurance'; Title IX 'Procedural specialities'; and Title X 'Public certification of certain Maritime Law proceedings'.

The following general characteristics of the LNM stand out:

- As indicated in the Preamble to the LNM, the Act does not seek a 'mere updating and compilation' but also to adapt it 'to the present practice of sea transport'. The private regulations governing maritime navigation prior to the LNM were set out basically in Book III of the Spanish Code of Commerce of 1885. Spanish legal doctrine unanimously came to consider these regulations as obsolete in regard to current maritime traffic, with Book III of the Code of Commerce being described as 'outdated and archaic',[3] 'quasi-Medieval'[4] and already 'antiquated at the time

1 This paper has been produced in the course of the research project: 'Transport as a driver of socio-economic development: legal solutions', subsidised by the Spanish Ministry of Economy and Competitiveness and by the European Regional Development Fund (MINECO/ERDF, ref. DER2015-65424-C4-1-P, principal researcher: JM. Martín Osante).

2 This decision differs from the route taken to reform maritime legislation in France (where the Code of Commerce was superseded by a number of special acts and regulations) and in Germany (where the regulations governing maritime trade in Book V of the Handelsgesetzbuch (HGB) are maintained). However, it is closer to the procedures used in Italy, the former GDR, Greece, Scandinavia and a number of Latin American countries such as Argentina, Mexico and Chile, where there is (or was, in the case of the GDR) a single unit of law covering maritime navigation, without prejudice to the relevant regulations for its implementation.

3 See J. Garrigues, *Curso de Derecho mercantil*, II, 1st edn (Madrid, Imprenta Aguirre, 1940), p. 589.

4 See R. Uría, 'En torno a la reforma de la legislación marítima', in R. Uría and others, *Estudios Jurídicos en Homenaje a Joaquín Garrigues*, I (Madrid, Tecnos, 1971), p. 433.

of its birth' in that the type of navigation that it reflected was a 'venerable historical relic'[5]. It was also pointed out that Spanish maritime legislation contained 'huge gaps'[6] and was poorly suited to meeting the needs of modern maritime navigation.[7] In short, it was considered that the new legislation must not be limited to merely updating the previous regulations. The LNM therefore left behind the regulations of the Code of Commerce and adopted a new set of regulations more suited to modern maritime traffic, which is very different from that of 1885.

- The LNM regulates only maritime navigation. It does not extend to air navigation, so it does not follow the line taken by Italy of covering maritime and air navigation in a single regulation.[8] Article 1.1 of the LNM states that 'The object of this Act is to regulate the legal situations and relations arising from maritime navigation'. The term 'maritime navigation' is then defined in subsections 2 and 3 of Article 1 of the LNM. Article 1.2 states as follows:

> '2. In addition to that performed in offshore sea waters, maritime navigation is also considered to include that which takes place on the waters of rivers, canals, lakes or natural or artificial reservoirs when these are accessible by ship from the sea, but only within tidal waters, as well as the navigable reaches of rivers up to where ports of general interest exist.'

Article 1 ends with paragraph 3, which excludes inland or continental waters from the scope of application of the LNM:

> '3. Outside the cases considered in the preceding Section, navigation within inland waters shall be governed by the regulatory legislation for the public water domain and by the other applicable provisions.'

---

5 Cf J.M. Muñoz Planas, 'Código de comercio y Derecho marítimo', in J.M. Muñoz Planas and others, *Centenario del Código de comercio*, I, Ministerio de Justicia (Madrid, 1986), pp. 402–407.

6 See J. Girón, 'Problemas en torno al estado actual de nuestra legislación marítima', *Lección inaugural del Instituto Consulado de Bilbao de Derecho y Economía pronunciada en la Universidad de Deusto el 14 de abril de 1975* (Bilbao, Universidad de Deusto, 1975), p. 12.

7 As indicated in all the following: A. Menéndez & J.L. Iglesias, 'Prólogo', in A. Menéndez & J.L. Iglesias, *Código de las Leyes marítimas* (Madrid, 1980), p. 10; J.M. Eizaguirre, 'La forma de la reforma', in J.M. Eizaguirre and others, *La reforma del Derecho marítimo. Congreso de Bilbao 1993* (Bilbao, 1995), p. 13; I. Arroyo, 'La reforma del seguro marítimo español', in I. Arroyo & E. Beltrán, *La reforma de la legislación marítima* (Navarra, Aranzadi, 1999), pp. 145–150; and F. S. Calero, 'Sobre la reforma de la legislación marítima. (Breve alusión al régimen proyectado de algunos contratos)', in I. Arroyo & E. Beltrán, *La reforma de la legislación marítima*, cit., pp. 127–129.

8 Although come Spanish authors, such as URÍA, op. cit., p. 433 et seq., proposed an overall view of maritime and air navigation as a whole, along the lines of the *Codice della navigazione* of 1942, which reflected the ideas of the so-called Neapolitan school of shipping law, whose leading proponent was Antonio Scialoja (see A. Scialoja 'La sistemazione scientifica del diritto marittimo' [1928] I *Rivista del diritto commerciale* 1 et seq.; A. Scialoja, *Sistema del Diritto della Navigazione*, 3rd edn, Rome, Foro Italiano, 1933, p. 3 et seq.; and more recently S. Zunarelli & M.M. Comenale, *Manuale di diritto della navigazione e dei trasporti*, 3rd edn (2016 Assago-Padova, Cedam), p. 50). The majority position in Spanish legal doctrine runs counter to this unitary concept of shipping law, as evidenced in all the following: A. Recalde, 'Derecho marítimo, Derecho de la navegación, Derecho del transporte: Concepto, sistema y especialidad', in J.M. Eizaguirre (ed.), *Diez años de Derecho marítimo donostiarra* (Vitoria, 2003), pp. 224–226; A. Recalde, 'El objeto y el ámbito material de la Ley de navegación marítima', in A. Emparanza & J.M. Martin Osante, *Comentarios sobre la Ley de navegación marítima*, Madrid (Marcial Pons, 2015), pp. 40–41.

- The LNM includes both private law and public law regulations, as stated in the Preamble:

  'The Act regulates the framework for activities inherent to maritime traffic, comprised of the actual geographic setting and the physical spaces that make it possible, as well as instruments and vehicles (. . .) That wide scope involves this Act including practically all aspects of navigation, both of Public as well as Private Law.'

  Accordingly, Title I (under the heading 'On administrative organisation of navigation') covers aspects of public maritime law. This again reflects the idea of a single, joint regulatory path and a single legislative text covering private and public aspects of maritime navigation. This path was abandoned in the codifications of the nineteenth century, in which there was a 'privatisation' of maritime law,[9] though this privatisation was already hinted at in Spain in the Bilbao Ordinances of 1737.[10]

  However, the regulation of public maritime law in the LNM is limited, given that the main source of Spanish public maritime law is the consolidated text of the State Ports and Merchant Navy Act (SPMNA/LPEMM) (Royal Legislative Decree 2/2011 of 5 September),[11] which establishes the basic administrative legal framework for ports, the merchant navy and maritime navigation.
- Undertaking the reform through a single piece of legislation rather than enacting various special acts proved to be the right decision,[12] given that only through a single act can the unity of the system be guaranteed. This facilitates the integrated, harmonious application of the legislation, and makes it possible to overcome gaps by resorting to analogy as envisaged in Article 2.1 of the LNM, thus avoiding the problems that frequently arise of coordination between different special acts.
- In view of the system of sources adopted in Article 2 of the LNM, it was decided that the regulation should be classed as 'special' rather than 'autonomous', given that there is subsidiary recourse to common law: 'Under supplementary terms, the complementary laws, regulations, practices, and customs related to maritime navigation shall apply. Failing all that, and where resorting to analogy is impossible,

9 Cf A. Menéndez & J.L. Iglesias, 'Prólogo', in A. Menéndez & J.L. Iglesias, *Código de las Leyes marítimas* (Madrid, 1980), p. 13; and A. Menéndez, 'La reforma de la legislación marítima', in I. Arroyo & E. Beltrán, *La reforma de la legislación marítima* (Navarra, Aranzadi, 1999), p. 122.

10 As specified in A. Recalde, 'Derecho marítimo, Derecho de la navegación, Derecho del transporte: Concepto, sistema y especialidad', in J.M. Eizaguirre (ed.), *Diez años de Derecho marítimo donostiarra* (Vitoria, 2003), p. 218; and A. Recalde, 'El objeto y el ámbito material de la Ley de navegación marítima', in A. Emparanza & J.M. Martin Osante, *Comentarios sobre la Ley de navegación marítima* (Madrid, Marcial Pons, 2015), p. 36.

11 Official Gazette of Spain n. 253, 20.10.2011.

12 Accordingly, J. Girón, 'Problemas en torno al estado actual de nuestra legislación marítima', *Lección inaugural del Instituto Consulado de Bilbao de Derecho y Economía pronunciada en la Universidad de Deusto el 14 de abril de 1975* (Bilbao, Universidad de Deusto, 1975), p. 13 et seq.; and J.M. Eizaguirre, 'La forma de la reforma', in J.M. Eizaguirre and others, *La reforma del Derecho marítimo. Congreso de Bilbao 1993* (Bilbao, 1995), pp. 16–18; J.M. Eizaguirre., 'Las fuentes del Derecho marítimo proyectado', in *Diez años de Derecho marítimo donostiarra* (Vitoria, 2003), pp. 12–13.

Spanish civil law shall apply'. It is not, therefore, a closed, autonomous system but one that is open to common law.[13]

- The LNM regulates not only mercantile, commercial and for-profit maritime navigation but extends also to navigation for purposes other than trade or profit (recreational, for research, etc.)[14]. In this regard, it must be taken into account that the LNM repeals the previous framework as set out in Book III of the Spanish Code of Commerce of 1885. Specifically, as indicated in title of that Book ('Maritime Trade'), the regulations governing maritime navigation set out there were drawn up taking into account only commercial maritime navigation, and more specifically the carriage of goods and, to a lesser extent, passengers.[15] Because it was limited to the regulation of commercial maritime navigation, the 1885 Code did not envisage or cover maritime navigation for recreational, sporting, research or fishing purposes.[16] Moreover, the connections between maritime navigation and commercial navigation, and between maritime law and mercantile law, appear not only in the Spanish Code but also in other mercantile codes of the nineteenth century.[17]

Changes in maritime navigation since the entry into force of the Code of Commerce of 1885 have resulted in a situation in which navigation is employed for a wide range of purposes (research, recreation, sport, fishing, towing, assistance, etc.) apart from the trade purposes that were the focus of attention of the legislators at that time. Hitherto, maritime navigation for sporting, recreational and other non-mercantile purposes had no specific governing regulations under Spanish law. This led to considerable legal uncertainty among operators in the sector, despite the fact that there were specific, albeit disperse, regulations for some specific aspects of private law governing non-commercial navigation (e.g. compulsory civil liability insurance for sporting or recreational vessels).

13 In the opinion of J.M. Eizaguirre., 'Las fuentes del Derecho marítimo proyectado', in *Diez años de Derecho marítimo donostiarra* (Vitoria, 2003), p. 20, the term 'common law' is used incorrectly here and should be replaced by 'Civil Code' or 'civil law'. Note that Article 1 of the *Codice della Navigazione* refers expressly to "*diritto civile*", cf S. Zunarelli & M.M. Comenale, *Manuale di diritto della navigazione e dei trasporti*, 3rd edn (Assago-Padova, Cedam), 2016, pp. 70–71, which highlights the similarity in terms of sources between Article 1 of the *Codice* and Article 2.1 of Spanish Act 14/2014.

14 As indicated by I. Arroyo, 'Título Preliminar. Disposiciones generales', in I. Arroyo & J.A. Rueda, *Comentarios a la Ley 14/2014, de 24 de julio, de navegación marítima* (Cizur Menor, 2016), p. 68.

15 Thus, J. Garrigues, *Curso de Derecho mercantil*, II, 8th ed., revised by F. Sánchez Calero (Madrid, Imprenta Aguirre, 1983), p. 550; J. Girón, 'Problemas en torno al estado actual de nuestra legislación marítima', *Lección inaugural del Instituto Consulado de Bilbao de Derecho y Economía pronunciada en la Universidad de Deusto el 14 de abril de 1975* (Bilbao, Universidad de Deusto, 1975), p. 15; J. Duque, Voz: 'Naviero', *NEJ Seix, T. XVII* (Barcelona, 1982) p. 149; J.M. Gondra, 'La labor del intérprete ante el Derecho marítimo (Reflexiones en torno a las pretendidas peculiaridades del Derecho marítimo en el plano de la metodología interpretativa)', *BAEDM, 1984*, n. 3, p. 76; and J.L. Pulido Begines, 'Qué es y qué debe ser el Derecho marítimo?', in J.L. García-Pita (ed.), *Estudios de Derecho marítimo* (Cizur Menor, Aranzadi, 2012), p. 58.

16 Cf J.L. Gabaldón García & J.M. Ruiz Soroa, *Manual de Derecho de la navegación marítima*, 3rd edn (Madrid-Barcelona, Marcial Pons, 2006), p. 24.

17 See A. Recalde, 'El objeto y el ámbito material de la Ley de navegación marítima', in A. Emparanza & J.M. Martin Osante, *Comentarios sobre la Ley de navegación marítima* (Madrid, Marcial Pons, 2015), p. 42.

The current LNM solves the problems of legal uncertainty that arose from Book III of the Code of Commerce in dealing with navigation for non-mercantile purposes, resulting from the fact that it was not easy to determine what regulations applied to such navigation.[18] The solution applied in the LNM consists of making the Act applicable to all maritime navigation regardless of whether it is for commercial (carrying of goods, passengers, etc) or other (recreation, sports, etc) purposes.

2 Spanish Maritime Navigation Law (LNM): background

The origins of the reform of Spanish maritime legislation must be sought as far back as the commission awarded by the Spanish Association of Maritime Law to Fernando Sánchez Calero in 1978 to draw up a draft maritime insurance contract bill. The proposed wording was discussed at a meeting of the Committee of the Spanish Association of Maritime Law, with special attention given to the relevant observations made by associations of insurers (UNESPA) and shipowners (ANAVE), and the text was completed in 1980.[19] This first draft was followed by others: one in 1982 by Ignacio Arroyo and José María Ruiz Soroa, another in 1983 and another in 1987. The draft maritime insurance contract bill was finally completed in 1991 at the Mercantile Law Section of the General Codification Committee, with Fernando Sánchez Calero as the proponent.[20] The intention of this bill, among others, was to tackle the problem of the exclusion of maritime insurance from Act 50/1980 of 8 October (the Insurance Contracts Act) and the common practice in Spain of incorporating British clauses into insurance contracts.

There is also a draft bill on contracts for the use of vessels that dates from February 1994,[21] also drawn up at the Mercantile Law Section of the General Codification Committee in the form of a specific proposal prepared under the leadership of Professor Duque Domínguez with the participation of Messrs Ruiz Soroa, Rodríguez Artigas and García Luengo. Together with these draft bills, an initial outline was drawn up for a draft bill on limitation of liability arising from claims in maritime law and accidents in maritime navigation. This outline was prepared by Justino F. Duque Domínguez and José María Ruiz Soroa.

18 In this regard, see J.M. Martín Osante, 'La aplicabilidad del Código de Comercio a la navegación de recreo', [2002] *Revista de Derecho Mercantil* 305 et seq., n. 243.

19 The text of the first draft bill on maritime insurance of 1980 can be seen in [1981] I *Anuario de Derecho Marítimo* 979–994; and in [1980] *Revista Española de Seguros*, nº 24 495–513.

20 The development of the said draft bill can be seen in F. Sánchez Calero, 'Sobre la reforma de la legislación marítima. (Breve alusión al régimen proyectado de algunos contratos)', in I. Arroyo & E. Beltrán, *La reforma de la legislación marítima*, pp. 77–79.

21 Both bills (maritime insurance & use of vessels) were published in 'Materiales para la Reforma del Derecho Marítimo' [1996] *Boletín del Ministerio de Justicia e Interior*, Year L, April, for information and assessment in all areas of legal practice and theory, and for the information of the general public, to paraphrase Juan Luis Ibarra Robles (speaking as Director General for Codification and International Legal Cooperation and Deputy Chair of the General Committee on Codification) in the prologue of the said publication (p. 7). A monographic study on the draft bill on contracts for use of vessels can be found in J.M. Eizaguirre (Coord.), *III Jornadas de Derecho Marítimo de San Sebastián. El Anteproyecto de Contratos de Utilización del Buque* (Donostia, Librería Carmelo, 1996). The full text of the draft bill on maritime insurance contracts of 1991 can be found in [1994] XI *Anuario de Derecho Marítimo* 1161–1181; and in [1993] 73 & 74 *Revista Española de Seguros* 89–102.

However, the complex and over-long process for the writing and approval of the LNM began in earnest with the commissioning by the General Codification Committee of the members of the Special Section for the Reform of Maritime Law to prepare a general maritime navigation Act.[22] The members of the Special Section were Professors Justino F. Duque Domínguez (Chair), Carmen Alonso Ledesma, José Luis Gabaldón García, José María Ruiz Soroa and Aníbal Sánchez Andrés; the mercantile and property registrar Enrique Albert Piñolé; the civil law notary Manuel Ángel Rueda Pérez; and the Assistant Director General for Maritime Regulations and Structure Luis Miguel Guérez Roig. The Section worked on this commission to draw up a general maritime navigation Act until late 2004, when the Proposal for a Draft Bill for a General Maritime Navigation Act was published.[23]

The text of the 2004 proposal, which comprised 597 articles, was prefaced with an interesting explanatory report and memorandum. That report is an aid for subsequently understanding and interpreting the precepts and principles that inspired the proposed structure, as it gives comprehensive details of what domestic, foreign and international regulations served to inspire the authors to write the articles, the fundamental aspects of each title, the principal new features, the goals pursued, the reasons why particular solutions were chosen from various options, etc.[24] Similarly, the memorandum provides explanations and justifications of a different sort for the articles that follow.

The 2004 proposal was succeeded by the General Maritime Navigation Bill of 2006,[25] the General Maritime Navigation Bill of 2008[26] and finally the Maritime Navigation Bill of 2013,[27] which went through the relevant procedural stages and was passed into law as the LNM.

3 Spanish Maritime Navigation Law and international Conventions[28]

3.1 Preliminary points

The legal framework covering maritime navigation is characterised by a broad range of uniform or international regulations in a number of sectors, such as carriage of freight, carriage of passengers, collisions, salvage, privileges, limitation of liability, marine pollution, arrest of ships, etc., that coexist with internal or domestic maritime legislation. This double

22 A study of the procedural steps leading to Act 14/2014 from the original proposal dated 2004 can be found in J.C. Fuentes Gómez, 'El largo proceso de elaboración de la Ley de navegación marítima', in Asociación Española de Derecho Marítimo, *Comentarios a la Ley de navegación marítima* (Madrid, Dykinson, 2015), p. 29 et seq.

23 This proposal was published in *Propuesta de Anteproyecto de Ley General de la Navegación Marítima*, Madrid, Ministry of Justice, 2004.

24 The report is reminiscent of *Relazione alla Maestà del Re Imperatore del Ministro Guardasigilli (Grandi). Presentata nell'udienza del 30 de marzo 1942-XX, per l'approvazione del testo definitivo del Codice della Navigazione*, which explains the contents of the various articles of what was to become the *Codice della Navigazione* of 1942.

25 Official Parliamentary Journal. Lower House. 8th Legislature. Series A. Issue 111–1. 10.11.2006.

26 Official Parliamentary Journal. Lower House. 9th Legislature. Series A. Issue 14–1. 19.12.2008.

27 Official Parliamentary Journal. Lower House. 10th Legislature. Series A. Issue 73–1. 29.11.2013.

28 A highly interesting source of information on this issue is J.M. Ruiz Soroa, 'El Derecho uniforme en la Ley de Navegación Marítima', in A. Emparanza & J.M. Martín Osante (eds.), *Comentarios sobre la Ley de Navegación Marítima* (Madrid, Marcial Pons, 2015), p. 49 et seq.

regulation – internal and international – is a source of contradictions and leads to situations of great legal uncertainty for operators, as it is often no simple matter to determine whether internal or international regulations must be applied.[29]

In this regard it must be taken into account that international Conventions are directly applicable in Spain and form part of the body of law once they have been ratified and published in the BOE [Spanish Official Gazette], in line with Article 96.1 of the Spanish Constitution and Article 1.5 of the Spanish Civil Code. Nor can international Conventions be repealed or modified by internal Spanish legislation. Specifically, the provisions of such Conventions can be repealed, amended or suspended only in the manner envisaged in the treaties themselves or under the general rules and regulations of international law.

A distinction must be drawn here between universal and non-universal Conventions.[30] Universal Conventions are those which are applicable to both international and domestic events (e.g. the 1993 Maritime Liens and Mortgages Convention,[31] the 1989 Salvage Convention[32] and the 1976 International Convention on Limitation of Liability for Maritime Claims),[33] while non-universal Conventions are applicable to international but not to domestic events (e.g. the 1910 Collision Convention,[34] the Hague-Visby Rules,[35] the 1974 Athens Convention 1974[36] and the Arrest of Ships Convention 1999).[37]

One of the goals of the LNM is precisely to coordinate its contents with international maritime law so as to overcome the current contradictions between the different international Conventions in force in Spain and the various domestic provisions governing the relevant matters, as indicated in Point 1 of its Preamble.[38] Accordingly, Article 2 of the LNM establishes under the heading 'Sources and interpretation' that:

> '1. This Act shall be applied as long as it does not oppose the terms set forth in the international treaties in force in Spain and the legal provisions of the European Union that regulate the same matters (. . .)',

and

> '2. In all cases, for interpretation of the provisions of this Act, the provisions contained in the international treaties in force in Spain and the convenience of promoting uniform regulation of the matters it forms shall apply.'

29 See J.L. Pulido Begines, *Curso de Derecho de la navegación marítima* (Madrid, Tecnos, 2015), p. 37.

30 As pointed out by J.M. Ruiz Soroa, 'El Derecho uniforme en la Ley de Navegación Marítima', in A. Emparanza & J.M. Martín Osante (eds.), *Comentarios sobre la Ley de Navegación Marítima* (Madrid, Marcial Pons, 2015), p. 52.

31 The International Convention on Maritime Liens and Mortgages (Geneva, 1993).

32 The International Convention on Salvage (London, 1989).

33 The Convention on Limitation of Liability for Maritime Claims (London, 1976).

34 Convention for the Unification of Certain Rules of Law with respect to Collisions between Vessels (Brussels, 1910).

35 The Hague Rules as Amended by the Brussels Protocol 1968.

36 Athens Convention relating to the Carriage of Passengers and their Luggage by Sea, 1974 (Athens, 1974).

37 International Convention on the Arrest of Ships (Geneva, 1999).

38 Similarly, A.B. Campuzano & E. Sanjuan, 'El derecho marítimo en España. La Ley de navegación marítima', in A.B. Campuzano & E. Sanjuan (eds.), *Comentarios a la Ley de navegación marítima* (Valencia, Tirant lo Blanch, 2016), p. 22.

This goal of ensuring uniformity seeks to put an end to the much-criticised dual provisions that exist in such matters in many fields in which Spain has ratified various international Conventions on the one hand but has domestic legislation on the other that often fails to comply with those Conventions. This is pointed out in Point II of the Preamble to the LNM.[39]

In any case, these lines will show whether or not the legislative technique used in Spanish law is conducive to the uniformity of maritime law, and whether or not the internal regulations adopted in Spanish law are necessary, taking into account that international Conventions ratified by Spain are already part of its internal legal system. On the other hand, the scope of Article 2 of the LNM will be examined. That article establishes the priority application of the Conventions over domestic legislation, and the need for the rules of Spanish law to be interpreted in accordance with the provisions of international law so as to foster uniformity.

3.2 Legislative technique used

The legislative technique used in the LNM to coordinate the national regulation with the contents of the international Conventions is different from that adopted in the Proposal of 2004. In the Proposal it was decided to reproduce the full contents of the Conventions in the internal law. Indeed, the Proposal regulated completely the different maritime institutions, including institutions that were already regulated in international Conventions which were previously part of the Spanish domestic legal system and whose scope of application extended to domestic factual cases.[40] In these cases where maritime institutions are regulated by universal Conventions (applicable to internal and international cases), the Spanish legislator's wording in the 2004 Proposal tried to match that employed in those Conventions, but using terms more suitable to our legal system. The writers of the Proposal recognize this in the Explanatory Memorandum:

> 'When writing the precepts of the Law incorporated into the conventions, it has been sought to use the appropriate concepts and terminology to our own legal system; this technique has the advantage that it offers a compact text without the need for the person applying the rule to refer to texts other than the general included in the Law.'[41]

On the other hand, the writers also adopted a regulation for the maritime institutions contemplated in non-universal Conventions (not applicable to internal cases).

The legislative technique of the Proposal of 2004 consisted, in short, in a duplication of the texts of the international Conventions in the internal law, although the duplication was not literal – some slight modifications were introduced into the internal law, or the contents

39 Along these lines, J.M. Alcántara, 'Los tratados internacionales en la nueva Ley de navegación marítima', in Asociación Española de Derecho Marítimo *Comentarios a la Ley de navegación marítima* (Madrid, Dykinson, 2015), p. 45.

40 Like observes, J.M. Ruiz Soroa, 'El Derecho uniforme en la Ley de Navegación Marítima', in A. Emparanza & J.M. Martín Osante (eds.), *Comentarios sobre la Ley de Navegación Marítima* (Madrid, Marcial Pons, 2015), p. 50.

41 See *Memorandum* (paragraph 'planteamientos generales') in the *Propuesta de Anteproyecto de Ley General de la Navegación Marítima*, Madrid, Ministerio de Justicia, 2004, p. 14.

of the Conventions were partially reproduced.[42] This technique was criticized because it presented the inconvenience of generating a double regulation of the same maritime institutions, the international regulation (the Conventions) which was already part of the Spanish legal system due to its publication in the Official State Gazette, and the internal regulation (Spanish internal maritime navigation law) which reproduced – with nuances – the text of the Conventions.[43] Additionally, the modification of the international Conventions would not have an immediate reflection in the Spanish internal maritime navigation law, as it would be necessary to modify the internal law (to adjust it to the Convention), so the reforms could not present the necessary agility for a better protection of the maritime sector.[44] The criticism of this 2004 legislator's option and the problems created by the duplication of regulations led to the rejection of this technique.

The legislative technique of the 2004 Proposal, or rather the duplication of the Conventions, was replaced by the referral to the Conventions. The Spanish legislator, taking as a starting point the text of 2004, started to eliminate its duplications of the Conventions, with the intention of suppressing the international and national double regulation. Instead of reproducing at all the Conventions, the Spanish legislator regulates the maritime institutions conducting a referral to the existing international Convention regarding to the specific maritime institution. This technique is already present in General Maritime Navigation Bill of 2006, as well as in the later ones of 2008 and 2013, and in the current law (LNM).[45] Specifically, the referral made by the LNM to international Conventions is double, a general one in its Article 2, recognizing the hierarchical superiority of international Conventions, and the specific referrals foreseen in each institution that already had an international regulatory Convention.[46]

The Article 2 LNM establishes:

> '1. This Act shall be applied as long as it does not oppose the terms set forth in the international treaties in force in Spain and the legal provisions of the European Union that regulate the same matters (. . .)',

42 In this sense, J.M. Alcántara, 'Propuesta de Anteproyecto de Ley General de la Navegación Marítima. Algunas reflexiones desde la plaza y una valoración', [2005] 178 &179 *Derecho de los Negocios* p. 11, 14.

43 See J.C. Fuentes Gómez, 'El largo proceso de elaboración de la Ley de navegación marítima', in Asociación Española de Derecho Marítimo, *Comentarios a la Ley de navegación marítima* (Madrid, Dykinson, 2015), p. 31.

44 In this line, J.M. Alcántara, 'Los tratados internacionales en la nueva Ley de navegación marítima', in Asociación Española de Derecho Marítimo *Comentarios a la Ley de navegación marítima* (Madrid, Dykinson, 2015), p. 49.

45 This change of legislative technique, from the full duplication to the simple referral, deserves a positive valuation to the General Council of the Judiciary, like explains in its *Informe al Anteproyecto de Ley de navegación marítima*, Madrid, December 20, 2012, pp. 28–30: 'In the dilemma between a tedious regulation, which makes a transposition to our internal law of the regulation contained in the mentioned international instruments, or the use of the technique of referrals to the content of the international texts applicable to the different aspects of maritime navigation, the text of the Preliminary Bill chooses this second possibility. This, which is also what the 2006 and 2008 Preliminary Bills did, contrasts with the technique followed in the 2004 Proposal, where the content of each convention was included in the articles, adapting it to the concepts and terminology appropriate to our legal system (. . .) the option accepted in the Preliminary Bill deserves a favourable opinion, although it might be advisable to introduce some greater precision in the referral provisions to the text of the Treaties.'

46 Just as specifies, J.M. Ruiz Soroa, 'El Derecho uniforme en la Ley de Navegación Marítima', in A. Emparanza & J.M. Martín Osante (eds.), *Comentarios sobre la Ley de Navegación Marítima* (Madrid, Marcial Pons, 2015), pp. 50–51.

admitting with it, explicitly, that the Conventions will have preferential application with respect to the internal law.

The LNM also incorporates several specific referrals to the Conventions. Indeed, the aforementioned law frequently uses the technique of referral to the international Convention in force in Spain, to determine the source applicable to a particular maritime institution (maritime liens and mortgages, limitation of liability, collision, salvage, arrest of ships, etc.). In other words, the national law itself establishes that the regulation of a particular maritime institution is the one contained in the international Convention. However, the Spanish legislator does not limit itself to including this referral to the international Convention but, after this referral, it proceeds to regulate some specific aspects of the different maritime institutions, thus increasing the possibilities of friction between the two (international and national) legal texts.

The specific referrals that the LNM completes to the international Conventions are:

Maritime liens: Article 122 LNM 'Legal regime of maritime liens'. 'Maritime liens shall be governed by the terms set forth in the International Convention on Maritime Liens and Mortgages, done at Geneva, on 6th May 1993.'

Carriage of goods. Liability of the carrier for loss, damage or delay: Article 277 LNM 'Liability regime'. '2. Contracts for national or international carriage of goods by sea under the bill of lading regime and liability of the carrier shall be governed by the Convention for the Unification of Certain Rules of Law relating to Bills of Lading, done in Brussels, on 25th August 1924, the protocols that amend it to which Spain is a party and this Act.'

Passage contract. Article 298 LNM 'Regime of liability'. '1. The liability of the carrier shall be governed, in all cases, by the International Convention relating to the Carriage of Passengers and their Luggage by Sea, done at Athens on 13th December 1974 (PYE/PAL), the Protocols that amend it to which Spain is a party, the provisions of the European Union and this Act.' '2. The provisions of this Chapter shall imperatively apply to all maritime passage contracts. Contractual clauses that are directly or indirectly aimed at attenuating or avoiding such liability to the detriment of the holder of the right to demand such compensation shall not take effect.'

Collisions. Article 339.1 LNM 'Legal regime and concept of collision'. 'Collision shall be regulated by the term set forth in the Convention for the Unification of Certain Rules of Law with respect to Collisions between Vessels, done at Brussels, on 23rd September 1910, the other conventions on such matters to which Spain is a party, and by the provisions of this Chapter.'

Salvage. Article 357 LNM 'Legal regime'. 'Salvage shall be governed by the International Convention on Salvage, done at London on 28th April 1989, by the Protocols that amend it to which Spain is a party and by the provisions of this Chapter.'

Limitation of liability. Article 392 LNM 'Right to limit liability'. 'The right to limit liability in claims arising from a same accident shall be governed by the terms set forth in the Protocol of 1996 that amends the Convention on Limitation of Liability for Maritime Claims, done at London on 19th November 1976, with the reservations made by Spain in the Instrument of Adhesion, and in this Title.'

Arrest of ships. Article 470.1 LNM 'Nature and regulation of the measure'. '1. The injunctive measure of arrest of ships, both Spanish as well as foreign, shall be governed by the International Convention on the Arrest of Ships, done at Geneva on 12th March 1999, by the terms set forth in this Act and, under supplementary terms, by those established in Act 1/2000, dated 7th January, on Civil Procedure. Such a measure shall necessarily involve immobilization of the ship in the port where it is located.'

3.2 *Consequences of the legislative technique applied.*

3.2.1 General referral to the international Conventions

The general referral of the Article 2.1 LNM (under the title 'Sources and interpretation'), '1. This Act shall be applied as long as it does not oppose the terms set forth in the international treaties in force in Spain (. . .)', in which the hierarchical superiority of the International Conventions is recognized, is unnecessary, as it reiterates what is already provided in Article 96.1 of the Spanish Constitution and in the Article 1.5 of the Spanish Civil Code.[47] This forecast contained in Article 2.1 LNM does not add anything with respect to what has already been foreseen in our system, so its absence would not alter the source regime.

As regards the reference contained in Article 2.2 LNM, '2. In all cases, for interpretation of the provisions of this Act, the provisions contained in the international treaties in force in Spain and the convenience of promoting uniform regulation of the matters it forms shall apply', its purpose is the uniform application of the provisions of international Conventions. However, as has been already indicated,[48] it is a rule that has no possibility of effective practical implementation, given that there is not a unique judiciary that applies the Convention and sets uniform criteria for interpreting and applying the Conventions – each Member State shall apply the Conventions through its respective national court and the decision of the Supreme Court of a Member State is not binding for other Member States. It should be added that LNM is an internal law and, in its provisions, together with the referral to the Conventions, there are Articles regulating maritime institutions either complementing or putting aside the Convention. In this case, in which the internal law does not follow the Convention, it cannot be used as an interpretive criterion 'the convenience of promoting uniform regulation', because the origin of the rule is not international but internal, and the purpose of the internal regulation is precisely to depart from the uniformity.[49]

3.2.2 Specific referral to conventions applicable to internal and international cases.

The specific referrals made by the LNM to universal Conventions, that is, applicable to internal and international cases, are in Articles 122 LNM (referral to the Convention on

47 In this sense, also consider unnecessary the referral about the priority of the International conventions of the Article, J.M. Alcántara, 'Los tratados internacionales en la nueva Ley de navegación marítima', in Asociación Española de Derecho Marítimo *Comentarios a la Ley de navegación marítima* (Madrid, Dykinson, 2015), p. 48; and I. Arroyo, 'Título Preliminar. Disposiciones generales', in I. Arroyo & J.A. Rueda, *Comentarios a la Ley 14/2014, de 24 de julio, de navegación marítima* (Cizur Menor, 2016), p. 84.

48 I. Arroyo, 'Título Preliminar. Disposiciones generales', in I. Arroyo & J.A. Rueda, *Comentarios a la Ley 14/2014, de 24 de julio, de navegación marítima* (Cizur Menor, 2016), p. 86.

49 Thus, J.M. Ruiz Soroa, 'El Derecho uniforme en la Ley de Navegación Marítima', in A. Emparanza & J.M. Martín Osante (eds.), *Comentarios sobre la Ley de Navegación Marítima* (Madrid, Marcial Pons, 2015), p. 51.

Maritime Liens and Mortgages, done at Geneva, on 6 May 1993), 357 LNM (referral to the International Convention on Salvage, done at London on 28 April 1989) and 392 LNM (referral to the Protocol of 1996 that amends the Convention on Limitation of Liability for Maritime Claims, done at London on 19 November 1976). These referrals would come to reiterate what the Articles 96.1 Spanish Constitution and 1.5 Spanish Civil Code already stipulate, that is, that regulations governing the aforementioned maritime institutions are those contained in the international Conventions. The Conventions belong to our internal legal system once they are published in the BOE [Spanish Official Gazette], and they constitute the applicable norm to the maritime institutions contemplated in aforesaid Conventions. The aforementioned specific referrals of the LNM add nothing to what our system plans in general terms for matters regulated in international Conventions. In this sense, the referrals are redundant, but at the same time clarificatory, as they specify the legal regime applicable to maritime liens, salvage and limitation of liability.

However, doubts arise about the legislative technique used because the Spanish legislator (LNM) is not limited to making a specific referral to the Conventions, but then specifies that the regulatory source is not only the Convention to which it refers, but also the (internal) provisions that are added in the LNM itself.[50] Thus, together with the referral to the Convention, we have an additional regulation in the internal law (LNM).

In this sense, the provisions adopted by the LNM, additional to the Convention (to which the LNM is forwarded), could complement the Convention, when regulating those aspects which the Convention itself leaves the Member States to being regulated by their internal laws. These LNM internal rules are perfectly valid, by observing the system of sources, in particular, they do not contradict the Convention, since they are adopted within the margins of the Convention and under the provisions of the Convention. Such internal provisions are referred to in the Preamble of the LNM, Section II: 'This also explains the legislative technique used, based on referral to the conventions in force in each matter, reserving to the Act the role of providing content to the spaces that such international treaties leave to the States.'[51] These spaces would be completed with the Articles of the LNM which follow the referral to the international Convention. Among these articles could be found, for example, the Articles 399.2 and 403 LNM about liability limitation.[52]

Nevertheless, not all provisions of the LNM, additional to the referral to the Conventions, are limited to filling in the spaces that the conventions leave to the internal law.[53] In the LNM we can find Articles reiterating aspects already regulated in the international

50 Lays out and solves these doubts in the right way, J.M. Ruiz Soroa, 'El Derecho uniforme en la Ley de Navegación Marítima', in A. Emparanza & J.M. Martín Osante (eds.), *Comentarios sobre la Ley de Navegación Marítima* (Madrid, Marcial Pons, 2015), pp. 52–54.

51 In the same way, A.B. Campuzano & E. Sanjuan, 'El derecho marítimo en España. La Ley de navegación marítima', in A.B. Campuzano & E. Sanjuan (eds.), *Comentarios a la Ley de navegación marítima* (Valencia, Tirant lo Blanch, 2016), p. 23.

52 The Preamble of the LNM in its section IX refers to this issue, highlighting how the LNM completes the regime of limitation of liability provided in the International Convention LLMC 1976/96: 'Title VII, which concerns limitation of liability, simplifies the previous – domestic and international – regimes, which are fairly confusing. It does so based on the Convention on Limitation of Liability for Maritime Claims, done at London on 19 November 1976 (LLMC), amended by the Protocol of 1996, the regime of which *is completed in this Title*.'

53 In this sense, J.M. Alcántara, 'Los tratados internacionales en la nueva Ley de navegación marítima', in Asociación Española de Derecho Marítimo *Comentarios a la Ley de navegación marítima* (Madrid, Dykinson, 2015), p. 57.

Conventions, that is, applicable to internal and international cases. These provisions of the LNM generate a double regulation, internal (LNM) and international (the Convention referred by the LNM itself), about the same maritime institution. This happens, for example, with the Articles 396 LNM (claims subject to limitation) and 397 LNM (claims excluded from limitation). And this double regulation is what the Spanish legislator plans to avoid with the LNM, as pointed out in the Preamble, Section II:

> 'This objective of uniformity implies the aim to put an end to the much-criticized dual provisions that exist in such matters in many fields in which, on one hand, Spain has ratified different international conventions and, on the other, we have domestic legislation that, in many cases, does not comply with these.'

These provisions of the LNM, which regulate issues already regulated in the Convention have no legal effect, as the Convention is hierarchically superior and given that the LNM regulates issues that is has no need to regulate, because they are already provided for in the Convention, and the Convention is already part of our domestic legal system.[54] This double regulation, as we have pointed out, should not generate legal problems, if the Articles of the LNM and the Conventions (LLMC) present the same wording, but problems may arise if the drafts of the two regulations do not coincide.[55] In any case, the internal provisions referred to, which reiterate the contents of the universal Conventions, should not have been incorporated in the LNM, since the Conventions are already part of our system and the referrals by the LNM to the Conventions would be sufficient to confirm their application to internal or domestic cases.

3.2.3 Specific referrals to conventions applicable only to international cases

The LNM contains referrals to international Conventions whose scope of application is limited to cases with an international element, in order to specify the regulatory rules of a maritime institution. This happens, for example, with Article 339 LNM regarding collision (which refers to the 1910 Convention on the unification of certain rules of law relating to collision between vessels) or Article 470 LNM relating to the arrest of ships (which refers to the 1999 International Convention on the Arrest of Ships). As a consequence of these referrals, the internal or domestic governing regulation of the maritime institution (collision, arrest) will be the international Convention, since the Spanish legislator so decided. Since the internal cases were outside the scope of the Conventions, the LNM had the facility of freely regulating those institutions and has chosen to regulate them by referrals to international Conventions.[56]

---

54 See J.M. Ruiz Soroa, 'El Derecho uniforme en la Ley de Navegación Marítima', in A. Emparanza & J.M. Martín Osante (eds.), *Comentarios sobre la Ley de Navegación Marítima* (Madrid, Marcial Pons, 2015), pp. 53–54, who lays out how these rules of the LNM which overwhelm the universal convention space have no legal effect.

55 Thus, J.M. Ruiz Soroa, 'El Derecho uniforme en la Ley de Navegación Marítima', in A. Emparanza & J.M. Martín Osante (eds.), *Comentarios sobre la Ley de Navegación Marítima* (Madrid, Marcial Pons, 2015), p. 54; and, similarly, J.M. Alcántara, 'Los tratados internacionales en la nueva Ley de navegación marítima', in Asociación Española de Derecho Marítimo *Comentarios a la Ley de navegación marítima* (Madrid, Dykinson, 2015), pp. 57, 60.

56 Cfr. A.B. Campuzano & E. Sanjuan, 'El derecho marítimo en España. La Ley de navegación marítima', in A.B. Campuzano & E. Sanjuan (eds.), *Comentarios a la Ley de navegación marítima* (Valencia, Tirant lo Blanch, 2016), p. 23.

The above-mentioned option of the LNM of regulating some maritime institutions' internal cases by referrals to the international Conventions (not applicable to internal cases), means that the regulation of internal cases is planned in the Convention. But, the regulatory status of the Conventions is the same as for an internal law, that is, it does not have higher status than that of the internal law (the LNM), because it is the internal legislator who, through the LNM, adopts the provisions of the Convention as regulation, for cases that were not planned in the aforementioned Convention.[57] Likewise, the Spanish legislator can complement, modify, expand or reduce the contents of these Conventions through the LNM, because the regulation of the Convention takes internal law status and, therefore, the LNM can be fully adjusted to the provisions of the Convention, but may also deviate from it according to what the Spanish legislator considers appropriate, because the LNM is free to decide how it regulates those internal cases (cases that were outside the scope of the Convention).[58]

And indeed, the Spanish legislator is not limited to referring to the Conventions to set the regulation of the collision or the arrest, but after the referral to the Convention adopts an additional regulation in the LNM that comes to nuance, complement or directly deviate from the Convention. This is the case with Article 342 LNM, which establishes the regime of joint and several liability of ship operators for both personal and material damages caused to third parties arising from the shared blame approach, while the 1910 Collision Convention (Article 4) provides joint and several liability only for personal injuries and not for materials.

Therefore, in the final version of the LNM great effort has been made to eliminate the double regulation of maritime institutions, internal and international, but, as we have already indicated throughout this work, it has not been possible to eliminate that double regulation, so problems of interpretation can arise and the judges must make an effort to try to solve them.[59]

57 See J.M. Ruiz Soroa, 'El Derecho uniforme en la Ley de Navegación Marítima', in A. Emparanza & J.M. Martín Osante (eds.), *Comentarios sobre la Ley de Navegación Marítima* (Madrid, Marcial Pons, 2015), p. 55.

58 See J.M. Ruiz Soroa, 'El Derecho uniforme en la Ley de Navegación Marítima', in A. Emparanza & J.M. Martín Osante (eds.), *Comentarios sobre la Ley de Navegación Marítima* (Madrid, Marcial Pons, 2015), pp. 55–56.

59 Some conclusions in this line, criticism of the legislative technique used by LNM regarding its relationship to international conventions, can be found in J.M. Ruiz Soroa, 'El Derecho uniforme en la Ley de Navegación Marítima', in A. Emparanza & J.M. Martín Osante (eds.), *Comentarios sobre la Ley de Navegación Marítima* (Madrid, Marcial Pons, 2015), p. 60; and, similarly, J.M. Alcántara, 'Los tratados internacionales en la nueva Ley de navegación marítima', in Asociación Española de Derecho Marítimo *Comentarios a la Ley de navegación marítima* (Madrid, Dykinson, 2015), p. 60.

CHAPTER 19

Recent national maritime law codifications – reasons and scope

The Polish perspective as compared with other selected jurisdictions

Dr Justyna Nawrot and Dr Zuzanna Pepłowska-Dąbrowska[1]

1 Introduction

There have been several recent attempts to draft new national maritime codes or proceed with substantive amendments to the existing Acts. Changes have already been adopted, for example in Germany, France, Spain, Turkey and, most recently, in Japan and Belgium. In Poland a draft proposal for the new maritime code has already been presented.[2] In fact, as Professor Van Hooydonk puts it, over the last few years we have witnessed the 'renaissance of the maritime codes'.[3] There are various reasons for the new codifications or substantial amendments to them. Regardless of their origin, those reasons have to be of serious gravity in light of the need to safeguard the legal certainty principle and the stability of the code. Nevertheless, any efforts taken by national authorities require consideration of practical needs and the cross-border nature of shipping activity. Those two issues have always formed a core basis of the development of maritime law.

Some legislators have adopted the more ambitious path of creating a more comprehensive Act, incorporating both private and public law norms relating to activities on seas, whereas other Acts concentrated on private law aspects. Finally, new Acts have adopted several mechanisms aiming at preserving the uniformity of maritime law on the international scale. Those methods include *inter alia* referring to the internationally recognised principles of maritime law. These three issues will be discussed below. At the same time, the Polish experience will be taken into consideration and compared with that of other jurisdictions.

2 Underlying reasons

The necessity to conform with international law is often raised as one of the reasons for the new codification of maritime law or substantive amendments to it. That is the case with the Spanish Maritime Navigation Law (Ley de Navegación Marítima, LNM) of 24 July 2014.[4]

1 The authors declare that the conducted research was funded by the National Science Centre, Poland, under the contract UMO – 2016/22/E/HS5/00050 Problems of contemporary maritime codes.

2 Text of the proposal in Polish in (2018) XXXV *Prawo Morskie* with an overview in English.

3 E. Van Hooydonk, 'The renaissance of maritime codes – a need for international guidance?' (2015) 21 *Journal of International Maritime Law* 5.

4 In force since 25.09.2014; official translation into English available at: http://servicios.mpr.es/VisorPublicaciones/visordocumentosicopo.aspx?NIPO=051140300&SUBNIPO= (visited 20 August 2019).

The preamble to the new Spanish Act explains the reasons for its adoption, pointing to the need to bring the regulation into line with international law. It follows that under the previous Spanish law there were incidents in which the national law was not in line with the ratified international conventions. Thus, it was necessary to adopt several mechanisms which aim at guaranteeing uniformity of maritime law.[5] Adapting the national law to the current shipping practice was another reason for endorsing the new Act. The LNM superseded Book III of the Spanish Commercial Code of 1885, which to a large extent reproduced the former Code of 1829. Thus, the old regulation was outdated and did not respond to new aspects of maritime practice such as containerization or multimodal transport.[6] Finally, a few issues requiring substantial reformulation were identified – namely protection of the maritime environment, underwater cultural heritage, fishing, use of territorial seas as well as immigration.[7] The new Act also had also advantage of organizing the Spanish maritime law, which was spread over many different regulations, acts and decrees.[8] As Professor Arroyo Martínez explains, the intention was to create a single comprehensive body of maritime law answering the needs of modern shipping practice.[9]

In Belgium, conformity with international law was also given as a reason for the new maritime code. However, it seems that the primary goal was to answer the needs of maritime practice and thus to promote the development and increase the attractiveness of the maritime sector in Belgium. The regulation of maritime law in Book II of the Belgian Commercial Code, whose basic text dates back to 1879, was seen as totally outdated both in its maritime practice and in its compliance with foreign legislation. Therefore, the Commission for Maritime Law (Commission de Droit Maritime Belge) described the need for its fundamental modernization as urgent and indispensable.[10]

Similarly, the Japanese maritime law was codified in the late-nineteenth century. It was, in fact, the oldest maritime law in Asia. However, with little amendment it became outdated and not responsive to current reality. Even its language was archaic and difficult to follow.[11] With new maritime laws in the neighbouring countries (China, Vietnam and South Korea), Japan needed to modernize its Commercial Code so as to become more competitive. The revision was part of a thorough reform of the Japanese legal system, commencing in the mid-1990s.[12]

In Germany, Book 5 of the German Commercial Code of 1897 was criticized as being outdated, too. Many sections of the Book contained gaps that needed to be filled in.

5 I. Arroyo Martínez, 'The New Spanish Maritime Navigation Act 2014, The Need for Uniformity and the International Maritime Conventions' (2015) *Il Diritto Marittimo, Fasc. II*, 421.

6 I. Arroyo Martínez, España: el proyecto de ley general de la navegación marítima, XXVI *Anuario de Derecho Marítimo* 219.

7 Ley 14/2014, de 24 de julio, de Navegación Marítima, Preámbulo.

8 I. Arroyo Martínez, 'The New Spanish Maritime Navigation Act 2014, The Need for Uniformity and the International Maritime Conventions' (2015) *Il Diritto Marittimo, Fasc. II*, 422.

9 Id.

10 E. Van Hooydonk, La revision de la loi maritime belge: arrière-plan, objectifs et méthode de travail, en : livre vert : nouvelle loi maritime Belge. Document de consultation en vue de la préparation d'un nouveau code maritime belge, ed. E. Van Hooydonk, www.droitmaritime.be/Documenten/LivreVert_221007.pdf (visited 20 August 2019), p. 15.

11 S. Kozuka, Japan's Maritime Law Reform in an International and Regional Context (2013) 30 *Australian and New Zealand Maritime Law Journal* 125.

12 T. Fujita, Maritime Law Reform in Japan (2014) *CMI Yearbook, Annuaire* 413. More on Japanese reform in Ch. 17 above.

A totally new Book 5 replaced the earlier law that had remained practically unchanged for more than 100 years.

Against that background, the Polish attempt to draft a new maritime code may seem a little odd as the current Polish maritime code was introduced in 2001, and thus it is relatively young. Bearing that in mind and appreciating the value of a stable maritime code, the Polish Codification Commission for Maritime Law began its work with no assumption of adopting a new code. However, after a thorough revision, it became clear that there were good grounds for the new Act and mere amendments to the existing Act would not be satisfactory.

The Polish Codification Commission for Maritime Law, in fact, agreed that the majority of the regulation required changes. Specifically, international developments had called the current maritime code into question. Firstly, since it was adopted it had undergone multiple amendments and thus its content required a thorough reorganization. Secondly, there were some international Acts that needed to be introduced into the Polish legal system (including the Athens 2002 Convention and the Nairobi Wreck Removal Convention).[13] The need to clarify the requirements for a ship's nationality and the need to bring the requirements into line with the EU law and the case law of the Court of Justice of the EU, were also among the main reasons for some substantial changes.

3 Scope of the new codes

During its work, the Polish Codification Commission raised the question whether the new maritime code should be a comprehensive Act, covering private as well as public law elements, or whether it should be focused on a shipping law. The former option would mean a return to the traditions of the first Polish maritime code of 1961, whereas the latter solution would be a continuation of the path taken in 2001 with the current maritime code. Currently, maritime safety and security issues, as well as other public law matters, are regulated outside the maritime code, in separate Acts.[14] The same applies to maritime labour law.[15] Therefore, the maritime code of 2001 is predominantly private law in nature, with only indispensable public law regulation. As Professor Łopuski puts it, the carriage of goods by sea regulation forms the core of this maritime code. The authors of this paper recognize that including public law regulations into the maritime code would have its advantages. Nowadays, making a clear distinction between public and private law is difficult, if not impossible. Even shipping law codes include provisions of public nature which are indispensable for shipping.

13 More on the draft proposal content, see J. Nawrot, Z. Pepłowska-Dąbrowska, 'National Report: Maritime Legislation in Poland and the Proposals of the Codification Commission for Maritime Law' (2017) 23 *Journal of International Maritime Law* 220–227.

14 The most important legal regulations dealing with public issues of maritime law are: Ustawa o bezpieczeństwie morskim of 2011 (Act on Maritime Safety), Consolidated text: *Journal of Laws* 2016, item 281; Ustawa o ochronie żeglugi i portów morskich (Shipping and Port Security Act of 2008), *Journal of Laws* 2008, No. 171, item 1055 and Ustawa o zapobieganiu zanieczyszczaniu morza przez statki (Act for the Prevention of Pollution from Ships of 1995, Consolidated text: *Journal of Laws* 2017, item 2000.

15 Ustawa o pracy na morzu (Maritime Labour Act of 2015), Consolidated text: *Journal of Laws* 2018, item 616.

Historically, maritime public and private law regulation was indispensable. It is sufficient to mention the Rolls of Oleron, Barcelona's Consolato del Mare and Hanzeatic Visby law, all of which contain not only typical private law regulations such as general average, liability in case of collision of ships and bottomry, but also navigational requirements, ship surveys, the principle of deviation and safe ports, i.e. institutions typical of modern maritime public law. The first national codifications, such as Colbert's Ordonnance de la Marine of 1681, also contain regulations of both private and public nature.[16] As Professor Łopuski states,[17] the clear distinction of private and public maritime law became a reality in the eighteenth century, the era of great codification, when private maritime law became part of national civil or commercial codes. In other words, maritime law has gone through the process of privatization and commercialization.[18] Consequently, the twentieth century's need for maritime law unification had to face the problem of this public law–private law distinction.

The new big threat that shipping (especially oil transport by sea) began to pose to the marine environment was a new factor behind the urgent need to rethink the boundaries between public and private maritime law in the twentieth century. The oil tanker disasters of the twentieth century revealed the weakness of the sceptical attitude of the private maritime sector to the protection of marine environment against oil pollution. Lord Devlin's famous report of 1967 presented after the *Torrey Canyon* disaster suggested solutions such as high limits of liability, the shipowner's absolute liability and compulsory insurance requirements. As a result, private law instruments responding to some extent to public goals were adopted as new solutions, first in the International Convention on Civil Liability for Oil Pollution Damage 1969, and later in other liability conventions. There was also a need to introduce maritime law regulations which, in addition to seeking compromise between states representing different maritime interests, could provide a real answer to global problems arising from new threats and the entanglement of private and public aspects of maritime law. The role of states in the administration of shipping became crucial, leading to the growing importance of maritime public law. The new approach resulted in the display of new issues in maritime law related to the exploitation of marine resources, protection of the marine environment and maritime safety. Maritime law was penetrated not only by the norms of the civil and commercial law but also by the norms of administrative, labour and criminal law. Consequently, the philosophy of maritime law changed, as reflected in international legislation and modification of primary maritime law institutions.

The Polish Codification Commission for Maritime Law noticed that merging public and private law under a new maritime code would demand the incorporation of extensive safety and security regulation. Finally, the current scope of the maritime code was upheld. Although there are benefits from a comprehensive code, two arguments outweigh them. Firstly, the provisions of public law are frequently changing, which would necessitate multiple future amendments to the code. The second reason has a more practical dimension. Such a code would be far bigger than the existing one. In recent times public

16 A. Recalde Castells, 'El objeto y el ámbito material de la Ley de Navegación Marítima' in A. Emperanza Sobejano, J.M. Martin Osante (eds), *Comentarios sobre la Ley de Navegación Marítima* (Madrid 2015), p. 36.

17 J. Łopuski, *Prawo morskie*, vol. I, Bydgoszcz 1996, p. 26.

18 A. Recalde Castells, 'El objeto y el ámbito material de la Ley de Navegación Marítima' in A. Emperanza Sobejano, J M. Martin Osante (eds), *Comentarios sobre la Ley de Navegación Marítima* (Madrid 2015), p. 36.

law provisions have grown considerably, and incorporating these into the code would be quite complicated. Thus, a decision was made to uphold the private law nature of the Polish maritime code.

On the other hand, those countries that have emancipated maritime law from general commercial law by new Acts tend to produce more comprehensive Acts, covering not only private law matters, but also public issues to a larger extent.

That is the case with the Spanish LNM, which contains 524 Articles, not to mention additional and final provisions. Its Preamble explains that a wide range of the LNM is dictated by the fact that it is aimed as a normative framework for activities inherent in maritime traffic in general. It includes private as well as public law norms. Specifically, its Title I on administrative organization of navigation, based on the United Nations Convention for the Law of the Sea (UNCLOS), is strictly public in nature. Parts of Title II are of a public law nature, too.[19]

It may be interesting to learn that, initially, the Spanish Act was supposed to be of a solely private law nature, as in the Code of Commerce. However, the broader option prevailed, following the example of older foreign codes, such as the Italian Code of 1942.[20] As a result, the LNM is not restricted to shipping issues. Professor Arroyo Martínez claims that, in this way, the new law overcomes the mercantile character of the coding era of the nineteenth century.[21] This approach made it possible to revise the formal division between private and public maritime law introduced by the Ordenanzas de Bilbao of 1737 and preserved by the introduction of the maritime law regulation of private nature into the Spanish Commercial Code.[22] It may be interesting to note, however, that the initial LNM project included more aspects of public law character, including a chapter on pollution prevention and safety of lives at sea.[23] Those parts were omitted from the Act as finally adopted. Moreover, the reference literature draws attention to the fact that the integration of public and private law norms in the LNM is not complete and that the law is in fact still preoccupied with the regulation of relations between private subjects.[24] On top of that, despite the declaration provided in its Preamble, the LNM cannot be seen as a complete Act, i.e. covering all aspects of maritime law, as it leaves outside the legal norms in respect of ports, for example.[25] Nevertheless, it remains a very ambitious Act, which is seen by some authors as a sign of maritime law autonomy in relation to commercial law in general.[26] Despite the

---

19 J.P. Rodríguez Delgado, 'El Derecho Marítimo se hace mayor: la avanzado autonomía del Derecho Marítimo tras la aprobación de la Ley de Navegación Marítima' (2015) XXXII *Anuario de derecho marítimo* 139.

20 I. Arroyo Martínez, 'The New Spanish Maritime Navigation Act 2014, The Need for Uniformity and the International Maritime Conventions' (2015) *Il Diritto Marittimo, Fasc. II*, 423.

21 I. Arroyo Martínez, 'Titulo preliminar, Disposiciones generales' in I. Arroyo Martínez and J.-A. Rueda Martínez (eds), *Comentarios a la Ley 14/2014 de 24 de Julio, de navegación marítima* (Thomson Reuters 2016), p. 67.

22 A. Recalde Castells, 'El objeto y el ámbito material de la Ley de Navegación Marítima' in A. Emperanza Sobejano, J. M. Martin Osante (eds), *Comentarios sobre la Ley de Navegación Marítima* (Madrid 2015), p. 36.

23 Proyecto de Ley General de Navegación Marítima, Boletín Oficial de las Cortes Generales, 19 de diciembre de 2008, Núm. 14–1.

24 Id., p. 37.

25 I. Arroyo Martínez, 'Titulo preliminar, Disposiciones generales' in I. Arroyo Martínez and J.-A. Rueda Martínez (eds), *Comentarios a la Ley 14/2014 de 24 de Julio, de navegación marítima* (Thomson Reuters 2016), p. 71.

26 J.P. Rodríguez Delgado, 'El Derecho Marítimo se hace mayor: la avanzado autonomía del Derecho Marítimo tras la aprobación de la Ley de Navegación Marítima' (2015) XXXII *Anuario de derecho marítimo* 134–167;

breadth of the codified subject matter, the new Act is not called Código but simply Ley. In fact, the Act assumes that only after it has been combined with other laws regulating maritime institutions, including State Ports and the Merchant Navy Act, will it become the Spanish Maritime Navigation Code.[27] Our understanding is that the task has not so far been fulfilled by the government, despite the three-year deadline. It follows that even such a broad regulation has not merited being called 'the code'.

The new Belgian Navigation Code (Code belge de la navigation) is even broader, covering a number of public law issues, including safety and security matters, pollution prevention, maritime accident investigation, as well as sanctions.[28] It is also broad enough to cover maritime crimes as piracy. It follows from the commentary to the draft written by the Commission for Maritime Law that codification was an opportunity to coordinate existing public laws concerning navigation and to put an end to their fragmentation.[29] Maritime public law has already been amended and brought up to date.[30]

4 Methods of preserving uniformity, principles of maritime law

It is interesting to observe that new codes (whether in force, or still at the proposal stage) adopt certain mechanisms aiming at preserving the uniformity of maritime law. One of the methods employed is the recourse and incorporation of maritime law principles, which may be adopted to serve different roles in a code.

Recognition of the principles and importance of maritime law has been already discussed in the maritime law doctrine. Professor Van Hooydonk cites extensive doctrine and case law, describing them as internationally (if not even universally) accepted rules of maritime law, bound with customs and usages.[31] Moreover, the principles of maritime law have been at the center of attention of the CMI working group, which undertook the task of preparing an elementary description of the typical concepts and rules of maritime law that might be regarded as being internationally accepted and common to most, if not all, legal systems and traditions.[32]

As Professor Van Hooydonk notes, many states have, in their national laws, recognized maritime principles as sources of law. One example is the new Belgian Navigation Code (Code belge de la navigation) which contains a provision recognizing usages and general principles as particular sources of maritime law.[33] The former are understood as having general or quasi-general application in the field of activity or in the place concerned, whereas the latter are defined as internationally recognized principles that constitute the basis of the

I. Arroyo Martínez, 'Titulo preliminar, Disposiciones generales' in I. Arroyo Martínez and J.-A. Rueda Martínez (eds), *Comentarios a la Ley 14/2014 de 24 de Julio, de navegación marítima* (Thomson Reuters 2016), p. 71.

27 Ley 14/2014, de 24 de julio, de Navegación Marítima, Disposición final novena. Habilitación al Gobierno.

28 Code belge de la navigation, http://www.dekamer.be/kvvcr/showpage.cfm?section=%7Cflwb&language=fr&cfm=flwbn.cfm?lang=N&dossierID=3536&legislat=54 (visited 21 August 2019).

29 Commission de Droit Maritime, Ébauche de Code Belge de la Navigation, Droit Public, Onzième Livre Bleu, http://droitmaritime.be/ (visited 21 August 2019).

30 Id, p. 10.

31 E. Van Hooydonk, 'Towards a worldwide restatement of general principles of maritime law' (2014) 20 *Journal of International Maritime Law* 170.

32 CMI IWG, 'Towards a compilation of principles of the Lex Maritima' (2016) *CMI Yearbook* 260.

33 Code belge de la navigation, Art. 1.1.2.4.

maritime law order.[34] Moreover, the Commission of Maritime Law proposed that maritime law principles should be included in the group of indicators considered while interpreting the code's and other maritime law provisions.[35] Although the proposal for a new maritime code was amended after it left the Commission of Maritime Law, the norm recognizing general principles as particular sources of maritime law remained in the adopted Act.

The Spanish LNM also recognizes the importance of the usages in defining the content of law. It states that supplementary applicable sources of maritime law are practices and customs related to maritime navigation.[36] They are indicated among other sources of maritime law, in the third place, next to complementary laws and regulations.

In Poland, there has been a discussion within the Codification Commission for Maritime Law on the inclusion of maritime law principles into the drafted code. It took place before the CMI group was set, and before the Belgian or Spanish comparative material was available. Initially, it was proposed that quite an extensive section on the principles of maritime law should be included within the general part of the new maritime code. This idea included provisions that defined the proposed principles, namely those referring to the obligation to protect the safety of life at sea, to the protection of the maritime environment, to freedom of shipping as well as provisions regarding the interpretation of contracts. Some emphasised the meaning of port customs and international commercial customs as well as current technological developments. The importance of international cooperation as one of the important duties of state maritime authorities was also stressed.

The proposed provisions, however, were seen by the majority of the Codification Commission as being too general and of a declaratory character. In fact, they were principles of maritime public law and it was decided that the code would not include matters of maritime safety and security. Yet, one of the proposed provisions which stressed the importance of usage in shipping was seen as necessary in the new draft. In the end, the Codification Commission for Maritime Law gave up the idea of including a separate section entitled 'Maritime law principles'. Instead, it decided to include a provision on the role of maritime usage and practice which the parties had established between them. The proposed provision is modelled on the Convention on the International Sale of Goods (CISG), rather than the UNIDROIT Principles of International Commercial Contracts or Principles of European Contract Law (PECL). Therefore, in the end no enumeration of maritime law principles exists in the Polish draft maritime code, nor have there been any attempts to define such maritime law principles. Only a norm on the binding force of usage and practice for contractual arrangement has been included, which is common for private law regulations. Nonetheless, since maritime principles derive from and are bound up with usages, it can be claimed that they are present in the Polish draft of the new maritime code.

It is argued that identification and employment of the principles of maritime law in national codification may serve as a tool for unification of maritime law internationally.[37] There are, however, other methods employed towards this aim. Except for references to the usages, the proposed draft of the new Polish maritime code introduces another way

34 Id., Art. 1.1.1.1 §2 2°.

35 Art. 2.14 §2 of the draft proposal as prepared by the Belgian Commission for Maritime Law.

36 Ley 14/2014, de 24 de julio, de Navegación Marítima, Artículo 2.

37 E. Van Hooydonk, 'Towards a worldwide restatement of general principles of maritime law' (2014) 20 *Journal of International Maritime Law* 170.

to warrant such uniformity. It sets an interpretative rule which aims in the same direction. The rule in question requires interpretation and application of maritime law provisions which are based on international conventions having regard to the promotion of worldwide uniformity of maritime law. Such provisions are also found in the project of the Belgian new code[38] or Spanish law.[39] They introduce an obligation to interpret norms derived from international conventions independently of preconceptions derived from domestic law. That may be achieved by reference to the legislative history of an international instrument at stake, international case law and scholarly critique.[40] In that respect the initiative by the CMI and Singapore University to create an information system whose aim is to exchange judicial decisions based on international conventions is very interesting and most welcome. Such a tool may be of great help in fulfilling the requirements of proposed or adopted new norms. That system has worked well in the case of commercial court judgments and arbitral decisions based on the CISG, where CLOUT (Case Law On UNCITRAL Texts) has been created.[41]

5 Concluding remarks

One of the general conclusions that can be drawn from the conducted research is that development of maritime law, besides its specificity resulting from the perils of the sea, is historically coupled with the general development of the concept of state and law. This was reflected in the ancient regulations, through medieval usages and codes, as well as in the codification processes of the eighteenth and nineteenth centuries, which aimed at strengthening the position of the central authorities and domestic legal orders. It seems that nowadays, when boundaries between public and private maritime law require revision, the tendency to create comprehensive maritime codes is likely to increase. Adopting complex maritime codes remains in line with the changes in the IMO's approach to maritime law. This can be concluded from the latest IMO conventions, as the Nairobi Wreck Removal Convention adopted in 2007 or the Hong Kong International Convention for the Safe and Environmentally Sound Recycling of Ships adopted in 2009, in which both aspects of maritime law – private and public – are involved.

The second important factor affecting development of maritime law through the ages is technological development and the development of available navigational techniques. Rapid technological development in shipping is also a factor that should prompt the creation of systemic rather than detailed (prescriptive) national legislation reflected in maritime codes.

Finally, the authors of this chapter would like to explain why they dedicated their research to the issue of national legislation. It is true that national legislation plays a subordinate role in the field of maritime law, which is predominantly regulated by internationally

38 Article 1.2.6. Interprétation. However it interesting to note that this provision was removed from the final act.

39 Ley 14/2014, Artículo 2. Fuentes e interpretación.

40 That summary was used by J.O. Honnold when describing similar provision at the CISG, John O. Honnold, *Uniform Law for International Sales under the 1980 United Nations Convention* (1999 Kluwer Law International), p. 15.

41 http://www.uncitral.org/uncitral/en/case_law.html (visited 29 August 2019).

binding acts.[42] Nevertheless, the significance of national legislation is still valid, especially as unification of maritime law on the international scale has been struggling with the low rate of ratification of international instruments. That phenomenon is sometimes also seen as a trigger for national legislators to act, who, failing to achieve consensus in the international arena, turn to unilateral regulation. In fact, this was suggested as a reason for the recent amendment to the German maritime code, in which solutions of the Rotterdam Rules were followed.[43] That was certainly one of the reasons for taking on the task of preparing a Polish draft proposal for a new maritime code. Certain regulations of the Rotterdam Rules seemed necessary, and thus were included in the draft proposal, without (so far) any prospects of being adopted on the international forum.

In our concluding remarks, we should also comment on the future of the Polish proposal for a new Maritime Code. Although the final draft proposal was finished and delivered to the Ministry for Maritime Economy and Inland Navigation in June 2018, its fate seems unclear. In fact, the Codification Commission was suspended before delivering the final draft proposal. Thus, its members continued work on the draft for more than a year in their own capacity. So far there have been no actions concerning the draft proposal undertaken by the proper Ministry.

42 E. Van Hooydonk, 'Towards a worldwide restatement of general principles of maritime law' (2014) 20 *Journal of International Maritime Law* 171.

43 J. Chuah, 'The new German Act on the Reform of Trade Law' (2013) 19 (1) *Journal of International Maritime Law* 6.

INDEX

For Product Safety Concerns and Information please contact our EU representative GPSR@taylorandfrancis.com
Taylor & Francis Verlag GmbH, Kaufingerstraße 24, 80331 München, Germany

www.ingramcontent.com/pod-product-compliance
Lightning Source LLC
LaVergne TN
LVHW080646011026
849160LV00014B/1343
* 9 7 8 1 0 3 2 0 8 1 9 6 0 *